NEW LABOUR, NEW WELFARE STATE?

The 'third way' in British social policy

Edited by Martin Powell

The POLICY
PP
PRESS

First published in Great Britain in 1999 by

The Policy Press
University of Bristol
34 Tyndall's Park Road
Bristol BS8 1PY
UK

Tel +44 (01)117 954 6800
Fax +44 (0)117 973 7308
e-mail tpp@bristol.ac.uk
http://www.bristol.ac.uk/Publications/TPP

British Library Cataloguing in Publication Data
A catalogue record for this book is available from the British Library

ISBN 1 86134 151 2

Martin Powell is Lecturer in Social Policy in the Department of Social and Policy Sciences, University of Bath.

Cover design by Qube Design Associates, Bristol.

Photograph of Tony Blair at Crampton Primary School supplied by kind permission of Joanne O'Brien of Format Photographers, London.

Printed and bound in Great Britain by Hobbs the Printers Ltd, Southampton.

Contents

Notes on contributors		vi
List of tables and figures		x
List of acronyms		xi
one	Introduction *Martin Powell*	1
two	Public expenditure and the public/private mix *Tania Burchardt and John Hills*	29
three	New Labour's health policy: the new healthcare state *Calum Paton*	51
four	The personal social services and community care *Norman Johnson*	77
five	Education, education, education *Yolande Muschamp, Ian Jamieson and Hugh Lauder*	101
six	Housing policy under New Labour *Peter A. Kemp*	123
seven	New Labour and social security *Martin Hewitt*	149
eight	New Labour and employment, training and employee relations *Peter Cressey*	171
nine	The new politics of law and order: Labour, crime and justice *Sarah Charman and Stephen P. Savage*	191
ten	Citizenship *Hartley Dean*	213
eleven	Accountability *John Rouse and George Smith*	235
twelve	Bridging the Atlantic: the Democratic (Party) origins of Welfare to Work *Desmond King and Mark Wickham-Jones*	257
thirteen	Conclusion *Martin Powell*	281
Bibliography		301
Index		339

Notes on contributors

Tania Burchardt is a research officer at the ESRC Research Centre for Analysis of Social Exclusion (CASE) at the London School of Economics. Her research interests include the relationship between public and private welfare and definitions of social exclusion. Recent publications include *Private welfare and public policy* (co-author, York Publishing Services, 1999) and *Private welfare insurance and social security: Pushing the boundaries* (co-author, York Publishing Services, 1997).

Sarah Charman lectures in criminal justice studies at the School of Social and Historical Studies, University of Portsmouth. She has published a range of papers on police management and pressure groups in criminal justice and is currently completing a book on the Association of Chief Police Officers (with Stephen Cope and Stephen Savage).

Peter Cressey is Senior Lecturer in Sociology and Industrial Relations in the Department of Social and Policy Sciences, University of Bath. His research interests cover the fields of social dialogue and industrial relations and the related field of employee participation. He is currently coordinating a Leonardo Project on social dialogue and human resource development. He has published widely on the subject of employment and was the co-editor of *Work and employment in Europe* (Routledge, 1995).

Hartley Dean is Professor of Social Policy at the University of Luton. His publications include *Social security and social control* (Routledge, 1991), *Dependency culture: The explosion of a myth* (Harvester Wheatsheaf, 1992, with Peter Taylor-Gooby), *Welfare, law and citizenship* (Prentice Hall/ Harvester Wheatsheaf, 1996) and *Poverty, riches and social citizenship* (Macmillan, 1999, with Margaret Melrose).

Martin Hewitt lectures in social policy in the Department of Social Sciences, University of Hertfordshire. His research interests and publications are in the areas of social need and new social movements, including *Welfare, ideology and need* (Harvester Wheatsheaf, 1992) and a book on social policy and human nature which will be published in 1999. He is currently researching (with Martin Powell) the new welfare state.

John Hills is Director of the ESRC Research Centre for Analysis of Social Exclusion and Professor of Social Policy at the London School of Economics. His recent publications include *Private welfare and public policy* (co-author,York Publishing Services, 1999), *The state of welfare:The economics of social spending* (co-editor, Oxford University Press, 1998) and *Income and wealth:The latest evidence* (Joseph Rowntree Foundation, 1998).

Ian Jamieson is Professor of Education and Dean of the Faculty of Humanities and Social Sciences at the University of Bath. His main research interests include the relations between schooling and work, educational evaluation, and school effectiveness and improvement. He is the editor of the *Journal of Education and Work*. He has recently co-authored *School effectiveness and school improvement* (Pitman,1996) and *Effective teaching and learning in work-related contexts* (DfEE, 1997).

Norman Johnson is Professor of Social Policy in the School of Social and Historical Studies at the University of Portsmouth. His main research interests are in the voluntary sector and mixed economies of welfare, where he has published widely. Current work includes a study of contracting in the personal social services, and the impact of the New Deal on voluntary organisations. His most recent book is *Mixed economies of welfare* (Prentice Hall, 1998).

Peter Kemp is currently a Professor in the Department of Urban Studies at the University of Glasgow. He was previously the Joseph Rowntree Professor of Housing Policy and founding Director of the Centre for Housing Policy at the University of York. He teaches social security, 'social exclusion' and European social policy on the Social Policy degree programme at Glasgow. His research interests encompass housing and social security, particularly Housing Benefit. Recent publications include *A comparative study of housing allowances* (The Stationery Office, 1997).

Desmond King is Professor of Politics and Fellow of St John's College, University of Oxford. His publications include *The New Right: Politics, markets and citizenship* (1987), *Actively seeking work? The politics of unemployment and welfare in the United States and Britain* (University of Chicago Press, 1995) and *In the name of liberalism: Illiberal social policy in Britain and the United States* (Oxford University Press, 1999).

Hugh Lauder is Professor of Education at the University of Bath. He has recently co-edited *Education, culture, economy and society* (Oxford University Press, 1997) and co-authored a longitudinal study of education markets and their impact on school performance, *Trading in futures: Why markets in education don't work* (Open University Press, 1999). He is currently working on an ESRC project on *National routes to a high skills economy: A comparative study of Korea, Singapore, Germany and the UK*.

Yolande Muschamp is Director of Studies for the Education Department in the University of Bath. Her research interests are in primary education, curriculum and assessment and the work of teachers, with a recent major publication being a co-authored study entitled *Work and identity in the primary school* (Open University Press, 1997).

Calum Paton is Professor of Health Policy in the Centre for Health Planning and Management at Keele University. He has published a number of books and articles, with his most recent being *Competition and planning in the NHS. The consequences of the NHS reforms* (Stanley Thornes, 1998).

Martin Powell lectures in social policy in the Department of Social and Policy Sciences, University of Bath. He has published widely in the areas of health policy and social policy, including *Evaluating the NHS* (Open University Press, 1997). He is currently researching the new welfare state (with Martin Hewitt) and undertaking an ESRC project on *Understanding health variations and policy variations*.

John Rouse is Professor of Public Services Management and Dean of the Faculty of Law and Social Sciences at the University of Central England in Birmingham. His main teaching, research interests and publications are in the fields of public service performance management and local governance.

Stephen Savage is Professor of Criminology at the Institute of Criminal Justice Studies, University of Portsmouth. He has published widely on social and public policy, criminal justice and policing. His major publications include *The theories of Talcott Parsons* (Macmillan, 1989), *Public policy in Britain* (co-editor, Macmillan, 1994) and *Core issues in policy* (co-editor, Longman, 1996). He is currently completing a co-authored book on the Association of Chief Police Officers (with Sarah Charman and Stephen Cope) and an edited book on policy networks in criminal justice. He is also co-editor of *The International Journal of the Sociology of Law*.

George Smith lectures in social policy in the Department of Sociology at the University of Central England in Birmingham. He has worked in a central government ministry and in a new town development corporation. His publications have been on innovation and change in higher education and on various aspects of contemporary social policy.

Mark Wickham-Jones is Lecturer in Politics at the University of Bristol. His publications include *Economic strategy and the Labour Party* (Macmillan, 1996) and papers in such journals as the *British Journal of Political Science, Politics and Society*, *Policy & Politics* and *Political Quarterly*.

List of tables and figures

Tables

1.1	Dimensions of political approaches	14
2.1	Voters' attitudes to taxes and spending relative to the Labour Party	40
2.2	Growth in public spending and spending plans 1993/94 to 2001/02	43
4.1	Public expenditure in selected public services in the UK	77
6.1	Public sector new housing completions and Right to Buy sales in Britain (1980-95)	128
6.2	Housing tenure in Britain	131
6.3	Provision of rented housing in England	131
7.1	The Third Way in social security: a typology	163
11.1	Approaches to accountability in the welfare state	253

Figures

2.1	UK government welfare spending 1973/74 to 1997/98	30
2.2	Spending on the welfare state as a proportion of all government expenditure	31
2.3	Forms of privatisation	34
2.4	Expenditure on welfare	36
8.1	Trends in UK policy for active labour market policies	145
10.1	Taxonomy of political discourses and welfare regimes	216
10.2	Taxonomy of popular moral repertoires and discourses	228

List of acronyms

ACPO	Association of Chief Police Officers
ALMP	active labour market policy
APA	Association of Police Authorities
CBI	Confederation of British Industry
CCETSW	Central Council for Education and Training in Social Work
CCT	compulsory competitive tendering
CSR	Comprehensive Spending Review
CTC	city technology college
DLA	Disability Living Allowance
EC	European Commission
EEC	European Economic Community
EPA	Educational Priority Area
EU	European Union
EYDCP	Early Years Development and Childcare Plans
GDP	gross domestic product
GMS	grant-maintained school
GPFH	General Practitioner Fund Holding
ISMI	Income Support mortgage interest
IT	information technology
JSA	Job Seekers' Allowance
LEA	local education authority
LEC	Local Enterprise Company
LHCC	local health care cooperative
LMS	local management of schools
LSVT	large-scale voluntary transfer
MIRAS	mortgage interest relief at source
NEA	non-elected agency
NHS	National Health Service
NMW	national minimum wage
NTO	National Training Organisation
NVQ	National Vocational Qualification
PCG	primary care group
PFI	private finance initiative
PSBR	public sector borrowing requirement
RDA	Regional Development Agency

SEM	Special Employment Measure
SERPS	State Earnings Related Pension Scheme
SIP	Social Inclusion Partnership
SRB	Single Regeneration Budget
SPS	Stakeholder Pension Scheme
SSP	state second pension
TEC	Training and Enterprise Council
TPC	Tenant Participation Compact
TPP	Total Purchasing Pilot
TUC	Trades Union Congress
VFM	value-for-money
WTE	whole-time equivalent

ONE

Introduction

Martin Powell

This publication examines the question of whether the election of a
New Labour government in the UK in May 1997 is leading towards the
establishment of a new welfare state. This chapter provides the broad
framework for the book and discusses issues and raises questions that will
be examined in the remaining chapters. It starts by briefly locating the
British welfare state within its wider geographical and temporal context.
After a brief overview of changes to the welfare state inherited by Labour
and changes to the Labour Party, the chapter then focuses on Labour's
'Third Way', the claim for a distinctive set of policies that are different
from both the Old Left and the New Right. This sets up the main
questions to be addressed:

* To what extent does the policy of New Labour differ from Old Labour?
* To what extent does the policy of New Labour vary from the New
  Right?
* How far do any changes suggest a new welfare state?

In short, is New Labour associated with a 'new welfare state'?

British welfare state in context

Although this text is focused on the British welfare state, it is useful to
place it within a wider context. This section locates the British welfare
state within typologies of welfare states, and outlines the influences of
broader social, economic and political changes. The most widely used
typology is given by Esping-Andersen (1990) who distinguishes between
Nordic (Socialist), Continental West European (Conservative) and Anglo-
Saxon (Liberal) welfare states. Examples are Sweden, Germany and the
UK respectively. This typology is the basis for many accounts of
comparative social policy (for example, Ginsburg, 1992; Leibfried, 1993;
Pierson, 1998, Chapter 6; see also Giddens, 1998, pp 6-7). However, a

number of caveats should be pointed out. First, some accounts have argued for a fourth type of Southern European welfare state. Second, it has been noted that in some ways Britain sits uneasily in its category, with many important differences from other Liberal welfare states such as the United States. The third, and related, point is that the model tends to be based on services in cash rather than in kind so there may be differences within welfare states. For example, it can be argued that while the British benefit system may be characterised as 'Liberal', the National Health Service arguably has some 'Socialist' characteristics (for example, Powell, 1997a, 1997b). As Ginsburg (1992, p 23) puts it, Britain is an odd mixture of the 'Socialist' and 'Liberal' types.

Welfare states vary temporally as well as geographically. Like time, welfare states do not stand still. Their evolution depends on choices made within constraints. To paraphrase Karl Marx, welfare states make their own histories, but not within circumstances of their own choosing. The emergence of the 'classic welfare state' in Britain is usually dated to the 1945-51 Labour governments at the end of the Second World War (Timmins, 1996; Powell and Hewitt, 1998; Hughes and Lewis, 1998; Pierson, 1998). This child of its times is often associated with the names of Beveridge and Keynes. To a large extent it was based on a blueprint of the Beveridge Report of 1942. This was designed to deliver a 'National Minimum' by means of the centrepiece of a social insurance plan, underpinned by means-tested social assistance and supplemented by a superstructure of voluntary insurance. Allied to these cash benefits were services delivering education and healthcare. One of the key assumptions of the Beveridge Report was that the state would ensure 'full employment'. This was to be achieved by active intervention in the economy along the lines suggested by Keynes. It has been noted that 'the post-war settlement' is composed of political, economic, social and organisational elements (Hughes and Lewis, 1998). More specifically, it has been pointed out that the social settlement of the Beveridge welfare state is based on particular assumptions regarding the ideological triangle of nation, family and work. The Beveridgean citizen was the fully employed (and insured) married, white, able-bodied, male worker, with other categories of people – including women, ethnic minorities, disabled people, children and elderly people – experiencing highly conditional forms of welfare exclusion outside the 'normal' universalism (Williams, 1989; Ginsburg, 1992; Hughes and Lewis, 1998; Saraga, 1998; Ellison and Pierson, 1998; Mullard and Spicker, 1998; Pierson, 1998, Chapter 3).

It is generally agreed that the British welfare state has failed to keep pace with half a century of economic and social changes (see Commission on Social Justice, 1994; DSS, 1998a; Ellison and Pierson, 1998; Hughes and Lewis, 1998; Jordan, 1998; Giddens, 1998; Blair, 1998a; Pierson, 1998): the economic sphere has changed since Keynes, and the social sphere has changed since Beveridge. It is often said that the Labour government of the 1970s abandoned the pursuit of Keynesian economics and the goal of full employment. It is claimed that the rise of 'globalisation' has reduced a government's room to manouvere: 'Keynesianism in one country' no longer appears to be a feasible policy option. Similarly, Beveridge's world has disappeared in that we now have an ageing population, a changed family structure and many working women. Hewitt (1993, 1998) claims that with the rise of new social movements, previously marginalised and largely invisible groups have been changed into 'new welfare subjects'. This has the result that axes of division, 'difference' or inequality beyond the socioeconomic such as 'race', gender, age and disability, which were formerly regarded as belonging to 'nature' and biology, are now viewed as social divisions (Hughes and Lewis, 1998; Saraga, 1998; Ellison and Pierson, 1998; Pierson, 1998). In short, we have "social policy in a changing society" (Mullard and Spicker, 1998).

New welfare state?

There have been many varied and conflicting accounts of change in social policy in the UK during the last 20 years or so. It is generally agreed that 'something happened' (Clarke et al, 1994, p 1), but there is little consensus beyond this point. It is clear that the welfare state has changed, but it would be surprising if there had been no change: it has always been changing. The debate is about the significance and pace of change. Has this been such to warrant a new term since the 'old' welfare state no longer fits? This section outlines the evolution of the welfare state in the period of Conservative government in the years 1979-97, and discusses their significance in terms of a new welfare state.

There are a number of accounts which chart social policy changes of the Conservative government (for example, Pierson, 1996b; Timmins, 1996; Alcock, 1997a; Ellison and Pierson, 1998; Glennerster and Hills, 1998; Hughes and Lewis, 1998; Jones and MacGregor, 1998; Pierson, 1998). The broad aims of Conservative social policy include rolling back the State, promoting choice and consumerism, encouraging the mixed economy of welfare and reducing welfare dependency (Wilding, 1992,

1997; Johnson, 1990). In their attempt to 'roll back the State', the Conservatives steadily reduced the basic rate of income tax and dramatically reduced the level of the higher rate tax. They made attempts to trim expenditure commitments such as uprating pensions in line with prices rather than earnings and seeking 'efficiency savings' in many policy areas. However, with the major exception of housing, expenditure in most policy sectors grew.

In the area of choice and competition, the 1980 Housing Act gave council tenants the chance to buy their houses at a generously discounted price. The 1980 Education Act introduced some degree of parental choice in the selection of schools, and introduced the Assisted Places Scheme which provided state support for some children to attend selected private schools. The third term of 1987-92 saw the introduction of 'quasi-markets' in many areas of welfare. Quasi-markets were intended to deliver the benefits of the private market to the welfare state at zero cost to the consumer. For example, schools and hospitals were funded on the basis of the money following the student or patient respectively. The idea was that this would allow, as in economic markets, popular institutions to flourish as a result of consumer choice.

Sectors of the mixed economy of welfare other than the State were encouraged to thrive. For example, the attractions of private pensions and private health insurance were enhanced with tax relief. New tenancy agreements aimed to revive the private rented sector in housing. The importance of the voluntary and informal sectors of welfare was stressed.

To reduce welfare dependency (and to reduce costs), the government in word and deed aimed to make life on benefits less attractive. For example, Job Seekers' Allowance (JSA) replaced unemployment benefit. Eligibility for Invalidity Benefit was tightened. Initiatives to reduce fraud were introduced. There were calls to restore responsibility through strengthening the ('traditional') family. The 1991 Child Support Act set out to transfer financial obligations from the State to 'absent parents'. Groups such as lone parents became 'folk devils'. There was a clear trend away from universal towards selective benefits. In the case of the Social Fund, grants became loans. All this meant greater inequality in terms of a growing gap between the 'successful' and the 'unsuccessful'.

The Conservative legacy left a changed welfare landscape, but perhaps more importantly, challenged certain assumptions. For example, the government had won elections in times of high levels of unemployment. Despite contrary evidence from opinion polls, the voters appeared to support low taxation parties. However, there is still continuing debate as

4

to the extent to which the Conservatives reformed the welfare state or created a new welfare state (see, for example, Hughes and Lewis, 1998; Pierson, 1998). Verdicts vary from significant change ('the end of the welfare state') to little change ('the resilient welfare state') (see Powell and Hewitt, 1997, 1998). This is due to the conceptual problems of defining what changes would be associated with a new welfare state and the empirical problems of decoding the evidence. In a 'choose–a–date' chronology or in multiple bites at the chronological cherry, writers have dated the end of the classic welfare state in 1973, 1975, 1979, 1981, 1987, 1988 and 1989. Such a dispute about the timing of its demise implies varying (and often implicit) definitions of the welfare state (see Powell and Hewitt, 1997). The (often implicit) criteria behind a restructuring include equality, universalism, full employment, the mixed economy of welfare or welfare pluralism, privatisation, social expenditure and free services. 'Thick economic accounts' that emphasise full employment and public expenditure suggest that the Labour government of the 1970s saw the end of the classic welfare state. On the other hand, 'thin political accounts' seek to 'play up' changes made after 1979 by the Conservative government, such as the increased use of means-testing as a mechanism of service delivery (Powell and Hewitt, 1997). Those associated with the 'resilient welfare state thesis' argue that the first two terms of the Conservative government (1979-87) saw few major changes to the welfare state. They continue that it was the third term of Conservative government after 1987 with the introduction of quasi-markets that saw the vital break. A final group argues for the continued resilience of the welfare state, pointing to the 'implementation gap': the difference between the rhetoric and reality of the Conservative governments. It remains unclear whether the welfare state has been restructured, and if so the criteria of restructuring and when it was restructured are also unclear.

New Labour

There have been a number of accounts of the transformation of the Labour Party from the failures of government in the late 1970s and the electoral wilderness of the 1980s that led to the landslide election victory of New Labour in 1997 (Hughes and Wintour, 1990; Heffernan and Marqusee, 1992; Seyd, 1992; Smith and Spear, 1992; McSmith, 1993; Shaw, 1984, 1996; Jones, 1996; Ellison, 1997; Taylor, 1997; Heffernan, 1998; Driver and Martell, 1998).

It is generally considered that the Labour Party moved to the Left after its election defeat of 1979 (Heffernan and Marqusee, 1992, Chapter 1) and at the 1983 General Election presented a 'Left' set of policies including ones on economic planning, public ownership, redistribution of wealth, nuclear disarmament and withdrawal from the European Economic Community (EEC) (Heffernan and Marqusee, 1992, p 26; Smith, 1992a, p 6; Jones, 1996, p 111). The Party suffered its worst ever defeat at the 1983 General Election. As Thorpe (1997, p 211) argues, Labour's performance then has become a byword for inefficiency and incompetence. The manifesto was termed by a member of the Shadow Cabinet "the longest suicide note in history". Shortly after the election defeat, Neil Kinnock replaced Michael Foot as Party leader, and the Party began to change both the 'product', by diluting or abandoning some policies that were perceived as electoral liabilities, and the 'packaging', through more professional presentation and campaigning. However, it is widely held that this early period saw more changes in presentation than in policy (Smith, 1992a; Shaw, 1996, Chapter 3; Jones, 1996, Chapter 3; Driver and Martell, 1998). Most commentators argue that Labour ran a more successful campaign at the 1987 General Election, but only marginally improved their electoral position (Hughes and Wintour, 1990; Smith, 1992a, 1992b). This led to more fundamental change – if the more successful campaign of 1987 failed to sell the goods, then the goods would have to change. The result was the 'Policy Review' and the 'Labour listens' campaign (Heffernan and Marqusee, 1992; Shaw, 1996; Jones, 1996; Taylor, 1997; Driver and Martell, 1998). These more fundamental changes in policy and presentation gave Labour a lead in the opinion polls in the period leading up to the 1992 General Election, but it unexpectedly lost at the ballot box, resulting in a 'defeat from the jaws of victory' (Heffernan and Marqusee, 1992). Labour's Achilles' heels were perceived to be their tax and expenditure policy and the issue of trust. First, Labour's spending plans were costed by the Conservatives at an extra £35 billion over five years. Shadow Chancellor John Smith's 'mildly redistributive budget' meant more tax for those earning more than £21,000 (McSmith, 1993, Chapters 15-17) which many saw as a vote-loser (Shaw, 1996, p 225). Second, several members of the Shadow Cabinet claimed that the mistrust of Labour by the voters associated with events beginning before 1979 still lingered on. More significantly, a Labour rising star named Tony Blair argued in 1992 that since 1979 "Labour has not been trusted to fulfil the aspirations of the majority of people in a modern world" (in McSmith, 1993, pp 237-9). Shortly after the numbing election defeat, Smith replaced

Kinnock as Party leader. Smith's style of leadership was characterised as 'masterly inactivity'. In the words of the subtitle of his biography, he was "playing the long game" (McSmith, 1993), which involved setting up committees and working parties, including the Commission on Social Justice, while relying on the Conservatives to make mistakes. Smith's death in 1994 and his replacement as leader by Tony Blair is said to mark a decisive break. In contrast with Smith, Blair is a man in a hurry, a member of the 'frantics' rather than the 'long-gamers' camp (see McSmith, 1993, pp 235-6). Blair quickly introduced 'one member one vote' and amended the historic Clause 4 in the Party Constitution, which committed the Party – at least on paper – to common ownership of the means of production, distribution and exchange (Taylor, 1997, Chapter 7). This highly symbolic act of shedding old ideological baggage has been seen as the birth of the 'new Party'. According to Tony Wright MP (1996, pp 135-6), it is the Labour Party's Bad Godesberg (where the German Socialist Party – the SDP – transferred itself into a Social Democratic Party), marking its transformation from a Socialist to a Social Democratic Party. The 'Road to the Manifesto' of 1996 contained five key pledges that were to form the core of the 1997 election manifesto. As White (1996b) noted, the word 'new' appeared 107 times and socialism once. A comparison with the 1992 manifesto showed the stripping out of liabilities. By this means, it was claimed that "Blair lays the ghost of old Labour" (White, 1996a).

The fate of the welfare state under a New Labour government is not clear. However, the welfare state is little mentioned in many of these accounts. Much of the focus is on organisational issues and the jettisoning of perceived unpopular policies such as unilateral nuclear disarmament, trade unions, taxes and Europe. It appears to be generally concluded that Labour's social policy did not need to – and substantially did not – change. As Timmins (1996, p 368) puts it: "For more than a decade Labour simply stopped thinking constructively about the welfare state. It was, after all, their welfare state ... they were damn well going to defend it, warts and all...." This hiatus may be deduced by the relative neglect of social policy in accounts of policy change; when it is mentioned, it is claimed that little significant change has taken place. For example, Smith (1992c, p 220) argued that Labour continues to distance itself from the other Parties by its commitment to equality and the universal provision of welfare. Although it was forced to appear consumer- rather than producer-orientated, to shed its 'tax and spend' image, and to rethink some policies such as council house sales, "much of Labour's policy in health care, social security and education is similar to past policy" (Smith, 1992c, p 220). According to the most extended treatment of social policy, Alcock (1992, p 135) claimed that throughout most of the 1980s Labour's policy on welfare showed little change from the policies, though not necessarily the practice, of the 1960s and the 1970s. Although in other areas the Party experienced a swing to the Left in the early 1980s and later a swing back to the Right, it is difficult to detect any such ebb and flow on welfare issues. Although there was some retraction on unpopular policies, it was essentially a case of 'more of the same'. The Policy Review contained a wealth of new ideas, but led to limited returns except for the subordination of welfare reform to economic policy priorities. It represented the culmination of a gradual development of the scope of Labour's policies for welfare while in opposition. Elliott (1993, p 161) argues that of the four pillars of the post-war settlement, only the welfare state remained inviolate.

Other accounts argue that a policy convergence between the two main political parties has taken place (Dean, 1994, p 105; George and Miller, 1994, pp 215-18). Wilding (1992, p 209) considers that an enduring legacy of Thatcherism's impact on the welfare state lies in its impact on the Labour Party as it moved significantly and substantially and accepted many of Thatcherism's policies. Powell and Hewitt (1998) argue that a new policy agenda clearly emerged, but that it is too early to point to a new policy consensus.

The 1997 election manifesto (Labour Party, 1997a) claimed that:

> **We will be the party of welfare reform. It set out 10 commitments that form our bond of trust with the people. Over the five years' term of office of a Labour government:**
>
> **education will be our number one priority, and we will increase the share of national income spent on education;**
>
> **there will be no increase in the basis or top rates of income tax;**
>
> **stable economic growth with low inflation;**
>
> **250,000 young unemployed off benefit and into work;**
>
> **rebuild the NHS, reducing spending on administration and increasing spending on patient care;**
>
> **tough on crime and tough on the causes of crime, and halve the time it takes persistent juvenile offenders to come to court.**

> We will help build strong families and strong communities, and
> lay the foundations of a modern welfare state in pensions and
> community care;
>
> safeguard our environment, and develop an integrated transport
> policy;
>
> clean up politics, decentralise political power throughout the UK
> and put the funding of political parties on a proper and
> accountable basis;
>
> we will give Britain the leadership in Europe which Britain and
> Europe need.

The manifesto concluded with five pledges that were largely drawn from
the previous years 'Road to the Manifesto'. These were printed on cards
that were distributed during the election campaign. It is said that most
'New Labour' MPs carry one of these cards in their pockets and that the
most devout have their pledges engraved on their heart. The election
manifesto says that as "a first step towards a better Britain", Labour will:

> ... cut class sizes to 30 or under for 5-, 6- and 7-year-olds by
> using money from the assisted places scheme;
>
> introduce fast-track punishment for persistent young offenders
> by halving the time from arrest to sentencing;
>
> cut NHS waiting lists by treating an extra 100,000 patients as a
> first step by releasing £100m saved from NHS red tape;
>
> get 250,000 under-25-year-olds off benefit and into work by using
> money from a windfall levy on the privatised utilities;
>
> not increase income tax rates, cut VAT on heating to 5% and
> maintain inflation and interest rates as low as possible.

Although some of these pledges are vague and almost unmeasurable, the
importance of the welfare state in New Labour's programme is clear. At
least in terms of ends, many of the key pledges are not very different from
the Conservatives. This is hardly surprising. After all, few parties promise
to increase class sizes or NHS waiting lists. There appear to be some
differences in means. Raising money from abolishing the Assisted Places
Scheme in education and a windfall tax on the privatised utilities placed
clear (blue or red?) water between the parties. Labour proposed to cut

very different red tape in the NHS from that cut by the Conservatives. However, perhaps the most significant pledge was the one not to increase the basic and higher rates of income tax, with a long-term objective of a starting rate of ten pence in the pound. The Party leadership declared that Labour would no longer be a 'tax and spend' Party. This position on income tax closed off the direct route of raising more money from the rich, the traditional pastime for Labour Chancellors: for example, Denis Healey's promise in the 1970s to tax the rich until the pips squeaked. The manifesto promised no return to the 'penal tax rates of the 1970s'. Labour had bitterly opposed the Conservatives reducing the top rate of tax to 40% in 1988: now this level was seen as perfectly reasonable. It follows that any extra revenue would have to be found via the routes of tax allowances and National Insurance, closing tax loopholes and tightening capital gains and inheritance tax. However, significant redistribution was ruled out in the hunt for the Middle England vote. Only the Liberal Democrats argued for higher taxation, which led to the *Daily Telegraph* (1997) calling them "the party of the left". McKibbin (1997) claims that New Labour shares many of the characteristics of "very old Labour", the party of Ramsay MacDonald, with Gordon Brown's claim to be the 'Iron Chancellor' being compared with MacDonald's Chancellor, Philip Snowden.

Perhaps the most important difference between the Parties was the issue of credibility or trust. Voters do not decide on the basis of pledges alone: they appear to put stress on ability to deliver. If differences in ideology narrow, then reliability becomes more important. For example, in the 1997 election the Natural Law Party pledged economic prosperity, perfect health, ideal education, lower taxes and reduced crime. In 'menu' terms alone, this appears very tempting and their low poll ratings must be explained in terms of the electorate's failure to believe in delivery. It could be argued that the Conservatives had lost the 1997 election in September 1992 with Britain's exit from the European Exchange Rate Mechanism, while the now-electable Labour Party was not tainted by failure, and voters were willing to give them a try. In this sense, the electorate in 1997 chose not the Tory devil they knew and blamed for breaching trust on its tax promises, but the deep purple sea of Labour. They rejected the Red Flag in 1983, but were willing to grasp the thornless red rose in 1997. After the 1987 Election, Labour frontbencher Bryan Gould claimed that "It's not our policies they don't like, it's us" (Hughes and Wintour, 1990, p 128). It could be argued that in 1997 this for Labour had been reversed in that the Conservative Party won, but Conservative MPs lost. Writing before the 1997 Election, McKibbin

(1997) argues that if Labour wins, it will do so for two reasons: because it is not the Conservative Party, and because it is not very different from the Conservative Party.

Reforming the welfare state

In the first Queen's Speech debate, Blair launched a crusade for welfare reform singling out modernisation of the £90 billion a year welfare system as the 'big idea' of the government. He claimed that: "We have reached the limit of the public's willingness simply to fund an unreformed welfare system through ever higher taxes and spending". Frank Field was appointed Minister of Welfare Reform, with a brief to 'think the unthinkable' (Jones, 1997; Webster, 1997; Grice and Smith, 1997). Field, in an article written just before his appointment, argued that: "The British electorate want high Continental benefit levels and low American tax rates. There is no way this dream can be met". He concluded that "we must cut welfare expenditure in this Parliament" (Field, 1997d). The key was to seek new forms of collective – but not State – provision such as Friendly Societies (Field, 1996a, 1996b, 1997a). At the 1997 Labour Party Conference, both Blair and the Chancellor Gordon Brown spoke of a fundamental reform of the welfare state. *The Guardian* (1997b) claimed that welfare reform was the issue on which most words were expended during the party conference season.

Chronology of policies

1997

May   Queen's Speech: 26 Bills and three White Papers. Modernisation of welfare state as big idea, including proposals on education, NHS and Welfare to Work.

July   Budget. Money for schools and hospitals. Pension funds and privatised utilities taxed. White Paper on education, *Excellence in schools*.

September Labour Party Conference. Speeches by Blair and Brown cover welfare reform. Brown pledges "full employment for the 21st century".

November 'Pre-Budget' statement outlining tax and benefit reforms and expansion of childcare.

December House of Commons backbench revolt on Labour continuing Conservative plans for benefit cuts for single parents; termed by critics 'Tory measure' and 'Peter Lilley memorial Bill'; White Paper on the NHS, *The new NHS*.

1998

February Green Paper on public health, *Our healthier nation*, presents a 'third way' on public health.

March Green Paper on welfare reform, *New ambitions for our country*. Budget "spares middle class". More spending on health, public transport and education; 'Making work pay' through tax credits and childcare tax credits.

May Green Paper on childcare, *Meeting the childcare challenge*, outlines a national childcare strategy; White Paper, *Fairness at work*.

July White paper, *Modern public services for Britain* (Comprehensive Spending Review). More money on 'good welfare' (health, education) compared to 'bad welfare' (social security); a promise to "decrease the bills of social failure". Green Paper, *Children first* promises a "new approach to child support". Green Paper, *Beating fraud is everyone's business*. Cabinet reshuffle: Secretary of State for Social Security Harriet Harman sacked; Minister for Welfare Reform Frank Field resigns. Alistair Darling appointed Secretary of State for Social Security. The government's first *Annual Report* published: good start made in "a year of welfare reform".

September Labour Party Conference. Blair, Brown and Darling praise achievements in welfare, but warn of challenges and difficult times ahead. Social Exclusion Unit publishes *Bringing Britain together*, a report on the poorest neighbourhoods.

November Queen's Speech. Welfare reform widely seen to be main item on agenda. Proposed measures on NHS, crime, welfare and local government. White Paper, *Modernising social services*; Green Paper, *Supporting families*; Acheson Report on Inequalities in Health published, advocating reducing inequalities between rich and poor.

December Green Paper, *A new contract for welfare: Partnerships in pensions*.

The Third Way

In his introduction to the 1997 manifesto, Tony Blair claimed that "In each area of policy a new and distinctive approach has been mapped out, one that differs from the old left and the Conservative right" (Labour Party, 1997a; cf Commission on Social Justice, 1994; Giddens, 1994; Miliband, 1994, p 87; Mandelson and Liddle, 1996, pp 17-18; Wright, 1996, pp 131-6). This is the politics of the 'Third Way' (Field, 1997a; Blair, 1998a; *Economist*, 1998; Halpern and Mikosz, 1998; Hargreaves and Christie, 1998; Le Grand, 1998; Giddens, 1998; White, 1998). There is continuing debate about the Third Way. Blair (1998a) and Giddens (1998) view it as a modernised or renewed social democracy. On the other hand, it is seen as a more non-ideological, pragmatic, policy-driven practice with theory lagging behind (Le Grand, 1998; Halpern and Mikosz, 1998). Some see the emergence of 'the third way international' going beyond the 'brain-dead politics' or the 'idle rhetoric' of Left and Right. This is based on Bill Clinton's 1992 campaign manifesto: "The change we must make isn't liberal or conservative. It's both, and it's different" (Lloyd and Bilefsky, 1998; Walker, 1998). There is little agreement on the international roots of the Third Way. While commentators such as Driver and Martell (1998) and Jordan (1998) argue for a transatlantic route, Blair (1998a) and Giddens (1998) point to links across the Channel towards European social democracy.

In his introduction to the Green Paper, *A new contract for welfare: New ambitions for our country* (DSS, 1998a, p v) Blair describes a third way of building a welfare state for the 21st century: not dismantling welfare, leaving it as a low-grade safety net for the destitute; nor keeping it unreformed and underperforming; but reforming it on the basis of a new contract between citizen and State. The Green Paper sees the Third Way as the third age of the four ages of welfare. The first age is the Elizabethan Poor Law which was concerned with stopping outright destitution. The second age focused on alleviating poverty through insurance-based cash-benefit systems. The welfare state now faces a choice of futures: a privatised future, with the welfare state becoming a residual safety net for the poorest and most marginalised; the status quo, but with more generous benefits; or the government's Third Way, which promotes opportunity and empowerment instead of dependence. This is based on the principles that work is the best route out of poverty for those who can work and that it offers dignity and security to those who are unable to work. The system combines public and private provision in a new partnership for the new age (DSS, 1998a, p 19). These policies will move the welfare state towards a fourth age by the year 2020.

This section uses the 'Third Way' as a loose framework by which to examine changes in the welfare state to see whether they tend more towards a continuation of Old Labour, a convergence with the New Right or a distinctive Third Way. Some of the main dimensions are shown in Table 1.1. They are based on themes emerging from New Labour documents, as well as a variety of sources including Le Grand (1998), White (1998), Driver and Martell (1998), Giddens (1998), Blair (1998a), Halpern and Misokz (1998).

The Commission on Social Justice (1994) set out three potential approaches to social and economic policy. The 'levellers' – the Old Left – were seen as being concerned with the distribution of wealth, but neglecting its production. Social justice is to be achieved primarily through the benefits system. The 'deregulators' – the New Right – believe in achieving social justice through reducing public services and freeing the markets, which would deliver extremes of affluence on poverty. The Commission's preferred alternative was for the 'middle way' of 'Investor's Britain'. This approach combines the ethics of community with the dynamics of a market economy. It is based on security as the foundation of change, but achieves security by redistributing opportunities rather than just redistributing income. The welfare state must be transformed

Table 1.1: Dimensions of political approaches

Dimension	Old Left	Third Way	New Right
Approach	Leveller	Investor	Deregulator
Outcome	Equality	Inclusion	Inequality
Citizenship	Rights	Both rights and responsibilities	Responsibilities
Mixed economy of welfare	State	Public/private; civil society	Private
Mode	Command and control	Cooperation/ partnership	Competition
Expenditure	High	Pragmatic	Low
Benefits	High	Low?	Low
Accountability	Central State/ upwards	Both?	Market/downwards
Politics	Left	Left of centre?/ post-ideological	Right

from a safety net in times of trouble to a springboard for economic opportunity. Paid work for a fair wage is the most secure and sustainable way out of poverty and, to this end, access to education and training must be improved. This has parallels with Giddens' view of the third way as being:

> ... **investment in human capital wherever possible, rather than the direct provision of economic maintenance. In place of the welfare state we should put the social investment state, operating in the context of a positive welfare society. (Giddens, 1998, p 117)**

The key concerns of the Third Way of an investor's welfare state may be seen in four areas: an active, preventive welfare state; the centrality of work; the distribution of opportunities rather than income; and the balancing of rights and responsibilities.

The issue of prevention differentiates an active from a passive welfare state. This has clear similarities with Giddens' (1998) discussion of positive as opposed to negative welfare. *Our healthier nation* (DoH, 1998c) is concerned with ensuring people do not fall ill in the first place. While the traditional NHS was largely concerned with 'repair', the 'new NHS' will be more active in preventing illness. The Social Exclusion Unit (1998b) stresses causes rather than effects, claiming that the New Deals for the unemployed, lone parents and disabled people, together with the government's actions on failing schools, crime reduction and public health, already represent a watershed in terms of starting to address the key causes of social exclusion rather than just dealing with its effects. Similarly, *A new contract for welfare: New ambitions for our country* (DSS, 1998a, p 20) argues that "Welfare is not only about acting after events have occurred ... the welfare system should be proactive, preventing poverty by ensuring that people have the right education, training and support".

The same document spells out the centrality of work:

> **The new welfare state should help and encourage people of working age to work where they are capable of doing so. The Government's aim is to rebuild the welfare state around work. (DSS, 1998a, p 23)**

> **Our ambition is nothing less than a change of culture among benefit claimants, employers and public servants – with rights**

> **and responsibilities on all sides. Those making the shift from welfare into work will be provided with positive assistance, not just a benefit payment. (DSS, 1998a, p 24)**

According to Miliband (1994, pp 88-9) the traditional welfare state was socially active when citizens were economically passive. Today's welfare state must be active throughout people's lives. Welfare has to be preventive rather than ameliorative, economic as well as social: the most potent social policy is a successful economic policy. The centrality of work to New Labour's Third Way is emphasised by Driver and Martell (1998), Jordan (1998) and Halpern and Mikosz (1998). Much of this is political common ground. The problem comes with the balance between carrots and sticks. Under the slogan of 'Making Work Pay' it is intended that the minimum wage and a partial fusing of the tax and benefit system will ensure that people who move from welfare to work should be financially better off. The proposed Working Families Tax Credit scheme, which will replace Family Credit from October 1999, will offer more generous support to working families with children and will mean that every working family with a full-time worker has an income of at least £180 a week. A more generous provision towards childcare costs will be made with a Childcare Tax Credit, covering 70% of childcare costs for low- and middle-income families. However, in contrast to its earlier opposition, Labour will introduce new financial penalties against the 'workshy', essentially bringing in an American-style 'workfare' system. One minister (who has obviously never watched daytime TV) was reported to say that "The public will not support a social security system that appears to tell people they can sit in bed all day watching television and drawing benefit". However, the link between work and welfare is nothing new. Delivering welfare under conditions of 'less eligibility' was a central tenet of the New Poor Law of 1834. Similar concerns of work incentives were familiar to Beveridge and assumptions about seeking work were built into the welfare state. However, during times of full employment these were rarely vigorously pursued (Hewitt and Powell, 1998). In short, the welfare state has always, in theory, been active. The Third Way appears distinctive only in the balance between carrots and sticks. While the New Poor Law and the New Right are largely concerned with the stick of minimal benefits and the Old Left are concerned with the carrot of high benefits, but higher wages, the Third Way consists of a minimum wage backed by education and training and fiscal attractions of work, but underpinned by elements of compulsion and arguably low benefits.

It is claimed that Old Labour redistributed money through taxes and benefits. A letter to the *Financial Times* (see Lister, 1998) lamenting the government's attempt to "erase from the map" the issue of redistribution was signed by 54 academics (the 'FT 54'). In a response, Field (1997b) argued that the government had not rejected fiscal redistribution, pointing to the transfer of £3.5 billion from the privatised utilities to finance the Welfare to Work programme. However, more significantly, he claimed that "simply increasing benefit levels is an inadequate and inappropriate means of tackling divisions in our society". The raison d'être of the government's policy is the enhancing of opportunities. The government "has a different programme from previous governments – of combining fiscal redistribution with a major emphasis on the redistribution of opportunities".

Taking Field's points in turn, although there has been little direct distribution, there may be some hidden or backdoor redistribution – redistribution through stealth. For example, in addition to the windfall tax on privatised utilities, the July 1997 Budget reduced tax relief on mortgages and health insurance and contained a 'smash and grab on pensions'. The Chair of the National Association of Pension Funds claimed that this amounted to the "biggest attack on pension provision since the war", taking £50 billion of extra contributions in the next 10 years. "Even Robert Maxwell only took £400m" (Webster, 1997; Merrell and Durman, 1997). It has been argued that the middle class has been hit by de facto tax increases involving increasing stamp duties on high-priced houses, changes to tax credits on pensions, tuition fees for higher education and increased council tax bills after local capping limits were relaxed (McCartney and Jamieson, 1997; Grice, 1997b)

It has been claimed that the Third Way redefines equality and redistribution from equality of outcome to equality of opportunity (Le Grand, 1998; White, 1998; Daniel, 1998). Shaw (1996, pp 218, 227) comments that New Labour views equality as an outdated concept and that the old objectives of equality and social justice have either been abandoned or diluted. However, it is more accurate to argue that they have been redefined. In 1996, Gordon Brown emphasised that:

> **For far too long we have used the tax and benefit system to compensate people for their poverty rather than doing something more fundamental – tackling the root causes of poverty and inequality ... the road to equality of opportunity starts not with tax rates, but with jobs, education and the reform of the welfare**

state and redistributing existing resources efficiently and equitably. (in Oppenheim, 1997a, p 4)

As Oppenheim puts it, Brown has redrawn Labour's map of equality – emphasising lifetime equality of opportunity rather than equality of outcome and focusing on the primary distribution of endowments rather than on secondary redistribution through taxes and benefits. She points out several strengths to this approach: it offers a wider and more dynamic notion of redistribution; it is a preventive strategy; it is about empowering individuals. However, there are important caveats to the emphasis on primary distribution: redistributing endowments does not come cheap. There will always be a need for some secondary redistribution: primary redistribution is a long-term strategy (Oppenheim, 1997a, p 5). Shaw (1996, p 228) claims that New Labour is in effect embracing the American vision of an economically and socially mobile society where everyone has the opportunity to procure for themselves the place in the social and economic hierarchy which their energy and talents merit. It is claimed that New Labour now offers 'genuine' or 'real' equality of opportunity which is differentiated from the Right's conception of a meritocratic society – 'the open road rather than equal start', which was savagely attacked by Tawney (1964) as 'The Tadpole Society'. However, it is not clear how 'opportunities' are to be redistributed (Taylor, 1997; Lister, 1997a). Crosland (1964), who appeared to have stronger antipathies to educational selection within the state system and towards private education than New Labour, argued that equality of opportunity was insufficient.

It is possible to argue that 'from equality to social inclusion' effectively encapsulates an important paradigm shift in thinking about the welfare state (Lister, 1998, p 215). According to Giddens (1998, p 102), the new politics defines equality as inclusion and inequality as exclusion. Similarly, for Field (1998), "the theme running through welfare reform should be inclusion". However, as Levitas (1996) and Lister (1998) point out, different conceptions of inclusion are possible, and Labour's emphasis is on paid work and education as *the* mechanisms of inclusion. In a telling phrase, Wright (1996, p 143) argues that New Labour must be "egalitarian enough to be socially inclusive". More recently, Blair (1998a, p 12) claims that "we seek a diverse but inclusive society". Field's (1998) claim that the principle that all people – rich and poor – should be included in the welfare contract is as valid today as ever has resonances of more traditional socialist views of inclusion associated with services such as education and healthcare advocated by those as diverse as Bevan and Crosland (Powell,

1995). Arguing for redistribution of both cash and kind to achieve an inclusive society (Smith, 1996; Field, 1998) appears little different from the 'Strategy of equality' or more accurately the 'Strategy for fraternity' of Tawney (1964) (see Le Grand, 1982; Powell, 1995).

The redefinition of equality is associated with the redefinition of citizenship. According to the new Clause 4 of the Labour Party Constitution, "the rights we enjoy reflect the duties we owe". Halpern and Mikosz (1998, p 37) claim that one of the key principles that appear to underlie the Third Way thinking is a notion of personal responsibility. According to Giddens (1998, p 65) "One might suggest as a prime motto for the new politics, no rights without responsibilities". The Third Way of citizenship moves from 'dutiless rights' towards 'conditional welfare'. The main conditions are connected with work obligations, but there are also suggestions that tenancies in council housing should be conditional on behaviour (Dwyer, 1998; Dean with Melrose, 1999). According to *Children first* (DSS, 1998h), the government wishes to develop an active family policy which links children's rights and parents' responsibilities. Similarly, *Supporting families* (Home Office, 1998a) is concerned with providing practical support to help parents do the best they can for their children. Blair (1998a, p 13) claims that this Third Way approach, giving "support where it is needed most, matching rights and responsibilities", goes beyond the old argument between those who did not care about the family and those who want to turn the clock back to a time before women went out to work. Wilkinson (1998) sees the potential for a third way in family policy, while Giddens (1998, pp 89-98) outlines 'the democratic family', a politics of the family beyond neo-liberalism and old-style social democracy. On the other hand, critics such as Silva and Smart (1999) argue that there is a good deal of continuity between the Conservatives and New Labour regarding the definition of 'strong' and 'problem' families.

According to *A new contract for welfare: New ambitions for our country* (DSS, 1998a, p 19) the Third Way "is about combining public and private provision in a new partnership for the new age". Smith (1996, pp 13-14) rejects the dogma that either the State or the market is always the best provider: "surely it is time to get away from the sterile lines of public and private and instead to look at how the two can best work together in the interests of the citizen". He continues that "The public and private sectors should work in partnership to ensure that, wherever possible, people are insured against foreseeable risks and make provision for their retirement" (Smith, 1996, p 33). It is claimed that "occupational pensions ... are arguably the biggest welfare success story of the century". Pensions are the most developed and most successful example of a public–private partnership (DSS, 1998a, p 34). However, it is noted that this partnership has failed to deliver a decent standard of living for all pensioners. The pledge (DSS, 1998a) to increase the basic pension at least in line with prices (rather than earnings) is a clear return to Beveridgean subsistence, rejecting later bi-partisan agreements on increasing pensions in line with the larger of increases in either earnings or prices, and a second state pension (SERPS) (Hewitt and Powell, 1998). Labour now works with rather than against the market and, in 'partnership' with its new ally, intends to introduce a private finance initiative (PFI) 'mark 2' which critics claim will 'out-Tory the Tories'. In addition to the PFI, other public/private partnerships in areas such as Education Action Zones (Gerwirtz, 1998; Power and Whitty, 1999), the London Underground (*Economist*, 1998) and 'privatising' benefit offices (described in Opposition as a 'crass, dogma-driven move' – see Powell and Hewitt, 1998) have been suggested. Many critics argue that there is a thin line between public/private partnerships and 'privatisation'. It has been suggested that a common theme linking these disparate partnerships is a willingness to blur the boundary between State and public provision; but if so, why the continued ritualistic hostility to private schools and private medicine? (*Economist*, 1998). For example, some Conservative 'public/private partnerships' such as the Assisted Places Scheme and nursery vouchers are to be abolished.

It has been claimed that Labour is moving towards a 'DIY' welfare state (Grice, 1997a; see Klein and Millar, 1995). For some Labour politicians such as Frank Field, this DIY appears to be based on a revival of mutual aid rather than simply being based on the private sector (see also Hirst, 1994, 1998; Wright, 1996; Giddens, 1998; Blair, 1998a). Field (1997a) argues that we need to break out of the 'welfare equals State' mentality, but states that:

> **I want to make one point crystal clear: the re-drawing of the boundaries between state and individual responsibility is not simply an exercise in downsizing state responsibility [but] crucial to the recreation of a civil society based on a partnership between individuals, organisations and Government.**

For Giddens (1998, p 69) the new mixed economy involves government acting in partnership with agencies in civil society to foster community renewal and development. Similarly, Hargreaves (1998, p 76) argues that government must find ways of bringing the third sector into its reforms of the welfare state. Giddens (1998, pp 78-9) continues that the fostering of an active civil society is a basic part of the Third Way. Government can and must play a major part in renewing civic culture, where the theme of community is fundamental. According to Blair (1998a, pp 7, 12-14) a major policy objective is "a strong civil society enshrining rights and responsibilities ... where the government is a partner to strong communities".

In areas such as the NHS, New Labour rejects the command and control of Old Left and competition of New Right and favours the partnership and cooperation of Third Way. It has pledged to 'abolish the internal market' in the NHS. To this end it is replacing the 'two-tier' system of General Practitioner Fund Holding (GPFH) with primary care groups (PCGs) and is reducing the competitive structure in the NHS by means of mergers and promoting partnership between trusts and health authorities, but is keeping the 'purchaser/provider split'. In local government, it is replacing compulsory competitive tendering (CCT) with a new, wider regime of 'Best Value'. However, in both the NHS and local government competition is being reduced and redefined, but not abolished (see for example, Boyne, 1998; Klein, 1998; Paton, 1998; Powell, 1999).

In contrast to Old Labour, New Labour rejects the view that high social expenditure is 'a good thing' (Mandelson and Liddle, 1996, p 26). According to the 1997 Labour General Election Manifesto, the myth that the solution to every problem is increased spending has been comprehensively dispelled under the Conservatives. The Labour focus is on the most effective use of public money between and across government departments. New Labour will be wise spenders, not big spenders. This appears to have two main elements. First, Blair and Brown have contrasted 'good' and 'bad' spending. 'Investment' in services such as education and health is 'good'. However, part of the social security budget is 'bad' – 'the bills of economic and social failure'. As Blair explains:

> **... part of the budget is spending on pensions, child benefit, and people with disabilities: good, we like that. The other part is spending on unemployment and people on benefit when they should be at work: bad, we want to decrease that. (Blair, 1998b, col 408)**

Second, the level of public spending is no longer the best measure of the effectiveness of government action in the public interest (Miliband, 1994, p 88). The Comprehensive Spending Review ties money to reform and modernisation, ensuring that it is well and wisely spent and goes to the front-line of services. It is what money is actually spent on that counts more than how much money is spent. New Labour stresses that this is the case for the NHS – which is the direct opposite of the weapon with which it used to beat the Conservatives. The Conservative argument of the 1980s, that a service should be judged by outputs rather than inputs, has belatedly been accepted. This has progressed furthest in social security. Chris Smith wrote:

> **I despair of those who argue that it is somehow a cause of the Left in politics to spend more on social security and social support. It isn't a mark of progressive success if you are spending more and more on a benefit system. If that were in fact the case, then Peter Lilley would be earning full marks in the pantheon of socialist heroes. (Smith, 1996, p 12)**

In 1997 Brown challenged "the myth that the solution to every problem was increased spending and that in some way the more public spending there was the better we were fulfilling the public interest" (in Oppenheim, 1997a, pp 7-8). According to the Commission on Social Justice (1994, p 104), "A higher social security budget is a sign of economic failure, not social success". Similarly, Field (1997a) argues that "spending on welfare is, all too often, spending on failure".

As Lister (1997a) shows, this argument has transferred from the global to the individual levels. Proposals for better benefits are dismissed as 'old fashioned' or 'Old Labour'. There has been a subtle shift from arguing that tackling poverty cannot simply be about extra money for those on benefit to a position that it is not about better benefits. After earlier bitter attacks, New Labour now agrees with the Conservatives that pension increases should be linked to prices rather than earnings. Essentially, this approach views benefits in terms of absolute as opposed to relative poverty; moving from Peter Townsend's ideas of relative poverty and back to the Beveridge concept of subsistence income (Hewitt and Powell, 1998). It has been reported that Prime Minister Tony Blair has decreed that there should be no improvements in benefit levels, so that life on benefits is less attractive (or less eligible) (Lister, 1997a).

The locus of power under New Labour is unclear. There have been some moves towards greater devolution such as in Scotland and Wales. The autonomy of local authorities has been increased in that they are allowed to spend the capital receipts from the sale of council houses, have greater choice about Best Value and have a more relaxed regime associated with the capping of local council tax. On the other hand, in a number of areas there are the opposite signs of centralisation such as the Secretary of State being given greater reserve powers, the use of 'name and shame' comparisons, threats and actual sacking of managers. Klein (1998) writes of the new highly centralised NHS adopting a command-and-control strategy. Blair (1998a, p 16) suggests that the underlying philosophy is "intervention in inverse proportion to success". Different points of the White Paper, *The new National Health Service: Modern, dependable* (DoH, 1997), suggest greater powers for the centre, professionals, representative bodies and consumers. It is difficult to predict the outcomes of a series of power struggles in the NHS.

Finally, it is unclear what Labour's new politics involves. On the one hand, it is claimed that values have not changed, but are placed in a modern setting. It has been claimed that Keir Hardie and Clement Attlee would have approved of New Labour policies. Blair (1998c) argues that the Third Way returns to the human values of the Left – justice, solidarity, freedom – but rethinks how they are delivered. On the other hand, Labour may be seen as 'post-ideological':

> **We will be a radical government. But the definition of radicalism will not be that of doctrine, whether of left or right, but of achievement. New Labour is a party of ideas and ideals but not of outdated ideology. What counts is what works. (Blair, 1998e)**

It is possible to see a new 'end-of-ideology thesis' in which the debate on the welfare state is shifted on to the secondary technical issues of delivery and efficiency.

Content outline

The following chapters will address the main research questions identified at the beginning of this chapter, using the Third Way as a broad framework: is Labour continuing the policies of the Old Left or the New Right, or following a distinctive policy agenda? However, it is not easy to supply definitive answers to these questions. First, there is continuing debate in arenas such as *Renewal, New Statesman* and the *Nexus* on-line discussions concerning the nature of the 'Third Way'. Second, there is the problem of decoding the new political language: to deconstruct the soundbite. The Third Way is partly a new political language, or rather a redefinition of the old political language (McElroy, 1997; Daniel, 1998). The old linguistic battle lines have been abandoned for newer less sharply drawn positions. Many have their own interpretations of the new 'hurrah words' such as social inclusion, social cohesion, stakeholding and individual freedom. This makes it necessary to enquire whether terms such as equality and redistribution now have different meanings. Third, in the early days of the government, it may be difficult to disentangle policy rhetoric from reality: implemented policies may be different from those that are promised.

In spite of these difficulties, the following chapters attempt a provisional verdict on the direction and speed of policy change. Each chapter is intended to be self-contained. This means that the book need not necessarily be read in chapter order, but may be consulted according to areas of interest. It follows that there will be some overlap between chapters in the sense that some topics (such as 'Welfare to Work') will be found in more than one chapter. However, cross-referencing to other relevant chapters is provided.

In Chapter Two, Tania Burchardt and John Hills focus on the vital area of public expenditure and the public/private mix, which has implications for all policy sectors. As Blair recognises:

> ... taxation goes to the heart of the Third Way. In the Eighties, the issue of tax was more important than any other in holding back the left. (Blair, 1998a, p 15)

Burchardt and Hills provide important contextual material which shapes debates in many policy areas, including the volume of public expenditure, the competing priorities within public expenditure, and the distinctions between production and finance within the mixed economy of welfare. The significance of Labour's Comprehensive Spending Review is stressed, and it is suggested that, contrary to some critics, Labour's budgets have had some redistributive tendencies.

The core of the book consists of chapters on the main policy sectors of welfare. In Chapter Three Calum Paton focuses on the NHS, arguably the embodiment of the welfare state for Old Labour. He argues that behind the rhetoric of Labour's 'new NHS' lies a number of tensions. In many ways, Labour is attempting to adapt Conservative policies: the internal market is evolving rather than being abolished. However, Paton emphasises the relatively neglected area of policy implementation (rather than formulation). There may be some differences between the intentions and the outcomes of policy (cf Klein, 1998). This makes speculation about the final shape of the new welfare state difficult.

Norman Johnson in Chapter Four examines personal social services and community care, which has not (yet) received much of Labour's attention. While he points to many policies which are continued from the Conservatives, there are perhaps some signs of points of departure, notably with respect to carers, childcare and the family. Johnson also emphasises communitarianism as an important ingredient in Labour's policy mix.

New Labour has often claimed that education is its first priority (for example, Labour Party, 1997a; Blair, 1998a). To reflect this importance, Chapter Five has three authors – Yolande Muschamp, Ian Jamieson and Hugh Lauder – giving an account of 'Education, education, education'. Although there are many similarities with Conservative policy, possible areas of discontinuity include the emphasis given to lifelong learning and nursery education and the introduction of Education Action Zones. The authors raise the point that the stress placed on inspection implies a 'low trust policy' in professional groups (cf Johnson's discussion on social workers in Chapter Four).

In Chapter Six Peter Kemp addresses the topic of housing. Like personal social services, housing was an area with no clear policy agenda. Nevertheless, housing illustrates some of the key themes to New Labour: a pragmatic acceptance of the market, social exclusion, joined-up government, Best Value, the tension between central and local control, and the Comprehensive Spending Review. Kemp examines the apparent paradox that while the political significance of housing has declined, it has been a favoured area in terms of expenditure. The answer appears to be that the importance of housing policy lies with its links with social exclusion.

The centrality of paid work to New Labour has already been stressed. In Chapter Seven, Martin Hewitt analyses social security, focusing on New Labour's claim to provide "work for those who can; security for those who cannot". He sketches out the main themes of Third Way in social security, including issues such as benefit levels, the structure of entitlement to benefit, the governance of social security and the changing dimensions of citizenship.

The following chapter by Peter Cressey places work in the wider framework of employment. A particular strength of this account is its clear exploration of the influence of Europe in the shape of European

Directives and the Social Chapter. However, Britain exhibits a complex mix of influences, including many continuities with the Conservatives, but some discontinuities. The New Deal is placed within the framework of wider debates about active versus passive labour market policies.

In Chapter Nine Sarah Charman and Stephen Savage inspect the area of criminal justice, which has been termed "critical to the third way" (Blair, 1998a, p 12). 'Law and order' has always been seen as Conservative territory, a possible vote-loser for Labour, where the Party was out of line with popular opinion (Mandelson and Liddle, 1996). It was in this area that the young(er) Blair first made his mark coining the phrase "tough on crime; tough on the causes of crime". Charman and Savage argue that Labour has been remarkably successful in turning this issue around. They warn against equating rhetoric with policy (cf Paton in Chapter Three), pointing out that accounts which see an essential similarity between Labour Home Secretary Jack Straw and the Conservative Home Secretary Michael Howard (cf Driver and Martell, 1998) are too simplistic. 'Mr Straward' does not exist.

The following chapters discuss issues that cut across different policy areas. Hartley Dean in Chapter Ten not only examines the changing nature of citizenship under New Labour, but also locates this within a framework which provides important conceptual advances on the debate on the competing traditions of citizenship. He stresses the rise of duties and conditional citizenship within New Labour thinking. In particular, he focuses on the importance of waged work within the Blair/Clinton orthodoxy.

In Chapter Eleven John Rouse and George Smith analyse accountability. They trace the changes from the traditional model of public accountability in the post-war consensus – the Westminster model – to the new public management of the Conservative years and the 'differentiated polity'. They show how concepts such as decentralisation, devolution, and consumerism came on to Labour's agenda and fused into a new emergent strategy for accountability. After examining democratic renewal and the nature of the new politics (cf Giddens' [1998] notion of the new democratic state), they suggest some of the main themes of a third way of accountability.

Desmond King and Mark Wickham-Jones in Chapter Twelve compare the approach of New Labour in the UK and the Democrats in the USA in the key area of Welfare to Work, pointing to a 'remarkable turnaround' in Labour's attitude to conditionality. Like Chapter Eight, they locate New Labour within the wider comparative context and illustrate the complexities of policy transfer between countries.

The concluding chapter summarises the main themes from the individual chapters and attempts to answer the questions posed at the beginning of the book. This is a difficult task for two reasons. First, many of the contributors stress the provisional nature of their verdicts. In some areas, policy developments are less advanced and the evaluations are more speculative. A number of contributors warn against confusing policy rhetoric with outcomes. Second, there are some differences between the views of the contributors. Some areas are seen to have more policy continuity with the Conservatives than others, although it may be more accurate to argue that Labour has adapted Conservative policy, or reformed the Conservative reforms to greater or lesser degrees in different policy sectors. However, some contributors tentatively suggest some evidence of an emergent 'Third Way'. A number of themes, including centrality of work, the new conditionality of citizenship and the redefinition of redistribution and equality, appear in many different chapters. While there are some clear signs of the emergence of a new welfare state, its exact shape is still far from clear.

TWO

Public expenditure and the public/private mix

Tania Burchardt and John Hills

Introduction

If there is one area where New Labour seems clearly distinct from the Old, it is public spending. It seems inconceivable that a senior Labour politician today would argue that government should 'launch a massive programme of expansion' to spend its way out of recession, as the Leader of the Labour Party did in the early 1980s. The apparent closeness that New Labour has to prominent figures in the world of business suggests an acceptance of and by the private sector unimaginable 15 years ago. This chapter examines the transformation – if transformation it is – with respect to any change in position by both Conservative and Labour towards public expenditure during the period. It then assesses the significance of this transformation for Labour's policy in government.

'Rolling back the State': Conservative policy 1979-97

Public expenditure

During the eight decades from the turn of the century to the year before Margaret Thatcher came into office, the share of the nation's income spent on the welfare state grew from 2% of GDP to 24% (Glennerster, 1998a). By the end of the succeeding two decades, it stood at just 25% of GDP – a far slower rate of growth than previously. Some important change had taken place. However, as Figure 2.1 illustrates, it would be a mistake to think of the arrival of Thatcherism as the decisive break – welfare spending fell sharply in 1976-79 in relation to GDP before rising again slightly in the early years of Conservative rule. It was the oil crisis of 1976, and the resulting International Monetary Fund intervention, that preceded a reduction, not the change in government.

Figure 2.1: UK government welfare spending 1973/74 to 1997/98

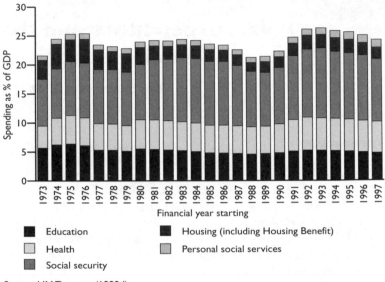

Source: HM Treasury (1998d)

Whatever the initial trigger for a downturn in welfare spending, there can be no doubting the Conservatives' commitment to reducing it still further. The first White Paper on public spending declared: "Public expenditure is at the heart of Britain's present economic difficulties" (HM Treasury, 1979). Glennerster (1998b) identifies four possible reasons for this approach:

- the levels of taxation required to finance public spending had become unsustainable;
- as the real post-tax income of families fell in the immediate aftermath of 1976, public attitudes towards public spending and the taxes required to pay for it were unfavourable;
- fiercer global economic competition and the need to sustain international trade meant limited opportunities to raise revenue from employers;
- other advanced countries were stabilising tax rates over the period, which, given potential movements of capital to areas with low taxes, exerted a downward pressure on UK tax rates.

The power of a new doctrine, monetarism, adopted with fervour by the incoming government, could be added to this list. After all, the international constraints were not binding: the UK was never a high-tax country. Tax as a share of GDP was in the middle of the international range in the mid-1970s. By restraining growth in the tax ratio, the UK was in the lower half of the industrialised country range by the start of the 1990s (Hills, 1996, Figures 4.2 and 4.3, pp 73-4).

A determination to reduce public expenditure is not in itself sufficient to achieve it. It was particularly difficult to control welfare spending. Figure 2.2 shows that welfare spending accounted for a higher percentage of government expenditure towards the end of the Conservative period of office compared to the figure for 1979. Lack of success in reducing – as opposed to restraining – the share of spending that went on welfare was not for want of trying. Three of the key measures are discussed below.

Targeting

For the 'New Right', the primary objective of welfare was poverty relief. That part of benefit expenditure which went to better-off families, such as some social insurance benefits and universal non-contributory benefits, was considered unnecessary, and better targeting on the poor would mean more efficient use of public money and facilitate lower tax rates. As a result of numerous changes to the benefit system – notably the linking of

Figure 2.2: Spending on the welfare state as a proportion of all government expenditure (%)

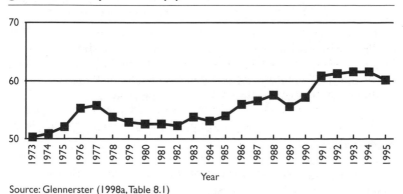

Year

Source: Glennerster (1998a, Table 8.1)

the basic pension to prices rather than earnings and eligibility restrictions on unemployment benefit – use of means-testing grew. In 1995/96 expenditure via the benefit system totalled at 22% of social security spending (excluding housing benefit), up from 9% in 1979/80 (Evans, 1998, Table 7A.1, pp 304-7). Similarly, as private renting was deregulated and subsidies to social housing cut back, support for tenants shifted on to a more means-tested basis, through Housing Benefit.

Cutting capital spending

Cuts in public investment would mean that the effects would not be felt as immediately as would follow a reduction in revenue spending. For example, in education, spending as a whole reduced only slightly as a proportion of GDP in the first years of the Conservative government, but capital spending was cut in real terms by nearly one third, falling from £1.7 billion in 1979/80 to £1.2 billion by 1984/85, and remaining at that level until the end of the decade[1]. In housing, public spending as a whole fell from 3.3% of GDP in 1979/80 to 2.1% in 1996/97, while capital spending more than halved in real terms, from £8.5 billion to £3 billion[2]. Overall, public sector net investment fell from 2.8% of GDP in 1979/80 to 0.9% in 1996/97 (HM Treasury, 1998c, Table A6).

Privatisation

This crucial strand of the Conservative's strategy is discussed in detail in the next section.

The Conservatives did not succeed in making substantial inroads into public expenditure on welfare – it rose and fell with the economic cycle and was very nearly the same proportion of GDP in 1996 as in 1979. However, spending would have continued to rise as it did in the period 1945-76 if a tough approach had not been taken. This is in the context of there being upward pressures on spending during the period, from an ageing population, high unemployment, a growth in the number of lone parents, and increased demand for health and education as living standards rose.

Public/private mix

The Conservative desire to keep public spending under control was one motivation for their promotion of private sector involvement in welfare, but it was by no means the only one. There were powerful political and ideological reasons too: opening up public providers to competition from outside and within undermined the power of public sector unions and of local authorities; encouraging individuals to opt out of State services by making their own provision fostered a sense of individual responsibility and facilitated a growth in private welfare markets. To the Conservatives, traditional forms of welfare provision – local education authority (LEA)-maintained schools, the National Health Service (NHS), council housing, access to benefits for all – represented state-owned monopolies, big demands on public finances, and lack of consumer choice.

However, only in a few cases were services amenable to wholesale privatisation. Sales of state-owned corporations, from British Aerospace to British Rail, began soon after Thatcher came to power, and continued right up to the last days of the Major government, but council housing was the only part of the welfare state subject to wholesale privatisation. The 'Right to Buy' legislation of 1980 formalised existing arrangements for council tenants to purchase their homes and removed local authority discretion. Discounts relating to the duration of the tenancy were introduced and made more generous in 1984 and again in 1986. This was followed in the 1987-92 and 1992-97 administrations by attempts to encourage local authorities to sell or transfer whole sections of stock to tenant-based organisations, private landlords or housing associations. 'Right to Buy' proved hugely popular and 1.7 million housing units were sold to tenants between 1981 and 1995, contributing to the reduction in the proportion of total housing stock owned by local authorities from 30% to 19% (Hills, 1998).

In other areas private provision was encouraged but with continuing state finance. The second Conservative administration saw the intensification of efforts to 'contract-out' peripheral services such as hospital cleaning and catering to the private sector. Competitive tendering became compulsory for these services in 1986. Individual consumers were also offered financial incentives to choose private over public alternatives, by means of tax reliefs such as private medical insurance for those aged 60 and above, and grants such as the Assisted Places Scheme, which gave financial help to children from low-income families who gained a place at an independent school.

In some cases existing structures of service provision were retained, but perceived opportunities to reduce public finance were adopted. Examples include NHS eye tests and dentistry, in which free treatment was restricted to special groups from 1989 onwards, and social services, for which user charges became more widespread.

Finally, the Conservatives explored ways to privatise choice of service provision while retaining some public finance or control. The best-known example is the reform of second-tier pensions which permitted employees to opt out of the state scheme (SERPS) into either an occupational pension scheme or a personal pension plan, with the same or even more generous levels of tax reliefs and rebates. The initial take-up of personal pensions exceeded all expectations, with nearly five million people opting out between 1987 and 1993, although sales then flattened off as the extent of inappropriate purchases became apparent.

These many and varied forms of privatisation are summed up in Figure 2.3. The top half of the chart represents public provision, and the right-hand side represents public finance; the overlap in the top right-hand quadrant (white) contains publicly provided and financed services, such as NHS hospital care. Services in the inner circle differ from those in the outer ring in being publicly controlled, with the decision over what level of service should be provided and by whom being in the hands of a public body rather than individual consumers. Moves out of the inner-

Figure 2.3: Forms of privatisation

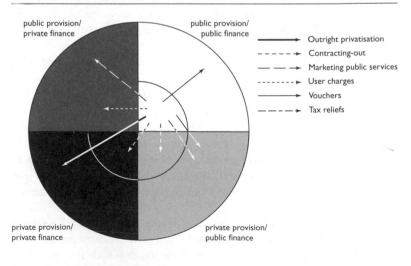

Source: Burchardt et al (1999)

circle white sector (public provision, finance and control) can be in any direction: directly to the opposite extreme (black outer ring: private provision, finance and control), or just to a neighbouring section, for example, left into private finance by making greater use of user charges, or down into private provision, by contracting-out, or out into private control by means of vouchers. More complex moves involve privatising two of the three dimensions, for example, by introducing tax reliefs for individually-purchased private alternatives (private provision and control, but retaining some public finance). Examples of all of these forms of privatisation can be found in the history of Conservative welfare policy since 1979.

What degree of success did the Conservatives have in their objective to minimise the role of the public sector? Figure 2.4 compares welfare expenditure in 1979 and 1995, divided as in Figure 2.3 along the three dimensions of provision, finance and control[3]. The changes need to be understood in the context of an overall growth in welfare expenditure of some 65% in real terms, but the picture which emerges in terms of shares of welfare expenditure is one of surprising constancy – with 'pure public' expenditure dominant in both years. However, its share of the total does fall from 52% to 49%. The 'pure public' sector fell faster for education, health, housing and personal social services, but was offset by considerable growth both in the amount of social security expenditure overall, driven by high unemployment and rising inequality, and in the proportion of social security classifiable as 'pure public'. At the same time the 'pure private' sector grew, largely as a result of the spread of owner-occupation. Public finance for private provision (bottom right quadrant) was the next largest sector overall, and grew as a result of contracting out and tax reliefs from 14% to 19% of total expenditure.

Constraints

Although the Conservatives met with some success in containing growing public expenditure, the welfare component within that overall budget continued to increase, and this despite determined and sustained attempts to reduce it. Part of the explanation for the difficulty they encountered is rising demand for welfare services: unemployment increased sharply soon after Margaret Thatcher came to power and remained high until the late 1980s; the elderly population was growing steadily, putting pressure on both health and pension expenditure; the rise in the number of lone

Figure 2.4: Expenditure on welfare

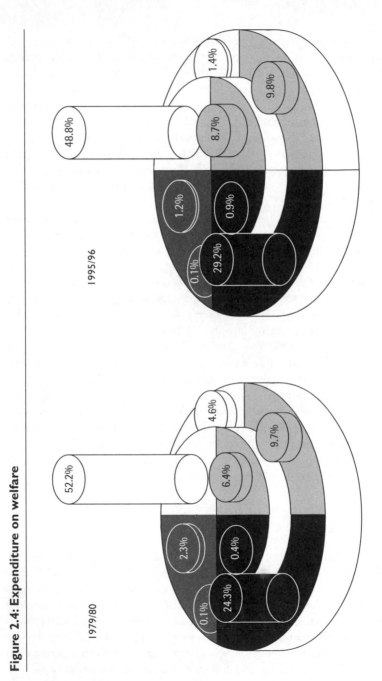

1979/80

1995/96

Source: Burchardt et al (1999)

parent families increased dependence on means-tested benefits. At the same time, the Conservatives were constrained by the continuing popularity of two of the major spending programmes, health and education, which together made up less than half of public welfare expenditure in 1979. Higher proportions of respondents to the British Social Attitudes Survey opted for health or education as first or second priority for public spending in 1996 than in 1983 (Judge et al, 1997, p 53). Privatisation appeared to offer a way out of the squeeze between rising demands and unwillingness to raise taxes, but again core programmes proved resistant to change. A plethora of initiatives were launched aimed at reducing public expenditure and marketising welfare services. However, most – with the exception of selling off housing stock – had only marginal effects on public finance. Shifts towards private provision of services, retaining tax-finance, were more marked.

Out with the Old, in with the New – changes in Labour's position 1979-97

Public expenditure

In Labour's 1983 election manifesto, Michael Foot outlined an Emergency Programme of Action, promising to launch a "massive programme for expansion" to spend the country out of recession (Labour Party, 1983). Just less than a decade later, when Britain was again suffering the effects of a period of economic stagnation, Neil Kinnock likewise had plans for a National Recovery Programme, but this one was to stimulate private investment alongside public funds and create "a government with which business can do business". The transformation in fiscal policy was complete in 1997, when Chancellor Gordon Brown committed the incoming Labour government to remaining within its predecessor's planned spending limit for the first two years.

Foot's proposed drive for expansion in 1983 was to cost an extra £11 billion in cash terms in government spending – 3.5% of GDP. The money, according to the manifesto, would come from oil revenues, reducing unemployment, taxing overseas investments, and borrowing. This last component was defended in classic Keynesian terms: in a recession, governments should borrow to generate employment and kick-start investment. Specific components of the Emergency Programme of Action included a huge public housebuilding initiative, a substantial increase in resources for social services, and investment in industry, especially public enterprises. On pensions, Labour promised a one-off increase in the basic pension and then to up-rate it in line with earnings – the Conservatives having linked up-rating to the less generous index of prices. Labour was also committed to raising Child Benefit, giving special help to one-parent families, and to a real increase of 3% per year in spending on the NHS.

The language of the 1987 manifesto was less stridently left wing, but policies on public spending were similar to those that had gone before: a 'Paying for Recovery' Programme would cost £6 billion a year (1.4% of GDP) for the first two years, paid for by reversing Thatcher's two pence in the pound income tax 'bribe', reversing tax cuts for the rich, reforming capital and taxation, and borrowing as much as a quarter of the cost of the whole programme. The commitment to restoring the earnings link for the basic state pension was retained, along with the same one-off increases in pensions and Child Benefit, although it was not specified how these would be paid for. The election campaign was dominated by lack of clarity from Labour as to how its plans would be financed.

Poor performance at the polls in 1987 prompted the Labour Party to undertake a major policy review, which reported in 1989. Kinnock's 'introduction' to the 1987 manifesto (Labour Party, 1987) signalled a change in attitude towards public spending: "We will not spend, nor will we promise to spend, more than the country can afford". However, he went on to hope that economic growth would be such that greater public spending would be possible, with – as ever – first priorities being health, education, and restoring the earnings link for the basic pension.

By the time of the 1992 election, these policies had been carefully costed and firmed up into an extra £1 billion for the NHS and £600 million over two years for education (together barely 0.3% of GDP). There was no mention in the manifesto of restoring the earnings link for the basic pension, although a one-off increase the same in nominal terms as that in the 1987 manifesto was promised – still a significant expenditure commitment – along with an increase in Child Benefit. A 'National Recovery Programme' would secure private investment alongside public funds and create "a government which business can do business with" (Labour Party, 1992).

Arguments about tax were once again a major feature of the election campaign, and a defeated Labour Party emerged determined to convince voters – next time round – that taxes, and public spending, would be kept under control. The search was on for a 'big idea' that could replace spending as the central plank of Labour's appeal. John Smith's Commission on Social Justice offered the concept of an 'Investor's Britain' as the key to future policy, combining the "ethics of community with the dynamics of a market economy" (Commission on Social Justice, 1994). The Commission rejected on the one hand an untrammelled free market approach, and on the other, a tax and spend nanny state, arguing instead that revenue could be raised in diverse ways and invested – rather than spent – on programmes that helped people to help themselves. On social security, they regarded an increase in the basic pension across the board as too expensive and proposed instead a "minimum pension guarantee" (Commission on Social Justice, 1994, p 269) which would rise in line with earnings, together with a universal second tier pension for those of working age. This was to be one element of a revitalised social insurance system.

However, with Tony Blair at the helm, even the Commission's more restrained (though uncosted) approach to spending was considered too radical. Instead, the 1997 election manifesto undertook to stick to spending totals set by the Conservatives for the first two years in office, thereby pulling the carpet from under the feet of opponents waiting in the wings to accuse Labour's spending plans of requiring additional taxation. However, the commitment bound Labour into a tight constraint, one possibly tighter than the one to which Conservatives themselves intended to keep. Labour's priorities were instead to be met by cutting out waste and reallocating money between budgets, and a windfall tax on excess profits of privatised utilities. Few concrete policies were offered on welfare, although comprehensive reviews were promised for pensions and long-term care. Education and health were to receive a larger share of government expenditure – but only as and when savings were made elsewhere.

Labour's analysis of its electoral woes was clear: voters feared spending promises would be paid for through higher taxation. The solution, to modernisers within the Party, was equally obvious: promise nothing except not to raise income tax. This was despite evidence from the British Social Attitudes Survey showing consistently large majorities in favour of higher taxes and spending on health and education, and a study of voters who switched allegiance from Labour during the 1992 election campaign, which found no evidence that they were particularly adverse to higher taxes (Heath et al, 1994, p 292). However, there is some indication that Labour's critique of its own position was correct, at least as far as its image with the electorate was concerned. Table 2.1 shows that in each of the

Table 2.1: Voters' attitudes to taxes and spending relative to the Labour Party (%)

	1983	1987	1992	1997
To Labour's Left	20	18	19	31
The same	21	24	24	31
To Labour's Right	59	57	57	38

Note: Based on British Election Surveys 1983 and 1987 and British Election Panel Study 1992-97.
Source: *Heath and Curtice* (1998, Table 1, p 5)

election years 1983, 1987 and 1992, a majority regarded themselves as 'to Labour's Right' on the issue of spending and taxation – but by 1997 the position was much more balanced. Combined results from these various sources suggest that the public wanted more public services and expressed that they would be at the least prepared to pay for them through higher taxes, but until the last election, thought that Labour would spend and tax *too much*.

Public/private mix

Given Labour's hostility to the private sector at the time, it may come as something of a surprise to read in the 1983 manifesto that in Michael Foot's opinion, "Without [a] continuing partnership to rebuild our country, all else will fail" (Labour Party, 1983). However, when reading on it becomes clear that the partnership to which he is referring is between government and the trade unions, not, as one would automatically assume in the 1990s, a partnership between public and private sectors. In the early 1980s Labour undertook to return to public ownership the industries privatised by Thatcher, to promote workers cooperatives and to support key public sector corporations. They opposed the Right to Buy initiative, and were committed to removing private practice from the NHS. On education, their 1983 manifesto stated, "Private schools are a major obstacle to a free and fair education system": a Labour government would withdraw their favourable tax treatment and abolish the Assisted Places Scheme.

Just as with their policies on public spending, there was no sudden transformation from Old to New Labour, but rather a gradual introduction of new terminology and an acceptance that there might be a place for market mechanisms in welfare. Four years later, in 1987, Labour stood on a platform of antiprivatisation, but was not opposed to private welfare per se. The enormous popularity of Right to Buy made it electorally impossible to continue to oppose it. On health, they promised to reduce prescription charges, but not to abolish them as they had in 1983, and pay beds, reflecting private practice within the NHS, were to be phased out, rather than immediately withdrawn.

The language of modernisation began to appear in the late-1980s, with Kinnock's major policy review, although some specific policies remain unchanged. Kinnock explicitly accepted that there might be a role for private provision of welfare services:

> **But it is no longer possible or as necessary as it used to be to draw strict dividing lines between 'public' and 'private'.... Instead of the Conservatives' dogma that public must be bad, private good, we offer a new framework for public and private services which put people first. (Labour Party, 1989)**

The Policy Review restated the Party's opposition to private practice in the NHS, but recommended a more indirect method for achieving its demise: to make the NHS so good that the need for private medicine would disappear. Hostility to private education was likewise tamed: their target became those private schools which select on pupils' attainment and parents' ability to pay, rather than private education in principle, and they recommended restricting tax breaks just to those schools with genuinely charitable aims.

The next major review of welfare policy took place under John Smith's leadership with the Commission on Social Justice. Its report reaffirmed a belief in the value of public/private partnerships, but pushed it one stage further: not only might services be efficiently provided by the private sector, they could also be partly financed from private sources. Employers, users, and private investors were all listed as being potential sources of finance for welfare. However, an entirely privatised future was rejected on the grounds that it would sacrifice social justice.

Labour moved in step-wise fashion, from opposition to the private sector itself, through an antiprivatisation stance, to an acceptance of a role for private provision of welfare, and then even some private finance. The final step was a conversion of acceptance to enthusiasm: Blair was determined to convince business leaders that they had a friend in Labour.

This process can be seen as simply a corollary of Labour's moves on public spending. The tighter the fiscal constraint, the more pressure there is to pass some responsibilities on to employers and consumers themselves. However, that cannot be the whole story: the acceptance of private provision, even if publicly financed, came before Labour embraced private finance. For some specific policies, such as Right to Buy, an electoral explanation seems sufficient – its popularity made continuing opposition untenable. More generally, the shift might have been one effect of waning trade union influence and the perception that wooing the corporate sector was increasingly important. What had been seen as wasteful competition came to be welcomed as the rigour of the market; what had been seen as protecting welfare provision from being polluted by profit came to be denounced as harbouring inefficiency.

'Prudence for a purpose' – Labour's policy in government

Public expenditure

Voters in the 1997 Election might have been forgiven for getting confused between the numerous pledges, contracts, and manifesto commitments that were issued above the signature of Tony Blair. However, one of these came across loud and clear: Labour would stick to the spending limits set by its predecessor for at least the first two years of the new Parliament. The Party was determined not to be susceptible to propaganda of the 'Labour's tax bombshell' variety this time round. Given that the electorate returned a Labour government with the largest majority since 1945, that strategy was clearly part of a successful formula. However, the question quickly arose, how would New Labour deliver distinctive policies while keeping within Conservative control totals? Prudence was evident, but where was the purpose?

The Chancellor set out two rules of fiscal policy in his first budget statement:

- to ensure that during the economic cycle, the government would borrow only to invest and that current spending would be met from taxation;
- to hold public debt as a proportion of national income at a prudent and stable level during the economic cycle.

This was followed in the 1998 Budget with the launch of 'The Code for Fiscal Stability', which enshrined in fiscal management the principles of "transparency, stability, responsibility, fairness and efficiency" (HM Treasury, 1998e, p 7). Both Budget speeches reiterated the government's commitment to adhere to the previous government's control totals for public spending and in June 1998 the Chancellor indicated his intention to extend tight fiscal constraints for the life of the Parliament (HM Treasury, 1998b).

However, within these totals, spending can be reallocated to reflect new priorities. To this end Labour set in train a Comprehensive Spending Review (CSR). Every spending department has been required to reassess its budget from a zero base, identifying inefficiencies and redistributing savings to newly-identified priorities. In a departure from the traditional pattern of annual spending rounds, the new departmental budgets have been agreed for three years. The results of this exercise were presented in July 1998 with a great deal of publicity being given to the increased spending plans for health and education (HM Treasury, 1998c). By comparing spending plans in cash for the next three years with the base of 1998/99 and then aggregating the differences, the government was able to claim 'increased spending' totalling £20 billion for the NHS and £19 billion for education.

While this type of hype may have the long-run effect of unduly raising expectations, there clearly has been a significant reallocation of priorities, as Table 2.2 shows. In aggregate, the government's preferred spending

Table 2.2: Growth in public spending and spending plans 1993/94 to 2001/02

	Real annual growth rates (%)			
	1993/94 to 1996/97	1996/97 to 1998/99	1998/99 to 2001/02 (planned)	1996/97 to 2001/02 (planned)
NHS (England)	2.1	2.3	4.7	3.7
Education (GB)	0.7	-0.2	5.1	2.9
Total Managed Expenditure	1.3	0.1	2.7	1.7
Social security (including Welfare to Work)	1.6	0.5	2.0	1.4
Defence	-4.3	-0.9	-1.4	-1.2
GDP	3.1	2.4	2.2	2.3

Source: HM Treasury (1998c, Tables A1, A2, A3 and A6, pp 106, 107, 109, 113)

measure – Total Managed Expenditure – grew by only 0.1% per year in real terms in the two years of adherence to its predecessor's spending plans, 1996/97 to 1998/99, falling from 41.9% to 40.0% of GDP. Within this total, real NHS spending grew almost as fast as GDP, but education spending fell in real terms.

The key effects of the CSR can be seen in the third column of the table. Total Managed Expenditure is planned to rise in relation to GDP by 2001/02 (to 40.7%, with all of this increase accounted for by capital rather than current spending). The NHS and education rise at nearly twice this rate in real terms. The space to achieve this is created by slower than average growth in other departments – not so much social security once you include items such as Welfare to Work spending, but rather areas such as agriculture (falling after the costs of the BSE crisis) and defence. As the table shows, defence spending was already falling before 1996. One measure of the realignment of spending in recent years is that in 1993/94 NHS spending (in England) was £31.9 billion and defence £25.1 billion; by 2001/02 they are planned to be £40.7 and £20.7 billion respectively (all figures in 1997/98 prices).

If you look at Labour's plans for the whole period 1996/97 to 2001/02, the overall effect is intended to be total spending growing more slowly than GDP, but health and education benefiting by somewhat faster growth – 3.7% and 2.9% respectively at an annualised rate. The effect is to raise their combined share of total spending by about 1.3 percentage points. In effect by the end of the period they will together be running at about £5 billion per year more in real terms than they would have been if spending shares had simply been left unchanged. This is less dramatic than the publicity about the CSR suggested. However, it is still significant: the additional resources for these two priority areas are almost as much as would have been raised by putting two pence on all income tax rates.

Flexibility on spending has also been manufactured by measures outside the departmental control totals. Labour promised not to increase the basic or higher rates of income tax, but revenue can and has been raised in other ways: in the first Budget a windfall tax on profits of privatised utilities was announced, due to bring the government £4.8 billion over two years (HM Treasury, 1997). This money was allocated to the Welfare to Work programme, aimed at getting young unemployed, lone parents, sick and disabled people, long-term unemployed and partners of unemployed people into employment. Other measures were considered to be part of the tax system and hence outside spending totals. Prominent among these is the Working Families Tax Credit (see Chapter Seven), the successor to Family Credit which provides more generous childcare provision and a reduced withdrawal rate as earnings rise. Renewed capital expenditure has been sanctioned, in the form of a 'release' of £4.2 billion in assets from the sale of council houses for tackling the backlog of repairs on local authority housing, and a £1.3 billion investment in the fabric of school buildings during the course of the Parliament (HM Treasury, 1998c).

Government plans are a notoriously poor guide to expenditure out-turn, so final judgement has to be withheld on the success of Labour's attempts to overhaul public spending. In particular, the Chancellor's strategy is dependent on continuing economic growth, which, in the light of the strong pound hitting manufacturing output and the East Asian economic crisis, can by no means be guaranteed. Nevertheless, the CSR signals a willingness to use surpluses, when they exist, for additional public investment rather than on tax cuts. It points to a rebalancing of public expenditure away from defence towards health, education and 'Welfare to Work' programmes. The two Budgets likewise indicate redistributive tendencies, for example by further reducing mortgage interest tax relief while increasing income support for children and pensioners. The question remains whether subsequent fiscal settlements will push resources in the same direction, pursuing the strategy of incremental change that was so successfully adopted by Margaret Thatcher to redistribute wealth in the opposite direction. However, the overall performance of the economy and an approaching general election could shift the balance back in favour of reining in public expenditure.

Public/private mix

The rhetoric of partnership is strong in government pronouncements. The Third Way is described as being about "combining public and private provision in a new partnership for the new age" (DSS, 1998a). The key principle for pensions (see Chapter Seven) outlined in the Green Paper written by former Minister for Welfare Reform Frank Field begins: "The public and private sectors should work in partnership". It goes on to describe measures to promote private saving and insurance. The private, voluntary and mutual sectors are also to be given a greater role in the delivery of welfare. In truth, public and private sectors have always worked in partnership; the trick is to get the most appropriate mix.

Specific proposals for the future of disability benefits followed the welfare reform Green Paper (DSS, 1998d). Most relied on reshaping public provision – decreasing the role of social insurance in favour of categorical benefits and greater reliance on means-testing – rather than bearing directly on the relationship with private provision. The one exception was the attempt to control the cost to the State of early retirement, by paying reduced Incapacity Benefit where the claimant was in receipt of an occupational or personal pension. This represents an odd type of public/private partnership: the government is effectively proposing to reduce the value of private cover individuals may already have purchased by deducting it at a rate of 50 pence in the pound from the state benefit they would otherwise have received.

The long-awaited pensions Green Paper explicitly stated the government's intention to rebalance pension income from its current 60% public and 40% private split, to 40% public and 60% private by the year 2050 (DSS, 1998e). Some of this shift would have occurred anyway, with private sector pension provision maturing and the value of the basic state pension falling in relative terms as a result of its value being linked to prices rather than earnings. The additional shift is to be achieved by using National Insurance rebates to encourage those on middle incomes to take out heavily regulated personal pensions ('stakeholder pensions'). For lower earners with a good employment record, the State will provide a flat-rate second pension which is more generous to them than its predecessor, SERPS. At the lower end, this in some ways will compensate for the falling relative value of the basic state pension. Underlying all this is a means-tested minimum income for all pensioners, the level of which is intended to rise, if possible, in line with earnings (DSS, 1998e). The Green Paper clearly signals a change in what are seen to be the appropriate roles of State and private provision: the former provides a secure minimum, while the latter (aided with National Insurance rebates) takes on the function of earnings-replacement.

Although it is too early for many proposed partnerships to have taken shape, there is some evidence of partnership in practice, particularly with the New Deal scheme (Chapters Seven, Eight and Twelve). This initiative for the young unemployed went national in April 1998, offering four options, all of which involve non-public-sector partners: a subsidised job with an employer, work with a voluntary organisation, work on the environment taskforce, or full-time education or training. By June 1998, 15,000 employers had signed New Deal agreements and the Employment Minister Andrew Smith was able to declare that it had "got off to an encouraging start" (New Deal website: http://www.dfee.gov.uk). In November 1998, 30 pilots involving offering the scheme to unemployed people aged 50 and above began, some of which are run by private sector companies. Partnerships do appear to be being pursued with renewed vigour, although employers and private sector training companies have been involved in many previous government-sponsored attempts to reduce the dole queue.

The private finance initiative (PFI) begun by the Conservatives has been continued and is being used for a new hospital building programme. Overall, the forecast for investment through PFI is £3 billion in 1998/99, more than seven times as high as the amount invested under the Conservatives in 1995/96. However, PFI could arguably be counted as public rather than private finance. In principle, private contractors take on some of the risk of the investment and borrowing is in the first instance private rather than public. However, contracts are eventually paid for from taxation. Payments for PFI are forecast to rise from £1 billion in 1998/99 to £2.5 billion in 2001/02 (HM Treasury, 1998a).

While the Green Paper on welfare reform, and subsequent policy announcements, suggest a willingness and even an eagerness to utilise private sector expertise, there are indications that Labour is aware of the potential drawbacks of all private solutions. 'A privatised future' is one of the two extremes which defines what the government's Third Way is not (the other being 'the status quo', with more money spent and no reform). Several sections of the welfare reform Green Paper refer to limitations of private provision, for example, on long-term care: "Private provision carries with it the risk of the market 'cherry picking' of the best risks, leaving the taxpayer to pick up the tab for the rest" (DSS, 1998a, p 39). References are made to the inadequacy of currently-available Mortgage Payment Protection policies and to uncertainties over interactions between the benefit system and credit insurance[4]. The Green Paper also explicitly recognised the need for careful regulation of private/public partnerships.

Some of the less successful Conservative initiatives to promote private welfare have been abandoned. A pilot scheme giving parents of four-year-olds vouchers to pay for places at a nursery of their choice is not being pursued, after it was shown that the main effect of the scheme was to increase the size of reception classes at State primary schools. The Assisted Places Scheme is also being wound up – one of the very few commitments from Labour on reversing Conservative policies to have survived since the early 1980s. Tax relief on private medical insurance for those aged 60 and above was likewise an early casualty.

One possible interpretation of Labour's policy on private sector involvement in welfare would be that they have learned from the mistakes of the last administration's overenthusiasm, but have not returned to the anti-business stance associated with Old Labour. Where the private sector can deliver welfare more efficiently, or has expertise that can benefit public providers, it will be drawn on, but the limitations are recognised. Set against that optimistic view is the fact that ministers do not appear to have realised the full costs of private provision – that requiring or expecting individuals to provide more cover for themselves, whether for income in retirement, their mortgage payments during unemployment, or earnings replacement during sickness, reduces the share of their income available for other purposes, including the payment of taxes. Likewise, services contracted out to the private sector, for example building new NHS hospitals, offering low-cost personal pensions, or running the New Deal, require careful regulation and monitoring. There is a danger that any efficiency gains may be more than offset by additional costs to the public purse.

Conclusion

> In each area of policy a new and distinctive approach has been mapped out, one that differs from the old left and the Conservative right. This is why new Labour is new. (Tony Blair in Introduction to 1997 Labour manifesto [Labour Party, 1997a])

Despite Blair's conviction, the rhetoric of New Labour is almost indistinguishable from that of the Conservatives on public spending and the role of the private sector in welfare: key phrases such as low taxation, fiscal prudence and partnership recur throughout government documents. The policy with which Labour came into office – sticking to Conservative spending totals – was designed so that you could not put a cigarette paper between them. The only additional revenue to be raised was through a windfall tax on the profits of privatised utilities. However, evidence of different priorities is now emerging, reaffirmed in the CSR. This includes:

- the use of economic growth to finance additional expenditure rather than to push public spending below 40% of GDP;
- a willingness to invest in public sector projects;
- new spending being planned for health and education and, for children and pensioners, on social security, paid for largely from economic growth and some rebalancing of departmental budgets;

- expenditure on the New Deal;
- a more cautious approach to private welfare.

Blair has said that Labour will have failed if it does not raise the living standards of the poorest during its term in office[5]. Budgets which redistribute resources in the same direction as the previous Budget, the minimum wage and the fulfilment of CSR targets, would go some way towards realising that goal. However, the overall performance of the economy is likely to become the key determinant of the achievability of Labour's twin commitments to keeping income tax rates low while increasing resources for health and education and providing, in the words of the Green Paper on welfare reform, "work for those who can and security for those who cannot" (Blair, 1998a, p iii).

Notes

[1] 1995/96 prices, adjusted by GDP deflator (Glennerster, 1998b, Table 3.1, p 37).
[2] 1995/96 prices, adjusted by GDP deflator (Hills, 1998, Table 5.1, p 134).
[3] Details in Burchardt et al (1999).
[4] See Burchardt and Hills (1997) for a discussion.
[5] Interviewed in *The Independent* 8 December 1997, quoted by Lister (1998, p 216).

THREE

New Labour's health policy: the new healthcare state

Calum Paton

Introduction

If a week is a long time in politics, then 18 years can change politics altogether. When Labour left office in May 1979, the National Health Service was in what the jargon would call a steady state. The Royal Commission on the NHS had basically given it a good report card in terms of financing and structure. In their 1979 election manifesto, the Conservatives did not promise significant change, focusing their energies instead on the economy and related issues such as trade union power.

In their 18 years out of office, Labour's health policy became reactive to Tory policy. The fact that Labour was both ideologically and practically committed to a model for the health service which involved public financing and public provision meant that what had been a radical policy in 1945 was a conservative policy 40 years later (and none the worse for that).

This chapter addresses two main themes:

- Is New Labour policy different to Old Labour?
- Has there been a convergence between Labour and Conservative policy?

In the case of health policy, the two questions are arguably even more closely related than in other areas. Hypothetically at least, New Labour policy is different to Old Labour because Labour's new health policy is a direct inheritance from Conservative policy. In that sense, it does not so much mean a convergence between Labour and Conservative policy as either adoption or adaption by Labour of Conservative policy from the outgoing Conservative government. Labour's policy may be conservative as defined by Disraeli – first opposing change, then adapting it. In other areas of social policy, convergence may be a more accurate term as well as a convenient one. New Labour has adopted many of the tenets of the 'new welfare state', different objectives and different policies have been articulated, at the level of a different emphasis at least, in areas such as education and employment. However, in health New Labour strategy is to seek to 'tidy up' the consequences of the internal market, inherited from the Tories. This chapter first examines Conservative health policy since 1979. It then outlines Labour's evolving policy, including aspects of policy implementation, before moving to assess Labour's new healthcare state.

Conservative health policy 1979-97

The Conservative government of 1979 inherited an NHS which was 'administered' rather than 'managed'. The Permanent Secretary and his department, responsible to ministers, were the nearest the NHS had to a corporate head office. Within the service, at regional, area and district levels, there were management teams operating on the basis of 'consensus management', of which the administrator was (at most) primus inter pares. This stemmed from the 1974 reorganisation, introduced by the Conservatives but planned in similar form by the 1960s Labour government. A further reorganisation of the NHS took place in 1982, under the Conservatives, which abolished the area tier from the health service structure and proclaimed devolution of planning functions to the level of the new district health authority. Barely was the ink dry and the chairs rearranged after this reorganisation when Roy Griffiths was invited by the then Secretary of State to conduct an enquiry into NHS staffing. This was soon generalised into an enquiry on the nature of – or rather absence of – general management in the NHS.

The Griffiths Report (1983) argued that the NHS lacked an apex: that there was no corporate board or head office responsible for looking downwards on to the service and managing it, as opposed to the role of traditional civil servants at the 'top of the office' who looked upwards to service the requirements of ministers. The first leg of Griffiths' recommendations concerned the creation of just such a board – the NHS Management Board, which has evolved today into the NHS Executive through various mutations. The second leg of the Griffiths recommendations concerned the institution of general management at regional, district and unit levels. (The units concerned hospital services and community health services, as well as other areas of service such as mental health units.) A further implication of these changes, as well as the supercession of consensus management, was that clinicians and health professionals were now intended to be responsible to their local corporate entity, and its general manager, rather than 'vertically upwards' via professional lines of accountability to the Department of Health. This laid the foundations for a centralism in NHS policy making and implementation which had never existed before – giving the lie to the rhetoric that it was the old NHS which had been about 'command and control'.

The Griffiths recommendations, mostly but not wholly implemented, represented the moderate influence of what has been termed 'the new public management' in the British NHS. While the late Sir Roy Griffiths was sympathetic to the NHS and to public healthcare, the Griffiths enquiry was known as the 'businessmen's enquiry' with some reason, since it introduced corporate business philosophy and techniques into the NHS. The most important substantive element of the Griffiths Report was that decision making, including decision making by doctors, should be taken in the light of devolved budgets so that services and finance would be considered together.

It is generally claimed that the most important change in the NHS resulted from the introduction of the 'internal market' as outlined in the White Paper of 1989, *Working for patients* (DoH, 1989a). This by and large became the 1990 NHS and Community Care Act, which was formally implemented on 1 April 1991 (see Butler, 1992; Paton, 1992, 1998; Klein, 1995).

This introduced a purchaser/provider split, with the aim of developing a market system in healthcare. Under this market system, variously referred to as a 'quasi-', 'internal' or 'managed' market, health authorities were allocated funding in order to purchase healthcare for their resident populations. However, they were no longer responsible for the provision of healthcare services. Hospitals (and other providers) became autonomous 'trusts', independent (both managerially and financially) from the local health authority. Such trusts were dependent for their survival on securing income from (any) purchasers who contracted with a provider unit for specific services at an agreed cost. As well as provider units being separated from health authorities, GPs were given the option of becoming fund holders, with (initially) limited budgets from which to purchase certain services on behalf of their patients. The emergence of GP Fund Holding (GPFH) was referred to as the 'wild card' in the government reforms (Glennerster et al, 1994). This was possibly because of its potential for unseen consequences but more probably because – by giving direct purchasing power to GPs, as independent contractors – there was greater potential for disruption to current patterns of healthcare provision.

There are three broad trends associated with the development of the internal market (Paton, 1998).

Firstly, it was rare that the money followed the patient – allegedly one of the benefits of the reforms. The reasons for this are complex. To begin with, the statement itself was always born more in political rhetoric than in a forward-looking analysis of the likely consequences of the reforms. The language of consumerism was used to justify an increasing stress on markets and the whole panoply of the reforms, although the survey by Paton (1998) highlighted that local populations played little part in determining purchasing priorities.

Secondly, anything resembling a functioning market was the exception rather than the rule. While the purchaser/provider split naturally created changed behaviour, it was not in the direction of a recognisable market. The study by Paton (1998) concluded that the mechanisms for determining service contracts were crude (largely based on historical data) and that health authorities' priorities reflected national concerns with little specific attention to locality purchasing. In contracting for services, localism predominated in terms of where purchasers placed their contracts. The typical health authority was likely to allocate about half of its budget to a single, local provider. At least 70% of the health authority's budget went to three providers only (all of which may have been local, including community and other trusts as well as acute providers). Consequently, competitive markets, involving a range of providers, both local and non-local, were largely absent.

Thirdly, the survey highlighted that the purchaser/provider split itself had significant transactions costs and rather more intangible or variable benefits. While most contracts were 'block' contracts, where purchasers bought services 'in bulk', transaction costs were particularly high for 'Extra Contractual Referrals' (ECRs), which were specially negotiated, 'one-off' contracts. The purchaser/provider split also created certain types of behaviour and incentives, many of which are perverse (Paton, 1995).

The research illustrated the high costs of introducing the internal market, both from a health authority and a provider perspective. It is ironical that having created the market, politicians then blamed managers for a mushrooming bureaucracy, resulting in persistent directives to all health authorities and trusts to cut management costs. The number of health authority staff involved in contracting, for example, varied between one and 30 whole-time equivalents (WTE), while in trusts the median number of staff involved in contracting was three, with an average contracting department budget standing at £174,000 per annum. The way in which expenditure on the finance and information functions has expanded is illustrated by the following example:

> **"In 1986, the finance department was very small, and one person from the district used to come in once every so often, waving a spreadsheet.... I now have nine accountants (three qualified), we have a business systems team, and we have an information systems team, so there have been quite considerable costs involved. We are talking of a department now costing close on half a million...."** (Chief executive of a mental health trust)

In short, Tory policies did not create a functioning market, or even a quasi-market, in healthcare. However, the structural upheaval and cost of the Tory reforms was substantial. This made any exercise in ignoring them, or starting with a blank sheet of paper, very difficult for Labour.

Although the creation of the internal market is the centrepiece of Conservative health policy, a number of other developments should be mentioned (Paton, 1998). First, the rhetoric of consumerism led to a raft of measures under the Patient's Charter (Klein, 1995; Powell, 1997a). Second, there were increasing concerns about the accountability of the NHS, with attention focused on the 'democratic deficit' of NHS quangos (Paton, 1992, 1998). Third, the development of the private finance initiative (PFI) meant that new hospitals would to a large degree be financed and managed by the private sector, with a crude analogy being the model of leasing photocopiers (Paton, 1998; Powell, 1999). Finally, there were broader developments in primary care (Glendinning, 1998). From 1 April 1996, GP fund holders as well as other GPs were 'accountable to' the new health authorities (DoH, 1996). This was to be used by Labour to build its 'evolutionary' model of 'primary-care commissioning' while also requiring GP purchasing groups to be accountable to the health authority. The 1997 NHS Primary Care Act allowed some derugulation and experimentation in the area of primary care. Another development to be 'moulded' by Labour was the Total Purchasing Pilot (TPP) (Mays et al, 1998). These pilot projects involved giving budgets for all health services jointly to the GPs covering a locality say, of 60,000 to 100,000 people. They were an extension of GPFH in two ways: covering more services and involving more GPs. Yet they were to be used by Labour in devising the primary care group (PCG) (see below) which was to become the linchpin of its policy. Was New Labour simply copying and moulding existing policy for the NHS?

Labour's evolving health policy

Labour was intrinsically hostile to the NHS Reforms of 1989/91. Nevertheless, their loss of the 1992 General Election meant that the eggs contained in the White Paper, *Working for patients* (DoH, 1989a), had become an omelette which apparently could not be unscrambled by 1997. Even had Labour won in 1992, the then leader Neil Kinnock has since stated that a key element of the reforms, the purchaser/provider split, would not have been reversed (Timmins, 1996). The 1992 Labour manifesto had been preceded by a policy document, 'Your good health', which suggested a repeal of the reforms at the level of aspiration, but also suggested that the distinction between planning and management in services would be retained while the market reforms were reversed. This neutral-sounding language was interpreted by some commentators to mean that Labour would reverse the purchaser/provider split, and simply separate the functions of planning and management within an integrated health authority, and by other commentators to mean that they would preserve the purchaser/provider split, with separately constituted health authorities and self-governing trusts running hospitals and other services.

Two documents of moderate significance were published during Labour's opposition between 1992 and 1997. In 1994, a consultation document entitled 'Health 2000' was published (when David Blunkett was Shadow Health Secretary). This used questions rather than answers as the basis for consultation. Secondly, and more significantly, in 1995, during Margaret Beckett's tenure as Shadow Health Secretary, 'Renewing the NHS' was published. This suggested that although the institution of the purchaser/provider split was more likely to stay, patient flows would be funded through a planning process rather than by contracts in a marketplace. The lack of clarity reflected the multiple drafting of the document: when the office of the Leader of the Opposition had its input (by now Tony Blair's office), the modernising/'no turning back' elements were grafted on rather than integrated. The detail was more anti-reforms than the headlines and soundbites.

When the Labour government was elected in 1997 a lot of political time had passed, even since 1995. 'No substantial change' was now to be the policy. However, Labour did express the aspiration to reintegrate the NHS, alongside statements that the internal market had provided many distractions and perverse incentives (Paton, 1995). It also acknowledged that there had been improvements to NHS policy and management while Labour was out of office which would not be overturned. This was later to be described as 'going with the grain' in Labour's own White Paper, *The new National Health Service: Modern, dependable* (DoH, 1997). Prior to this paper, some announcements and circulars had heralded Labour's approach, between its election in May 1997 and its December White Paper.

Labour in office was now pledged to keep the purchaser/provider split. This sounded to some like an ideological acceptance of 'the market'. The new soundbite was that Labour would abolish the market, but keep the split. However, if there isn't really a market, it amounted to little change from Tory policy. Or, turning it round the other way, if a purchaser/provider split means a bias to as much of a market as the politicians will allow (as purchasers are allowed to choose providers, presumably on market criteria), it means not abolishing the market after all. (You could abolish the split and keep the market, rather than the other way around, if health authorities were responsible for their services yet able to contract with other authorities for patients who were not, for whatever reason, treated locally. This would probably be less costly than the currently evolving arrangements!)

The reason Labour is keeping the split is not because research and experience has shown its benefits but because of an obsession with slogans about 'the future', 'new', 'No turning back' and the like. Labour's dilemma was to reconcile two opposing claims – on the one hand, 'the NHS is crumbling'; on the other hand, 'don't worry; we won't change much'. Understandably, Labour wished to minimise organisational disruption – ironically, the Tories had exhausted the service with such and had therefore cleverly entrenched their reforms. Yet despite seeking to impose its own stamp without structural change, Labour could not avoid this. This meant wholesale managerial change, initially by the back door, as any reading of the 1997 White Paper bears out and which ministerial instructions as to implementation were amplifying throughout 1998. The alleged aim was to 'reintegrate the NHS without reorganisation'. The danger was that there would be major reorganisation (yet again) without reintegrating the NHS.

The new NHS: modern, dependable?

On 9 December 1997, the Labour government published its White Paper for the NHS in England, entitled *The new National Health Service: Modern, dependable* (DoH, 1997). Separate papers were published for the other countries of the UK. In the foreword, the Prime Minister Tony Blair stated that "creating the NHS was the greatest act of modernisation ever achieved by a Labour government". Given the importance laid by New Labour on the term 'modernisation', this was an important statement. For defining the NHS per se as modernisation meant that it was less likely to be subjected to the type of fundamental review instigated for other aspects of the welfare state and consisting primarily of 'hard choices' (principally redistribution within static budgets, 'from the poor to the poor').

At the political level, Labour's agenda was to combine a reintegration of the NHS (after the fragmentation of the internal market) with an allegedly forward-looking policy which meant 'no turning back' to the 1970s and the situation prior to 18 years of Conservative government. Additional and related to this, there was a desire to avoid another fundamental structural reorganisation. A further requirement of Labour's new policy was that administrative costs were to be cut to allow more resources for 'front-line' patient care.

To a certain extent, 'old radicalism' (the socialism that dare not speak its name under New Labour) was to have more of a place in the pantheon of the NHS than elsewhere in society. However, it was to be linked to an alleged new pragmatism, if not new radicalism, which looked to the future. At one level, this was the politics of the soundbite. If everything has to be 'new', then simply defining the emergent policy as 'new' is the means to achieve it!

At the level of political overview, the internal market was to be abolished and GPFH was to be superseded. Yet the purchaser/provider split (now justified in Labour's language as merely the distinction between commissioning and service management) was to remain. The main change was that commissioning – seemingly synonymous with purchasing – was now to be entrusted to PCGs, rather than health authorities. Health authorities themselves, expected to become fewer in number through mergers over time, were to take ultimate responsibility for planning services (that is, for strategic decisions as to closing hospitals, merging hospitals and building new services). Yet PCGs, typically representing populations of around 100,000 and comprising around 50 GPs, community nurses and possibly other actors, were to be the purchasers.

One of the purposes of these groups was to seek to achieve a single unified budget for funding for all hospital and community services, prescribing and general practice infrastructure. It was no doubt hoped that this would lead to more effective and efficient use of resources, primarily by giving GPs responsibility for the 'seamless' and integrated care of patients.

The political motivation to avoid conflict with GPs was another reason behind the setting up of PCGs. It was believed that existing fund holders – especially large groups of fund holders, or consortia holding the total budget for hospital and community services – would see the new policy as an extension of their desired freedom without some of the disadvantages. Making all GPs responsible for commissioning would also end the criticism that the distinction between fund holding and non-fund holding GPs created a two-tier service.

This was nevertheless a risky strategy. Non-fund holding GPs did not generally want the responsibility of holding budgets. On the other side of the fence, different reactions were possible among fund holders. Some welcomed the Labour government's White Paper. However, others saw the new policy in essence as taking away their power yet increasing their responsibilities.

The ultimate effects of the new White Paper, when passed into legislation, would crucially depend on how much the new PCGs were taking the powers of the health authority. In the first instance, there was to be a range of different models of PCGs. This was in all likelihood making a virtue out of necessity (or as the White Paper put it somewhat more optimistically, "going with the grain"). The Labour government has inherited a spectrum of commissioning arrangements including: locality commissioning groups (groups of GPs working closely with their health authority to commission services); GPFH; multifunds and total purchasers as an extension of GPFH.

Concerning the range of models, there were to be four options for PCGs:

- the minimalist role – supporting the health authority in commissioning and acting only in an advisory capacity;
- taking devolved responsibility for managing the budget, but as part of the health authority;
- becoming freestanding bodies – trusts – but accountable to the health

authority to contract for secondary services;
* becoming freestanding bodies as above but with the added responsibility for providing community health services for the population (by implication as an alternative to contracting with community trusts for this purpose).

Despite the stress that the most appropriate model or models would be assessed in light of the objectives of providing effective care and also reducing administration and management costs by comparison with the previous government's internal market, it was also claimed that PCGs "... will be expected to progress along (the spectrum) so that in time all primary care groups assume fuller responsibilities" (DoH, 1997).

Added to this ambiguity was the possibility that the health authority would be the iron hand in a velvet glove. The White Paper (DoH, 1997, para 4.3) stated that among the health authority's tasks would be "deciding on the range and location of health care services for the health authority's residents, which should flow from and be part of, the Health Improvement Programme". This Health Improvement Programme was squarely the responsibility of the health authority. If the health authority was to decide on the range and location of healthcare services, then the role of the PCGs would simply be to purchase services from already-planned and 'commissioned' sources of provision.

Added to this was the health authority's revamped and enhanced responsibility for improving public health. Pending publication of the Green Paper entitled, *Our healthier nation* (DoH, 1998c) (which would be published in February 1998), it was stated in the White Paper that the health authority would work in partnership with local authorities and others to identify the most important local action that would make the most impact on the health of local people. This raises the question: If these crucial decisions are to be taken (quite rightly) by the health authority, what if PCGs wished to commission services out of line with these priorities?

This is the perennial question for the NHS: How can national and higher-tier priorities in pursuit of effective healthcare and a uniform NHS be reconciled with local freedoms in choosing priorities generally and services specifically? The different agendas embraced by the Labour government led it to face both ways on this issue. On the one hand, it wanted to stress local freedom. (An early paragraph in the White Paper said there will be no return to the 'command and control' of the NHS which had existed before the Conservatives' reforms.) On the other hand,

᭣t wished to reintegrate the service in pursuit of its truly national status. In theory at least, local choice can undermine this objective if different localities make different choices.

The irony is that the NHS which had existed before the Conservative reforms was characterised by anything but 'command and control'. One of the motivations for the Conservative reforms had been to command and control more effectively! New Labour inherited and enhanced this approach: performance management from above was heavily stressed in the new White Paper and national commissions to police it were announced.

Additionally, the Labour government had the objective of diminishing the 'transaction costs' which it defined as the hallmark of the internal market. Devolving purchasing responsibility to PCGs might well increase transaction costs, or at least prevent their diminution. Five PCGs within each health authority could be characterised as five mini-health authorities, replicating functions unnecessarily, not least by employing the type of staff (albeit on a larger scale) which GP fund holders had been employing. It would also be another reorganisation of the NHS in all but name (not that this would matter, if – as with the Conservative reforms throughout the 1980s and early 1990s – the aim was merely to avoid reorganisation at the soundbite level).

The more you look at the detail, the more ambiguity is discovered as to whether the internal market was in fact being abolished. If PCGs had the right to decide where to commission services from trusts (which were to remain in their post-'NHS reforms' state), then it was a question of theology as to whether the market was abolished or not. Or, to put it the other way around, if market forces had already waned under the Conservative government before 1997 after their short life between 1992 and around 1995, then the Labour government was not abolishing something which had already been abolished.

The Labour government seems to be squaring the circle by:

- defining the abolition of the internal market as the move to longer-term contracting (now rechristened service agreements);
- abolishing GPFH 'as we had known it';
- outlawing cost per case agreements between purchasers and providers, with their high administrative costs;
- allegedly abolishing ECRs through more refined purchasing.

Yet these are technical rather than strategic changes, and the last is arguably unachievable.

The new White Paper bore signs of extreme haste in drafting, as evidenced by the form of its drafting and the resort to stark lists of bullet points; a strange mix of technical detail and soundbite; a blurring of the distinction between innovations inherited from the outgoing government and new developments. As with the Conservative government's White Paper, *Working for patients* (DoH, 1989a), the devil would be in the detail – much of which was yet to be decided and which would no doubt be decided on the hoof.

Labour's White Paper had affinities with New Labour's approach to many policy areas. Its first priority was to be strict about the prospect for extra financing (Labour's additional money for the NHS was no different in all likelihood to what the Conservatives would have provided). Having appeased the economic orthodoxy of the Treasury, the next priority was to seek to offer a carrot to all main interest groups in healthcare. A major consequence of the Conservative reforms had been the mushrooming of special interests: fund holders and non-fund holders; hospital clinicians in greater conflict with GPs; the new management cadre and so on. Yet the danger now was promises based on a false prospectus. 'Doctors and nurses' were to be brought back to the centre of decision making – but it was often responsibilities rather than powers that they were to be given, not least, for rationing. All services, including prescribing budgets, were now to be cash-limited. On the bright side, stress on collaboration and the pursuit of what was called integrated care was at least likely to provide one of the bases for 'a new start' for the NHS from a government which had less ideological difficulty in accepting the principles of socialised medicine than had its predecessor.

Finally, the politics of the new policy involved 'tacking on' the aspiration of collaboration (not competition) to inherited structures which had been designed for competition. (New Labour, Old Conservative!)

It is interesting to compare the English White Paper with the Scottish White Paper. In Scotland, market mechanisms had not developed so far. GPFH, in particular, was more limited. As a result, the Scottish White Paper heralded a new (Scottish) NHS which was to be more 'integrated'. As well as the health boards (health authorities), there were to be (in the areas of most boards) one acute hospital trust and one primary care trust. However, the latter were different from the English primary care trusts, which were to be first purchasers and second providers. In Scotland, primary care trusts were to be providers: they were to contain all GP practices, and all community and mental health services. Instead of PCGs doing the purchasing, as in England, 'local health care cooperatives' (LHCCs) of GPs were to advise the health board (health authority). What is more, it seemed that the health boards in Scotland would have a more direct role in the affairs of trusts, for example, in capital allocations and services plans.

This difference can be interpreted as a pluralism throughout the UK, reflecting different desires and political traditions. However, it can also be interpreted as the type of streamlining which was no longer possible in England without another 'reorganisation': unscrambling the Tory omelette was not possible in England. What did seem likely was that in Scotland relative administrative and transaction costs would be lower and coherent planning more feasible.

Implementing Labour's health policy

National and local institutions

By the end of 1998, the Labour government's main priorities in implementing its new health policy could be discerned at national and local levels. At the national level the White Paper, *The new National Health Service: Modern, dependable*, (DoH, 1997) proposed the National Institute for Clinical Excellence and the Commission for Health Improvement. The former was to be responsible for 'service frameworks' in all specialities, which would set out appropriate forms of treatment, appropriate ways of delivering that treatment, criteria of cost-effectiveness, and (following the Calman-Hine Report on cancer services) criteria for establishing a 'hierarchy' of service availability, from the local to the regional. All in all, if taken ambitiously, this was a centralist planning agenda which would leave local actors (maybe rightly, of course) with little leeway for their local commissioning and collaborative decisions. However, the question then arose: What was the point of retaining and enhancing multifarious local purchasing and providing arrangements – not least in the light of the government's agenda to cut management costs?

The second initiative, the Commission for Health Improvement (soon to be irreverently known by its nickname Chimp) was to be the stick by which standards were to be enforced. Poorly performing trusts or health authorities (or trusts and health authorities unable to ensure good performance from their PCGs) would be visited by the 'men (and possibly women) in grey suits' – an echo of education policy. Again, the logic ran: if we are not subjecting you to the market, we have to have mechanisms for enforcing good performance.

At the local level, despite the desire to avoid structural reorganisation, the implementation of the policy of PCGs became arguably the biggest 'process'-obsessed reorganisation yet. The alternative forms of PCG (see above) were redefined as a chronology (by communication from Minister of State Alan Milburn in February 1998). All PCGs were expected to progress beyond levels one and two to become freestanding primary care trusts, eventually all embracing model four (which would mean that they would also be responsible for providing community services as well as purchasing hospital services).

Jockeying and conflicts soon arose over the question of who was to run the PCGs. The GPs, especially fund holders, clearly thought they were to run the groups. Yet the Labour Party had also held out the prospect of 'locality commissioning' involving professions other than doctors. Notably, nurses were anxious about their status in PCGs. Decisions about the composition of the boards of PCGs had to be taken quickly. In the end, given the ambivalence at best of much of the profession of GPs concerning PCGs at all, an inbuilt majority for doctors was soon dictated by ministers, who were eager to prevent damaging disputes with the doctors which could lead to the policy being stillborn. In the end, PCGs are to have boards composed of between four and seven doctors, one or two nurses, a lay member, a non-executive member of the 'parent' health authority, and an officer from the member of the local authority social services department.

It soon became clear that the policies of creating PCGs, on the one hand, and restricting 'management costs' in the new NHS, on the other hand, were at the very least in tension. Every PCG would acquire a chief officer – to become a chief executive when trust status was achieved. However, as a 'mini health authority' the PCG would require all the other functions as well – finance, personnel and the like. It was decided that these would be secured 'on contract' from the parent health authority – no doubt a provisional decision, following lessons to be learned from the further evolution of PCGs. It was made clear that the initial configuration of PCGs would only last a year or two, as further mergers would take place after the year 2000.

Next, a major problem arose over the fact that PCGs were to be controlled by GPs – holding 90% of the health service budget even though they were not even employees of the health service! They were independent contractors – and very much saw themselves as such. Apart from the minority of the profession who welcomed the possibility of salaried practice (an option taken further by some of the Primary Care Act pilot projects initiated by the previous Conservative government), most GPs did not see themselves as part of a corporate organisation known as a PCG. Even less did they see themselves as acting corporately or 'collaboratively' with the parent health authority – which they tended to see as a restricting hand or even an adversary rather than partner. 'On the ground', the new ethos of 'everybody collaborating with everybody else', despite the inheritance of fragmentary and multifarious purchasers and providers from the Conservative health policy, looked particularly threadbare. The prospect of sharpened competition between GP 'purchasers' and hospital clinicians seemed increasingly likely. With GPs controlling ever more of the NHS budget, the desire to pursue their own priorities, if not hobby horses, threatened priorities for services which might not always be in the interests of populations or patients as opposed to individual GP interests.

The Queen's Speech of November 1998 promised an NHS Bill, which would primarily end GPFH; institute PCGs, 'end the internal market' (yet again!) and impose further obligations on the medical profession through the policy of 'clinical governance'. Heralded in the White Paper, *The new National Health Service: Modern, dependable*, clinical governance was to be a system of quality control (and, hopefully, quality improvement) primarily for the medical profession. This policy had been given extra force by a series of scandals involving the medical profession in 1998, which strengthened ministers' resolve to achieve tighter 'performance management' of the clinical process.

Less centralist, at least in the image, was the initiative to create Health Action Zones. Initially, 12 pilot projects were approved and funded in 1998. Health Action Zones were to incorporate partnership between all sorts of different local agencies, embracing the health service, local government, other elements of the statutory sector and the voluntary sector. This is not the first time that the rhetoric of 'partnership' has been invoked for the NHS, but a reading of the history of similar initiatives does not suggest a reason for immediate optimism (Higgins, 1998; Hudson, 1998; Challis et al, 1988).

As Powell (1999) notes, increasing centralisation in the NHS stemming from the previous government's reforms (against the conventional wisdom about command and control disappearing) was at least temporarily accompanied by local variation in availability of services. It seems also that the policy of Health Action Zones will be to stress local priorities. As Powell puts it, "the new NHS may increasingly be a series of diverse local health services rather than one national service". If this is the trend which unfolds in practice the question is: Will the strong strain of centralism and 'comparison of local performance by national criteria' also contained in Labour's policy assert itself?

On issues such as this, Labour's Third Way is less a synthesis of the first and second ways (defined as centralism and localism, in this case) than a statement of both and a failure adequately to analyse the issues raised.

Community and medical power

In a similar vein is Labour's equivocation about consumerism. It naturally plays lip-service to representation of the community. Yet PCGs will not represent the community – they will be dominated by GPs. Representation of the community is a difficult matter and Labour is repeating the previous Conservative government's equivocation about whether to decide which services are available (and how they are provided) nationally or to leave it to local choice. There are a number of issues within this rationing debate. Firstly, need there be rationing at all? There are a number of arguments for making rationing – if it is necessary at all – implicit rather than explicit (Hunter, 1997). Making rationing explicit makes denial of care explicit for those who cannot afford to use the private sector. Such rationing may merely be to acknowledge reality, but decisions made by individuals as citizens, adjudicating between different types of care, are likely to be very different from the decisions made by the same citizens when they or their loved ones require care. To that extent, it is unlikely that explicit rationing as determined through public opinion can ever be made to 'stick'. Insiders with power will always be able to 'work the system'.

Secondly, if there need be rationing, should it be done locally or nationally – at what level and by which actors? In launching the White Paper, *The new National Health Service: Modern, dependable*, in December 1997, the then Minister of State for Health Alan Milburn claimed in an interview on BBC2's Newsnight with Jeremy Paxman (9 December) that the new approach would end rationing rather than begin it! Allowing the minister this effective rhetorical flourish, the government proposes no new thinking on this issue – while allowing discussion around agencies such as the National Institute for Clinical Excellence to emphasise that cost-effectiveness as well as merely clinical-effectiveness will enter into calculations about what is and is not available on the NHS. Secretary of State Frank Dobson's temporary banning of Viagra through public prescription does not really enhance the debate. Dobson's 'logic' was that this was not concerned with a life-threatening condition, implicitly rejecting vast areas of similar conditions in the NHS such as cataract surgery and hip-joint replacement.

Whether you talk about rationing or prioritisation, in the absence of expanded public financing for the NHS, hard choices (to use Labour's language) will be necessary. Labour also faces the decision as to whether it is doctors and professionals or 'managers' who are to make these hard choices. On the one hand, it continues and even extends the agenda of performance management and comparison through performance indicator from the previous government, giving power to managers to shape or at least constrain local priorities. On the other hand, Labour claimed in the White Paper, *The new National Health Service*, that decisions about how best to use resources for patient care are best made by those who treat patients and that such an approach is "at the heart of the proposals of the White Paper" (DoH, 1997). In reality, Labour is giving the decision to doctors – but doctors as managers rather than as doctors. GPs on PCGs will have to make hard decisions – not as individual doctors but as managers of the resource. Hospital clinical directors, responsible for their specialities, will have the responsibility of deciding how to spend resources, not least in line with national criteria and the need to achieve nationally-defined levels and types of performance. This will implicitly or explicitly give clinical directors more power over their consultant colleagues and make the collegiate consultant relationship in the hospital more of a hierarchy. Each provider trust board (hospital and non-hospital) has to have a board-level officer responsible for clinical governance, normally the medical director, who is directly responsible to the chief executive. To say that Labour is 'cutting management and re-empowering doctors' would be naïve – or rather to redefine power as responsibility by sleight of hand.

Inequalities in health

After the election of the Conservative government in 1979, discussion of inequalities in health was taboo in the Department of Health. In 1980, the then Secretary of State Patrick Jenkin gave the Black Report, *Inequalities in health* (Black et al, 1980), a rude reception (incidentally therefore guaranteeing publicity for it). Even when the issue came implicitly back on to the agenda in the early 1990s, the Secretary of State Virginia Bottomley insisted on talk of 'variations' rather than inequalities. The New Labour government established an Independent Inquiry into Inequalities in Health (Acheson, 1998), chaired by the former Chief Medical Officer Sir Donald Acheson. This produced its report at the end of November 1998 which reiterated a number of important factors. The causality runs from social and economic inequality to ill health, rather than the other way round, with sick individuals becoming poorer as the explanation for the correlation. This is now reinforced as much less important. Three crucial areas it emphasised are:

• correlation of income inequality and ill health;
• priority that should be given to the health of families with children;
• need to carry out a government-wide 'policy audit' such that all policy likely to have an impact on health is evaluated in terms of its impact on health inequalities.

As well as this, it updated the conclusions of the Black Report of 1980 and the so-called 'blacker' report produced by Margaret Whitehead in 1997 (Black et al, 1980; Whitehead, 1987).

This report provides a crucial pointer to whether Labour's Third Way is capable of squaring an important circle: How can social inequalities and therefore health inequalities be reduced without income redistribution? The current author humbly suggests the hypothesis that there is no Third Way in this area: either income inequalities can be reduced or health inequalities will not be reduced. Proponents of the Third Way argue that by investing in employment, social inequalities can be reduced without income redistribution – and that this 'Third Way' is more radical than simply redistributing income in a static manner. However, such a strategy is likely to be undermined by the dictates of competing in the global economy as currently constituted – dictates accepted and welcomed by the Blair government as perhaps its most significant revision from 'Old Labour'. In hard reality, this means competing by lowering relative incomes and benefits.

Globalisation means an auction for inward investment and an auction to avoid external capital flows, which consists of lowering comparative real wages, tax rates and therefore public expenditure. In this environment, and with New Labour actively resisting European moves to find a genuine Third Way to avoid the vicissitudes of globalised capitalism, the outlook for a systematic attack on inequalities and health, correlated as they are with inequalities in income, is bleak.

This is where the stress on prevention and promotion comes in. It is at least partly an implicit attempt to argue that 'special action' can overcome wider social and economic factors. The previous Conservative government's White Paper, *The health of the nation* (DoH, 1992), identified five priority areas for achieving this, but was criticised for concentrating on individual lifestyle and ignoring factors beyond the control of individuals. Labour produced a Green Paper on public health in February 1998, entitled *Our healthier nation* (DoH, 1998c). This again used the rhetoric of the Third Way, implying that concentration on both lifestyle and community and social factors was important. However, other initiatives and policies may hamper the agenda (such as issues around welfare benefits) and even individual causes of ill health (such as tobacco) are met with equivocal policy responses (such as the crusade to preserve duty free shopping by Prime Minister Blair!).

Partnership and complexity

Considering the detail of Labour's emergent health policy, two abiding impressions are left: firstly, there is the oxymoron of 'statutory voluntarism' and secondly, there is considerable complexity in implementing a profusion of often uncoordinated initiatives through a complex set of agencies.

The first impression comes from the fact that partnership, cooperation and collaboration are emphasised and mandated at every turn – but that the overall effect of this is difficult to gauge, to put it at its most optimistic.

The second impression arises from the fact that the government is not really abolishing many of the institutions of the previous government (other than replacing fund holding with the legal foundation for primary care trusts in the NHS Act promised in the Queen's Speech of 1998). Instead, it is adding to them, as it devises its piecemeal initiatives and seeks to present them as a new, or rather Third Way.

Equally, there is uncertainty – despite the frenetic activity and setting of tasks by ministers, surrounding some of the most central issues. For example, if annual contracting is to be replaced, is the new three- or five-year contract to be a cost and volume contract? Not a contract at all? We know from emerging guidelines that one means of seeking 'to abolish the internal market' is by implementing standard costs/prices which providers will be expected to meet. How will these be used in the commissioning/purchasing process? How does commissioning differ from purchasing in ministers' minds?

The problem is that while there is detailed instruction on process the strategic guidance by ministers who mandate that process is inadequate. It is not enough for ministers to say, as they have been saying frequently in 1998, that strategy is the responsibility of the Management Executive and senior managers, with ministers being responsible for policy. The danger is that policy aspirations contain and conceal ambiguities, which can only be resolved by a ministerial/managerial dialogue on how to translate policy into strategy. The implementation of policy 'feeds back' into the policy debate itself.

Ironically, just as the last government invested huge amounts of money to create a market that never was, the Labour government is investing more and more time and effort in 'reshaping' the inheritance of that market without either changing much (except at the level of the prescription of collaboration rather than competition) or achieving clear health-related objectives as a result. A promising sign is the evaluation of different models of primary care commissioning as they evolve, but even here the danger is that politically-chosen models will be set in stone before such evaluation can meaningfully report. In any case, the brief for such evaluation is not wide enough to embrace genuine alternatives for planning healthcare.

New Labour and a new welfare state?

While new ministers coming into office when Labour was elected in 1997 were clear at the general level about their goals, they relied for the detail on senior NHS management, based in the Executive in the Department of Health, who had lived and breathed the previous government's reforms. The previous government had created a Management Executive allegedly to take the NHS both out of politics and of the traditional Civil Service administration. Instead, the result was a politicised Management Executive. Now, the new government was relying on that same central management cadre. In the new environment they came to behave more like traditional civil servants than 'neutral' managers. They were at arm's length from the detail, yet had some influence in minimising challenge to the NHS reforms.

As well as considering such practical restrictions on radicalism, it is fair to conclude that New Labour has no 'big idea' for health policy. This is not a criticism in itself. It has already been pointed out that Labour's 'big idea' was the NHS itself and that preserving the NHS (a conservative policy) is the name of the game for subsequent Labour governments.

However, in 1997 to preserve 'the NHS as we knew it' would involve making changes in order to return to the situation which existed before the NHS reforms of 1989/91. This is not to imply that to defend the NHS Labour would involve having to 'return to 1979'. Modernisation in a technical sense, involving substantial changes to hospital and primary care sectors, would be quite consistent with returning to the status quo ante in the sense in which it is being defined here – prior to destabilising structural change based on New Right politics. (In particular Labour's confirmation of the PFI is likely in the long term to produce a lot of 'bad deals' for the NHS.)

New Labour's health policy faces a number of tensions. Firstly, to govern the NHS pragmatically while reintegrating it requires structural change – a fact which the New Labour government denies. (Otherwise, Labour is simply administering a Conservative-shaped NHS.) Labour claims that further change will be incremental, and that root-and-branch removal of the institutions of the 'new' NHS will not occur. As a result, many of the new power relationships and incentives brought about by the reforms would remain. In particular, the use of purchasing agencies to prioritise and ration care remains as the theoretical cornerstone of the purchasing function, despite Labour protestations that it is ending rationing rather than beginning it. This means less power to patients and 'front-line' doctors (doctors *qua* doctors) and more power to politicians and managers (even if the latter wear white coats).

Labour's critique of the NHS during Tory tenure in the early 1990s included the argument that there was a democratic deficit: only at the level of the nationally elected government was there popular control of the health policy, as quangos replaced even indirectly elected and appointed authorities throughout the service. One of the solutions proposed by Labour when in opposition was a regional tier throughout England as well as devolution in Scotland and Wales which would take over stewardship of health at the strategic level. However, this has now receded in England, unless the London Mayor and other developments revive it. Debates about elected health authorities and the possibility of elected local government commissioning health services have also receded – perhaps for very good reasons, pointing to work as a necessary good irrespective of its quality, conditions or pay (Paton, 1995).

In other areas, such as PCGs, Labour is implementing structural change:

the 'iron law of NHS reform' is that the more governments deny structural change, the larger that structural change is likely to be! The problem for Labour is that its structural changes (such as PCGs) are not well geared to its objective of cost-effective care management.

Secondly, there is a difference between New Labour's approach to the NHS and other areas of social and economic policy. New Labour is more like Old Labour in terms of the goals it believes in for the NHS – a universal, comprehensive and egalitarian service. Yet in practice, for the reasons just outlined in the paragraphs above, its approach to the NHS is more in tune with the philosophy of the out-going Conservative administration than in other areas of social policy: more Old Labour in theory; more Tory in practice.

In these areas of policy, Labour is ahead of the Tories – both in terms of Blairite 'hard choices' (choices which even Mrs Thatcher did not dare make) and being distinct from the Tories. It could be said that there is a convergence between Conservative and New Labour social and economic policy.

When it comes to the NHS, New Labour does not have a philosophy particularly distinct from Old Labour, but is struggling to carve out a policy distinct from the out-going Conservative administration in practice.

For Labour, modernisation in health policy could have been 'radical' if it had dismantled the new fragmentation inherited from the Conservatives, rather than adapted it. As things stand, there is the danger of creating inappropriate structures and policies in a move to combine equity, effectiveness and economy. As Anthony Crosland (1964) had put it many years before, "Labour had always been split between radicals and modernisers. The trouble was, the radicals lived in the past; whereas the modernisers were no longer radical". Despite Blairite rhetoric about the radical centre, this may well be the epitaph for Blairite health policy.

Another type of 'radicalism' on the NHS (this time, radicalism of the Right) would be for Labour to adopt the antithesis of the founding principles of the NHS: being universal and comprehensive. If Labour were to adopt a rationing approach which made services available in inverse proportion to ability to pay, then it could be argued that this would be a distinct policy for 'New Labour'. Yet, this would be highly dangerous: a service for the poor is a poor service, for economic as well as sociological reasons. Over time, those not eligible for NHS services would insure themselves privately, which is more expensive rather than cheaper. As a result, ongoing tax revolts would diminish the public purse available even for an NHS solely for the poor. The poor would in effect be 'paying for themselves through the public purse' and tax revolts would then extend to the poor as well, diminishing public services still further.

It seems in any case that Labour will not be going down this road. Ministers have recently been stressing that the NHS can be a fairly comprehensive and universal service. They stress its economy and value for money – not only because it invests in the health of the workforce to the economic benefit of all, but also because it does so cheaply. Both these claims are true.

New Labour seeks to have it both ways: it supports the NHS because it is the expression of solidarity and equity; at the same time because the NHS is cheap, New Labour's strategy is to proclaim its continuing adherence to 'health and education for all' while construing that adherence as being one of the State's key diminished responsibilities in the age of globalisation. In that age, the State's role, according to New Labour, is both to give global capitalism a 'human face' and also to facilitate economic absorption of the dictates of globalism. To that extent, the new healthcare state is about direct investment in productivity. Countries with more diffuse healthcare systems (as in France or the USA) can only envy the economy of the British healthcare state.

Thirdly, the complexity and fragmentation inherent in implementing policy in the new NHS has led central government to rely more (not less) on 'command and control'. By the end of 1998, the profusion of 'commands' by Department of Health circulars and executive letters was testing the patience of even the most willing senior managers.

Given such 'command and control' (whatever its effectiveness), claims that Labour's health policy represents a 'third way' must be treated with suspicion. The 'Third Way' is allegedly between the Scylla of 'hierarchy' and the Charybdis of the 'market'. There appears to be a fusion of academic analysis about hierarchies, markets and networks, on the one hand, and popular slogans about the same, on the other hand. It is sometimes argued that the NHS before the market was a type of Weberian hierarchical bureaucracy, with command and control its popular expression. After the internal market, some analysists depict an amalgam of market and networks as the source of both structure and agency (Ferlie et al, 1996).

This is fashionable but misleading. It is not a question of markets versus hierarchies. Internal markets in public services of the nature of the NHS require hierarchies and more 'command and control' than a modern, flexible planning system. The phrase 'hierarchy' derived from organisational economics confuses two elements. Firstly, there is the control of resources and organisations at a high enough level to prevent the perverse incentives of decentralised market forces in a public service – which recent research has noted (Paton, 1998). Secondly, there is 'hierarchy' in the often-pejorative sense of centralised bureaucratic control of operations within organisations. Disadvantages within the latter may be minimised without removing the former – and certainly without instituting internal markets. The 'market' was in practice the latest variant of command and control and represented the deepening of hierarchy – not its negation (Jenkins, 1995). New Labour's policy is tidying up the often-unintended fragmentation of the market and continuing with command and control. The so-called collaborative networks established in *The new National Health Service* (DoH, 1997) are in fact mandatory mechanisms for implementing central policy. (A clear example is on clinical quality, where the limited discretion left to hospitals on this matter in *The new National Health Service* has already been removed by a ministerial edict from Alan Milburn, Minister of State for Health, on 13 April 1998.)

Conclusion: Labour, the market and the State

The 'Third Way' is mostly rhetoric. Almost all New Labour policies are announced as a 'third way'; but you must look at the particular context to see which two alternatives the alleged 'third way' is coming between. On the economy generally, it appears to be between laissez-faire capitalism and redistributive welfare capitalism, with the 'Third Way' being a rather limited supply-side tinkering. On welfare reform, it is between collectivism in financing and universalism in provision, on the one hand, and pure individualism, on the other hand.

New Labour has argued for the centrality of market forces in the economy as a whole, even to the extent of altering Clause 4 of its Constitution to stress inter alia the vigour of market forces. However, in areas of social policy such as health and education the approach in practice is central control plus inspectorate – performance management backed up by central sanctions, in the pursuit of objectives.

The general thread is that the 'Third Way' rejects social democracy (never mind socialism) while asserting community, responsibility and opportunity rather than relying on laissez-faire in its purest form. However, in health the special status of the NHS ensures that more direct government control continues, which makes talk of a 'third way' rather superficial. What is more, rather than diminishing bureaucracy, the new healthcare state can validly be categorised as an example of the 'new bureaucracy'.

The jury is undoubtedly out on the effect of Labour's policy. If it can manage to reintegrate the NHS and provide it with some stability as well as some fiscal growth over time, then it may well go down as having 'saved the NHS'. However, the danger of the opposite result is quite a high one. If Labour fails to please the middle classes, who are the beneficiaries as much as the poor of a universal and comprehensive service, by preserving and strengthening that service, then it may be judged to have failed on its own terms.

FOUR

The personal social services and community care

Norman Johnson

Introduction

The personal social services are probably the least understood of the major areas of social provision reviewed in this book. Everyone has some idea, even if not wholly accurate and somewhat vague, of the functions of education, health, housing and social security services, but what the *personal* social services do, and who provides them, are far from clear. Baldock sums up the position:

> There is a residual quality to the personal social services. Their responsibilities can sometimes appear to be a ragbag of disparate social rescue activities that are left over by the other parts of the welfare system. They have been called the 'fifth social service': seen as last not only in terms of size but also in terms of resort; the service people turn to when all else has failed. (1998, p 306)

This lack of prominence is confirmed by the figures in Table 4.1 which compares public expenditure in selected public services: the personal social services are at the bottom of the list by a very considerable margin.

Table 4.1: Public expenditure in selected public services in the UK (£ billion)

Service	Public expenditure in 1995
Social security	102
Health services	41
Education	38
Public order and safety	14
Personal social services	9

Source: *Social Trends*, no 27, 1997

Given the restricted size of their resources, it might be tempting to dismiss the personal social services as an unimportant area of public policy. However, a quite different conclusion results from a consideration of the services they provide and their significance in the lives of vulnerable groups in the population.

The personal social services consist of social care (as distinct from healthcare) provided by local authority social services departments and a variety of related agencies for:

• children and families
• older people
• people with physical disabilities
• people with learning disabilities
• people with mental illness.

Services may be provided to individuals, groups or whole communities. They may be delivered in clients' own homes, in residential establishments or in daycare facilities. The settings, the perceived needs of particular client groups and the types of workers involved are closely interrelated, but the distinguishing characteristic of the tasks carried out by social services departments is their diversity. For example, social work is usually thought to be the key activity of the personal social services, but social work itself is ill-defined and may take many forms. Also, the great majority of the people employed by social services departments (86%) are not professionally qualified social workers. They are made up of administrative and clerical staff, workers in residential homes and in day centres, and those employed as homecare workers or in the meals-on-wheels service.

The earliest and most extensive development of community care was in the mental health services. Care in the community for mentally ill patients had been talked about since the late 1920s, but its statutory enactment came with the 1959 Mental Health Act. After that date the number of mentally ill people cared for in the community increased dramatically as the number of beds for mentally ill patients declined. Between 1961 and 1981 the average number of beds occupied daily by mentally ill people fell by almost 42% (from 165,100 to 96,400). The closure of psychiatric hospitals gathered pace in the 1980s. Between 1982 and 1992 the number of beds was further reduced by more than 30%. These figures relate to the United Kingdom; more recent figures relating to England show that between 1987/88 and 1997/98 the average daily number of beds available to mentally ill people fell by 4.5% a year.

However, there has been widespread criticism of the quality and quantity of community services for mentally ill people and fears have been expressed that the closure of hospitals without commensurate increases in support and supervision in the community could lead to greater criminality and endanger the public. This issue will be referred to again later on in this chapter when discussing New Labour's policies in relation to the personal social services.

In 1995, the number of children being looked after by local authorities in England, Wales and Northern Ireland was 57,000, of whom 64% lived with foster parents, and there were 38,000 children on child protection registers. These figures do not give a wholly accurate indication of the work carried out with children, since the work of the social services departments is not limited to children formally being looked after and those on child protection registers. A number of highly publicised child abuse cases, some of them allegedly mishandled by social workers, has meant that the work of social services departments in childcare and protection has received more media attention, and as a result is more readily recognised by the general public than the services provided for other groups. It is therefore paradoxical that services for children in terms of the resources consumed and the numbers served are dwarfed by services for older people.

In 1997 there were 307,000 older people in residential homes. Although the majority were in private homes, local authorities paid the fees or a proportion of them when the older people themselves could not afford to do so. In a survey conducted in a week in September 1997 more than 756,000 meals were provided for 247,000 people by or on behalf of English local authorities. In the same week local authorities provided or paid for 2.6 million hours of homecare for 470,000 households. Elderly people are the chief beneficiaries of the meals and homecare services. The majority of day centre attendances are accounted for by people with learning disabilities. In the survey week in 1997 local authority social services departments in England provided or paid for 632,000 day centre places with 490,000 attendances. Although these figures are impressive and give an indication of the scale of the operations of the personal social services, three qualifications need to be borne in mind:

*   social services departments provide help for only a small minority of each client group; families always have been, and remain, the main providers of social care services;
*   many people will never have the need to use the personal social services

throughout their lives which is a sharp contrast to health services and education;

• increasingly, social services departments are becoming enablers rather than direct providers of services (see the section below on privatisation).

Having given a brief outline of the personal social services, attention now focuses on the policy context, beginning with the changes made during the Conservative government's 18 years in office in order to give an indication of New Labour's inheritance in this area of social policy.

Developments 1979-97

Community care

The long-standing debate about the meaning of community will not be entered into here. The most useful interpretation in the context of this chapter is a definition in terms of sets of relationships and the interactions they give rise to. These relationships may be based on: kinship; place (such as neighbourhoods); work or occupational group; religion; ethnic origin; political affiliation; leisure pursuits; shared adversity. As will be demonstrated, the most important of these relationships in terms of social care are those based on kinship.

In the 1960s community care was generally understood to mean care by statutory personnel working within the community. The crucial distinction was between care in the community and care in institutions. The claim that community care was superior, in most circumstances, to institutional care was heard with increasing frequency in several policy areas – most notably in mental health services and services for children. A shift in the meaning of community care began to emerge in the 1970s. However, this shift was from care *in* the community to care *by* the community. The significance of this change of meaning is that care *by* the community is principally care by family, friends and neighbours. This was most clearly stated by the White Paper on the care of elderly people:

> **Whatever level of public expenditure proves practicable, and however it is distributed, the primary sources of support and care are informal and voluntary. These spring from the personal ties of kinship, friendship and neighbourhood. They are irreplaceable. It is the role of public authorities to sustain and,**

where necessary, to develop – but never to replace – such support and care. Care *in* the community must increasingly mean care *by* the community. (DHSS, 1981, p 3)

This view was endorsed by the Audit Commission report (1986, p 11) *Making a reality of community care*, which emphasised the enabling role of local authorities who should encourage "patients and clients to do as much for themselves as possible ... with 'care' provided only where it is really needed".

These themes were repeated and made more explicit in the Griffiths Report (1988) on community care and in the White Paper (DoH, 1989b) and the subsequent National Health Service and Community Care Act of 1990. The thinking behind the community care changes introduced by the 1990 Act are to be found in the Griffiths Report (1988). The government accepted the report's recommendations and published a White Paper setting out the plans for legislation in greater detail (DoH, 1989b). The White Paper proposals, almost in their entirety, were incorporated into the Act. This made local authorities the lead agencies in community care, but required them to work in collaboration with health authorities and independent providers. Social services departments were obliged to produce three-year rolling community care plans which required the approval of the Secretary of State. Principally, the role of local authorities was to assess the community needs within their localities, to take steps to ensure that these were met and to monitor performance. The main change was a purchaser/provider split in which local authorities ceased to be the main direct providers of services: they were expected to make the maximum use of commercial and voluntary sector providers. The role of social services departments was to act "as the designers, organisers and purchasers of non-health care services, and not primarily as direct providers, making the maximum possible use of voluntary and private sector bodies" (Griffiths, 1988, p 1). Financial support of the voluntary sector was to change from grants to either contracts or fee-for-service arrangements, although small core grants would still be available. One of the objectives behind the community care plans was to enable the government to monitor the use of independent providers and the steps being taken to increase their contribution. The stated objective was to achieve greater efficiency and an extension of consumer choice through the introduction of competition. With some reluctance, the government rejected compulsory competitive tendering (CCT):

The Government believes that the wider use of service specification and tendering is likely to be one of the most effective ways of stimulating the non-statutory sector. It has decided against extending compulsory competitive tendering to social care services, and favours giving local authorities an opportunity to make greater use of service specifications, agency agreements and contracts in an evolutionary way. (DoH, 1989b, p 23)

No explanation for this decision was offered, but it seems likely that it was based on a recognition of the uneven distribution of alternative suppliers.

Care managers were to be responsible for assessing individuals' needs for community care and putting together, in consultation with clients, community care packages, calling on a variety of providers including voluntary and commercial agencies. The White Paper was careful to emphasise that assessment discussions with clients would need to be conducted within the constraints imposed by the availability and affordability of services and facilities. Consumers who could afford to do so would be expected to contribute towards the cost of provision, although specific charging policies would be left to the discretion of the local authority.

The role of the Department of Health's Social Services Inspectorate in advising and monitoring social services departments was strengthened and local authorities were required to establish independent inspection units. Both the 1989 Children Act and the 1990 NHS and Community Care Act required social services departments to set up complaints procedures.

With the implementation of the NHS and Community Care Act in 1993, the personal social services experienced the most far-reaching changes since the 1970 Local Authority Social Services Act brought social services departments into being in 1971. Changes in policy, practice, attitudes and values were all involved. Probably the most significant changes were those associated with the creation of internal markets and the move from direct provision to the enabling, regulation and financing of provision. All authorities were impelled to move in the same direction, but they did so at different speeds and with varying degrees of enthusiasm.

The NHS and Community Care Act (more clearly in the guidance papers that accompanied it) emphasised the importance of partnership in community care. Partnership has become one of the most frequently-used words in discussions of welfare arrangements. The Conservative governments of the 1980s and 1990s used it constantly, although there was little recognition of a possible conflict between competition and partnership. Partnership is frequently used to signify joint planning, commissioning and provision in community care. In this respect it may refer to partnerships: between independent providers and local authorities and/or health authorities; among providers; between statutory authorities. However, the forms of partnerships that have received most attention are partnerships between providers and users or their carers. One of the clearest expressions of this type of partnership is to be found in the 1989 Children Act. Marsh and Fisher illustrate this point:

> **The Children Act 1989 sets a framework for services which emphasises client involvement, participation, partnership and consultation. The Act provides for this in connection with requests for help and with child protection processes. It is particularly evident in the concept of parental responsibility continuing through changes of care, the emphasis put on maintaining the links between parents and children, and in the provision for local authorities to 'look after' children with minimal formality. (Marsh and Fisher, 1992, p 11)**

The very extensive guidelines accompanying the implementation of the 1989 Children Act also emphasised partnership. Particularly influential in promoting partnership was a government paper entitled *Working together under the Children Act 1989* (DoH, 1991). In addition, the Joseph Rowntree Foundation has published a series of studies (Common and Flynn, 1992; Marsh and Fisher, 1992; Newton and Marsh, 1993; Stevenson and Parsloe, 1993; Baldock and Ungerson, 1994; Goss and Miller, 1995) on the theme of partnership.

Several attempts have been made to evaluate the new arrangements: the Social Services Inspectorate has produced innumerable reports on specific aspects of the changes, there have been several reports from the Department of Health (1995) and the NHS Executive (1995) and from the Audit Commission (1993, 1994). Other work has been conducted by the King's Fund Centre and the Nuffield Institute (Henwood, 1995) and by Le Grand and Bartlett (1993), Bartlett et al (1994), Knapp et al (1994), Wistow et al (1994), Forder et al (1996). It would take up too much space to examine the findings of all of this work, but one or two comments might be in order. Some improvements were noted: a greater degree of accountability; greater flexibility and responsiveness; increased public knowledge of the personal social services; more importance attached to the views of users. Among the problems identified were: a lack of management information; inadequate coordination in joint-working arrangements; difficulties associated with managing markets; dissatisfaction with assessment procedures, rationing and charges; shortage of resources.

One of the problems in attempting to give an overall evaluation is that there are vast differences between local authority social services departments, not least in the quality of the services provided and the progress towards user-empowerment. There are differences, too, in the support given to carers. A second problem is that it is sometimes difficult to assign specific improvements or problems to changes in the system. The community care reforms are an aspect of privatisation: the community care statistics for 1997 show a marked increase in provision by commercial and voluntary agencies since 1993. However, the growth of privatisation began well before 1993 – especially in the case of residential care. A closer look at privatisation will demonstrate that it began to expand significantly in the 1980s and that this long-term trend was strengthened by the 1990 NHS and Community Care Act.

Privatisation

Privatisation is a term most commonly associated with the sale of public utilities, but the Conservative governments of the 1980s wished to see the expansion of commercial and voluntary sector provision in a whole range of services. Social care was no exception to this general policy.

As already indicated, the growth of private markets was most evident in the provision of residential care. In 1980 in the UK, local authorities owned 45.8% of all residential homes for older people and provided 62.7% of the places; the private sector owned 34.7% of the homes, contributing 17.4% of the places; the voluntary sector owned 19.5% of the homes and provided 19.9% of the places. By 1995 the picture had changed dramatically: local authorities owned only 17% of the homes, providing 26.8% of the places; private homes constituted 67.8% of the total, providing 55.7% of the places; the voluntary sector owned 15.2% of the homes, contributing 17.5% of the places. The independent sector (private and voluntary sector combined) owned almost 83% of all homes and provided more than 73% of the places. Nursing homes demonstrate a similar division: in 1995, 73% of nursing home places were provided by the private sector, as compared with 6.5% provided by the voluntary sector and 20.5% provided by the public sector.

A *Statistical bulletin* (DoH, 1998a) gives details of three community services provided or paid for by social services departments: home help and homecare; meals; day centres. The figures permit some estimation of the impact of the 1990 NHS and Community Care Act. The bulletin says:

> **Local authorities, while still the main provider of all three services, continue to increase the use they make of voluntary and private sector providers. In particular 44% of home help/care contact hours were provided by the independent sector in 1997, compared with just 2% in 1992. (DoH, 1998a, p 2)**

The greatest proportionate contribution of the non-statutory sector in 1997 was in meals, delivering 41% of the meals going to people's homes and 65% of meals served at luncheon clubs. Day centre provision remains predominantly in the hands of local authorities – 78% in 1997. However, the proportion provided by the independent sector has risen steadily since 1992 from 10% in that year to 22% in 1997. The independent sector has made greater inroads into services for adults than it has into services for children and families. A joint survey by the Local Government Association and the Association of Directors of Social Services (1998) demonstrated that the public sector still provided 72% of services for children and families, but only 47% of services for adults.

Voluntary associations have long employed professional social workers – the NSPCC and Barnardos are two examples of several organisations working in the area of childcare and child protection. Profit-oriented agencies in social work are much less common, but there were some developments in this direction during the 1980s. The new community care arrangements could lead to the employment of social workers by companies specialising in the field of domiciliary care.

Private consultants and trainers are more numerous than they were in the 1970s. The 1989 Children Act gave rise to a deluge of training courses and training packs, and there are training companies specialising in such areas as race awareness and antidiscriminatory practice. There are consultants in every area of social work, but probably the best known and most numerous are to be found in child abuse. Social work careers consultants advertise in the professional weeklies and, less grandly, there are employment agencies offering advice on full-time or part-time employment and providing temporary workers and locums.

New Labour and the personal social services

The lack of prominence given to the personal social services, their essentially residual position, was described at the beginning of the chapter. The community care reforms raised their profile and they became the object of intense research and media interest. Baldock and Ungerson, in a study of consumerism in community care, said that:

> ... it might even be argued that, in Britain, community care has found itself at the forefront of a significant renegotiation of the post-war welfare settlement, as regards the established rights of citizenship and the social entitlements and obligations they entail. (Baldock and Ungerson, 1994, p 6)

The research interest remains, but the media has switched its attention to those areas of social policy that the new government has identified as its major priorities. In its manifesto and the election campaign, the Labour Party identified education as its number one priority closely followed by health. Welfare to Work and law and order were also highlighted. The personal social services were alluded to obliquely with references to community, families, pre-school facilities and carers.

Since 1997, the government's promises to reduce class sizes and expand pre-school and after-school provision, to reduce hospital waiting lists, and to provide everyone with either work or work-based training, have occupied the centre ground of political debate and have been the main focus of the media. Much less attention has been accorded to the personal social services. The degree to which these priorities are reflected in the allocation of resources is disputed. On the one hand, the Department of Health Statistics Division shows that the total budgets for 1997/98 were 94% higher in real terms than in 1986/87 (DoH, 1998a). On the other hand, a survey by the Local Government Association and the Association of Directors of Social Services, published in June 1998, reported that social services departments faced an average shortfall of 3.4% against their spending plans despite an increase in government funding of 1.2% in real terms. Cuts in services were planned by 54% of local authorities and 60% were either increasing charges, imposing them for the first time or increasing exemption thresholds. Other cost-cutting strategies included restricting access to services and increasing the fees paid to independent providers by less than inflation. Pressures were particularly acute, the Local Government Association/Association of Directors of Social Services claimed, because of the effects of accumulated reductions in central government funding in previous years – from 1992/93 to 1997/98 a fall of 6.1% in real terms taking inflation and demographic trends into account.

During 1998, several adjustments to spending on the personal social services were instituted. For example, in July extra resources were promised to overhaul care in the community for people with mental health problems. The proposals are an attempt to respond to demands for a greater emphasis on public safety in mental health policy stemming from several high-profile homicides. The Secretary of State Frank Dobson said that community care had failed. The plans, an extension of changes being considered by the previous Conservative administration, include the establishment of outreach teams to keep round-the-clock track of psychiatric patients and the building of special units open for 24 hours a day and staffed by nurses. These plans were confirmed and extended in December: an additional element was the power to enforce treatment. An extra £700 million over three years, less than had been anticipated, was allocated to bring the plans to fruition. More generally, the three-year Comprehensive Spending Review (CSR), published in July 1998, gave councils an extra £2.2 billion. In addition, £3.6 million was released from the sale of council houses and councils were expected to raise £2.75 billion from the sale of assets. An interesting aspect of the financial settlement was £800 million for what was termed 'a new deal for communities' to tackle unemployment, crime and low educational standards in about 20 of the country's poorest housing estates. However, the Chancellor's calculations were based on the presumption of a 5% increase in council tax. Local authorities claimed that even with this increase there would still be a shortfall in 1999–2000 of £1 billion. Looking further ahead, the White Paper, *Modernising social services*, published at the end of November 1998, promised £3 billion extra resources during the next three years and the establishment of a social services modernisation fund into which would be paid £1.3 billion (DoH, 1998b).

Rulings by the High Court and the Law Lords before the election had important implications for the resources of social services departments. In one of these cases the High Court ruled that local authorities, in deciding about subsidising a residential placement, could take the financial position of elderly people into account even when their assets fell below the £16,000 threshold at which local authorities were expected to meet part of the costs. This ruling was overturned by the Court of Appeal. Another decision by the Law Lords eased the financial pressure on social services departments by ruling that Gloucestershire Council was entitled to withdraw homecare services on the grounds that it could not afford them. Since taking office the Labour government, in the person of Paul Boateng, the Junior Minister in the Department of Health with responsibility for the personal social services, has supported both decisions. The government confirmed the Court of Appeal's decision that local authorities were required to subsidise the cost of residential care once personal assets fell below £16,000, but it refused to back a private House of Lords Bill which would have prevented local authorities withdrawing care services on the grounds of inadequate resources.

It is widely accepted that the most efficient and effective use of resources, and thus the quality of community care, are dependent on partnerships. This was stressed by the Conservative government and New Labour has, if anything, given it even greater emphasis. For example, a statutory duty is to be laid on local authorities and health authorities to work together to promote the well-being of their local communities. *Modernising social services* devotes a chapter to partnership. Among the partnerships identified are those involving the NHS, housing, education, criminal justice agencies, the employment service, the voluntary sector and users, carers and their representatives (DoH, 1998b). Many of the emergent or proposed partnerships are multiagency. One example is the Youth Offending Teams which will involve partnerships between social services, education, health authorities, the police and the probation service. The programmes aimed at tackling drugs misuse will include the same range of agencies working collaboratively with housing authorities and appropriate voluntary organisations. The Home Office (1998c) has issued guidelines for improved collaboration between local authorities and voluntary agencies through the development of compacts.

The extra resources already referred to are not the only signs that the government is beginning to take a more active interest in the personal social services. For example, in the election campaign the Labour Party promised to look at ways of ensuring more effective support for carers. The role and needs of carers received more attention during the 1980s and in 1995 the Carers (Recognition and Services) Act, promoted by a Labour MP, was passed. A statement by the Chief Executive of the Carers National Association described the day that the Act received the Royal Assent as "one of the most significant so far in the history of the carers' movement" (Carers National Association, 1997, p 2). In 1998, the government set up a working party to look again at the issue. The December statement about the future of pensions included greater recognition of the needs of carers by granting credited contributions to those unable to work because of caring responsibilities. A second indication of the government's greater willingness to take action in this area is the projected launch of a major childcare strategy (see also Chapter Seven) to improve the management of family and children's services. This was first intimated in the 1998 report of the Chief Inspector of the Social Services Inspectorate. The report, like several before it, was highly critical of the inconsistent quality of the work done for children and families and the complete absence of a coherent strategy in many authorities. In September 1998, the government announced a drive to deliver a new deal for children looked after by local authorities. A team of experts seconded from social services, education and the voluntary sector will be charged with ensuring that the demanding targets which will be set for local authority children's services are attained. In early November 1998, the government stated that £330 million was to be made available to strengthen procedures designed to ensure the safety of children and young people in children's homes, foster care and boarding schools. Among the changes to be implemented are more training and more stringent vetting of people applying for jobs which would bring them into contact with children. The government plans three levels of police checks: basic for those not in direct contact with children; intermediate for those coming into direct contact but only under supervision; enhanced for jobs involving unsupervised work with children. A few days after the announcement of the new deal for children, a ministerial statement promised to iron out the widely differing standards of care provided for elderly people and disabled people. The impetus for these initiatives came mainly from growing public concern about the treatment of children and older people in residential care. There have been several widely publicised instances of the sexual and physical abuse of children in local authority, voluntary and private homes, in some cases stretching over many years and with connections to paedophile rings. The standards of care provided for elderly people in residential establishments has also given rise to concern, with standards ranging from the very good, through neglect to definite ill-treatment. Nor is abuse restricted to residential care; it also occurs in domiciliary care of all types, including foster care. The White Paper (DoH, 1998b) proposes new arrangements intended to secure more effective protection of those being cared for. A network of independent regional inspectorates will take over the present regulatory functions of local and health authorities: the new regulatory bodies will have responsibility for both residential and domiciliary care agencies. The inspectorates will be required to appoint children's rights officers, who will be high-ranking officials with the task of ensuring that the work for children is not swamped by the greater volume of work for adults. The White Paper (1998b, p 49) also promises "to legislate as soon as Parliamentary time allows to create new and stronger duties on councils to support care leavers up to at least 18; and to discourage discharge below that age in cases where it is premature". One of the duties of the inspectorates will be to apply national performance indicators. Daycare for adults and field social work will not at first come within the remit of the inspectorates. However, social workers do not entirely escape the regulatory net. New Labour has already accepted the recommendations of an inquiry begun by the previous Conservative government into the organisation of training for social work. In line with the recommendations, the government proposes to abolish the Central Council for Education and Training in Social Work (CCETSW) and replace it with an employment-led National Training Organisation (NTO). The new organisation, to be called the Training Organisation for the Personal Social Services, will be one of many such structures and, as its title suggests, its remit will go well beyond social work training to cover the training needs of *all* personal social services employees. The White Paper takes this a stage further with a proposal to establish a General Social Care Council to regulate both the conduct and training of all social care staff. Initially, the Council would register only those with professional social work qualifications and other care workers who had reached National Vocational Qualification (NVQ) Level 3. However, other levels of staff would be included as adequate training provision became available in sufficient quantity. In December 1998 a further regulatory agency was promised for 1999 – a Disability Rights Commission with an annual budget of £11 million.

During the election the Labour Party represented itself as the Party of the Family. Since community care is mainly family care the changes made in family policy are relevant to the personal social services. The 1998 Green Paper on welfare reform talked of the need to support children and families, and Harriet Harman, the Secretary of State for Social Security (until the July 1998 Cabinet reshuffle) has pointed out that "no fewer than seven Cabinet Ministers have a major interest in childcare" (Harman, 1998, p 3). However, the previous Conservative government went further than Labour in having a Minister for the Family who sat in the Cabinet. Labour's efforts in this direction are closely tied in with the aims of its Welfare to Work initiative, the central philosophy of which is that whenever possible everyone (including lone parents) should work. However, if parents are to work affordable childcare of an acceptable quality has to be made available. Labour has promised to ensure that daycare will be available for all children aged four with extensions for younger children when resources allow. Another development is the allocation of £300 million to provide an extra million places during the next five years in after-school clubs. These fill the gap between the end of the school day and the end of the parents' working day. Another attempt to encourage lone parents back into the labour force is the proposed tax credit for childcare. Under this scheme, low-income families will have up to 70% of their childcare expenses paid, the amount varying according to the number of children and the level of income.

In fashioning New Labour, Blair constantly emphasised the importance of community which he claimed was the true basis of socialism. An influential work by Selbourne (1997) lends weight to the argument that civic duty should be given more prominence in theories of socialism. In some ways this bears some relationship to Tawney's (1964) emphasis on fellowship and fraternity. However, in Tawney's day there was no Amitai Etzioni and the term communitarianism had not been invented. It is interesting to note that Driver and Martell (1997) see communitarianism as a response to both neo-liberalism and old social democracy.

> **New Labour sell community as the hangover cure to the excesses of Conservative individualism. Community will create social cohesion out of the market culture of self-interest.... If communitarianism is New Labour's answer to Thatcherism, so too is it Tony Blair's rebuff to Old Labour. Community will restore the moral balance to society by setting out duties and obligations as well as rights. And where Old Labour looked to the state for action, New Labour talks of *reinventing government* through collective action in the community. (Driver and Martell, 1997, pp 27-8)**

This quotation suggests unequivocal responses to the two major questions addressed in this book. In this respect, at least, New Labour departs from both Old Labour and the Conservative Party.

Etzioni (1995) has been promoting communitarianism with an almost religious zeal since 1990, and New Labour, more particularly Tony Blair, former Minister of Welfare Reform Frank Field and Home Secretary Jack Straw, have been influenced by communitarian ideology. The emphasis on communitarianism is on duties and responsibilities rather than rights (see also Chapter Ten); Etzioni has called for a moratorium on any new rights and has suggested that some existing rights may need to be foregone so that people can focus on service to others and civic duties. Among the cures for a society dominated by selfishness, greed and materialism is a return to traditional family values, reversing the 'parental deficit'. Divorce would be made more difficult and moral education would be introduced into the school curriculum.

Communitarianism is at its strongest in exposing the shortcomings of stark individualism. Bell (1993), for example, sees communitarianism as presenting a challenge to liberal individualism. He criticises Western governments for failing to recognise the importance of both local democracy and community. Blair levels much the same criticisms at Old Labour and contemporary conservatism. But communitarianism has also enabled New Labour to abandon notions of social class. Driver and Martell (1997, p 43) argue that the various strands of communitarianism in New Labour can be seen "as part of a wider shift from social democracy to 'liberal conservatism' in Labour ideas". There is a strong prescriptive and ethical or moral element in New Labour's communitarianism. Communities are distinguished by shared moral values which are seen as a means of restoring social cohesion.

Communitarianism has implications for policy which go well beyond the personal social services and community care, but it has a particular significance in this area. Most simply, the explicit recognition of communities as vital units of social organisation is bound to add to the significance of community care. Communitarianism implies decentralisation and an enhanced role for local agencies. Greater use will be made of independent organisations, both voluntary and commercial. New Labour sees the voluntary sector as an essential element of a civil society encouraging active citizenship. The voluntary sector has already taken on a bigger and more formal role in the provision of social care services, but a communitarian philosophy emphasising duties, responsibility and civic obligation will push the voluntary sector even further to centre stage as the mixed economy of care develops. Mikosz (1998, p 13), in a discussion of New Labour's Third Way, writes of "the rediscovery of the 'civic sphere', that is, of voluntary and mutual organisations which are neither state nor private and whose existence strengthens the fabric of society (the idea of social capital)". The larger voluntary organisations, as already indicated, employ paid staff, but implicit in communitarianism is an increase in volunteering which is favoured because it gives people the opportunity to serve others and indirectly to benefit the whole community. The community also benefits if people help themselves rather than relying on state support. This has several strands. The first is a very general point about self-reliance and taking responsibility for your own welfare. There is a clear relationship here to New Labour's notion of a stakeholder society. A second strand, also closely related, is the role of the family in providing care for its members. The family has been a conspicuous feature of American communitarian analysis, but the family has also been given prominence by New Labour. Driver and Martell (1997, p 38) cite several instances in which Blair has stressed the importance of the family and its role in bringing children up to become self-reliant individuals and good citizens. More recent examples include the Prime Minister's address to the 1998 Labour Party Conference and a Consultative Document on the future of the family published in November 1998 (Home Office, 1998a) which argued that marriage was the best basis for rearing children and the family should be "at the heart of our society and the basis of our future as a country". Among the proposals is the establishment of a National Family and Parenting Institute.

A third strand within the self-reliance theme of communitarianism is mutual aid or self-help. Frank Field, one of the architects of Labour's new approach to welfare and a staunch advocate of stakeholder welfare, made the following comment in 1996:"Any new settlement will be dominated by the emerging values which prize ownership and control. What I have called the growing social autonomy of voters – wishing to do 'their own thing' determined on a basis of free association – will be the touchstone of the new welfare" (Field, 1996b, p 11). Within the voluntary sector, self-help groups are probably the most innovative, and certainly the fastest growing, segment. Numerous among these are consumers' groups – including users of personal social services – which may campaign for a strengthening and extension of social rights. Communitarians would applaud the principle of mutual aid, but would be much less enthusiastic about the advocacy role of mutual aid groups. New Labour, on the other hand, has constantly emphasised the empowerment of users and carers. This emphasis was very obvious in the Policy Review (Labour Party, 1989, p 7) in which Neil Kinnock admitted that in the past Labour had "the reputation of being more concerned with protecting the interests of the producers of goods and services rather than the interests of consumers". He claimed that this reputation was undeserved, but that in future Labour would indisputably become the Party of the Consumer. New Labour pushed this message home throughout the election and after taking office. One of Field's arguments for stakeholder welfare is that it gives consumers more control over their own welfare.

In emphasising the importance of community, voluntary organisations, self-help and families New Labour is firmly committed to mixed economies of welfare. However, a fully pluralist system requires markets. New Labour, in contrast to the Labour Party of the 1970s, has embraced markets with some enthusiasm, not only in commerce and industry but also in welfare. New Labour seems to have no problems with welfare for profit and in this respect it is closer to the Conservative Party it replaced in government than it is to Old Labour. New Labour's unequivocal acceptance of markets is illustrated in a Fabian pamphlet, written by Tony Blair, in which the Prime Minister states that "with the right policies, market mechanisms are critical to meeting social objectives, entrepreneurial zeal can promote social justice, and new technology represents an opportunity, not a threat" (Blair, 1998a, p 4). The same is true of New Labour's support for competition (albeit in a modified form) in public services. This commitment is clear from the government's guidelines for replacing CCT in local services with a duty of achieving Best Value: a duty that "local authorities will owe to local people, both as taxpayers and customers of local authority services" (DETR/Welsh Office, 1997). The replacement of CCT will be fully achieved only after primary legislation. In the meantime, about 30 projects have been set up to demonstrate what can be accomplished, and it is expected that all local authorities will take steps towards Best Value ahead of legislation. For its part, the government is relaxing the regulations surrounding CCT which is expected to become less bureaucratic in nature and more transparent. However, the guidelines state that "in most service areas, there will be a clear presumption in favour of open competition" (DETR/Welsh Office, 1997). The same document, in setting out the principles of Best Value, modifies some of the earlier, more stark statements about competition:

> **Competition will continue to be an important management tool, a test of best value and an important feature in performance plans. But it will not be the only management tool and it is not in itself enough to demonstrate that Best Value is being achieved. (DETR/Welsh Office, 1997)**

Best Value will apply to all local authority departments, including those, such as social services departments, that have not been subject to CCT. Most social services departments introduced elements of tendering, particularly for bigger contracts, and it is difficult to say how this will be affected by the Best Value initiative. Presumably the Social Services

Inspectorate and the Audit Commission will be interested in the steps taken to secure Best Value in social care services.

Having looked at New Labour's inheritance and some of their major policies in relation to the personal social services, it is time to readdress the major questions posed by this book. Is New Labour's approach to the personal social services significantly different from that of both Old Labour, on the one hand, and Conservative policies on the other? If there are differences, is the approach of New Labour sufficiently distinct in this area to constitute an element of a new welfare state?

Old Labour, New Labour and Conservative approaches to the personal social services

When Labour was last in power, mixed economies of welfare and the reappraisal of the role of the central state were only beginning to be seriously considered. This is where the most significant differences between Old and New Labour arise. Throughout the 1960s and into the 1970s the Labour Party was in favour of State provision which also implied State finance and State regulation. The voluntary sector was reluctantly tolerated, but it was to play an essentially subsidiary role in supplementing or complementing State services. Welfare for profit was anathema and where it existed the Labour Party of that time said it should be separate from the State. Internal markets were not part of Old Labour's thinking and the idea of social services departments becoming enablers and purchasers rather than direct providers was similarly not on Old Labour's agenda. Partnerships with independent providers and contracts in social care were not relevant. As this chapter has demonstrated, and as is very clear in the White Paper, New Labour is no less committed than the previous government to partnerships of all types.

Some of the themes that have become the hallmark of New Labour had their first expression (although somewhat tentative) in the Policy Review of 1989, which exhibited, for example, a greater willingness to address the issue of markets, an acceptance that markets are the most appropriate means of efficiently distributing many goods and services and that competition is one way of securing consumer choice. However, the review went to some length to point to the drawbacks of markets in education, health and social care. In relation to community care the review categorically rejects the policy which reduces the role of local authorities as direct providers:

> We ... entirely reject any suggestion that local authorities and
> other statutory agencies should only be purchasers of services,
> leaving provision to the private and non-statutory sectors. Public
> services are, and will continue to be, the principal means of
> meeting need, ensuring equality of access, and securing quality
> in community care. (Labour Party, 1989, p 51)

New Labour under Blair is much more prepared to accept internal markets
in social care; markets, competition and contracting will continue, although
competitive tendering will give way to Best Value. Charges and their
associated means tests will remain. In the personal social services, New
Labour has adopted many of the major principles of Conservative policy.
The main differences are those of emphasis and tone. For example, while
markets and competition are accepted, it is recognised that these are
insufficient on their own to guarantee equity, efficiency, effective high
quality services and user empowerment. Whereas the Conservatives saw
markets and competition almost as the sole policy vehicle, New Labour
takes the view that they are part of a broader strategy which includes
efforts to ensure that as many people as possible have a stake in society
and that those who are unable to participate in the market economy are
given the necessary support. According to communitarians, economic
success depends on social cohesion which, in turn, implies the moderation
of competitive individualism by principles of mutualism, fellowship and
social responsibility, all of which have important implications for the
personal social services and community care. The neo-liberal elements
within the Conservative Party, particularly in the 1980s, based their support
of markets on a crude form of individualism, in which the relentless
pursuit of self-interest was seen as acceptable behaviour. Driver and Martell
point to the differences between New Labour's support for the market
economy and the neo-liberal approach:

> Labour's communitarianism challenges the neo-liberal market
> model in three ways. First, it denies that successful economies
> live by competitive individualism alone: community values, like
> cooperation and collaboration are just as vital to a successful
> market system. Second, it challenges the neo-liberal assumption
> that general welfare is best left to the free play of private enterprise.
> There is a role not just for government but for collective action
> through the intermediate institutions of civil society. Third,

market individualism, it is argued, has eroded those institutions
seen as vital for social cohesion. (Driver and Martell, 1997, p 33)

Social cohesion is claimed to be one of the main benefits of a
communitarian approach. But communitarianism is about localism and
the question arises as to the degree to which local cohesion can be
transposed into the national arena.

New Labour's espousal of communitarianism is closely intertwined
with its policies of decentralisation and vigorous but responsive local
government (see Chapter Eleven). Old Labour was supportive of local
government, but paradoxically it was also highly centralist. This centralist
tradition began to be eroded during Labour's opposition years and
decentralisation and the devolution of power were firmly endorsed in the
1997 election manifesto. The previous administration had also talked
about decentralisation, but Margaret Thatcher's antipathy towards local
government, although somewhat eased under the following Conservative
Prime Minister John Major, led to an attack on local authorities' functions,
finance and autonomy. Under the Conservative governments of the 1980s
and 1990s the power of the central state, on balance, increased. For different
reasons, there are similar contradictions in New Labour's approach to
decentralisation: there is a general preference for decentralisation, but this
chapter has identified several measures in the personal social services leading
to greater central control. The Audit Commission and the Social Services
Inspectorate and existing ministerial powers now have a range of new
regulatory and supervisory bodies to oversee and the powers of the
Secretary of State have been increased.

These centralist tendencies in New Labour's policies in relation to the
personal social services are also a reflection of an antipathy towards and a
mistrust of professionalism. This is bound up with the Party leadership's
commitment to communitarianism which has within it very strong
elements of antiprofessionalism. The previous Conservative administration
had been highly critical of the social work profession, making scathing
remarks about its inappropriate concern with 'political correctness'. It
was considerations such as these that gave the impetus to Conservative
initiatives to reform social work training – initiatives developed and
extended by the new government. New Labour's approaches are little
different to those of the Conservatives in that they are based on a perceived
need to supervise and regulate professional social workers. Labour has
gone much further in this respect than the Conservatives. Nowhere is

this more explicit than in the extensive powers proposed for the General Social Care Council.

In the 1970s there was much talk of more participatory social services in Labour circles and this became a much more significant aspect of policy in the Policy Review (Labour Party, 1989) as Old Labour began to give way to New Labour. There was a greatly increased emphasis on consumerism and the empowerment of users and less emphasis on producers:

> **While Labour has done a great deal in practice to protect the consumer, more attention has been given in the past to the interests of the people at work who produce and deliver the goods. This has meant, for example, that the specific needs of women, who are often the main users of many services, have not always been fully considered. This report puts the balance right. Its priority is how to give consumers more power and better protection. (Labour Party, 1989, p 41)**

New Labour has reiterated this theme, emphasising in particular the involvement and empowerment of the users of public services whether the services are provided directly by statutory agencies or by independent contractors. In this, New Labour is continuing, possibly extending, the policies of its predecessor. One of the stated aims of the Conservative community care reforms was the empowerment of users.

New Labour clearly favours mixed economies of welfare in which the role of the central and local state as direct providers of services is diminished. This has become the new orthodoxy and it fits in well with many aspects of communitarianism. As already indicated, communitarians strongly favour voluntary action and mutual aid. In the Fabian pamphlet already referred to Blair states:

> **A key challenge of progressive politics is to use the state as an enabling force, protecting effective communities and voluntary organisations and encouraging their growth to tackle new needs, in partnership as appropriate. (Blair, 1998a, p 4)**

This statement could just as easily have been made by John Major and his colleagues.

New Labour's emphasis on the family is also virtually indistinguishable from Conservative policies in this area. The Consultative Document on the future of the family is just one indication of this (Home Office, 1998a). One of the main characteristics of community care in mixed economies of welfare is that it expects families to assume a greater degree of responsibility for the care of their members. Paradoxically, while New Labour shares this expectation, its Welfare to Work policies may diminish the capacity of families to provide care. The government is committed to doing more to support carers, but the reliance on families will undoubtedly continue. It may be seen as an aspect of the communitarian emphasis on duties and responsibility. The philosophy is that rights and duties are inextricably linked, but in this sphere at present there is an imbalance: there are few rights and many duties.

Conclusion

The personal social services and community care under New Labour have been paid much less attention, both within and outside the Party, than have education, health, Welfare to Work and social security. However, in many ways this area of policy can be usefully employed to begin to answer the central question posed by this book: To what extent does New Labour's approach in welfare differ from that of both Old Labour and of the Conservatives, and are any differences sufficient to justify talking of a new welfare state?

Along with President Clinton, Blair claims to be following a 'third way'. In Blair's case, this means steering a middle course between old-style social democracy and the competitive individualism of the Conservatives. A good example of the middle way is to consider the relationship between rights and duties in the three approaches: Old Labour emphasised rights and said little about duties and obligations; the Conservatives said a great deal about duties and were less clear about rights; New Labour tries to balance rights with reciprocal duties (see Chapter Ten). In the personal social services and community care there would be rights to certain levels and standards of care either in the community or in residential establishments. There is also a right to have a personal assessment of needs and to be fully involved in this process and in any decisions about the services to be provided. There is a right to complain. In this way, services are said to be needs-led, but in practice, there are always limited resources in relation to demand. What emerges is a resources-led service with the customer having to make the best of what is available. What is available is determined by the resources and policies of the provider. The duties might include: doing everything possible to manage without asking for help; families looking after their own members; a willingness to pay for services and make economical use of whatever is provided. The problem is that in the personal social services there is a lack of clarity about what your rights are and certainly a lack of knowledge on the part of consumers and potential consumers. Vulnerable people may not be willing or able to insist on their rights (for example, not wishing to complain). The enforcement of rights may also be difficult.

New Labour has departed from traditional Labour in its greater willingness in the personal social services to accept a fully pluralist system, involving voluntary organisations, volunteers, mutual aid, and commercial providers. Internal markets, competition, charges and means tests are also now acceptable. The claim to be steering a *middle* course has to be questioned. New Labour has moved a long way from Old Labour and there has been considerable convergence with Conservative policies. As already noted, the main differences are those of emphasis and tone. New Labour's acceptance of markets and competition is more qualified than that of the Conservatives and competitive individualism is rejected in favour of communitarian ideals of mutuality, responsibility and civic duty.

In the rest of this Parliament, as the Labour government implements its education, health, criminal justice and Welfare to Work reforms, it may begin to pay more attention to the personal social services and community care. The White Paper on social services (DoH, 1998b) gives a clearer indication of the government's intentions in the personal social services, but the Queen's Speech opening the 1998/99 Session made no provision for legislation to implement the proposals. Once legislation is published, we will be in a better position to evaluate Labour's policies in this area and to judge the extent to which they contribute to a new welfare state.

FIVE

Education, education, education

Yolande Muschamp, Ian Jamieson and Hugh Lauder

Introduction

The Labour Party manifesto of 1979 gave only three short pages to education, but by 1997 the title 'Education, education, education' headed the manifesto and education was declared to be the Party's first priority. The few paragraphs of the earlier document had evolved into a detailed programme of reforms. In the intervening years the successive Conservative governments had introduced what Gipps (1994) referred to as an "explosion of developments", the most fundamental changes to the education system in the England and Wales since the Education Act of 1944. The introduction of a Parents' Charter, open enrolment, the National Curriculum, the local management of schools (LMS) and the expansion of school inspection on an unprecedented scale had brought exposure to the education system which began with the 'Great Debate' instigated by James Callaghan as Prime Minister in his 1976 Ruskin Speech.

When evaluating educational policy the contribution of reforms to the development of a welfare state has been measured traditionally through their "promotion of wealth creation through preparation for economic production" and their promotion of "social justice and individual rights" (Pollard, 1997, p 364). From the 1940s to the 1970s wealth creation and social justice could be seen as the aims of the attempt to redistribute social goods on a more equitable basis which consisted in the first instance of a secondary education for all, comprehensive education and the raising of the school leaving age (Gewirtz, 1996). Inherent in the concept of social justice was the view that schools would produce equality of opportunity for children to achieve their educational potential regardless of their social grouping. During the 1980s and 1990s a crisis in confidence in the comprehensive system appears to have led the Conservative government to redefine equality of opportunity. Equality in educational achievement has given way to equality of access to provision with the development of the concept of 'equity' by the New Right (Brown and Lauder, 1997).

Comparing the Labour Party's manifesto of 1979 with that of 1997 reveals fundamental differences between the commitments given in each to the principle of equality of opportunity in education. There has been no reversal of Tory reforms with the return of a Labour government and yet it is not entirely possible to argue that the differences between the two Labour manifestos are the result of Labour adopting Tory policies. Labour's concept of a 'Third Way' would appear to be evident in the new gloss given to old Tory policies. The reluctance to abandon Tory policies might be explained by the tension between Labour's intention to modernise the schools and education system and its desire or perceived need to maintain the support of the middle-class voter which has created severe constraints on its choice of strategies for education reform.

Its dissatisfaction with the comprehensives, the weight of parental pressure to raise standards and the need to allay parents' fears of failing schools have required Labour to continue the Conservative's policy of open enrolment which allows parents to make the decision of which school is best for their child. Labour has abandoned the principle of comprehensive education leaving in place the Conservative diversification of education institutions which brought in new types of schools such as the city technology colleges (CTCs) and the 'opted-out' grant-maintained schools (GMS) and with it the partial selection of pupils. Arguably it has accepted the marketisation of education in order to promote the vision of parental choice. Whereas this may be an immediate response to establish the Party as a 'safe pair of hands' it also has the foundations of a radical transformation of schools. Labour's Third Way may be emerging – alongside its conventional remedies for underachievement – in the form of technological and pedagogic innovations and experiment.

Labour claims to be addressing educational failure, following the Tories in blaming and shaming the schools, while ensuring that the consumers of education take their share of responsibility. The onus on schools to reform has much in common with Old Labour's centrally prescribed policies for schools. For example, getting the basics right through providing guidance from literacy and numeracy taskforces and ensuring school effectiveness through creating central agencies such as the Standards and Effectiveness Unit. However, at the same time there is a third way in:

• the radical experimentation that is being encouraged in new partnership between industry, local education authorities and schools in the creation of Education Action Zones;

- the striking introduction of information technology in the National Grid for Learning;
- the reorganisation of vocational education;
- the promotion of lifelong learning.

By comparing Labour's 1979 and 1997 manifestos and taking into account the changes introduced by the intervening governments, this chapter will be able to examine the tensions which have arisen when introducing the policies in a climate of public concern over standards. It will attempt to explain the government's policies and to evaluate their potential contribution to a new welfare state.

Standards

There has been a crisis in successive governments' confidence in education, which has existed from the 1970s. This is reflected in a media-led public loss of educational consensus. It appears in the Labour Party manifesto of 1997:

> **Nearly half of our 11 year olds in England and Wales fail to reach expected standards in English and maths. Britain has a smaller share of 17 and 18 year olds in full time education. Nearly two-thirds of the British workforce lack vocational qualifications. (Labour Party, 1997a)**

P. Brown (1997) argues that the massive investment in education during the 1960s had not prevented the economic recession of the 1970s, nor had it brought about a redistribution of social goods. The symptoms of education failure were reflected in the growing number of complaints from industry that it was the schools which were responsible for youth unemployment, allowing the emerging powerful Right to claim that the attempt to enhance the educational achievement of working–class youth had created an unemployed group who "were now a source of economic liability" (P. Brown, 1997, p 397). This brought about a loss of confidence in the comprehensive schools attacked originally in the Black Papers and continuously promulgated as failing ever since by the New Right.

The Right was able to argue that the comprehensive system had failed to provide a suitable education for the working classes and that the practices of comprehensive schools had led to the dilution of standards, a levelling down. It survived all challenges to its argument that standards were declining. However, the 'standards' interest had not always belonged to the Right. It was a focus on standards that made up the central section of the Callaghan Green Paper *Education in schools: A consultative document* (DES, 1977) which concluded Callaghan's 'Great Debate' in education, initiated by his Ruskin speech. Daugherty (1995) suggests that the section 'standards and assessment' took forward the growing interest in a commonly prescribed curriculum for schools by hinting that a common curriculum would provide the basis of a standardised assessment system for judging standards in schools.

The comprehensive system was central to the 1979 manifesto. Standards would be raised by a continuing commitment to ensuring that there was universal education by the end of the 1980s. This was to be achieved by more than just removing selection to state schools but by abolishing subsidies to the private sector:

> **Independent schools still represent a major obstacle to equality of opportunity. Labour's aim is to end as soon as possible, fee-paying in such schools, while safeguarding schools for the handicapped. Labour will end as soon as possible the remaining public subsidies and public support to independent schools. (Labour Party, 1979, p 17)**

There was no mention yet of a common curriculum or assessment policy. Instead, the focus was on the quality of experience within the schools by reducing class size:

> **Already class sizes are the lowest ever recorded. The ratio of pupils to teachers is now only 23.6 in primary schools and 16.2 in secondary schools. Labour will continue to give high priority to reducing class size further. (Labour Party, 1979, p 17)**

To address the difficulties of youth unemployment the manifesto came close to identifying unemployment as the responsibility of the education system, by addressing the problem with educational measures rather than workplace initiatives. The Youth Opportunity Programmes would give colleges the role of finding work placements for 16- to 19-year-olds and an expansion of the Youth Service would aim to meet the social and recreational needs of youth. Through its attack on independent education and because of the responsibility it gave to colleges to address the problems of youth unemployment, Labour remained vulnerable to the accusation that mediocrity was being promoted in the name of social justice (P. Brown, 1997). This view would remain central to arguments from the Right as represented for example by the Hillgate Group:

> It must be remembered that the deterioration in British education has risen partly because schools have been treated as instruments for equalising, rather than instructing children. (Hillgate Group, 1987, quoted in P. Brown, 1997, p 398)

Despite the partial support by the Conservative governments for the comprehensive schools, Conservative continued to criticise this 'equality' issue where mixed ability teaching within comprehensive schools was leading to a dilution of standards in order to achieve equality of outcomes. However, this preoccupation with low standards remained throughout the period of Conservative government with the responsibility for failure increasingly being given to the teaching profession. Additionally, 'standards' almost became a moral issue with its link to 'character'. The Conservatives in their 1987 manifesto committed themselves to raising standards in education, asserting that:

> Parents want schools to provide their children with the knowledge, training and character that will fit them for today's world. (Conservative Party, 1987, p 1)

They stressed the importance of basic education skills and moral values of honesty, hard work and responsibility. These aims would be met with the introduction of a common National Curriculum and a programme of National Assessment. The Conservative government embarked on a series of reforms which was to transform the education system. This included restructuring (twice) the public examination system, introducing the National Curriculum and phased national tests, expanding school inspection, introducing regular teacher appraisal and the publication of league tables of school performance. These reforms were introduced alongside measures to increase the role and nature of involvement of parents and to increase accountability, both of which are discussed in the following sections.

Despite these changes the belief that standards were still falling persisted during the 1990s. This belief was reinforced by international comparisons of pupil performance and the commissioned discussion paper by Alexander,

Rose and Woodhead which became known in the media as 'the three wise men report'. In fact, Alexander claims that it was the government's intention to find a decline in standards:

> ... the political intentions which lay behind the commissioning of the discussion paper, for members of the government from Prime Minister Major downwards had made clear their presumption (1) that standards in primary education were falling and (2) that 'trendy' post-Plowden methods were to blame. If the discussion paper failed to deliver on the first part of the premise, the government's 'winter initiative' would look distinctly shaky. (Alexander, 1997, p 237)

With its promise to introduce a new focus on standards in primary schools Labour adopted the Conservative's policy of 'back to basics' while allowing innovation and experimentation in selected areas. This was made possible because the 'basic' core subjects of mathematics, English and science had been established by the introduction of the National Curriculum. Primary schools would be seen as the key to 'mastering the basics' through a focus on literacy and numeracy, baseline assessment and year-on-year targets for improvement. All of this built on the reforms made by the Conservatives. The emphasis in *Excellence in schools* (DfEE, 1997a) on 'a sound beginning' takes curriculum guidance beyond the school system. The Conservative government through the 1988 Education Reform Act had introduced the National Curriculum for pupils within the 11 years of compulsory schooling. School years were relabelled as Years 1 to 11 and the traditional division of infant, junior and secondary were replaced with Key Stages 1-4. Labour has extended curriculum guidance downwards and set challenging pre-school targets for local education authorities (LEAs) to devise Early Years Development and Childcare Plans (EYDCPs) to be in place, after Department for Education and Employment approval, in April 1999. The LEAs have a duty to secure places for all four-year-olds. Power and Whitty (1999, p 2) suggest this is some "indication that the welfare state should provide support for education, at least from the cradle if not to the grave". The EYDCPs require nursery providers to liaise with primary schools reflecting the government's view in the White Paper that nursery education will provide "the foundations of learning" (DfEE, 1997a).

The promise to reduce class size in primary schools was the only feature which had appeared in the 1979 manifesto and which differed radically from the policy of the Tories whose reforms through open enrolment and devolved budgets had led to an increase in class size. The Labour manifesto did not use the pupil–teacher ratio used in 1973 (23.6 in primary schools) but a target for average class size (30 pupils in Key Stage 1 for pupils aged five to seven) as if to emphasise the growing trends under the Conservatives towards larger classes. The reduction was to be achieved by using the money saved by phasing out the Assisted Places Scheme. Power and Whitty (1999) argue that using the first piece of education legislation passed under the new Labour government to abolish the scheme was a deliberate ploy by Labour to distance itself from the Conservatives and indicative of its commitment to 'benefit the many, not just the few'.

Within Key Stages 3 and 4 of the secondary phase of education, the Labour Party in its 1997 manifesto had strengthened its commitment to 'standards' and diluted its support for the comprehensive schools. It would raise standards by modernising the comprehensive school and introducing setting. Setting is the grouping of pupils into teaching groups or classes for different subjects according to their previous achievement. It differs from streaming where pupils are put into classes according to previous achievement but then stay in these classes for all subjects. This strategy seemed an attempt to destroy the popular belief that comprehensive schools relied on mixed ability teaching groups, rather than reflecting the reality that setting was common place in schools. (The recent call by the Office for Standards in Education [Ofsted] for primary schools [Ofsted, 1999] to set pupils by ability shows how this issue is still hotly debated.)

Although the Labour government supported comprehensive schools and guaranteed that there would be no return of selection at 11⁺ they reversed their 1979 disapproval of independent schools. They promised not to abolish good private schools or to change the status of grammar schools unless parents voted for a change. Brown and Lauder argue that in this situation there is a danger that the concept of equality of opportunity has become diluted (Brown and Lauder, 1997, p 187). They state that as a consequence the system is moving from one where funding is based on need to one where the market determines the level of resourcing. This can only serve to encourage "the creation of underfunded sink schools for the poor and havens of 'excellence' for the rich". The CTCs have remained and general support for diversity in the status of schools appears to be a feature of the government's policy. The Beacon Schools Initiative which allocates extra funding for outstanding schools to become models for less successful schools has continued this trend. As Mortimore and Mortimore point out:

> ... it seems entirely reasonable to expect schools which are doing well to act as models for those labouring under difficulties.... But teachers visiting – or being visited by staff – from beacon schools, which are privileged in terms of extra funding or in the type of pupils they attract, may grow resentful of the inequity rather than be impressed by the pedagogy. (Mortimore and Mortimore, 1998, p 210)

The Labour government promotes the argument, not supported by current research, that schools are able to produce equality of opportunity regardless of the mix of its intake (see Lauder et al, 1999; Mortimore and Whitty, 1997; Wells, 1993).

While the reduction in class sizes, the focus on literacy and numeracy targets and the Beacon Schools Initiative are attempts to improve schooling as it exists, other innovatory projects would suggest that there is a genuine intention by Labour to radically restructure the education system. This is reflected in the encouragement and freedom given to schools and LEAs to experiment with new partnerships and pedagogies which realise the potential of new technologies within the creation of Education Action Zones, which aim to raise educational standards in poor areas. The zones appeared to be a return to the Educational Priority Areas (EPAs) that had been established as a result of the Plowden Report (CACE, 1967) except that this time the zones would be selected by a bidding competition, a radical move towards the Conservative governments' strategies for the management of resources. They are not the systematic attempt to compensate pupils for the poor social and economic conditions of the inner cities seen in the 1960s and 1970s. The 25 successful bids to become Education Action Zones are charged with the responsibility to become "test beds for the schools system of the next century" (Secretary of State quoted in *The Guardian*, 24 June 1998, p 4) The successful bids are not from the traditional inner city areas identified as EPAs. Instead they include authorities such as Hereford, Norfolk and North Somerset. To qualify, the areas had to attract business sponsorship. By giving business a greater influence over how pupils are taught in the zones:

> Ministers are confident that they will provide Tony Blair with models for a third way in education, departing from the traditional

structure of local authority and independent schools. The school clusters usually managed by a local authority will have licence to depart from the central curriculum guidance, for example in Brighton and Newcastle it will be adapted to prepare 14 and 16 year olds for work. The regulation will allow zones to vary teachers rates of pay and conditions and in the Birmingham two zones there will be a 50 per cent increase in school opening hours. (J. Carvel, *The Guardian*, 24 June 1998, p 4)

Already the Education Action Zones have attracted criticism on the grounds that although the partnerships are new they are dominated by the existing LEAs. As Gewirtz (1998, p 9) points out, although the Education Action Zones are intended to "foster innovation in schools, they are being established against a background of support for more traditional pedagogical practices". Power and Whitty (1999, p 9) question whether the private companies involved in the Education Action Zones initiative see the zones as "testing beds for future commercial ventures elsewhere in the education system". These extensions are quite dubious and appear to have more to do with 'marketing' government policy than any concern with firmly grounded research. For example, the track record of private providers in managing schools has not to our knowledge even been documented far less published, and no private provider has experience of running an LEA. Given that LEAs are now charged with target setting and standard raising it would be expected that such a task would be best left to professionals with a proven track record.

The zones are complemented by an initiative not identified in 1979, that of bringing new technology into schools by a national partnership with industry. A National Grid for Learning will aim to connect every school in Britain to the information super-highway (DfEE, 1997b). It aims to provide a:

... national focus and agenda for harnessing new technologies to raise educational standards, and improve quality of life and Britain's international competitiveness, especially the new literacy and numeracy targets. (DfEE, 1997b, p 3)

The National Grid for Learning reflects the aims of the 1979 manifesto in that its purpose is to "remove barriers to learning, ensuring opportunities for access to all". Lottery money will be used to improve teachers' IT skills. A similar improvement in the training of teachers was brought about when the Teacher Training Agency introduced an information and communication technology element to the curriculum for all courses from September 1998. Ofsted will inspect this programme during 1998-99 to ensure the demanding standards are met by all teachers qualifying in 1999.

Choice

The increased involvement of industry, competitive practices, diversity and increased specialisation in schools by competitive bidding, builds directly on the major changes in the education system brought about by the Conservatives during the 1980s. P. Brown (1997) argues that the 1988 Act which introduced open enrolment, the Parent's Charter, the variation between schools by the establishment of CTCs and the expansion of the Assisted Places Scheme aimed to bring about a market in education which was to move the education system from meritocracy to "parentocracy where education becomes dependent on the wishes and wealth of parents rather than the ability and efforts of pupils" (P. Brown, 1997, p 394). The parent was redefined as consumer. Whitty argues that marketisation is now a world trend which aims to restructure and deregulate state education (Whitty, 1997). New Labour's general reaffirmation of Tory policies on markets is echoed in policies in New Zealand and parts of Canada, Australia and the United States. However, its policies on merit pay, the use of private providers as partners in Education Action Zones and as possible managers of LEAs – in January 1999 the government advertised for private companies to bid to take on education services in the LEAs judged to be failing by their Education Development Plans and inspection reports (Rafferty, 1999) – is a clear extension of market principles that have few parallels anywhere except, perhaps, the United States.

In England and Wales the quasi-market was to be identified as a decentralised system of autonomous institutions which gave increased parental choice of specialised forms of provision. As Gewirtz et al comment:

We should not be surprised by this for the market provides politicians with all the benefits of being seen to act decisively and very few of the problems of being blamed when things go wrong. (Gewirtz et al, 1995, p 1)

However, it has been shown in studies such as Gewirtz et al (1995) or Menter et al (1997) that in primary schools, severe constraints on parental choice are inherent in the market system, removing the real choice that has been promised by both governments as a part of their commitment to the involvement of parents in schooling. In the 1979 manifesto the initiative which appeared to be aimed directly at parents was the promise to provide nursery education "for 90 per cent of our 4 year olds and half of our 3 year olds by the early 1980s" (Labour Party, 1979); the second was the intention to provide income-related mandatory awards for 16- to 18-year-olds in order to remove the financial barriers which prevent many young people from low income families from continuing their education after 16. Both commitments were linked to welfare concerns in that they were more to do with support for the family than engagement with education issues. They reflect the intention to compensate disadvantaged children. By contrast, today's government's early years initiatives, such as the Sure Start Programme designed to support families with young children in areas of poverty, have a direct education interest in that they reflect pedagogic issues:

> **We know that children who benefit from nursery education – especially those from disadvantaged backgrounds – are more likely to succeed in primary school. (DfEE, 1997a, p 15)**

In this area there is still an attempt to target resources where the intake of pupils to nurseries suggests that there is most need. For example, the Early Years Development and Childcare Plans and the early excellence centres for under fives which will replace the nursery voucher scheme. The government has continued the central control of admissions policy, curriculum guidance, pedagogy and baseline assessment introduced by the Conservative government through Ofsted inspections.

The continuation of these initiatives is justified in the government's White Paper by its claim that it will provide 'a sound beginning'. However, there remains concern in the profession that initiatives may be introducing an education which is "too formal, too soon" (Sylva, 1997). However, it may be the perceptions of parents rather than those of the profession which have had the most influence on the reforms. This would reflect P. Brown's view of parentocracy. There is evidence of a divide between the teaching profession and parents in their evaluation of the reforms introduced by the Conservative government (see Hughes et al, 1994; Freedman et al, 1997). The Conservatives introduced a quasi-market into education which saw parents as consumers. Open enrolment gave parents the responsibility of choosing their child's school subject to the often severe constraints of each school's admissions policy. Schools which had met their admissions targets were not able to increase their intake so the choice of parents could be restricted (see Gewirtz et al, 1995; Menter et al, 1997; Whitty, 1997 and Adnett and Davies, 1999, for fuller accounts of the ways in which parents use this choice).

As well as being given a 'real choice', the powers and responsibility of parents would be increased, they would have greater representation on governing bodies and for the first time have direct representation on LEAs. To promote a culture in which parents felt responsibility for learning Labour committed itself to introducing contracts between school and parents and to asking schools to set homework. The parents would remain responsible for the attendance of their child at school and new referral units would be established to deal with the problems of truancy. The government has confirmed that legal steps should be taken against parents who fail to fulfil their responsibilities. Crozier (1998) agrees that the new partnership between school and parents is one of individual interests, although she adds another dimension to the concept of parental responsibility by arguing that partnership is actually 'surveillance' in two ways, both of parents and of teachers. To bring about a good partnership, schools:

> ... need to persuade parents and through parents the pupils, to adopt their value of what it means to be a 'good' parent and a 'good' pupil.... For those parents who share that agenda this may be acceptable; for others they are either left without a voice or tensions are created in the relationship. (Crozier, 1998, p 126)

She views the shift towards "self-helpism" as integral to "the demise of the welfare state and the rise of the market economy" (p 127).

However, this situation reveals tensions within the Labour policy. It is difficult to see how greater diversity in schools, with many schools given discretion to select a proportion of their pupils, can coexist with a commitment to comprehensive education. As Standing points out in her discussion of education choice for lone mothers, a market view of education assumes that everyone has equal access to resources. She states that "choice in education is a false concept, serving to increase existing inequalities of gender, race and class" (Standing, 1997, p 79).

Similar conclusions are made by Gewirtz et al (1995). Their discussion of the concept of choice perhaps explains why such a powerful term once brought into the schools admission process could not be removed:

In the *Parent's Charter* (DES, 1991) choice is powerfully promoted as a personal matter, a question of individual parents taking responsibility for their children's educational future.... This appeal to parents to 'consume' education idealises 'responsible consumerism', both typified and encouraged by the steady growth in consumer magazines and consumer programmes on TV and on the radio, all promoting the merits of being a responsible rational consumer. (Gewirtz et al, 1995, p 21)

Their typology of 'choosers', which is strongly class related, shows how the privileged and skilled choosers inevitably are overwhelmingly middle class. This class advantage is well documented elsewhere (see Glatter et al, 1997 for an international comparison). P. Brown takes this argument further by suggesting that it was because of this divisive outcome that the privatisation of education was pursued by authoritarian Conservatives,

... because the latter believe that if left to the free market, not only would the elite schools be preserved, but also the schooling for different social groups would 'diversify as society requires'. (P. Brown, 1997, p 399) [inverted commas show lines attributed to Scruton, 1984, p 160]

These measures would appear to be a continuation of the move made by the Conservatives towards Brown's 'parentocracy'. For parentocracy to become a reality the role of the LEA would end, there would be independent education for all, the variety and choice of schools would be maximised and parents would be free to move children between schools. A system of 'survival by results' would be needed and schools must fear failure (P. Brown, 1997, p 402). The 1988 Conservative Education Reform Act put many of these features into practice and it would appear that the Labour government is determined to continue this trend. The requirement for LEAs to draw up Education Development Plans and have them in place, after DfEE approval, by April 1999 will provide the basis for the assessment of LEAs.

Lifelong learning

The third education interest of the 1979 manifesto which could be interpreted as contributing to the welfare state was the commitment to provide greater access for working-class students (particularly adults) to enter further and higher education:

> **We want to see more workers given time off work for study. To this end, the places at the Open University have increased from 43,000 in 1974 to 80,000 in 1978. We propose to extend the present mandatory grant system. Labour supported the Adult Literacy Scheme and will ensure its continuation. (Labour Party, 1979, pp 17-18)**

In the 1997 manifesto this commitment to lifelong learning remains central. New Labour sees economic efficiency and social justice as two sides of the same coin (for example, Commission on Social Justice, 1994; Oppenheim, 1997a; Martell and Driver, 1998; see also Chapter One). Education and training are at the heart of the new agenda of investing in human capital, and removing barriers to employability (see Chapters Seven, Eight and Ten), adding the 'plus' to 'flexibility plus' (Driver and Martell, 1998, p 108). As the Commission on Social Justice (1994, p 120) puts it, "Lifelong learning is at the heart of our vision for a better country". International comparisons and the threat to the economic well-being of the country are used to justify this focus: "It is an economic necessity for the nation.... We will compete successfully on the basis of quality or not at all" (Labour Party, 1997a, p 1).

The manifesto links the issues of standards discussed above in the school context to the post-16 and lifelong learning commitments. Labour links the failure of 11-year-olds with the low numbers of 17- and 18-year-olds in full-time education and with the lack of vocational qualifications among nearly two thirds of the British workforce. Brine (1998) argues that the government now has a wider agenda and that the *White Paper: Education and training* (EC, 1995) has made the concerns expressed by the European Commission (EC) those of the Labour government. She argues that the EC recognised that unemployment, social exclusion and the free movement of people are concerns that can only be addressed by an approach to education and training which emphasises lifelong learning, the importance of languages and includes a European dimension. The 1990s has brought about a new agenda where it is no longer enough only to reduce unemployment but where the real concern must be to reduce social exclusion by improving chances and opportunities:

> **There is a fear that social exclusion will threaten economic growth**

and peaceful unity within and across the union and possibly, due
to the rise of fascism within the EU and post-communist states,
might eventually threaten external peaceful unity as well. (Brine,
1998, p 145)

The commitment to lifelong learning can be seen through the plans set
out in the White Paper *Excellence in schools* (DfEE, 1997a) to broaden A-
levels and upgrade vocational qualifications while ensuring rigorous
standards and key skills. The responsibility for training the workforce in
job-related skills will be given to employers although supported by funding
for the leaner via Individual Learning Accounts. Labour's support for the
Open University given in the 1979 manifesto remains: it will ask the
Open University to collaborate in a new University for Industry sponsored
by a private–public partnership and a remit to use new technology to
enhance skills and education.

The new University for Industry can be seen as addressing several of
Labour's policy interests. It was described by Gordon Brown as "a skills
ladder of opportunity that will allow the many, by their own efforts, to
benefit from the opportunities once only open to the few" (G. Brown,
1997a). It combines a commitment to the modernising Britain project,
with traditional concerns for equity and social inclusion, through a
partnership between individuals, companies and the State, delivered largely
through the medium of IT.

The skills deficit in the UK is quite distinct. While new entrants to
the UK labour market are gradually becoming as well qualified as those
of its international competitors, and this is particularly the case at degree
level, the UK has a legacy of significant under-qualification among older
workers. Moreover, in addition to inequalities between the generations,
access to and take up of training is socially skewed. The higher the level
of qualification, the greater the likelihood that an individual will receive
further training. The propensity to train is much higher in larger firms
than in the small- and medium-sized enterprises.

The University for Industry is seen as a supply-side policy solution to
these long-standing problems. The University for Industry is conceived
as a hub of a national learning network extending into the home and
workplace (Robertson, 1998). As Hillman explains, it will act as a catalogue
and broker of information on courses and training programmes, sustain
guidance services, and stimulate the mass marketing of learning
opportunities (Hillman, 1996). There are obvious parallels with one of
the great Labour success stories, the Open University:

> Just as the Open University has, since the 1960s, offered a thousand
> second chances in higher education through television in their
> homes, the new University for Industry can from the 1990s
> onwards, through satellite, cable and interactive technologies,
> bring lifelong learning direct to millions in their homes as well
> as workplaces. (G. Brown, 1997b)

The final piece of the jigsaw is provided by the concept of 'Individual Learning Accounts'. Labour plans to open one million Individual Learning Accounts, with some modest contribution from the government. It is hoped that employees and employers will top up this money. The learner can then exchange these for training/learning credits for education and training. The aim is that the Individual Learning Accounts will produce the necessary fiscal incentive for training.

Labour will create an extra 420,000 places in further education colleges and will double the number of nursery places for three-year-olds in the next three to four years (*Daily Telegraph*, 18 July 1998). This would seem to bear out Blair's (1998a, p 10) claim of the overriding priority given to education and training – not just to schools but to lifelong learning from nursery level to the 'third age'. However, some critics have contrasted the commitment to 'lifelong learning' with the ending of free tuition and the imposition of £1,000 a year fees for students in higher education, along with the phasing out of the student grant (for example, *The Times*, 2 October 1997). The 'greater access' to the expanding system of higher education – the equivalent of eight extra universities will be created over the next three years (*Daily Telegraph*, 16 July 1998) – is partly to be restricted to those willing to invest in their future 'human capital' (Driver and Martell, 1998).

Accountability

To what extent will the reforms introduced by the Labour Party meet the public aims of education? The fears expressed by Dale (1997) provide the perspective from which to approach this question:

> Underlying these debates is the fundamental question of how
> the public-good purposes of education relating to democracy
> and equity can be addressed when the governance of education
> is so fragmented. (Dale, 1997, p 280)

Crozier (1998) argues that the two-way nature of the surveillance which is inherent in the parent/school contracts introduced by Labour reflects the efforts that the government is making to ensure the central control of schools. Ironically, a policy begun by the Conservatives to increase the diversity and autonomy of schools has been accompanied by an unprecedented centralisation of education:

> **The market-in-practice in England is a subtle and multi-faceted instrument. It rests on a rhetoric of school autonomy and parental freedom of choice but delivers a very effective means of surrogate control. (Gewirtz et al, 1995, p 190)**

The surrogate control begun by the Conservatives in the form of a National Curriculum, national assessment and the publication of performance tables has been continued and increased by the Labour government. Its White Paper attempts to develop these initiatives by a commitment to 'more useful' performance tables and by establishing targets for performance of pupils in the national tests for literacy and numeracy.

The dramatic expansion by the Conservatives of school inspection with the establishment of Ofsted in 1989 has also remained central to this control. Added to this body is the Standards and Effectiveness Unit and other initiatives, listed here by Parliamentary Under Secretary of State Estelle Morris:

> **Ofsted inspection, school target setting, which will be introduced to all schools from September; Education Development Plans, which will provide a link between school-level targets and an LEA's overall strategy to raise standards; literacy and numeracy strategies; the new relationship between schools and LEAs and the planned induction programme for new teachers. (Morris, 1998)**

The 1979 manifesto had included nothing within this area. Again these reforms would appear to be a response to the Conservative reforms of the 1980s and 1990s. It would appear that the campaign against comprehensive schools discussed above had successfully linked educational failure with the teaching profession and that the Labour Party had very little choice but to continue with policies that addressed the problem of failing schools by continued rigorous inspection and control of the institutions and of the teachers themselves.

Blair (1998a, p 16) stresses rigorous inspection and the tough powers that ministers have to intervene in failing schools and education authorities. According to O'Leary (1999), "the end is nigh for 'state' education" as Education Secretary David Blunkett issued an 'unprecedented order' to remove key services from 'failing' LEA of Hackney, East London. A number of private companies have expressed interest in managing state schools. O'Leary concludes that "Within five years, a Labour government may be presiding over a school system that would have been the envy of Sir Keith Joseph and the architects of privatisation".

As Power and Whitty (1999, p 5) point out, the government continues to downplay the socioeconomic context in which the schools operate: "Implicit in much of New Labour is the idea that 'turning things around' is simply a matter of the right mind set".

Mortimore and Mortimore (1998) argue that the new Labour government's misunderstanding of the situation in which these schools found themselves caused them to lose an opportunity to address the problem of low standards. They argue that the problems of 18 schools identified by the government as failing had resulted in part from the policies of the previous government which the new government was now endorsing:

> **Some schools had been thrust into their unenviable position by the previous government's policies on 'opting out' and parental choice and by being pressurised by their respective local education authorities to accept 'hard to teach' pupils whom neighbouring schools (some of them grant maintained) had refused or excluded. (Mortimore and Mortimore, 1998, p 207)**

The justification for the policy of continuing Ofsted's public categorisation of failing schools and the 'naming and shaming' of them, may reflect Dale's recognition that it is the State's responsibility to act as guarantor of the public good which would be assessed through the country's competitiveness. It may be that once in place organisations such as Ofsted are difficult to remove. The continued high profile of Her Majesty's Chief Inspector Chris Woodhead and his appointment to the Standards Task Force, has surprised the profession. The Qualification and Curriculum Authority, continuing the work of its predecessor the School Curriculum and Assessment Authority, is surviving the huge interference in its management of and responsibility for the school curriculum by the National Literacy Task Force and the National Numeracy Project. The new Standards and Effectiveness Unit, in its remit, would appear also to overlap with the Qualification and Curriculum Authority's main functions but it is too early to tell how the two organisations will coexist. Similar tensions appear to exist in teacher training when both the Teacher Training Agency and Ofsted seem to have responsibility for ensuring the quality and standards of provision. The changes to the nature of teachers' work well discussed elsewhere (see Menter et al, 1997; Whitty, 1997) are likely to continue. Whitty argues that the:

> **... new arrangements for managing education and other public services can be seen as new ways of resolving the problems of accumulation and legitimation facing the state, in a situation where the traditional Keynsian welfare state is no longer deemed to be able to function effectively. (Whitty, 1997, p 301)**

The Green Paper, *Teachers, meeting the challenge of change* (DfEE, 1998a), calls for "a new vision of the teaching profession" with what would appear to be payment by results, despite a statement to the contrary, through proposals for extra pay for teachers "who are effective and whose pupils make good progress", a fast-track to headship for talented recruits and a new School Performance Award Scheme. The teacher on the new fast-track scheme would undergo a separate intensive programme of training which could include a two-week placement in the private sector. At a whole school level the School Performance Award Scheme proposes extra payment from a targeted national fund for the top percentage of schools decided via a range of performance indicators. The difficulty in agreeing performance indicators for schools is reflected in the confused explanation of which schools are likely to be rewarded. A school recently under special measures which "improved significantly" might receive an award whereas an "underperforming school would not, even if its raw exam and test results were apparently good". This would appear to suggest that the government expects to be able to identify underperfomance. Unfortunately the policy will continue to set school against school. As Mortimore and Mortimore (1998, p 207) point out, the school effectiveness literature demonstrates that it is "seldom possible to designate an entire school as 'effective' and attempts to describe schools uniformly as 'good or bad' are genuinely unhelpful".

Conclusion

In the area of raising standards it would appear that the association of Old Labour with a comprehensive system that levelled down and failed both the middle and working classes has created a new programme of policies for raising standards in the 1990s which are difficult to separate from those of the Conservatives. While pledging its support for the comprehensive system and by guaranteeing not to return to selection Labour is building on the Conservative reforms to increase marketisation and diversity between schools.

With respect to the links with the economy, the Labour government's skills policies share with its Anglo-Saxon counterparts an emphasis on the supply side with little or no attention being paid to the demand for skills. The consequence is that a significant part of the UK economy is trapped in a low skills equilibrium (Lauder et al, 1999). In essence, little has changed since Finegold and Soskice's classic 1988 paper. Despite an emphasis on raising basic skills, the Moser Committee on raising basic skills for adults and the Skills Task force have yet to produce their reports. Even then we can expect raised skills to provide little by way of improvement in the performance of the economy so long as the demand side is left unattended.

Another low trust policy with respect to the teaching profession which has characterised government policy concerns the mandated literacy and numeracy hours for primary schools. Under this policy the government prescribes not only the time but how it is to be used. In itself this intervention into the teachers' domain is based on a particular theory of how children best learn numeracy and literacy and allows little room for professional judgement or contextual factors to be taken into account. If the theory is misguided then the government's strategy for raising standards will be placed in jeopardy. As it is, the very fact that the government has taken such a low trust approach to teachers suggests that the trade-off which needs to be considered may be lower morale and hence less effective teaching. The fact that the government is finding it so difficult to recruit teachers and retain them may be one example of the 'down-side' to their policies.

Only in a few areas is it possible to identify the traditional concern for achieving equality of opportunity. One example is the setting of ambitious targets for nursery provision with welfare-related support and in the targets set for the national tests at age 11 in primary schools. It is too early to tell if any of the local initiatives to raise standards will work but Labour appears to have embarked on a high risk strategy. By leaving the schools to ensure that equality of opportunity is achieved rather than ensuring this through the regulation and distribution of resources by need, Labour may create a polarisation between 'sink' schools and oversubscribed high achieving popular schools while the genuine transformation of schools, the Third Way, remains on the sidelines.

SIX

Housing policy under New Labour

Peter A. Kemp

Introduction

It would be rather surprising if the Labour government of Prime Minister Blair were not pursing policies that were significantly different from those being pursued by the last Labour government. The Labour Party was out of office for 18 years and there were important social and economic developments in the intervening period. To some extent, policies have to change with the times, no matter who is in government. However, times have changed, not least because of the actions of the Conservative governments while Labour was in opposition.

During the decade following the 1979 General Election, the Conservative governments of Mrs Thatcher transformed the political economy and the public culture in Britain (Marquand, 1998a). Whereas some areas of the welfare state demonstrated considerable resilience in the face of what Marquand has aptly described as 'the Thatcher Blitzkrieg', housing experienced major change. Housing provision and, even more, housing policy and debates were substantially transformed under the Conservatives. Any government coming back to power after 18 years in opposition, whether it was New or Old Labour, would have to ensure that its agenda responded to such fundamental changes.

Mrs Thatcher's first government rushed in to legislate for changes in housing policy that it knew it wanted to implement. New Labour instead opted for a series of Comprehensive Spending Reviews (CSRs), including one for housing, which inevitably delayed the point at which major new changes would be introduced. The outcomes of the CSRs are only now becoming apparent and many important issues have yet to be decided. As a result, this chapter can only provide a provisional survey of housing policy under New Labour. The chapter begins by briefly reviewing the post-war development of housing policy prior to 1979, the year when the Callaghan Labour government left office, in order to explain the Conservative inheritance. The next section presents a brief overview of the main features of housing policy under the Conservative governments of Margaret Thatcher and John Major. The chapter then outlines the housing situation inherited by the New Labour government when it returned to office in 1997. Subsequent sections examine New Labour's housing policy aims and the outcome of the CSR for housing policy. The final two sections attempt to assess whether New Labour's housing policy represents a departure from Old Labour and also from that of the Conservatives.

The Conservative inheritance

The election of Mrs Thatcher's government in 1979 marked a major turning point in housing policy and provision in Britain. The new government was determined to 'roll back the State' in social and economic policy. In housing, this objective has to be seen in the context of the polarisation of provision that had been taking place since the early years of this century. To a large extent, Conservative housing policy during the 1980s and 1990s was a reaction against that polarisation and needs to be understood in the light of it. This section attempts to sketch out the main elements of that polarisation.

At the beginning of the century, private renting was the tenure of the masses, accounting for about 90% of the housing stock in 1914. Renting from private landlords has gradually declined since then and by 1979 accounted for only about 10% of the housing stock. During the same period, owner-occupation expanded from 10% to 55%. Local authority housing, which accounted for well under 1% of the stock in 1914, steadily expanded to a peak of 29% in 1971 and remained at that level until the Conservatives returned to office under Mrs Thatcher. As the privately rented sector declined, the housing market came increasingly to be dominated by owner-occupation and council housing. As a result, by the time that Mrs Thatcher came to power in 1979, households that could not afford to buy their home had few alternatives to council housing.

Throughout the post-war period, but particularly since the early 1960s, Conservative and Labour governments presented owner-occupation as the preferred tenure and sought to encourage expansion of this form of accommodation (see Malpass and Murie, 1994). Prior to 1979, council housing was used as the principal vehicle for the provision of new rented housing. While Labour governments tended to be true believers in the merits of council housing, Conservative governments were 'reluctant collectivists', acceding a major role to it in the absence of investment by private landlords (George and Wilding, 1976; Hamnett, 1987). In the 1950s and 1960s Conservative and Labour governments alike promoted large-scale council housebuilding programmes. These building programmes were sometimes aimed at general housing needs (including better-off working people) and sometimes more at rehousing people from slum clearance schemes (Merrett, 1979). Throughout most of this period, council housing was a popular choice for many working-class households and presented a cheaper and more attractive option than renting privately.

However, by the 1970s there was a growing disillusionment with council housing, both on the Left and on the Right of the political spectrum, particularly with high-rise flats and large-scale estates (Dunleavy, 1981). As owner-occupation gradually replaced private renting as the tenure of the masses, council housing lost some of its relative appeal (Murie, 1997). Whereas council housing seemed attractive by comparison with private renting, it seemed less so when compared with home ownership.

Britain was relatively unusual in having such a large council housing sector. In other countries in Western Europe, social housing has tended to take the form of housing associations and municipal housing companies rather than dwellings owned and managed by local councils (Harloe, 1995). Perhaps with that in mind, in the 1960s and especially in the 1970s, Conservative and Labour governments sought to promote housing associations as a 'third arm' of rented housing provision alongside council housing and private renting (Cullingworth, 1979). Run by voluntary committees, these not-for-profit organisations were regulated and funded by The Housing Corporation. The turning point in the history of this sector came in 1974, when a new financial regime was introduced to encourage new building and rehabilitation by housing associations. The 1974 Housing Act introduced large capital subsidies that enabled housing associations to provide accommodation at so-called 'fair rents' set by local rent officers. Under this new financial regime, the stock of dwellings owned and managed by associations began to expand significantly, albeit from a very low base. For Labour, housing associations complemented council housing by providing for special and other needs not well catered for by local authorities. For the Conservatives, housing associations were seen as a more ideologically acceptable rental alternative to municipal housing (see Back and Hamnett, 1985; Best, 1991, 1997).

In the mid-1970s, the Labour government carried out a major review of housing policy. The subsequent Housing Policy Review Green Paper (DoE, 1977), published two years before Mrs Thatcher came to power, reaffirmed Labour's commitment to home ownership. Although Labour had become less enthusiastic about council housing and accepted that mistakes had been made, it still believed that local authorities had an important and continuing role to play in the provision of rented housing. The Green Paper argued that:

> No one should forget the horrors of the Victorian slums which the local authorities have now banished from most of our cities. The public sector has made a notable contribution towards raising the general level of housing conditions across the country. (DoE, 1977, p 75)

Council housing was still seen by Labour as a public sector solution to the private market problem of substandard housing. It was one of the achievements of the subsequent Conservative governments that they were able to reverse this perception and present the private and voluntary sectors as the solution to the problem of public housing (Kemp, 1991). What is new about New Labour is that it has largely accepted the Conservatives' analysis of the housing problem.

Housing under the Conservatives 1979-97

The Conservatives came to power in 1979 with a clear manifesto commitment to increase home ownership and, in particular, to give council tenants a statutory right to buy their house at a substantial discount from its market value. The extension of the so-called 'property owning democracy' was a central feature of the Thatcherite project and was seen by the Conservatives as a vote-winner. Shortly after the 1979 General Election, Margaret Thatcher claimed that "thousands of people in council houses and new towns came out to support us for the first time because they wanted a chance to buy their own homes" (quoted in Forrest and Murie, 1988). Additional objectives were to reduce public spending on housing and to minimise the role of local authorities as landlords. A final and perhaps less important objective was to halt or even reverse the decline of the privately-rented sector.

The 'Right to Buy' policy was popular with the electorate and, so far as the Conservatives were concerned, successful in implementation (Forrest and Murie, 1988; Malpass and Murie, 1994). By 1986, more than one million council homes had been sold into owner-occupation. A decade later the figure had reached 1.5 million dwellings (Wilcox, 1997). In no

• other area of social policy has privatisation extended so far or with such widespread popular support. However, the impact of the Right to Buy has been uneven. Forrest and Murie (1988) have shown that, generally speaking, the better houses (rather than flats) in the better areas have been bought by the better off tenants. The poorer tenants, those living in flats and in the less attractive houses and those living in the less popular estates, have been left behind in the council sector. This differential impact of the Right to Buy scheme has helped to accentuate the socioeconomic 'residualisation' of council housing, a process that has been underway for several decades (Malpass, 1990). It has also helped to further undermine the image of council housing, which has increasingly come to be seen as housing for the poor and disadvantaged. Meanwhile, new entrants to council housing tended to be poorer than those leaving the sector (Burrows, 1997).

As well as being successful in extending home ownership, the Right to Buy scheme contributed to the Conservatives' other main objectives of minimising the role of council housing and – since the receipts from sales counted as negative spending – of reducing public expenditure. The total receipts from council house sales accounted for around two fifths of all privatisation proceeds between 1978/79 and 1988/89. Forrest and Murie (1988) have described council house sales as the biggest privatisation of them all.

The Conservatives were also very successful in implementing substantial cuts in public sector capital spending on housing. In constant 1995/96 prices, net capital expenditure on housing fell from £8.1 billion in 1978/79 to £3.0 billion in 1995/96, a reduction of 63% (Hills, 1998). The cuts in capital spending were reflected in the number of new local authority dwellings being completed, which virtually collapsed under the Conservatives. Completions of new public sector dwellings in Britain fell from 86,027 in 1980 to only 863 in 1996 (Wilcox, 1997). Council house sales exceeded new completions by local authorities reaching its peak in 1982 (see Table 6.1) and from that point the council sector began to decrease in size both absolutely and relatively for the first time in its history (Forrest and Murie, 1988).

In the period from 1979 until 1986, extending home ownership was the central focus of Conservative housing policy. Home ownership was elevated to the status of a Holy Grail and was presented as the solution to almost all housing problems (Forrest et al, 1990). Asked in the House of Commons about the growth in homelessness, Margaret Thatcher responded by recounting the number of extra people that had become owner-

Table 6.1: Public sector new housing completions and Right to Buy sales in Britain (1980-95)

	Housing completions (000s)	Right to Buy sales (000s)
1980	86	1
1981	66	82
1982	37	200
1983	35	142
1984	34	103
1985	27	94
1986	23	91
1987	20	106
1988	20	164
1989	18	186
1990	17	129
1991	10	75
1992	5	65
1993	3	61
1994	2	67
1995	2	51

Source: Wilcox (1997)

occupiers since she came to office. However, from 1986 there was an important shift in emphasis. Promoting owner-occupation remained an important policy objective, but attention was increasingly focused on the demunicipalisation of rented housing (Kemp, 1989).

In 1986, legislation was passed with the aim of smoothing the way to demunicipalisation. Meanwhile, the Conservatives engaged in a sustained ideological assault of council housing as a form of provision. Local authorities were criticised for being inefficient and paternalistic managers of their housing. Council housing, it was suggested, was a form of provision whose time had passed. One Minister for Housing, John Patten, argued that we should "get rid of these monoliths" and transfer council estates to agencies "who will be closer in touch with the needs and aspirations of individual tenants". Later in the same year his successor as Minister for Housing, William Waldegrave, could see "no arguments for generalised new build by councils, now or in the future" (quoted in Kemp, 1989, p 52).

A White Paper on housing, issued following the General Election of 1987, set out the new strategy for rented housing (DoE, 1987a). This formed part of the quasi-market reforms introduced by the Thatcher government, not just in housing, but also in education and the health service (Le Grand, 1990). The 1987 White Paper and subsequent legislation in 1988/89 envisaged a radical reform of rented housing. The main thrust of the reform was the demunicipalisation of rented housing and a shift towards a more market-oriented and pluralist system of rented housing provision. The Conservatives sought to shift local authorities away from their role as providers of rented housing, preferring them to act instead as 'enablers' facilitating provision by other agencies, including housing associations and private landlords.

So far as *new* rented housing was concerned, measures were taken to encourage an expansion of supply by housing associations and private landlords, while new restrictions of capital spending by local authorities made it difficult for them to provide new homes (and renovate existing ones). In relation to the *existing* stock of council houses, legislation was introduced to encourage tenants to opt for alternative landlords. As well as promoting transfers of the existing stock to alternative landlords, action was taken to improve value for money in the retained council stock. If a significant amount of rented housing was to remain under council ownership, then the Conservatives hoped to ensure that it was exposed to the 'disciplines of the market' and the managerialist imperatives that have been injected into public services more generally (Pollitt, 1993). This new managerialism involved three main elements: a more 'businesslike' financial framework for council housing accounts, statutory performance indicators, and compulsive competitive tendering (CCT).

The most successful instrument for shifting rented housing out of council housing and into alternative provision has proved to be so-called large-scale voluntary transfers (LSVTs). This initiative was originally developed from the bottom up by local authorities themselves, but was subsequently adopted and encouraged by the Conservative governments. The demand for LSVTs has come from councillors and officers rather than tenants (Kemp, 1989). In most cases, LSVTs involved the sale of the local authority's entire stock of rented houses – and the transfer of its staff – to a newly-formed housing association set up for the purpose, subject to a ballot of the tenants (Mullins et al, 1995). By April 1997, 54 councils (all of them in England) had divested themselves of their housing stock via an LSVT. Altogether, this involved the transfer to housing associations of more than one quarter of a million homes (Wilcox, 1997).

From the mid-1990s, the Chartered Institute of Housing and others began to explore ways of transferring housing which might allow councils to retain a greater degree of influence over their former housing stock than is the case with LSVT associations. In particular, the possibility of setting up local housing companies was explored in some depth. The Institute hoped to persuade the then government to exclude expenditure by 'arm's-length' local housing companies from the public sector borrowing requirement (PSBR), in line with the practice elsewhere in the European Union (EU) (Hawksworth and Wilcox, 1995).

One result of the measures introduced in 1988/89 was that rents in the private, housing association and council sectors increased significantly in real terms – more than retail prices as a whole and average earnings. These increases were the result of a number of factors. These included a reduction in 'bricks and mortar' subsidies that help to keep social housing rents below market levels, as well as rent deregulation on new lettings by private landlords and housing associations. Even registered 'fair rents' set by rent officers increased in real terms in the 1990s. The increase in rent levels led to an increase in the number of tenants on Housing Benefit which, in turn, led to the cost of Housing Benefit doubling in real terms between 1988/89 and 1995/96 (Hills, 1998; Kemp, 1998).

In the early 1990s, the Conservatives carried out what they referred to as a 'fundamental' spending review, including a review of Housing Benefit and Income Support mortgage interest payments (ISMI). One outcome was the introduction of restrictions on the amount of rent eligible for Housing Benefit for private tenants with deregulated lettings in 1996; some of the further restrictions planned for October 1997 were implemented by the New Labour government. Another outcome was a cutback in entitlement to ISMI for claimants aged less than 60. Instead of the ISMI safety net, the Conservatives wanted owner-occupiers to rely on private mortgage protection insurance (Burchardt and Hills, 1998; Ford and Kempson, 1997). Meanwhile, cutbacks in mortgage interest relief at source (MIRAS) were also made by the Chancellor. All three of these measures were a response to the rising PSBR in the face of the economic recession of the late 1980s and early 1990s.

What is perhaps most surprising given the Conservatives' heavy promotion of owner-occupation, was that the cutbacks in financial support for this tenure were introduced as the housing market was recovering from the slump of the late 1980s and early 1990s. This slump involved a downturn in property transactions, a sharp rise in mortgage arrears and repossessions, and the emergence of so-called 'negative equity' in which the value of the owner's home was less than the outstanding mortgage loan (see Forrest and Murie, 1994; Maclennan, 1997). Along with the deregulation of rents and new tenancy arrangements, the slump in the owner-occupied housing market helped to generate a modest revival of the privately-rented sector in the early 1990s (Crook and Kemp, 1996).

Labour's inheritance

By the time Labour returned to office in May 1997, the housing system and housing policy debates were significantly different from when the Party last held office (Malpass, 1998; Whitehead, 1997). In particular, major changes had taken place in the housing tenure mix over the previous 18 years. By 1996, the owner-occupied sector of the housing market had increased to 67% of all households in Britain (Table 6.2). The number of households renting accommodation fell in both relative and absolute terms. Table 6.3 shows the composition of the rented housing by type of landlord between 1979 and 1996. Within a smaller rented stock, the share owned

Table 6.2: Housing tenure in Britain

	1981		1996	
	000s	%	000s	%
Owner-occupiers	11,895	56	15,906	67
Private renters	2,339	11	2,387	10
Housing association	469	2	1,035	4
Council	6,380	30	4,512	19
Total	21,083	100	23,840	100

Source: calculated from Wilcox (1997)

Table 6.3: Provision of rented housing in England

	1979		1996	
	000s	%	000s	%
Local council	5,187	68	3,586	54
Housing association	362	5	946	14
Private landlord	2,042	27	2,116	32
All rented housing	7,591	43	6,648	32

Source: calculated from DoE (1987b) and Wilcox (1997)

by local authorities declined from around two thirds in 1979 to just more than half in 1996. The number of privately-rented homes continued to fall during the 1980s but recovered in the early 1990s. Private landlords owned a similar number of dwellings in 1979 and 1996 (though the numbers fell during the first decade from 1979 and then recovered) and hence their market share increased from just more than one quarter to almost one third of all rented homes. During the same period, housing associations almost trebled their market share and by 1996 accounted for one in seven tenant households.

In many respects, housing conditions had improved under the Conservatives and Britain was a better-housed nation compared with when Labour left office in 1979 (see Hills, 1998). Many more households were living in their preferred tenure of owner-occupation. Levels of satisfaction with housing had increased and hence, as Hills has pointed out, standards appear to have risen in line with rising expectations. The proportion of households living in dwellings that lacked basic amenities (such as an inside toilet) or central heating had fallen considerably. The state of repair of the housing stock as a whole also improved in the 1980s. On the other hand, on the new government's own estimate, there was a £10 billion repair backlog in the council housing sector alone. Space standards in new housing association dwellings have fallen since the introduction of the new financial regime in 1988/89 under which government grants were reduced and associations required to borrow funds from the private capital markets (Karn and Sheridan, 1994; Goodchild and Karn, 1997).

Despite significant improvements in housing conditions, in some respects the situation had deteriorated (see Hills, 1998; Malpass, 1998). The shortfall between the number of households and the number of fit dwellings had increased and the number of households living in crowded conditions was rising. Although the number of households accepted as homeless had begun to fall from the early 1990s, the total was still double the number in 1979. Likewise, the number of people sleeping rough had fallen in the 1990s following the implementation of the Conservative's Rough Sleepers Initiative under which accomodation, outreach and support services are targeted at people living on the streets, but was still apparently higher than it had been before the 1980s. Mortgage arrears and repossessions increased dramatically in the owner-occupied housing market slump of the late 1980s and early 1990s. Although both had fallen somewhat by the time Labour returned to office, they were still much higher than when they left office in 1979. A substantial number of homeowners remained in negative equity, although the preference for owning remained strong. Rents had increased significantly in real terms since 1979 and accounted for a larger share of disposable incomes (Hills, 1998).

Although local authority lettings fell in the early Thatcher years, they were at a similar level in 1994/95 as a decade earlier, despite the continued decline in the size of the stock. Meanwhile, the number of lettings made each year by housing associations had more than doubled (Hills, 1998). An important reason why local authorities were able to maintain their relettings was that the turnover of tenants had increased, reflecting a reduced demand for social housing and growing dissatisfaction with the accommodation on offer in some areas and on some estates (Burrows, 1997). As Labour returned to office, local councils and other landlords – mainly but not exclusively in the north of Britain – were acknowledging that they were facing low demand for their dwellings and even abandonment (Pawson, 1998). At the same time, there were parts of the country – mainly in the south of Britain, but not exclusively so – where there remained an acute shortage of affordable rented homes. This in part reflects the uneven economic and demographic restructuring of the British economy, with some areas experiencing labour shortages and population growth while others had high unemployment and population decline.

Lettings by social housing landlords were increasingly being made to homeless people rather than to applicants who had reached the top of the waiting list (Hills, 1998). The Conservative government had responded to this development by limiting local authorities' duty to rehouse homeless people and by requiring all council allocations and nominations to housing association tenancies to be made only to people registered on the waiting list. The changes were in part intended to prevent alleged queue jumping by homeless people including lone parents, although there was little evidence to support the notion that people were deliberating getting pregnant or making themselves homeless in order to obtain a council flat.

One major difference from 1979 was that housing had lost much of its political salience by the time that New Labour came to power. In the past, there have been times when housing was one of the most important issues on the domestic front, but this is no longer the case (Hills, 1998). Most households are now well housed and there is little pressure on the new Labour government from the contented majority (Galbraith, 1992) to make housing a major priority for extra public spending. This is perhaps less true in Scotland, where a much higher percentage of the population rent from the local council than is the case in England and

Wales. Insofar as there is pressure from the voters about housing it is more indirect, to do with mortgage interest rates, which increased significantly after Labour came to power, but subsequently declined.

There is public concern over *where* the projected increase of 4.4 million extra households in England will be accommodated – in greenfield, rural locations or on reused brownfield, urban sites – but less about *who* will supply the dwellings needed to house them. A debate exists about how many social rented homes should be constructed each year, but this argument is largely confined to the housing lobby and academics (for example, Holmans, 1995; Whitehead, 1997) rather than the wider public.

Housing policy under New Labour

Whereas the Conservatives came to power in 1979 with a clear agenda for housing (as discussed above), the same was not true of New Labour in 1997. Apart from a few specific manifesto commitments on housing (Malpass, 1998), it was not at all clear what Labour's housing policy objectives would be, nor what instruments it would use to pursue them. The setting up of the CSRs, including a housing review, served to defer any major announcements about Labour's approach to housing policy. It was not until June 1998 – 13 months after the general election – that Hilary Armstrong, the Minister for Housing, set out the key elements of Labour's housing policy in a speech to the Chartered Institute of Housing Annual Conference. Even then, she noted that her speech was "a few weeks too early" because the outcome of the housing CSR had not yet been announced.

The silences about Labour's housing policy were clearly something about which the Minister for Housing was defensive. In her speech to the Chartered Institute of Housing, Armstrong reminded her audience that the government had released nearly £1 billion of capital receipts for the improvement or construction of social rented homes, allocated an additional £21 million to expand the Rough Sleepers Initiative outside London and restored the right of access to permanent housing for statutorily homeless people.

> So let no-one say we've changed nothing. Let no-one say we're carrying on where the Tories left off. Yes, we've had policy reviews and spending reviews to get things right but we've spent

a year beginning to change what the Tories got most wrong.
(Armstrong, 1998, p 1)

The Housing Minister described Labour's aim as being to offer everyone "the opportunity of a decent home and so promote social cohesion, well-being and self-dependence". According to John Prescott, Secretary of State for the Environment, Transport and the Regions, in order to achieve that aim the housing CSR (discussed later in the chapter) needed to ensure that:

> ... **housing policy plays its part in tackling social exclusion; local authorities develop good quality housing strategies to act alongside their regeneration and other policies; and improve radically the delivery of housing services; and that tenants are empowered as customers of those services. (Prescott, 1998, p 1)**

This statement seems to indicate that housing policy is to be focused not so much on housing objectives as ensuring that housing plays its part in combating 'social exclusion' and in contributing to urban regeneration (cf Hills, 1998). It also implies that these problems are essentially ones to do with rundown council estates. This reading of the housing question is also apparent in Hilary Armstrong's speech to the Chartered Institute of Housing, in which she described the four 'cornerstones' on which Labour's housing policies and programmes would be built. These were: making the market work; empowering individuals; ensuring best value in public services; and strengthening communities.

Making the market work

According to Armstrong (1998), the government's "over-riding aim is to make the market work for all people". New Labour's approach to housing is underpinned by a clear acceptance of the market as the best way to provide shelter. However, this commitment to the market model is accompanied by an acknowledgement that the market does not work well for all people and hence government intervention is required to make it work. However, while accepting that intervention is required, the minister was careful to emphasise that it should be limited and, as shall be seen later, largely confined to addressing the problems of the social rented housing sector.

> If the housing market worked perfectly there would be no need
> or rationale for government intervention but the free market
> can not accommodate the needs and aspirations of all.
> Government must intervene – but that intervention must be
> limited and strategic, empowering and enabling, not centralising
> and controlling. (Armstrong, 1998, p 3)

Apparently, there will be no return in social housing to what Dunleavy (1981) has described as the 'statist' nature of welfare in Britain. New Labour has no intention of reversing the retreat from council housing begun by the Conservatives. Yet, in making the market work, New Labour:

> ... will exercise no preference between public or private sectors....
> I have no ideological objection to, nor ideological obsession with,
> the transfer of local authority housing. If it works, and it is what
> tenants want, transfer may be an appropriate option. What
> matters is what works. (Armstrong, 1998, p 4)

However, according to the Minister for Housing, a key element of Labour's approach is "the separation of local authorities' strategic role from their housing management role". What this appears to mean is that local authorities should focus on carrying out comprehensive need assessments and use them to inform their housing strategies and investment decisions. Housing associations – or 'registered social landlords' as Whitehall began to call them under the Major government – should continue to be the main provider of new social rented housing. Local authorities should consider transferring their stock to other types of social housing landlord and, where local authorities do continue to own rented homes, they should consider contracting out the management of them to housing associations.

Old Labour was committed to council housing and the Conservative governments of Margaret Thatcher and John Major wanted to *force* councils to get rid of it; but New Labour apparently wishes to *encourage* and incentivise councils to transfer the ownership, or at least the management, of their dwellings to other social housing landlords.

The Scottish Office is pursuing a more explicit policy of demunicipalisation under the Housing Minister, Calum MacDonald. The £300 million of extra spending on Scottish housing following the CSR (see below) will be linked to the development of New Housing Partnerships. A central feature of these partnerships is expected to be the transfer of council housing to 'community ownership' housing associations. These will be collectively owned and managed by boards made up of tenants, councillors and others drawn from the local community (Scottish Office, 1998). Whatever the merits of these new organisational forms, they are likely to face considerable opposition from local government unions committed to the defence of council housing controlled by councillors and run by housing managers.

While actions aimed at making the market work will be focused on social rented housing, limited intervention will also take place in the private housing market. The Minister reaffirmed Labour's pre-election pledge to introduce licensing for houses in multiple occupation, which contain some of the worst and most badly managed dwellings. Landlords will be granted a license to let such accommodation only if it meets certain minimum standards, and is adequately managed. Labour also intended to examine ways to ensure that landlords do not unfairly refuse to return deposits to tenants. In a move more akin to Old Labour, the government has also proposed to limit the rate of increase in registered fair rents, which in recent years have been well in excess of inflation and earnings growth.

On home ownership, the Minister made clear that she is in favour of it "where it meets individual or family aspirations and where they can afford it" (Armstrong, 1998). It apparently did not need saying that New Labour has no intention either of repealing the Right to Buy or ending the large discounts on property values which accompany it. Some minor reforms would be introduced to speed up the house buying process and the government would also take steps towards further leasehold reform. As for home buyers who find they cannot afford it, the government intends to encourage mortgage lenders to make repayments more flexible (for example, by repayment holidays 'when times get tough') and to develop an industry-wide standard for mortgage protection policies. No mention was made of reversing the Conservatives' cuts in ISMI.

Rough sleeping – the focus of the first report by the Prime Minister's Social Exclusion Unit (1998a) – will be tackled by a coordinated approach to the problem. The aim will be to reduce rough sleeping to as near to zero as possible. This will be achieved by:

* better coordination of housing, health, training and employment programmes aimed at rough sleepers;
* a new coordinating body in London led by a so-called 'Tsar';
* increased resources;

• action to prevent people leaving care, prisons and the armed forces from becoming homeless.

The homelessness lobby has welcomed the Social Exclusion Unit's proposals for tackling rough sleeping. However, concern has been expressed about the authoritarian tone of parts of the report, such as talk about the need to 'deliver clean streets' and the suggestion that the option of a hostel bed could be made contingent on participation in the Welfare to Work programme.

Empowering individuals

As well as strengthening the marketplace, new Labour's housing policy aims to empower social housing tenants and give them a stake in their communities. The Minster for Housing claimed that:

> **For too long this Century, the benefits system has combined with a paternalistic approach to council house allocations, to create a system where some families ... have exercised little or no choice within the housing market. The state has made choices on their behalf – where they will live; how much is their rent; even, although this is now largely a thing of the past, what colour the front door had to be. (Armstrong, 1998, p 9)**

Accordingly, Armstrong (1998, p 10) pledged that new Labour would:

> **... restore choice and power, self-reliance and personal responsibility to the social housing tenant. We will give tenants in council and housing association properties a direct say, a direct stake, in the running of their homes.**

In pursing the latter, Tenant Participation Compacts (TPCs) between local councils and their tenants would be introduced from April 1999. TPCs will set out common and minimum standards for tenant involvement in the management of their homes. Meanwhile, The Housing Corporation would be encouraged to strengthen its policies on tenant involvement in housing associations.

A related issue is 'antisocial behaviour' by 'difficult tenants', concern about which increased significantly during the Major government and continued under New Labour (Dwyer, 1998; Scott and Parkey, 1998). The Conservatives introduced a number of measures to deal with this apparent problem. The 1996 Housing Act gave local authorities power to grant 12-month 'probationary tenancies' for new tenants and made it easier for private and social landlords to evict tenants on the grounds of antisocial behaviour. New Labour's 1998 Crime and Disorder Act introduced a new 'community safety order' to cover cases of antisocial behaviour or violent harassment.

Dwyer (1998) argues that these developments in respect of 'antisocial tenants' represent an erosion of citizenship rights, presumably because tenants may lose their home if they do not conform to accepted modes of behaviour. At the margin, what is deemed to be 'acceptable' can be a matter of dispute. However, at the extreme, for those tenants experiencing violent harassment or racial abuse it could equally be argued that these new powers could help them to enjoy their citizenship rights to peaceful occupation of their home. The issue of 'problem tenants' is a complex one and not necessarily directly comparable with moves to make unemployment benefit more conditional on claimants' job search behaviour. Taking action to deal with it is consistent with Blair's stress on the need for duties and not just rights (see Chapter Ten).

Ensuring Best Value in public services

Like other areas of the public sector, local authority housing is to participate in a new drive to ensure continuous improvement in the organisation and delivery of services (DETR, 1998a). A new regime called Best Value is being introduced to replace CCT in local government. Although rather vague as yet, the basic idea behind Best Value is that by a process of annual planning, monitoring and performance review, the efficiency, effectiveness and quality of service delivery will improve. Local authorities' capital spending allocations will be linked to service reviews to encourage them to improve performance. Good performers may be rewarded with higher allocations and poor performers punished with lower allocations. It is proposed to shift local authority housing revenue accounts on to a resource accounting basis and to require councils to produce annual business plans, in order to improve the efficiency with which their housing is managed. The Audit Commission will be required to set up a Housing Inspectorate to check up on local authorities (a housing equivalent of Ofsted). The imposition of the Housing Inspectorate was a price that the Treasury appears to have extracted from the DETR in return for agreeing to increased spending on housing (see below). Finally, as in education, the government will give itself powers to take over the management and delivery of services from 'failing' local authorities.

New Labour intends to continue with the managerial and centralising tendencies of the Conservatives (cf Chapter Eleven), even if the instruments through which they are to be pursued are in some respects different. New Labour evidently prefers – at least in the first instance – to encourage rather than to coerce local authorities into achieving improved value for money. Yet central government under New Labour, as under the Conservatives, intends to proceed on the assumption that local authorities are knaves rather than knights (Le Grand, 1997). For all the talk about cooperation, it is clear that Whitehall under New Labour does not fully trust local government to deliver efficient and effective services.

Strengthening communities

Strengthening communities is seen by New Labour as a vital element of effective policies for tackling social exclusion in areas with the most social and economic deprivation – the 'worst neighbourhoods' as the government has referred to them. New Labour recognises that tackling these problems involves more than just improving housing condition and hence that it is necessary to link together housing, urban regeneration and other social policies.

The problems of the most deprived estates are to be tackled by the so-called New Deal for Communities. This particular new deal will bring together housing and urban regeneration spending together to improve neighbourhood management and service delivery and to improve economic opportunities for local people. Like many of the initiatives developed under the Conservatives, the New Deal for Communities will involve central and local government working in partnership with the private and voluntary sectors, initially in 17 'pathfinder areas'.

The New Deal for Communities forms part of the Labour government's national strategy for neighbourhood renewal, as set out in the Social Exclusion Unit's report, *Bringing Britain together* (Social Exclusion Unit, 1998b). This is the third report to be published by the Prime Minister's Social Exclusion Unit, following earlier reports on rough sleeping (see above) and school exclusions. It argues that the gap between the 'worst estates' (not a term likely to commend itself to the people living in them) and the rest of the country has grown much wider during the previous two decades. In his foreword to the report (Social Exclusion Unit, 1998, p 7), Prime Minister Blair argues that this is a situation that no civilised society should regard as tolerable:

> **It is simply not acceptable that so many children go to school hungry, or not at all, that so many teenagers grow up with no real prospect of a job and that so many pensioners are afraid to go out of their homes. It shames us as a nation, it wastes lives and we all have to pay the costs of dependency and social division.**

The report acknowledges that social and economic changes have been important factors behind the chronic problems of the most deprived neighbourhoods. It also argues that local and central government policies and practices have often made matters worse. Lack of coordination between Whitehall and local authorities and between different departments within both levels of government have meant that 'a joined-up problem has never been addressed in a joined up way'. Other reasons for the failure of government to tackle effectively the most deprived neighbourhoods include:

> **... the absence of effective national policies to deal with the structural causes of decline; a tendency to parachute solutions in from outside, rather than engaging local communities; and too much emphasis on physical renewal instead of better opportunities for local people. (Social Exclusion Unit, 1998b, p 9)**

As well as the New Deal for Communities, the national strategy for neighbourhood renewal will involve the Sure Start Programme aimed at supporting young people in deprived areas, the transfer of the Single Regeneration Budget (SRB) from central government to the new Regional Development Agencies (RDAs), and the targeting of Employment, Education and Health Action Zones on areas of severe social exclusion. An intensive programme of policy development has been set in train, involving 18 cross-cutting action teams drawn from 10 Whitehall departments and involving experts from outside government and people with 'on the ground' experience of deprived neighbourhoods. The intention is that this accelerated policy development will result in the production of a 'coherent national strategy' for England which, within a 10 to 20 year period, will result in significant progress towards tackling spatial concentrations of social exclusion. In Scotland, a number of Social Inclusion Partnerships (SIPs) are being set up, including area-based SIPs in communities facing the greatest hardship and thematic SIPs to promote social inclusion among particularly vulnerable groups.

The new national strategy for neighbourhood renewal goes well beyond the confines of housing policy. New Labour has explicitly acknowledged that housing-led renewal has often proved to be insufficient to tackle the deep-seated and multifaceted social and economic problems of the most deprived neighbourhoods. The new approach goes well beyond housing policy and encompasses the whole range of social policy areas. It will also be much more coordinated, intensive and sustained than previous attempts to tackle the problems of inner-city neighbourhoods and outlying estates. What is less clear is how far these locally-based initiatives – even in combination with national-level, supply-side policies such as Welfare to Work and the Working Families Tax Credit – will be able to solve these problems, some of which are the result of wider social and economic changes, such as the decline in demand for unskilled workers.

Comprehensive Spending Review

One of the apparent objectives behind the setting up of the CSRs was to shift resources into health and education without a fully commensurate increase in public spending and certainly without having to increase income tax rates. While the government has managed to achieve this objective, one unanticipated outcome so far as the housing lobby is concerned is that the resources devoted to housing and urban regeneration are also planned to increase significantly. Spending on these two areas is planned to increase by nearly £5 billion during the three years from 1999/00 to 2001/02, although once inflation is taken into account the amount is rather lower than this (the overall public expenditure context is examined in Chapter Two). Strictly speaking, this extra spending has not come from the 'release' of receipts from council house sales. It represents increased permissions to borrow in order to finance capital expenditure and therefore counts as additional public spending.

Most of the additional spending will involve capital expenditure by local authorities on improving their stock of dwellings and on urban regeneration programmes such as the New Deal for Communities. Not surprisingly, the housing pressure groups have welcomed this increase. However, they have also pointed out (for example, Blake, 1998) that the planned spend on housing during Labour's first term (1997/98 to 2001/ 02) will be very substantially *less* than that under the last Conservative government (1992/93 to 1996/97).

The overall aim for the housing CSR, according to the Deputy Prime Minister, was to "define the objectives of housing policy" for the New Labour government (Prescott, 1998). More than a year later, there are still major gaps in Labour's housing policy. The housing CSR announcement in July 1998 added little in the way of detail to the overview of policy presented by the Minister for Housing at the Chartered Institute of Housing Conference in June (discussed above). The statement on housing and urban regeneration policy (Prescott, 1998) was largely concerned with spending allocations and failed to address many of the key issues outlined by the government when it set up the CSR. As one commentator has pointed out: "Far from being a comprehensive statement of housing policy, this really is a three-year budget for housing. The big policy questions have yet to be answered" (Blake, 1998, p 21).

These big policy questions include the reform of Housing Benefit and support for homeowners, the balance between bricks and mortar subsidies and Housing Benefit, the level and structure of social housing rents, the role of housing in community care and the links between housing and Welfare to Work. Most of these questions concern the interface between housing and other aspects of social policy, including social security, income taxation, community care and employment (Kemp, 1998; Malpass, 1998). At the same time, many of them involve conflicts of interest between different government departments. Even more important, addressing some of these unresolved issues may require the government to make unpopular decisions or ones that will be perceived as attacks on vested interests.

Whether the outcome of the review of these remaining policy issues will be radical reforms or relatively minor changes, remains to be seen. It will partly depend on whether the government is willing to make the 'hard choices' of which Prime Minister Blair talked in the first few months of taking up office. This may prove difficult if Blair is to maintain the wide coalition of support on which his Party was elected to office. It appears that the realities of office are such that 'hard choices' are hard to make, even for a government with a landslide majority in the House of Commons.

New Labour, new housing policy?

Having sketched out housing policy under the Conservatives and the emerging policy under New Labour, this section addresses whether or not there has been convergence between the two parties over housing and whether New Labour is different from Old Labour. (The terms New and Old Labour are used here merely as convenient shorthand to refer to the Party before and after 'modernisation'.) Is New Labour simply carrying on where the Conservatives left off? Is there anything new and distinctive about New Labour that sets it apart from either Old Labour or the Conservatives?

Assessing whether New Labour policy has changed since 1979 is both easy and difficult. It is easy because Labour's policies clearly have changed compared with the last Labour government. However, that is hardly surprising, since the housing situation has also changed and hence Old Labour polices would probably have changed as well. It is rather more difficult to answer the counterfactual question of whether New Labour's policies are different from what they would have been if Labour had not modernised itself and its image. To answer that question it is necessary to speculate on how Old Labour would have responded to current circumstances.

An Old Labour government would almost certainly have continued to affirm its commitment to owner-occupation, as New Labour has also done. Old Labour might well have reversed the cuts in entitlement to ISMI and considered the introduction of a mortgage benefit scheme (perhaps paid for by abolishing the last vestiges of mortgage interest relief), both things which New Labour are unlikely, and certainly unwilling, to do. Old Labour would have wanted to abolish the Right to Buy and associated discounts, but would not have done so for fear of the electoral consequences. In contrast, New Labour shows no desire to get rid of the Right to Buy. Altogether, New Labour policy on home ownership is closer to Conservative policy than to Old Labour.

An Old Labour government would probably have given pride of place in social rented housing back to the local authorities. Unlike the present government, it is unlikely that an Old Labour government would continue with the demunicipalisation and fragmentation of social rented housing engineered by the Conservatives. Old Labour would probably have allowed local councils to recommence building new houses and would have refocused estate regeneration away from extensive reliance on housing associations.

It is possible that Old Labour might have acquiesced to the transfer of council housing to local housing companies, where local authorities wished to pursue that option and tenants agreed to it. Unlike the Conservatives and New Labour, they would probably have allowed the setting up of local housing companies that remain in the pocket of the local authority rather than at an 'arm's length'. Old Labour might possibly have agreed to exempt spending by local housing companies from the PSBR, whereas New Labour has ruled this out. Old Labour would have been much more likely to contemplate increased public spending on housing, over and above the Conservatives' and New Labour's spending limits. Old Labour would certainly have abolished CCT in housing management, but its not clear whether they would have seen a need to introduce the BestValue performance regime.

Under Old Labour, the role of housing associations in the demunicipalisation of rented housing would probably be downplayed or curtailed, but their role in rehabilitating the private sector housing stock would probably be re-emphasised. In this respect, the current government is more akin to the Conservatives than to Old Labour. The cuts in social housing grant (housing association grant in Scotland) would probably be reversed to some extent and the emphasis shifted back to bricks and mortar subsidies and away from Housing Benefit.

Old Labour would probably reverse the 1996 restrictions in Housing Benefit which affect tenants with deregulated tenancies. Unlike New Labour, they would almost certainly cancel all rather than just some of the October 1997 restrictions planned by the Conservatives. It is not yet clear what else New Labour will do with Housing Benefit (though they do hope to cut back the budget in the long term). Apart from reversing the 1996 restrictions and not implementing any of the 1997 ones, an Old Labour government would probably introduce restrictions on the amount of rent private landlords can charge tenants on Housing Benefit and would limit the amount of benefit payable on privately-rented (but not council) properties that are judged to be below standard.

Old Labour might consider introducing a registration scheme for all private landlords and would probably match the current government's intention to introduce a mandatory licensing system for houses in multiple occupation. Old Labour would almost certainly also match the current government's intention to limit the rate of increase in regulated rents. In these respects Old and New Labour are quite different from the Conservatives. However, unlike New Labour, an Old Labour government would probably reverse the automatic use of fixed-term, assured shorthold tenancies and revert to assured tenancies as the default tenancy.

Like the current government, an Old Labour one would almost certainly reverse the change in the homelessness legislation introduced by the Conservatives in 1996, but would have done so more wholeheartedly. It is also probable that an Old Labour government would succumb to the pressure from the housing rights lobby and extend the right to rehousing to homeless single people. New Labour has simply extended the legislation to cover young people who have been in care.

While these speculations refer to housing policy in Whitehall, the future of housing policy following devolution in Scotland and Wales remains unclear (see Chapter Eleven for more details of devolution). In Scotland, the new Parliament will be responsible for housing policy and it is likely that the outcome will be significantly different from that south of the border. There are already some important differences between housing in Scotland and England (such as the financial framework for local authority housing revenue accounts and the much broader role of Scottish Homes compared with The Housing Corporation). The two systems are likely to diverge much further once the new Scottish Parliament takes over (Goodlad, 1997). While there appears to be more sympathy with an Old Labour approach in Scotland than there is south of the border (especially in the Scottish National Party, strangely enough), the future is uncertain to some extent because the outcome of the pending Scottish Parliamentary elections is as yet unknown.

Conclusion

Although the aims and instruments of the government's housing policy are not yet fully formed, certain conclusions are apparent. Labour housing policy has certainly changed since 1979 and in many respects is different from that which would be pursued by an Old Labour government. New Labour has accepted some of the analysis and many of the policy prescriptions of the Conservatives. Even before 1979 Labour was a firm supporter of owner-occupation, but it is no longer opposed to the Right to Buy. Initial opposition gave way to acceptance that it is a highly popular policy, not just among council tenants but also among the voters at large. New Labour has also accepted that the privately-rented sector can have an important if limited role to play in the housing market. It has promised not to reverse the deregulation and tenancy reforms introduced by the Conservatives. Even so, it is proposing to limit increases in fair rents and this has led some to question whether this will be the thin end of an Old Labour wedge.

More significantly, Labour has taken on board, and appears committed to carrying through, the Conservatives' project of demunicipalising rented housing and creating a quasi-market in social housing. While New Labour has dropped CCT and intends to replace it with what it calls Best Value, this is simply managerialism by other means. Although New Labour is talking to local government with a softer voice, and sees the virtues of cooperation rather than hostility, it nonetheless intends to continue with much of the Conservatives' agenda for social rented housing. It is likely that the fragmentation of social rented housing that began under the Conservatives will continue under New labour.

Where Labour has a new story to tell it is in respect of social exclusion. Labour appears committed to tackling social exclusion which, insofar as it is to do with housing, has largely been defined to comprise rough sleeping and the problems of rundown council housing estates. To the extent that housing is one of the 'winners' from the CSRs, it is because it is seen as central to tackling the problems of social exclusion rather than because of arguments for better housing per se. Explaining why housing had been given the biggest percentage increase in its budget than any other area of policy in Scotland, the Minister for Housing in Scotland said that:

> ... good housing is absolutely essential to effective action on public health, on improving opportunities, on regenerating communities and on tackling social exclusion. That is why we have put housing at the top of the Government's agenda alongside health and education.... (Scottish Office, 1998, p 6)

If housing has lost much of its political salience, social exclusion has not and the housing budget has been increased because of it. Bramley (1997) has argued that housing policy is in decline or is becoming an adjunct to other areas of social policy. Meanwhile, Hills (1998) argues that housing policy has become part of social security and urban regeneration policy. To the extent that this 'end of housing policy' analysis is correct, it has become accentuated under New Labour.

[Author's note: I should like to thank Dr Jo Neale and the editor for helpful comments on an earlier version of this chapter.]

SEVEN

New Labour and social security

Martin Hewitt

Introduction

This chapter examines some of the key themes shaping New Labour's social security policy, assesses whether its policies continue or break with the Tories' legacy of 1997 and speculates on where Labour is taking social security. First, having posed the terms of the question of continuity or discontinuity, the chapter examines the changing needs of four social groups on which the government has focused: lone parents, unemployed poeple, disabled people and pensioners. Second, the chapter seeks to describe the government's 'Third Way' in social security in tackling the problems of these groups and in seeking a path that departs from the policies of Old Labour and New Tories. Finally, it outlines the changing direction of welfare under Labour. The next two sections will be largely descriptive in content and the last more speculative.

The question of continuity or discontinuity – between the social policies of New Tory and New Labour, of Old and New Labour, and of the classic and new welfare states – is central to the analysis of social policy today (Powell and Hewitt 1998). However, it becomes an increasingly complex question the more you attempt to disentangle the lines of continuity and discontinuity.

At first glance, some continuity with the social policies of the former Tory government is evident. Labour stuck to Tory expenditure plans for the first two years of government and will not raise levels of income tax during the remaining three years (Chapter Two). It implemented Tory plans not to up-rate the Income Support premium for lone parents and One Parent Benefit but to remove these benefits altogether from new claimants – reforms passed by Parliament despite considerable public dismay.

In other areas the new government has broken continuity with the previous government. Most significantly it has announced an increase of £56 billion in public spending in its Comprehensive Spending Review (CSR) for the final three years of government, although little of this is intended for social security. It has promised to keep the basic pension which the Tories proposed privatising. Although it has not restored the important linkage Old Labour installed in 1974 between earnings and long-term benefits for pensioners and the long-term sick and disabled (Timmins, 1996, p 344), which the Tories scrapped in 1980, it has introduced an income guarantee tied to earnings for pensioners receiving Income Support, and is proposing to introduce an income guarantee for severely disabled people (see below) (*The Guardian*, 10 March 1999).

Yet Labour has gone further than the Tory government's workfare initiatives. The Job Seekers' Allowance (JSA) not only remains on the statute book (despite Labour's earlier pledge to restore unemployment benefit), but the New Deal programme has systematically advanced a Welfare to Work strategy with potentially wide-reaching implications for welfare reform and restructuring. One of the most fundamental reforms is the introduction of a tax credit scheme for working families. In particular, the New Deal and tax credits mark out a new path for welfare in furthering labour market participation. This stands as a departure from the traditional role of social security in redistributing provisions to the out-of-work poor and other groups in need. It suggests that Labour has freed itself of the 'public burden' model of welfare that weighed down post-war governments until the 1970s. After 20 months in government, it is fair to pass an initial judgement on New Labour's progress as breaking with some Tory policies while consolidating others.

This complex journey across political boundaries and time zones can be seen in the origins of Labour's rhetoric for Welfare to Work about "reforming the benefits system so that it gives people *a hand up, not just a handout*" (Labour Party, 1997c, p 12; emphasis added). This 1960s US 'War on Poverty' slogan was reintroduced into social policy discourse by the Conservative Charles Murray in his attack on the American dependency culture in his influential text *Losing ground* (1984, p 22). It was then taken up in Bill Clinton's 1994 campaign of welfare reform as "a stepping stone not a way of life" (Crine, 1994, p 9) and adopted in the UK by the Commission on Social Justice when it argued the case that "the welfare state must offer a hand-up rather than a handout" (Commission on Social Justice, 1994, p 224). From there it was but a short step to where it gained its latest spin in the hands of New Labour.

In social security policy as elsewhere, New Labour is seeking to tread a path marked by lines of continuity and discontinuity in a delicate balancing act that is seen as appropriate for the transformed times that occasion the movement into the new millennium. It involves combining what under Old Labour and the New Right were seen as opposite attitudes and principles. This means:

- **keeping faith with parts of Labour's tradition of collectivism and solidarity while introducing a philosophy of personal independence in keeping with the realities of a more competitive world;**

- **encouraging self-interest, which the Tories sought to foster with their enterprise culture and attack on welfare dependency, while securing a greater sense of inclusiveness;**

- **recognising above all that the system of welfare must change because the world has changed, 'beyond the recognition of Beveridge's generation'. (DSS, 1998a, p iv)**

Consequently the government is treading a path partly laid by the Tories while at the same time endeavouring to stake out new territory. As a signpost for this journey, it is guiding policy down the 'Third Way' between Old Labour and New Right. According to the first Green Paper on welfare reform (hereafter the Welfare Green Paper), the welfare state now faces a choice of three futures:

> ... a privatised future, with the welfare state becoming a residual safety net for the poorest and most marginalised; the status quo but with more generous and costly benefits; or the government's *third way* – promoting opportunity instead of dependence, with the welfare state for the broad mass of people, but in new ways to fit the modern world. (DSS, 1998a, p 19, emphasis added)

The argument around the two 'extremes' of privatised and statist welfare reoccurs throughout the welfare reform Green Papers (DSS, 1998a, 1998c, 1998d, 1998e) as a discursive device for constructing the government's case for the Third Way.

A sense of the challenge social security poses can be seen in the Department of Social Security's *Welfare reform focus files* (1998b). In 1996/97 spending on social security was £93 billion. This amounted to 32% of total public spending and the largest programme of government expenditure, almost twice that on health and social services, nearly three times that on education and more than the £72 billion total raised by income tax (DSS, 1998b, no 1, pp 1-2). By comparison, in 1979/80 social security spending was £49 billion (DSS, 1998b, no 1, p 5). Even the small underspend of £2.7 million against the Conservative's projected spending on social security for the two years 1997-99 (Hencke, 1998) only delays the moment when annual spending eventually reaches £100 billion. The government is further challenged by the growing population of claimants such as disabled people, unemployed people, pensioners and families on Income Support, and the rising proportion of GDP – 5% in 1950 and 13% in 1997 – devoted to social security (DSS, 1998b, no 1, pp 2-3). However, while the proportion of wealth that Britain devotes to social security has been increasing, the number of people living in poverty has also grown, with one in four people in 1996 living on less than half average income (after housing costs) compared with one in 10 in 1979 (DSS, 1998b, p 4). Income distribution through social security is no longer going to the poorest. For example, in 1979 the poorest fifth of households received 42% of all benefits spending; by 1994/95 this had fallen to 30% (1998b, p 6). For these reasons the government rests its case for welfare reform. However, despite the concern of British politicians about the high levels of social security spending, from a European perspective the UK ranks ninth out of 11 European Union (EU) states in social protection expenditure, with only Italy and Portugal falling behind (ONS, 1998, p 140).

Tony Blair summarises Labour's approach to social security in the Green Paper as rebuilding "the system around work and security. Work for those who can; security for those who cannot" (DSS, 1998a, p iii) – a mantra often repeated on the government front-bench (see Chapters Eight and Twelve). Achieving this twofold work and welfare objective points to the difficult task of maintaining in an even-handed way a united society capable of meeting the needs of those who can and those who cannot work. Initially, the government's major policy announcements on the New Deal and tax credit programmes stressed the first objective. Subsequently, policies for those who cannot work have come on stream, especially for the disabled (DSS, 1998c, 1998d) and pensioners (DSS, 1998e. However, in terms of policy presentation as well as implementation, the stress is firmly on the first objective – a work ethic for the new welfare state – with all claimants of working age, bar a few exceptions, required to attend an interview to receive information on work as well as benefits and other services (the 'single gateway'). The government seems intent not only on shifting the philosophy of welfare from supporting a passive dependency culture to promoting an active regime of work for all who can, but also to shift as many people as it can from the claimant to worker status. In general terms, Labour is continuing the process of welfare restructuring along the workfare lines of the Tories. Jessop has described – in somewhat broad stroke terms – the shift from the 'Keynesian Welfare State' to the 'Schumpeterian Welfare State', whose purpose it is to "subordinate social policy to the needs of labour market flexibility and/ or to the constraints of international competition" (Jessop, 1994, p 24). In this transformation, social security policy subordinates welfare provision for the basic needs of all to the needs of the modern employment market for labour flexibility.

New Labour and the poor

In general, the design of New Labour's welfare reforms is shaped by its perception of the problems faced by the poor, and especially by lone parents, the unemployed, people with disability and pensioners – the fastest growing groups of poor whose growth has contributed to the rising cost of social security. Apart from the concern expressed by the former Minister for Welfare Reform Frank Field about means-testing and its contribution to benefit fraud (1996a, p 11) and the government's concern about the growth in social security spending, the case for welfare reform is made largely in terms of the intrinsic problems presented by these social groups. In this respect, the approach to welfare reform is little different from the Conservatives' whose reforms were also driven by preconceptions about certain types of claimants. The Conservatives eventually crystallised their thinking about dependency – and about welfare bureaucracy – around the idea that individuals perform best when market forces are unleashed. Hence, the comprehensive programme of 'bringing the market to the state' (see Pierson, 1996a, p 159) which transformed the public sector in the 1980s and 1990s. Whatever Labour has done in other sectors to reverse this, little has changed in social security where the long-term project of encouraging greater reliance on private social security provision continues steadily. In treading a similar path to the Tories', New Labour will have to make its mark in a different direction if it is to fulfil its vision of being a radical government of welfare reform. The idea of personal fulfilment through work as the collective duty of all appears to offer this route. Hence, the centrality of the New Deal in the government's welfare reform programme. Here it can aim for a more comprehensive achievement than the Tories' piecemeal achievements in workfare and conditional welfare (see Lilley, 1995, p 12) which avoids some of their mistakes, especially in widening the use of means-testing. In this sense, comprehensive achievement alludes to the standard that Beveridge set for welfare reform. Tony Blair implies as much when he notes in his introduction to the welfare Green Paper that "there has been no truly comprehensive review of the welfare state in all its elements since Beveridge" (DSS, 1998a, p iii). However, if the New Deal is less than successful in achieving its work and welfare objectives, Labour's achievements may turn out to be less comprehensive and more piecemeal. The dilemma facing New Labour is that its claim to be pursuing a radical agenda, the Third Way, could result in a less than radical outcome if it fails to modernise the rundown welfare system and to reduce the growing ranks of the poor.

To attempt to make some sense of these speculations the main policies for the four groups of claimants who pose the most concern for the government will be described, before going on to examine whether these policies constitute a new third way in social security.

Lone parent families

The increase in lone parent families results from important changes in family structure over the last three decades, such as the declining number of people marrying and the rising number divorcing. The population of lone parents has grown significantly from 600,000 in 1971 to 1.7 million in 1996, the majority of whom are women and comprise divorced and separated people with an increasing number of single never-married mothers (DSS, 1998b, no 7, p 5). It is estimated that 2.7 million children live in lone parent families and six out of 10 lone parents live in poverty, accounting for nearly one in four of the people living in poverty in this country (MacDermott et al, 1998, p 5). One consequence of this trend has been a fourfold increase in lone parents on Income Support, from 250,000 in 1971 to just more than 1.1 million in 1996. The number of lone parents claiming Family Credit has tripled between 1988 and 1996 (DSS, 1998b, no 7, pp 5-6). However, the most recent figures for lone parents on Income Support in 1996-97 show a small fall for the first time since 1993 to less than one million (DSS, 1998f).

The government's response to these trends has been to decree that help:

... should be provided for children in poorer families on the

basis of identifiable needs of children, not on whether there happens to be one parent or two. So there is no case for a one-parent benefit, and the government will not return to that approach. (DSS, 1998a, p 57)

In essence, such a return would discriminate against two-parent families and their children. Consequently, the former Tory government's plans to end the lone parent rate of the Income Support family premium and One Parent Benefit for new claimants were implemented in April and July 1998 respectively. Claimants who had received these benefits before these dates will continue to do so until their entitlement circumstances change. However, such reforms ignore the evidence of the *extra* child-related costs of lone parent families compared with two-parent families (summarised in MacDermott et al, 1998, pp 17-18).

The government's solution for lone parent family poverty is to encourage more parents into the labour market with the added support of in-work benefits. The expectation is that parents should actively consider work once their children are old enough to start school rather than old enough to leave school at 16, as used to be the case. Under the New Deal for Lone Parents, they, like others of working age, are required to attend a gateway interview with a personal adviser.

Unemployed

The unemployed represent a large proportion of the poor, some of whom are lone parents, disabled, young or long-term unemployed. For these people who belong to the growing number of workless households in Britain, the New Deal represents the centrepiece in Labour's welfare to work strategy. Between 1979 and 1996, households with no one in employment have more than doubled from less than one in 10 to just less than one in five working-age households, making a total of 3.4 million workless households (DSS, 1998b, no 3, p 2). This is at least in part caused by the disincentive effect of means-tested social security benefits (Gregg and Wadsworth, 1996).

Given these problems, the government is adopting a 'make work pay' strategy by extending and increasing the value of in-work benefits such as tax credits and by supporting provisions such as education, training and the National Childcare Strategy which is investing £300 million in out-of-school childcare places and £540 million in Sure Start initiatives targeted at pre-school children and their families to prevent social exclusion in deprived areas (DSS, 1998c, p 6). By contrast the Conservatives widened incentives to come off benefit and go to work by reducing benefit levels relative to wages (Oppenheim, 1997b, p 52). They left childcare strategies to the market, entry to which was aided by tax, benefit and voucher payments. Labour's New Deal provides 18- to 24-year-olds who are normally unemployed for six months with four opportunities: private sector employment where the employer receives a six-month £60 per week subsidy; full-time education or training; voluntary work experience in the non-profit sector; environmental taskforce work. Each gateway offers the individual employment preparation and personal job-search advice. For those older than 25 and unemployed for at least two years, the New Deal for the Long-Term Unemployed provides a six-month £75-a-week job subsidy for employers, benefit rule changes to improve access to full-time education or training and personalised advice, counselling and help. The personalised service provides a means of filtering out unwarranted benefit claims. For the young and long-term unemployed, staying on benefit will be penalised by a benefit reduction and eventual withdrawal – penalties the Tories introduced with the JSA, but which Labour has combined with more positive measures to find work. In this Labour is continuing the stricter benefits regime introduced by the Tories (Finn, 1998). There are no similar New Deal provisions for those younger than 18. One consequence of this is that employers may prefer New Deal workers rather than those younger than 18 because of the subsidy that comes with the former, thus lowering the chances of school-leavers finding work (Chatrik and Convery, 1998, p 8).

Second, the national minimum wage (NMW) should provide extra incentives to the unemployed to enter low paid employment. It will increase the incomes of poorer households with one or more persons in work, make working for low wages more attractive, reduce claims for in-work means-tested benefits, and increase payment of tax and National Insurance contributions (Sutherland, 1998, p 13). However, using a computerised tax-benefit model, Sutherland has shown that for a hypothetical NMW of £3.50 there would be a reduction of only 6% in the number of low-waged employees still facing high marginal rates of tax (defined as 60% or more), and a positive 'revenue effect' (in increased tax receipts and reduced benefit payments) of £1.1 billion (Sutherland, 1998, p 14).

Finally, the government is focusing welfare increasingly on in-work support paid through tax rather than social security by introducing the

Working Families Tax Credit, an earned credit which tapers off as earnings rise to provide a minimum income of £200 a week for a family with one child. This "will offer more generous support to working families, reducing the number facing high marginal tax rates and improving incentives" (DSS, 1998a, p 58). It will replace means-tested Family Credit which now goes to about 757,000 working people in families with children (DSS, 1998g). In extending this approach, the government is introducing a Child Tax Credit for all standard-rate tax payers, a Disabled Person's Tax Credit to replace the Disability Working Allowance and a Childcare Tax Credit to cover 70% of childcare costs of up to £100 a week for low-income working families with one child. Tax credits will soften the impact of the benefit trap that discourages claimants from joining the labour market, by giving more credits to families on low earnings up to the tax credit threshold. However, studies of tax credits in other countries are providing a mixed assessment of their likely value in the UK (for example, Mendelson, 1998).

Disability

For the government, society's treatment of disabled people stands as "the mark of a civilised society, expressing our mutual obligation to help disabled people play a full role in society" (DSS, 1998c, p 11). This role involves either work for disabled people who can or security for those who cannot. The question for observers of government policy is whether this twofold aim can be achieved even-handedly – a further mark of a civilised society founded on mutual obligations. However, it is generally recognised when issues of obligation are in question that you cannot start from the premise that duties should underpin rights in the same way for all people – some require the means in the first place to fulfil their duties (see Doyal and Gough, 1991, p 94). There are some individuals who are less well-placed than others to fulfil their duties and so morally have a claim on more resources for need-satisfaction in order to fulfil their duties. With this caveat in mind, how should we understand the thinking behind Labour's social security policies for disabled people?

Responding early to the government's Welfare to Work strategy, the Social Security Advisory Committee's review of policies for the disabled (SSAC, 1997) defined the issue of the incentives differential between work and welfare as being central to its new agenda[1]. Of the eight issues it discusses, four address the question of work incentives for people with disabilities, namely issues about:

- **the extent to which the benefit system should make provision for long-term sickness or disability (other than the additional costs directly attributable to disability) at a different rate from that for long-term unemployment;**

- **whether in respect of inability to work, the benefit system should reward those who have previously worked to a greater extent than those who have not or have been unable to do so;**

- **whether it is practical to develop a structure that provides a greater incentive for those currently treated as incapable of work ... to move from benefit dependency into work to at least some extent, without unfairly penalising or stigmatising those who are incapable of any work;**

- **whether ... a structure can be developed that encourages those who can work, either for a part of a week or episodically, or can work full time but with limited capacity, but does not penalise those who, having attempted to do so, cannot, for good reason, sustain the attempt. (SSAC, 1997, pp 2-3)**

Coming so soon after the 1997 Election, the Social Security Advisory Committee's report not only questioned taken-for-granted assumptions about the needs of disabled people, but provided a significant bridgehead between the Conservative and Labour governments for developing a conditional philosophy which supports welfare claims based increasingly on 'desert', focusing on people's behaviour, rather than needs-based criteria.

The government for its part has expressed concern about the increasing expenditure on benefits for sick and disabled people, from just more than £5 billion in 1979 to £24 billion in 1996/97, representing one of the fastest growing areas of social security (DSS, 1998b, no 4, p 1). Sickness and disability are the most important factors contributing to the growth in workless households during the last decade (DSS, 1998b, p 5). Incapacity Benefit and Disability Living Allowance (DLA) are two benefits for which the rise in claims posed an early problem for the new government. The Integrity Benefits Project was launched by the outgoing government as a way of checking the entitlement of DLA claimants on the highest rate. The government withdrew this somewhat belatedly at the end of 1998 after growing outcry from disability groups. However, the entitlement tests for Incapacity Benefit and DLA are currently being reviewed (DSS, 1998a, p 54). Incapacity Benefit is moving towards an 'all work test' that determines the work capacities as well as incapacities of the disabled (DSS, 1998c, p 15) and the DLA Advisory Board is proposing a more rigorous medical test of entitlement (Brindle, 1998).

The government is introducing a complex package of benefit reforms for disabled people. The overall outcome is likely to increase the size of the group of disabled people who can work compared to those who cannot. To ensure that more enter the labour market, all people with disabilities or long-term illness (excluding those receiving DLA) must attend a gateway interview (DSS, 1998c, p 14). However, the problem with applying the Welfare to Work strategy to disabled people is that four million of the 6.5 million disabled people are over retirement age and outside its scope and that disabled people seeking work face employer discrimination (Brindle and MacAskill, 1997). Welfare to Work can do nothing for the first problem and little for the second, except attempt, together with more effective legal protection, to change the employers' views of disabled workers. Consequently, the government has accepted the case for establishing a Disability Rights Commission.

For those who cannot work, three reforms are of note. First, the government is proposing a new disability income guarantee for the poorest and most severely disabled receiving the higher rate of non-means-tested DLA (for individuals needing 24-hour care) and means-tested Income Support to secure an income substantially above the Income Support minimum. Second, Incapacity Benefit is to be confined to individuals who have had to give up work because of disability or long-term illness and will be withdrawn from the long-term unemployed approaching retirement age. To achieve this and "strengthen the link between work and entitlement", Incapacity Benefit entitlements are to be changed for new claimants so that only recent National Insurance contributions count (DSS, 1998c, p 16). Third, Incapacity Benefit is to be clawed back for claimants receiving occupational or private pensions, on the grounds that this mix of public and private benefits constitutes a wasteful "duplication of provision" (DSS, 1998c). These reforms raise further social policy issues about the continuing contraction of National Insurance entitlements, the extension of means-testing to the better-off and the future mix of benefits – the implications of which, discussed in the next main section, help to further define the government's 'Third Way'.

Pensioners

Britain like other Western societies is an ageing society whose elderly need increasing levels of welfare resources. The basic state retirement pension alone is the most expensive single benefit currently costing about £30 billion, about one third of social security expenditure (DSS, 1998e, p 17). Added to this, £7 billion is spent on the state earnings related pension scheme (SERPS) and income-related and disability benefits for pensioners, and £7 billion on National Insurance rebates to people contracted-out of SERPS. The Conservatives sought to contain expenditure on pensions by cutting the link with earnings in 1980, cutting the value of the SERPS in 1988 and in early 1997 proposing a privatised pension scheme to cover the costs of basic and additional pensions for the majority (Jones and Shrimsley, 1997).

By the mid-1990s politicians began to adopt a more optimistic view of the future of pensioners in the light of the fact that average pensioner incomes were rising faster than average earnings as a whole. However, this trend disguises growing inequalities in pensioners' income. Between 1979 and 1996, the income of the poorest tenth of pensioners had risen by 31%, and the richest tenth by 78% (DSS 1998b, no 6, p 2). Pensioners are over-represented at the lower end of the distribution of income: about one in four households in the bottom 20% of the overall distribution are pensioners (DSS, 1998b). Nonetheless, the fact that the higher you go up the pensioner income ladder, the smaller the proportion of income is made up of state pension and means-tested benefits and the larger the proportion made up of SERPS, occupational and private pensions and savings, leads the government to argue that "the flourishing public–private partnership has delivered a substantial increase in average living standards for pensioners" (DSS, 1998a, p 36).

The Labour government's Green Paper on pensions confirms the intention to continue down the path of mixed provision: a "new public–private partnership building on the best features of state and private provision" (DSS, 1998e, p 30). In advancing its case for the Third Way, the government is dismissing the two 'extreme alternatives': universal state provision which would be "unaffordable and poorly targeted" and private provision which would be impractical because the poor "could not afford to make sufficient contributions to produce a decent income in retirement" (1998e, pp 29-30). In this vein it rejects Frank Field's and others' arguments for a compulsory second pension. Three key proposals are of note. Unlike the Tories' proposals, the Paper restates Labour's commitment to keeping the basic state pension as "a key building block of the pension system" (1998e, p 30). This is being underwritten for pensioners on Income Support by a new minimum income guarantee which raises their income above the basic Income Support level by a guarantee uprated according to earnings. The guarantee is the main device to ensure that poorer pensioners on Income Suport receive an income above the means-tested minimum. This implies that in the short term the 600,000 pensioners entitled to Income Support but not claiming can now be persuaded to claim or be more effectively targeted. However, more realistically, the government recognises that there are still 'deep-rooted problems' attached to claiming the minimum income guarantee which more effective publicity about entitlement and more automatic delivery system may not overcome (DSS, 1998e, p 36).

The second key proposal is a new state second pension (SSP) to replace SERPS, which it is envisaged will double the value of SERPS for people earning up to £9,000 a year and give additional benefit to earners between £9,000 and £18,500 a year. For earners in this bracket who already are, or wish to become, members of occupational, private or stakeholder pensions, there will be increased rebates making these funded pensions more attractive. The position of those above £18,500 will remain unchanged (DSS, 1998e, p 40). The third proposal is to legislate to enable private insurance companies and mutual organisations to offer stakeholder pension schemes (SPSs) to individuals without occupational pensions or suitable private pensions. These should have approved governance structures, lower marketing and administrative costs than private pensions, no penalties if people stop contributing and simpler tax rules (DSS, 1998e, pp 50-1). However, these proposals do not commit SPS to the democratic principle of the mutualist philosophy of Field, where members would own their assets and control the organisation through representative boards (Field, 1996a, pp 100-1). Instead, the outlined model for the approved governance structure requires only that these schemes are run by boards of trustees in conformity with trust law (DSS, 1998c, p 52), where elected representation is optional.

The discussion of the SSP's role has a transitional air about it. It aims to boost the pension entitlements of those on low incomes and carers to cut reliance on means-tested benefits and in the 'first stage' to help moderate earners build up better second pensions. This will be done by increasing the value of National Insurance rebates for earners in the £9,000 to £18,500 bracket who opt for a stakeholder or other funded scheme. In the 'second stage' (assuming Labour is returned in 2002), when the SPS is established, the SSP will become a flat-rate scheme for low earners, with moderates and high earners joining funded schemes (DSS, 1998e, pp 39-40). This raises questions about Labour's plans for pensions thereafter, from the late-2000s. The Green Paper does not address this. One possibility is that a flat-rate SSP could absorb the basic pension, leaving those not covered to means-tested provisions; alternatively it could be extended into a more adequate universal state pension. However, whatever the future, the government's timetable does not envisage legislating for the SSP until April 2002, just before the next election.

While in the long-run Britain faces a significant challenge in developing pensions policy – seen in the changing support ratio over the next half century as the numbers who are of pension age increases by one third and those of working age decline by 30% (DSS, 1998e, p 13) – its position is better than other industrialised countries such as Germany, Canada and Japan. Further, in Britain, based on *current* policies, the share of GDP supporting pensions will fall between 2025 and 2050 (DSS, 1998e), because of the growing role of private pensions and the link between the basic state pension and prices rather than earnings. It is the government's awareness of the way these trends have undermined state provisions during the last two decades that motivates its dual focus on improving the public–private partnership in pensions and raising the income of the poorest pensioners.

The Third Way in social security

This section examines in what ways the policies described above constitute a distinctive 'Third Way' for social security that differs from the two paths followed by Labour in the post-war decades and by Conservative governments between 1979 and 1997. The Third Way can be described as seeking to redefine four dimensions of social security policy: the level of benefit; the structure of benefit entitlement; government regulation; and citizenship (see Table 7.1).

First, on benefit levels, the Beveridge Report recommended fixing benefits to subsistence rather than earnings (Beveridge, 1942, p 14; see Hewitt and Powell, 1998, p 97). However, in 1974 Labour tied long-term benefit levels to annual increases in earnings or prices whichever rose the higher as a commitment to ensuring that social security achieved some degree of redistribution, at least in maintaining the living standards of the poor relative to those of the working population. In 1980 the Conservatives

Table 7.1: The Third Way in social security: a typology

Dimensions	Old Left	Third Way	New Right
Benefit levels tied to	earnings	prices for some and earnings for others	prices
Structure of entitlement	national minimum for all and additional private insurance for some	NMW and basic pension; growing 'inclusive' public and private provision	growing privately provided minimum and state provided residual benefits
Governance of social security	central command and state monopoly	partnership and dialogue between state and private sectors	deregulation of state monopoly
Citizenship	rights to benefits	rights to benefits come with duties	duties, with minimum rights

undid this arrangement and left benefits tied to prices alone, so contributing to a long-term decline in the level of benefits in relation to earnings and causing growing impoverishment for poor families on benefit. This departure represented a significant point of disagreement between Old Labour and New Tories. However, New Labour has avoided committing itself to returning to dual-track indexation for benefits on the grounds of its prohibitive cost. In this sense, it has been open to Baroness Castle's charge, voiced at the 1996 Labour Party Conference, of depriving pensioners of increases in earnings above inflation during the past two decades (Castle and Townsend, 1998). Labour's approach here suggests a general reluctance to use social security to redistribute income – a significant departure from Tawney's arguments in the interwar years to use government-financed social services as a principal means to combat inequality (1964; see also Le Grand, 1982; Powell, 1995). At best the minimum income guarantees for pensioners and disabled people will raise benefits relative to earnings in 1999 for these two recipient groups alone, leaving others dependent on Income Support indexed to prices. In conclusion, the Third Way implies fixing benefit levels to earnings for some of the poorest on means-tested Income Support lifting others off means-tested out-of-work benefits through Welfare to Work measures and leaving the rest to benefits tied to prices.

Changes in the structure of state and non-state benefit entitlements since Beveridge represent a further point of difference between post-war Old Labour (and Old Conservatives) and the new Thatcherite Tories of the 1980s and 1990s. Between the two, New Labour now seeks a third way. The Beveridge reforms of the late 1940s provided a national minimum for all (assuming full-employment) on which *in addition* individuals were encouraged to build up occupational or private entitlements. The Beveridge tradition among Old Labourites and Old Conservatives was clear on the importance of the national minimum – although small earnings-related additions were introduced in the 1960s and 1970s culminating in the provision of more substantial SERPS additions in 1978. Any provision outside the State was in addition to the minimum, enhancing individual choice and protection beyond what the State provided (Powell and Hewitt, 1998, pp 4-5). For individuals who were not covered by National Insurance, the safety net of means-tested national assistance and, from 1966, supplementary benefit was provided. In effect, the State guaranteed universal coverage for all workers with entitlements based on regular contributions.

The cross-Party agreement on these essential elements of the post-war consensus on social security was abandoned in the 1980s when the Tories replaced National Insurance sickness and maternity benefits with statutory sickness and maternity pay provided for up to 28 weeks by employers on whom claimants would now have to rely. In 1996, the government replaced National Insurance unemployment benefit with the JSA. Entitlement to JSA is either based on National Insurance contributions or means-tested, with all recipients entering into a job seekers' agreement. JSA reduces the entitlement period from 12 to six months and introduces workfare conditions of entitlement, which in various forms were trailed by the Thatcher governments of the 1980s (see Finn, 1998). The remaining principal National Insurance benefit, the basic state pension, was allowed to decline in value as a result of severing its link with earnings. Shortly before the last election, the Major government announced long-term plans to replace the statutory National Insurance basic pension and SERPS with compulsory private pensions with the government providing top-up guarantees to a minimum pension level for poorer workers. All of these measures substantially undermined the contributory principle in National Insurance. The pension proposals would have constituted the final nail in Beveridge's National Insurance coffin. A further extension of private provision for basic needs occurred in 1995 with the removal of Income Support mortgage benefit for the first nine months from sick or unemployed claimants less than 60 years of age, with the advice that workers should look to private insurance as the alternative. The consequence of these changes after nearly two decades of growing unemployment and rising inflation has been to replace the state national minimum with a residual level of means-tested benefits and to end the principle whereby the State alone is responsible for basic benefits, on top of which non-state bodies provide various additions.

The Welfare Green Paper's account of the difference between Old Labour and New Tories – as a dramatic choice between a privatised future with residual state welfare and a costly welfare state (DSS, 1998a, p 2) – enables the government to articulate a third way to re-shape social security entitlements. Instead of returning to universal state provision for basic needs, the government wants to strengthen universal entitlement to welfare in a fundamentally different way which involves a more targeted, diversified and gradualist approach based on a greater public–private mix. (In changing the principle of universalism Labour has also changed the terminology to 'inclusivity'.) This approach can be seen most clearly in the pensions proposals where in the long run the government aims to establish a flat-rate contributory SSP for people who cannot afford a funded second pension, with funded pensions for the rest. Instead of compulsion as the means to secure universal adequate pension cover for future generations of pensioners, the government has chosen to adopt a more evolutionary approach. However, this approach carries two long-term optimistic assumptions:

* it assumes that existing private financial institutions can adapt to the diverse financial circumstances and patterns of work of different social groups and develop a wide range of user-friendly products for their needs – an assumption that this highly competitive industry may be unable to realise;
* in the long term it implies an optimistic assumption shared with Beveridge, that over time as the present generation of pensioners is replaced by better covered pensioners, Income Support will become increasingly residual, thus reversing a 50 years trend whereby Income Support and its predecessors came to assume a mass role for the poorer pensioners and others.

A second aspect of the new structure of state and non-state provision is seen in the government's Working Families Tax Credit. To qualify for credits, employees must disclose their circumstances to their employers who must declare their earnings and circumstances to the Inland Revenue. While this reform is likely to achieve a more universal cover, it is confined to working families – unlike, for example, a more radically universal basic income approach. Tax credits depart from the traditional sense of universal provision in other ways too. For example, by using this in-work benefit (or tax credit) to raise the income of the low paid to a level higher than individuals receive from means-tested out-of-work benefits, the government is rejigging the less eligible principle in a way appropriate for an enlarged low-waged sector; in effect, out-of-work claimants are made less eligible than in-work claimants. Using the tax system normally means paying benefits to the senior working male member of the tax unit rather than the mother as with Family Credit thus depriving mothers of an important source of money under their control. The hope that partners will enter into an agreement with each other to decide whether one partner receives the credit or the other a cash equivalent benefit assumes that all families are governed by a democratic code (cf the 'new democratic family' of Giddens, 1998). This assumption ignores the contrary finding of studies that show that female partners tend to receive less than their fair share of household income (for example, Goode et al, 1998). The NMW introduces a further though lower level of universal protection to ensure that no adult worker is paid less than £3.60 an hour.

To summarise, the Third Way to structure benefit entitlement forecloses any return to the post-war principle of universal benefits and provides instead an inclusive but variegated structure of provisions for a range of social groups, including the proposed pension reforms, working tax credits, NMW and higher income guarantees.

Evidence that New Labour is no longer committed to the traditional universal principle came in Chancellor Gordon Brown's confirmation in his CSR in July 1998 that the government would be withdrawing Child Benefit from mothers with children older than 16 and replacing it with a means-tested benefit for young people older than 16 at school or college (G. Brown, 1998c). The government is intending to tax higher rate taxpayers on any future increase in Child Benefit, planned to rise by £2.50 in April 1999 (DSS, 1998a, p 58). Further evidence of Labour's fundamental rethink of its universalist philosophy was given in the *Daily Telegraph* report where Harriet Harman, the former Secretary for Social Security, announced the new pension guarantee as "a new Labour way of helping pensioners". The report quoted a source close to Harman as saying: "The old Labour way was for universal increases across the board. This is targeting those who need it most" (Copley, 1998). However, despite the conviction of Labour modernisers that universalism is wasteful, Ruth Lister has argued to the contrary "that it is means-testing and not universalism which is anachronistic, for the former is ill-suited to modern conditions of rapid change, fluctuating incomes and insecurity" (Lister, 1997a, p 16).

The third feature of the government's Third Way concerns the governance and regulation of social security. In 1948, the Labour government introduced a centralised State monopoly over basic benefits. The Tories, by contrast, facing very different social and economic circumstances in the 1980s and 1990s have deregulated much State provision, encouraging individuals to pursue self-interest over collective interest, private producers to compete for custom (with some pension firms adopting unacceptable sales tactics) and both customers and producers to face market risks with reduced government support.

By contrast, New Labour, in pursuit of the Third Way, is seeking to follow the path of cooperation and dialogue. The notion of a new democracy of dialogue has been developed in Tony Giddens' work on the future of welfare (1994, 1998). The style and appearance of governance is noticeably more consultative and consensual than previously. In social security, as for other policies, the government has set up several reviews especially in the areas of pensions, disability and elderly care (on which the forthcoming Royal Commission will be the first for more than 20 years). It has appointed members of committees not only from government, business and the established professions, but from groups such as trade unions, social scientists, social workers and the police. Consultative Green Papers have encouraged and in some cases succeeded in attracting wide public response. The Welfare Green Paper reports ongoing consultation with various groups of claimants in developing its welfare reform strategy (for example, lone parent and disability organisations; DSS, 1998a, pp 26, 55). Governance by cooperation is seen in relationships between the public and private sectors which are promoted as part of the 'new partnerships' especially in the pension sector. This is a principle that the Beveridge Report encouraged (Beveridge, 1942, pp 6-7). The new government is setting up new bodies such as the Disability Rights Commission, is giving wider remits to the Financial Services Authority and is an 'active partner' in negotiating with financial sector bodies, representing mortgage lenders, insurers and banks, to produce better mortgage payment protection policies (DSS, 1998a, p 40). It sees the need to promote pension awareness through education and proposes that pension providers should provide annual pensions statements to every adult (DSS, 1998e, p 31). The Prime Minister and senior colleagues took their proposals to Labour Party members around the country on the 'welfare roadshow'. These new attempts at dialogue are seen from one viewpoint only, that of the welfare provider – the government – and not the recipient. When the dialogue becomes unscripted, different voices can be heard – as when the welfare roadshow in Wood Green, North London, admitted non-Labour Party members of the public to Gordon Brown's 'appearance', many of whom seized the opportunity to deliver a highly critical line on the government's welfare reforms (MacAskill, 1998).

New Labour's philosophy of citizenship (see Chapter Ten) defines the fourth feature of its Third Way in social security. Here again the rationale is one of seeking to reconcile two notions that had previously represented opposing approaches, namely citizenship based on rights and on duties. For Old Labour the national minimum ensured that in principle the basic needs of all citizens were met and that in particular contributory and non-contributory social security protected all from want. The idea that all members of the human race share at least a modicum of basic needs and so enjoy universal rights to welfare stood as a fundamental view of human nature on which citizenship claims to State welfare were based for much of this century (Hewitt, 1998, pp 62-3). The rise of the New Right replaced this belief with a more individualist notion of human nature which argued that our basic needs are first and foremost the responsibility of individuals earning their livelihood and satisfying their needs in the marketplace and that only in extreme circumstances should the State provide welfare for its citizens' basic needs. Citizenship was conceived largely as a matter of the duties and responsibilities of the individual (to be reliable workers, good parents, law-abiding citizens and so forth). Rights were increasingly confined to residual forms of welfare which met only subsistence needs with entitlements based on means-testing. With the numbers of the unemployed and poor rising throughout the 1980s and 1990s social security took on an increasingly residual demeanour, and the conditional nature of social rights became more marked, with workfare conditions becoming more formalised with the introduction of the JSA in 1996.

The Third Way for Labour has meant articulating a philosophy of citizenship that conjoins notions of rights and duties, most explicitly stated in Tony Blair's *Spectator Lecture* in 1995 on 'The rights we enjoy, the duties we owe' (1996a, pp 236-43). In this light, Labour has adopted a more conditional approach to citizenship rights to social security, retaining the Tories' JSA and promoting a New Deal which stresses the obligations individuals owe in claiming their rights to welfare (Dwyer, 1998). Although the spirit of conditionality has replaced unconditionality, the government has so far limited the compulsory element in conditional welfare to penalising the unemployed who refuse New Deal opportunities.

Plant has described the Labour government's approach to social inclusion as a shift in thinking from "one based on citizenship, status and rights, to one based on obligation and achievement" (1997a, p 3). In a more flexible labour market individuals are expected to take more responsibility than previously for their own employability by acquiring the skills, education and, in some cases, job experience the government provides. Both the individual and the government acquire new obligations: the individual to seek work and training; the government to provide training and sometimes work. Plant recognises that the assumption that rights are contingent on performing duties rests on the government as well as the individual. In the shifting meaning of citizenship, a government that once took responsibility for providing unconditional welfare must now, in the new climate of conditional citizenship, act as the 'employer of last resort' when the labour market fails to provide jobs for all (Plant, 1997a, p 31). Elsewhere Plant argues that the State carries "a correlative duty ... to provide work or training so that the worker has a right to work or train under this general duty" (1997b, p 96).

Conclusion

In the context of greater global competition and economic insecurity at the end of the 20th century, Labour is constructing a two-part division of welfare based on "rebuilding the system around work and security". Unlike the earlier social divisions of the Poor Law and classic welfare state, the distinction between work and security is meant to portray the unity of inclusive welfare rather than division and exclusion. However, the stress on rewarding work in the government's policy and rhetoric is in danger of overshadowing the needs of the most vulnerable who cannot work.

Labour is committed to continuing Tory policies for affordable social security which actively encourages participation in work, including low paid and relatively insecure work. The concept of 'active' social security policy has come to replace the 'passive' policies that resulted from the continuation of Beveridge's measures in the context of an entirely different economic climate (Commission on Social Justice, 1994, p 221). The rhetoric of active versus passive and opportunity versus dependency provides dominant themes defining the Third Way in the government's Green Papers on welfare. An active welfare state based on changing the structure of incentives by raising benefit levels and enhancing support for the poor in work over the levels received by the out-of-work poor defines the thrust of Labour's social security strategy. To this end, the New Deal, tax credits, the NMW, reduced National Insurance entitlements and the single gateway are among the measures designed to shift more lone parents, unemployed and disabled people off out-of-work benefits and into work. At the same time Labour is introducing new more targeted measures to provide better help to those who cannot work, especially disabled people and pensioners. For both groups, those in- and out-of-work, social security provisions are becoming more individualised and diversified and less reliant on the broad distinctions associated with the classic welfare state, such as the national minimum, the means-tested residual minimum and less eligibility (between the independent in work and the dependent on welfare). Between the two broad approaches – for those who either can or cannot work – will eventually fall groups for whom the New Deal and new out-of-work benefits have little to offer. It is too early to quantify the size of these traditionally residual groups of lone parents, unemployed and disabled, whose needs could be passed over by Labour's twofold approach and who will remain dependent on Tory policies that Labour has so far no plans to scrap, principally means-tested Income Support and the social fund. The worst scenario would be for Labour inadvertently to create from its rhetoric, about the poor who can and the poor who can't work, a third welfare division of those left behind. By contrast, the most optimistic scenario would see these groups benefit from the growing body of policies targeted at social exclusion – ranging from the Sure Start initiatives for the under-fives to targeted Education, Health and Employment Zones in poorer areas – and equipped to benefit from schooling and new work opportunities. Otherwise, for Labour's poor and excluded, under the Third Way there is no third option.

Note

[1] I owe this point to Michael Daly of Oxford Brookes University.

EIGHT

New Labour and employment, training and employee relations

Peter Cressey

Introduction

The issues of employment, labour market structures, training and industrial relations have been critical ones for the Labour Party throughout the whole of this century. They have been pivotal areas cementing the links between the trade unions and the Party, they have secured broader working-class support through employment rights reform and have determined the general economic strategy adopted – be it Keynesian or neo-Keynesian. However, the shifts in Labour Party thinking since its last period in government in relation to these issues do appear to be fundamental and hence capable of unscrambling that trade union relationship, lessening working-class support and providing an alternative vision of the future from that of macro demand management. The main changes are exemplified in the 1996 Labour Party publication *Building prosperity: Flexibility, efficiency and fairness at work* and repeated in the recently published Employment Relations Bill (January 1999). Assessing what actual changes have been inaugurated since coming to power in the raft of proposals and reforms Labour has enacted will give some idea of the direction in which the government is going.

In general it appears that the Labour government has gone for a minimalist approach in relation to employee rights at work, to the regulation of business and to the involvement of trade unions in deciding and implementing policies. Deregulation will stay. Competitive flexibility continues to be a central plank. Many of the trade union laws will be kept firmly in place. On the latter Tony Blair said in the Foreword to the White Paper *Fairness at work*:

> **There will be no going back. The days of strikes without ballots, mass picketing, closed shops and secondary action are over.** *Even after the changes we propose, Britain will have the most lightly regulated*

labour market of any leading economy in the world. (DTI, 1998, p 1; emphasis added)

Such statements seem to give credence to the numerous critics (Gray, 1998; Coates and Barratt Brown, 1996; Davey, 1998) who point to a continuity with the previous government and the adoption by New Labour of key elements of the Thatcherite programme. However, this is not the whole picture. In addition to these affirmations there appears to be some discontinuities of policy especially in the area of job creation, training and Europe. In these three areas differences in approach from the Tories are in evidence with 'New Labour' drawing on other national experiences and some 'Old Labour' sources for its inspiration. The influence of the US Democratic Party, especially in the creation of the 'Welfare to Work' programme, is outlined in Chapter Twelve. Elsewhere, Davey (1998) has indicated how global has been the reach of New Labour's trawl for new policy initiatives:

> **Apart from its acceptance of a number of Thatcherite reforms, new Labour's search for a fresh identity has been global rather than indigenous. It has turned to the American Democrats for lessons on how to win power, the Australian Labour governments of Hawkes and Keating on how to retain it, and to the Asia-Pacific for a vision of the future. (Davey, 1998, p 78)**

Nor is that all. In the area of employment, employee relations and training there is the growing influence of Europe and with it the pull of the more 'corporatist' stakeholder model of 'social partnership'. Such a model offers an easier accommodation with strands of Old Labour thinking with its emphasis on the centrality of trade union involvement in decision making, social rights advance, higher welfare spending and structural intervention in the labour market. To Guest (1997), in terms of the employment relationship broadly conceived, the UK stands between two models: the European one with its "legislative framework and pluralist assumptions" and the American model that rejects regulation and puts faith in the "value of market forces". Both of these models can claim success in recent times. The European model, while doing badly at job creation, scores better in terms of societal consensus, social inclusion and representational justice. The free market model has been signally more successful in labour market terms but less so in inclusivity, representation and welfare. For Guest the question is whether New Labour can give birth to a 'third way' that will offer at the same time both "justice and jobs" (1997, p 1).

This chapter will look at New Labour's policies in the labour market and employment relations areas to see if this hybrid model is being realised or if the pressures of office are forcing the government into a more pragmatic accommodation with the previous government's agenda and approach. It will then look at the issues of job creation (specifically at the plans for Welfare to Work) and also training, employability and the plans for skills development. The second substantive section will identify the key policy changes in terms of employee representation and the reforms emanating from Europe, including those on consultation and information provision. The chapter will conclude by asking to what extent New Labour policies have a deep ambivalence within them that will make them ultimately unsustainable over the longer term.

Employment and job creation

The United Kingdom has pursued a number of different job creation strategies in the past 20 years. These have moved from direct intervention via job creation measures and job subsidies towards the current activation measures designed to get the long-term unemployed off benefit and into work. The forms of labour market policies that successive governments have supported do show elements of continuity, especially regarding the trends towards flexibilisation and activation. Farnham and Lupton (1994) describe the employment and labour market policies pursued by the Tories as confronting two central problem areas for the economy. The first was what has been described as the 'British labour problem' where trade union regulation had introduced rigidities in pay, working time and employment patterns. In this vision, restrictive practices and the relatively low productivity of the British economy can be laid at the door of powerful unions. It was the government's responsibility to redress this by flexibilising and deregulating the labour market. The second problem area identified by them was the 'British training problem' where industrial growth is deemed to be held back by a chronic shortage of skilled workers both in the technical and supervisory fields. This meant that "British firms made less efficient use of their labour and were restricted to the employment of simpler technologies" (Farnham and Lupton, 1994, p 97).

The British economy needed a number of supply-side measures relating to training, reskilling and upgrading the labour stock. These were supplemented by a series of measures to discipline those that were out of work to force them into taking jobs that they may not have done voluntarily.

The two problems together shaped the approach to employment policy during the 18 years of Conservative rule. There was a concerted attack on trade unions, a reorganisation of the power relationship between employers and employees, an individualising of the employment contract and a restructuring of the apparatus of training and job-search facilities. The installation of an 'enterprise culture' meant the imposition of new disciplines both inside and outside work. The unemployed and those on benefit had greater compulsion to undertake job searches and enter the labour market.

The next section will briefly describe the range of labour market policies used, highlight the difference between active and passive labour market policies, describe the format and range of the active policies undertaken within the UK and finally show the way in which policy has swung from one particular approach to another. The chapter will then concentrate on the new government's activation agenda with particular emphasis on the 'New Deal'.

The job creation legacy

The attempts to manage the labour market only really begin following the end of the long post-war boom in the early 1970s. During each decade since 1970 changes in labour market policy are evident and with these changes differential emphasis has been put on what job creation and employment training schemes should be achieving.

Labour market policies are made up of passive and active measures. Passive measures are those that support the unemployed and offer varying levels of compensation. They include the use of unemployment benefit, redundancy payments, post-redundancy wage guarantees, early retirement arrangements and other similar compensatory schemes. By the late 1980s in the UK 75% of all monies devoted to tackling unemployment went on such passive measures, a pattern repeated in most OECD countries (Towers, 1994). Active labour market policies (ALMPs) are much more diverse in their format and operation. The OECD gives a set of distinguishing characteristics. It divides ALMPs into four main types of programme:

- employment training: including both formal classroom training and on-the-job training;
- subsidies to employment: these can be paid either to employers or to employees;
- job-search assistance: included here are job clubs, individual counselling, incentive payments and so on;
- direct job creation: using company or public authority schemes to employ workers or by aiding business start-ups, coops and so on.

Labour in the 1970s used a number of 'special employment measures' based on direct job creation and job subsidies as well as the development of supportive 'passive' labour market policies. However, since then detectable shifts of policy have occurred. As a result of political changes and because of burgeoning costs due to cyclical variations in the proportion of long-term unemployment in the overall figures, policy has undergone a change. Successive policy programmes are represented in the highly simplified diagram in Figure 8.1.

This representation shows a return to direct job subsidies especially as a method of reducing youth unemployment. This is concurrent with emphasis on the supply-side aspects of employability primarily through redressing the inadequacies of the unemployed, training them into appropriate skills in demand, and discerning what labour market

Figure 8.1: Trends in UK policy for active labour market policies

Job creation/
job subsidies
———————>
Employment training

    Employment training
    ———————>
    Job-search assistance

        Job-search assistance
        ———————>
        Benefit changes

            Job creation subsidies
            ———————>
            Job search and
            training

| 1970s | 1980s | 1990s | 1999 |

Dominant policy
Subsidiary policy

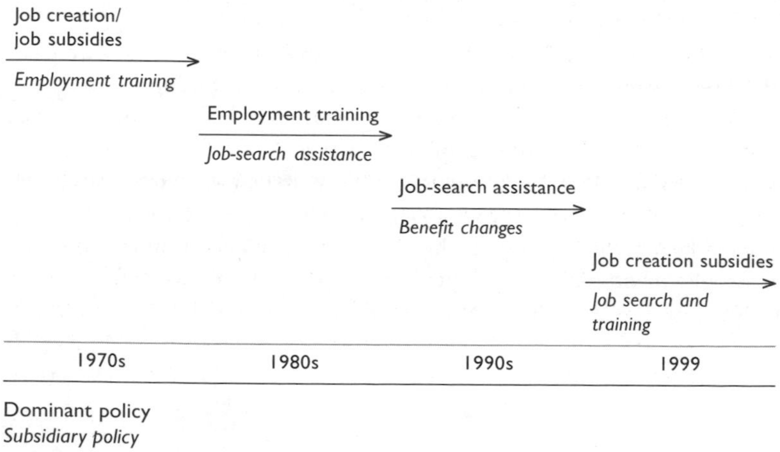

employment trends need to be met. Over the longer term the Conservatives lessened the force of the employment training route as the main way to reduce claimant unemployment preferring instead intensive counselling, guaranteed job interviews, job-search seminars and compulsory attendance at job clubs. These measures, combined with the Restart programme (introduced in 1986), had dramatic effects on reducing the number of claimant unemployed and were seen as a policy success by the previous government. However, evaluation studies have been sanguine about the employment creation effect that these cheap supply-side policies had, pointing to them as coercive mechanisms for forcing claimants into either non-registration (still unemployed but off the register) or low paid, unskilled marginal jobs in the deregulated labour market (Disney et al, 1992; Layard and Philpot, 1991). As Gregg trenchantly puts it:

> **The other major development has been the shift towards a set of policies to drive down the reservation wage of groups of workers who it was felt had priced themselves out of work.... This then completed the shift in emphasis from raising the demand for labour at the going rate to matching the wage with skill levels so that labour will be demanded. Coupled with *Restart* and benefit regulations that require active job search, it produces a consistent policy response if the problem of unemployment persistence is too high reservation wages and too little job search by the unemployed, coupled with growing problems with skill acquisition by the young, skill maintenance when unemployed, and a skill mismatch. (Gregg, 1990, p 52)**

The introduction of the Job Seekers' Allowance (JSA) (1996) completed this trend and added more restrictions and a tightening of the rules regarding claimant eligibility while providing little towards financing or creating the jobs for those claimants.

Conservative Party policy in the 1990s switched away from direct job creation and job subsidies to employers, which were seen as distortive of the market and of wage rates. They were also seen as continuing rigidities in employment contracts – especially through the reinforcement of the 'going rate' – and as pre-empting employer decisions about job creation.

New Deal

It seems on the surface that the new policy encapsulated in the 'Welfare to Work' scheme, or 'New Deal' as it is popularly known, is a change in direction for Labour (see also Chapters Seven and Twelve). The New Deal includes within it almost all of the four elements of an active labour market policy – mixing subsidies, job-search assistance, training and direct job creation. Within it job subsidies of £60/week are paid directly to employers for six months if they take a 16- to 24-year-old into employment. There is a training grant of £750 for each participant and a 'gateway' period of intensive counselling, advice and guidance. The young participant will be offered four choices:

- subsidised employment;
- full-time basic skills training/education;
- a job with a voluntary sector organisation for six months;
- the opportunity to join an environmental taskforce and undertake necessary community improvements.

What will not be on offer is the ability to refuse one of the four options and remain on benefit. The package also includes the possibility of 'taster'employment (short placement spells), the use of mentors, special assistance with childcare and increased help for disabled people, lone parents and ethnic minorities. Such a scheme has raised pro and anti sentiments within the Labour Party, its left wing and wider audiences. Among the arguments in favour is that it:

- appears redistributive in that it takes billions of pounds in windfall tax out of the super large utilities and targets this at some of the poorest sections of the community;
- is interventionist in style and brings the State back into taking some responsibility for the labour market and employment levels;
- is national and therefore does not rely on voluntary schemes of variable quality in different geographical areas; it is also large enough to make a difference – in the first three years up to 250,000 participants should have undertaken at least one of the options;
- will offer an upgraded personal service to the young unemployed – the Employment Service has been prevailed on to change its culture and offer genuine help and advice to 'clients' in a manner qualitatively different to that which went before. (Denny, 1998)

These arguments are balanced by a high level of hostility that has focused on the following points:

- It is punitive inasmuch as it does not offer a fifth option of not taking any of the preferred options. This breaks with the Labour past in a decisive way and has laid the policy open to charges of workfarism. Gray (1998) sees this as the direct continuation of the earlier Tory policy 'Project Work' that was the first post-war compulsory work programme where those unemployed for more than two years had to undertake a 13-week spell of work on a benefits plus £10 basis. The sanction of loss of benefit for refusing work in that scheme has been continued in the New Deal. Meager (1998, p 39) indicates that "scheme participation as a condition for benefit" is the prime feature of "workfare approaches".
- It is potentially short term since no extension of the initial three-year windfall tax has been guaranteed. The existence and persistence of youth unemployment cannot be dealt with by short-term fixes.
- It may will not provide long-term jobs in significant numbers nor quality training that could affect the skills stock of the country. Historically, the larger the job creation scheme the "harder it appears to offer genuine work to participants without displacing private-sector activity" (Meager, 1998, p 37). Because of the long queue of applicants, turnover (or churning) has to be built into the scheme in order to meet targets for helping the 250,000.
- For many critics the issue is of a more general nature in that it represents a new form of discipline being enforced on the unemployed and by extension the employed labour force. The arguments put forward by Gray (1998) suggest that because the impact on long-term jobs will be so low it can only be an attempt to impose a new work discipline and work ethic. Many of Frank Field's pronouncements, pointing to work as a necessary good irrespective of its quality, conditions or pay (Field, 1995) seem to echo this.
- The criticisms of Coates and Barratt Brown (1996) reflect a deeper unease that the 'New Deal' tackles the issue of unemployment in a limited way rather than grasping the fundamentals. For them an imposition of a shorter working week and work-sharing could have made a far greater and longer lasting impact. Choosing this package effectively steers Labour away from other more radical policies that could have meant much more when combined at the European level. Hence new Labour's failure to make common cause with Lionel Jospin

when he proposed financing public spending on unemployment through Euro–Bonds. This, together with a wider agreement on shorter working hours with no loss of pay for the workers, could have made a significant impact on unemployment across the spectrum (Gray, 1998, p 6).

• There is a more economistic criticism of job activation strategies as a way of helping the young and long-term unemployed. Much of the evaluation of the Special Employment Measures (SEMs) programmes of the 1970s focused on quantifying the cost per job of direct work creation and job subsidies through such concepts as deadweight, job substitution and displacement and 'churning'. Deadweight is where subsidies are expended on jobs that would have been created anyway by employers without subsidy. Displacement or substitution of employment is the situation where the job created by the programme/subsidy results in the loss or transfer of a job from elsewhere. Churning describes a situation where individuals continually return to ALMP programmes and distort or disguise the actual effect on the unemployed. Each of these essentially 'economistic' concepts seeks to measure the quantitative effectiveness of programmes. Much of the evaluation of SEMs in the UK has been of this type, assessing the extent to which the measures have ensured a net return on monies expended. What it has shown is that the job creation schemes do have a high deadweight component meaning the public money is being paid to employers for employing people they would have taken on anyway. They also tend to substitute scheme members for other categories of unemployed meaning that again there is little net overall benefit from the scheme. Most empirical research (OECD, 1996; McGregor et al, 1996; Auer, 1996; Meager, 1998) tends to be in agreement that smaller more targeted schemes work better when combined with personal and individual job-search advice. They have less deadweight and substitution effects and when combined with training suited to local labour market conditions can be more successful in job retention terms over the medium to long term. Particular studies of 'workfare' schemes that contain tighter benefits or benefit sanctions show little evidence of success (Meager, 1998, p 41). When considering 'compulsion' after undertaking a review of international practice it was found that there was:

... no convincing evidence that compulsory participation improves the performance of active measures ... compulsion

> may further stigmatise the LTU [long-term unemployed], with
> employers aware that they participate in a scheme simply to
> secure benefit entitlement rather than through positive jobsearch
> motivation. (Meager, 1998, p 41)

Because the New Deal has had such a short period of operation it is difficult to evaluate its effects at this stage. In the past very little of the evaluatory concern has been on the actual quality of the jobs created or on the social impact and longer-term employability of the employees. However, this aspect is crucial from a sustainable point of view as the general perspective of providers and doers might be that the process and output of the programmes as economically low and psychologically unrewarding, 'not proper work'. Many accounts of drop-out rates indicate that this can be a problem for many such schemes (Layard and Philpot, 1991). However, this does not mean that all schemes are like this and many such as the Wise Group scheme in Glasgow demonstrated that community objectives, high value output and good training can be reconciled.

Overall then the introduction of the New Deal has brought with it uncertainties about the style and approach of New Labour. The trade unions while welcoming in general the package have had reservations about the scheme, in particular, its compulsory element and effect on wages and existing workers. UNISON, for instance, has issued a detailed briefing to its branches itemising the issues that need to be dealt with under the Welfare to Work heading (www.unison.org.uk). In its opinion there should be no difference in contracts, the scheme participants should be given equal representation rights, no existing worker should be displaced as a result and a 'normal' rate of pay should be offered. It also seeks to gain agreement that those taken on be retained after the six month subsidy ends. It wants training to be of a recognised quality and be delivered with a 'supporter' who has appropriate training and recognition within their job. Elements such as these would qualitatively transform the content and experience of the scheme and imbue it with positive and solidaristic elements. It is too early to say if this or the more slimmed down version of the programme will emerge in the longer run.

Training

When the previous labour administration left office in 1979, Panitch (1980) could speak of Britain being a semi-corporatist state. This was especially true of the training and skills development area which was linked to national plans and frameworks. There were in existence institutions such as the National Economic Development Office (NEDO) with its overall and sectoral planning arms, industry training boards, the Manpower Services Commission and various other State and semi-State agencies. Since that time virtually all of these institutions have disappeared and there has been a return to voluntarism and a move away from direct State involvement in training and its provision. Farnham and Lupton (1994) attribute this shift towards free-market solutions to the 'British training problem' that emphasises 'flexibility' and the inculcation of an enterprise culture. Nowhere is this more marked than in the ending of the industry training boards and of the Manpower Services Commission. Both were seen as corporatist and tripartite hangovers where union power continued. With their closure the privatisation of training could flourish to the extent that by the end of the 1980s three quarters of training places, although financed by the State, were provided by companies or private agencies. The Training and Enterprise Councils (TECs) are the culmination of this process of 'marketisation' as now 82 local and regional TECs undertake local training. They are financed through commercial contracts with the government and they then sub-contract training to local agencies on a competitive basis. The outcome of this process has been a decentralisation of training provision and an increased variability in content and quality. It also stands as another example of the sub-contract State where government denudes itself of core responsibilities (Gray, 1998, p 5).

New Labour's agenda is emerging and retains much of what went before, so agencies such as TECs, Business Link, Business Connect and Local Enterprise Companies (LECs) continue to be the key providers or 'partners' in training. However, the emphasis on flexibility has changed. The older Tory approach stressed numerical flexibility – arrangements such as temporary contracts, fixed period working, sub-contract formats and greater part-time work. For Marginson a new language of flexibility is emerging:

> **In contrast, new Labour is stressing the importance of increasing qualitative flexibility, through training and the acquisition of new skills, so as to make workers more adaptable. (Marginson, 1998)**

The government strategy is to pursue the modernisation of skills through the inauguration of 'lifelong learning'. Learning becomes something that an individual undertakes throughout their 'work career' and not one restricted to given times, to narrow job demands or particular employers. In line with European Union (EU) developments it is now *employability* within firms, local and national labour markets that is to be prioritised rather than a simple qualifications increase. It shifts responsibility for employment away from the State having to underwrite full employment and moves it to the individual who by dint of their learning efforts can deal with the dynamics of the labour market. To support this a number of new initiatives have been started such as the University For Industry. This national scheme aims to provide comprehensive advice and provision of basic training to people at any stage in their development. It seeks to improve the availability and quality of learning materials, link existing provision and stimulate demand through the use of computer-based training possibilities. Alongside this is the development of Individual Learning Accounts. The government has promised to create initially one million accounts with £150 in them. These Individual Learning Accounts can be augmented by other money from individual and corporate sources throughout a career to give people easy access to a range of training when they need it. The government is also supporting corporate programmes such as Investors in People. This award is given to British companies that achieve a pre-set standard of training excellence, employee development and good communication practice. The Investors in People standard aims to enhance training and development provision for employees, with the intention of improving an organisation's business performance. So far more than 4,000 organisations have received the award. Investors in People is attractive to business for many reasons, due to its association of business improvement with a better trained and motivated workforce, giving employees a better understanding of the business and promoting staff involvement. Together these schemes form the basis for the Lifelong Learning Initiative that has been put forward.

In addition there is now a requirement from Europe that the government undertakes a plan for skills development under Objective 4 of the European Structural Funds. The first such plan was created in November 1997 and covers the period up to 1999. This includes within it the government's analysis of and plans for skills development and adaptation across the country. It also has to set up performance indicators to monitor skills and an implementation programme to fund their improvement (DfEE, 1997e).

Because of the newness of the Lifelong Learning Initiative we must await the substantive proposals and the likely impact of the University for

Industry. However, what is evident is a reluctance to change back to the tripartite structures of the past. Trade unions are one of the partners involved in shaping policy but they do not have a privileged place within it. The key partners include employers, individuals, education and training providers, government and the trade union. As such the latter are one among a host of stakeholders with an input to match.

Employee relations

The 1997 election manifestos of the Conservative Party and Labour Party did differ considerably. The former wished to maintain Britain's opt out of the Social Charter, exempt the UK from the European Working Time Directive, ensure that strike action would have to be approved by a majority of affected members and enable the public to sue trade unions where strikes had a 'disproportionate effect'. For Labour there was a full programme of reforms, a number of which were diametrically opposed to Tory policies. It signed up to the Social Charter soon after the election, it favoured implementation of the European Working Time Directive and it has sought to selectively dismantle some of the more onerous restrictions on trade union activity. In addition, the long awaited national minimum wage would be decided by a newly-created Low Pay Commission. Trade union recognition procedures were to be created and staff at Government Commission Headquarters were to have their rights to trade union membership restored.

All in all the new strategy sought to get rid of the worst excesses of ultra-restrictionist trade union laws and replace these with a set of minimum standards across the economy. At the same time trade union recognition and the extension of the European elements of the Social Charter would at last restore equal treatment to UK workers. For Gennard all the reforms taken together signalled a "new employment relationship, based on partnership, between employers and employees" (Gennard, 1998, p 10). This culminated in the publication in the May 1998 by Margaret Beckett of the White Paper entitled *Fairness at work* (DTI, 1998). As well as giving details of the government's proposed statutory trade union recognition procedure, the White Paper outlines a range of other employment law reforms in areas such as individual employee protection against unfair dismissal, dismissals during disputes, representation during grievance and disciplinary procedures, maternity rights and parental and family leave. Three elements of the new policy warrant comment: the trade union recognition procedures, the minimum pay provisions and the acceptance of European employment reforms.

Trade union recognition

The White Paper sets out proposals for legislation to provide for trade union recognition where this is favoured by a majority of an appropriate group of employees. The proposals draw on the joint statement on recognition agreed between the Confederation of British Industry (CBI) and the Trades Union Congress (TUC) in December 1997. There will be a statutory procedure under which, in the absence of voluntary agreement with an employer, unions holding a certificate of independence may refer claims for recognition to a revamped Central Arbitration Committee. Evidence of reasonable support among the employees concerned will be a condition for the Central Arbitration Committee proceeding with the application. In the event of continuing disagreement between employer and union over the appropriateness of the bargaining unit proposed by the union, the Central Arbitration Committee will determine its scope. Where the employer then accepts that the union enjoys the support of a majority of the bargaining unit, or the union can demonstrate that it has more than 50% of the bargaining unit in membership, the Central Arbitration Committee will issue a declaration that the union is to be recognised. Otherwise, the Central Arbitration Committee will arrange for a secret ballot of the bargaining unit to be conducted and will issue a declaration that the union is to be recognised if a majority of those voting and at least 40% of those eligible to vote have supported recognition. Where a union achieves recognition via the statutory procedure, the employer and the union must try to reach a procedure agreement setting out how they will conduct collective bargaining.

The reaction from the social partners has been mixed. The CBI's Director General Adair Turner said that the government has listened to key business concerns and "the approach to statutory trade union recognition, while not welcome, should be workable" (Turner, 1998). The CBI is worried about the proposed right of employees to be represented by a union official over grievances or disciplinary matters, which could create substantial burdens, particularly for small firms. The employers bodies have also been lobbying hard to persuade the government to change the procedure whereby automatic union recognition is granted where half the workforce were already in union membership. The TUC has been supportive of the measure and sees it as an important tool in restoring trade union density across all sections of employment. However, it has opposed two elements. The first is the specification of 40% of the eligible membership as the threshold for recognition, which it says places unrealistic obstacles in the way. The second issue is the exemption of firms below 20 employees from the legislation, which it says represents omitting a large percentage of the overall working population. To Hall the outcome is a compromise:

> **After months of lobbying and counter-lobbying by the TUC and within the government by 'old' and 'new' Labour, the recognition proposals appear ultimately to have been shaped by the overriding priority given within Downing Street to maintaining the Labour government's business-friendly credentials. On the headline issues, the White Paper's formula – including a 40% 'yes' vote threshold and an exemption for small firms – is rather closer to the CBI's negotiating position than to the TUC's. But other aspects, such as the absence of a specific threshold of employee support for recognition applications and the approach to be taken on defining the bargaining unit, are more welcome to the TUC. (Hall, 1997)**

The subsequent Bill published at the end of January 1999 did concede some small points to the employers lobby, for instance the idea of unlimited compensation for unfair dismissal was dropped and a ceiling of £50,000 put in its place. The main trade union recognition proposals have largely gone through unscathed with the 40% vote confirmed and the automatic union recognition clause granted in cases where 50% of workers are in union membership. This latter clause may not have the major impact the employers envisaged since less than one quarter of workers are now union members (*The Independent*, 15 September 1998). However, the report points out that the effect could be more marked in particular sectors. Marginson (1998) also indicates that of all the workplaces without union recognition at present only 2% of them have union levels of more than 50%.

Minimum pay

Since the abolition of the national wages councils pay levels have been subject to little regulation apart from market constraints. This has resulted in pockets of poverty pay and wide variations in rewards. The incoming government moved quickly to fulfil a manifesto commitment and established the Low Pay Commission. The Commission's task has been to take evidence and then make recommendations to the government on the appropriate level for the national minimum wage. In the Summer of 1998 it proposed that the minimum wage be £3.60 per hour rising to £3.70 in June 2000. The key area of controversy has been the inclusion or exclusion of 16- to 25-year-olds within the ambit of the legislation. The government required the Commission to set a lower rate for this age group and this has been set at £3.00 (1999) and £3.20 (2000). The Low Pay Commission is to stay in existence and monitor and oversee the effects of the minimum wage on the labour market.

Two issues centrally concerned the employers. The first was the impact on competitiveness and with that ultimately jobs in the economy: setting the wage too high would effectively mean exporting jobs to higher productivity economies. The second concern was that any raising of pay thresholds would then entail a knock-on effect as other more highly paid workers sought to re-establish pay differentials (Gennard, 1998, p 8). Trade unions on the other hand were looking for a base level of more than £4.00 per hour and one that started at the age of 18. The out-turn does appear once more to favour the employers stance, as Edwards notes:

> **The rate of GBP 3.60 is around the level at which many employers were arguing that the effects would be manageable. This outcome reflects the watchwords of caution and pragmatism running through the LPC [Low Pay Commission] report ... the Government's response was to lower the development rate to GBP 3.00 (and also to accept the GBP 3.60 adult rate without any commitment to raising it to the recommended GBP 3.70 in 2000). (Edwards, 1998)**

One of the reasons given for the overall approach was the likely effect that the minimum pay would have upon the New Deal proposals on helping unemployed people into the labour market. According to the Low Pay Commission report the commissioners were keen to avoid any disincentive for employers to become involved in training schemes under the New Deal (Low Pay Commission, 1998, paras 5.26-29). Edwards regards the outcome as a "significant achievement" given the very different concerns that the trade unions, employers and government had at the outset.

In recent studies the impact of the minimum wage has been estimated and this shows that between 1.7 and 2.1 million employees look set to benefit from it (*Labour Market Trends*, 1998). The main recipients are women in part-time employment where currently 52% earn below the national minimum wage and younger workers who also are disproportionately affected.

Europe and employment policy

The speed with which the government signed up to the Social Charter gave grounds to think that this represented a new turn in British government policy towards Europe. The European concept of 'social partnership' with extended rights and consultation given to the employers and trade unions seems to fit with the New Labour vision of a new partnership based on consensus rather than conflict. Since signing up there has been backing given to the new Working Time Directive that is likely to have a large impact in the UK, but also less enthusiasm for certain aspects of the Social Charter especially the proposals for the establishment of a formal information and consultation mechanism in UK firms. In relation to the latter this does show how far the Blair government has gone in accepting an employers' perspective on European legislation and regulation.

As with many of the items of European social policy this issue has a long history, effectively first mooted in the early 1970s as the Fifth Directive on Company Law and subsequently seeing the light of day as the European Company. In order to expedite matters the European Commission (EC) set up an expert group under the chairmanship of the former EC Vice-president Etienne Davignon, in order to try and identify a possible solution which would meet everyone's concerns. The Davignon Group's report was presented to the EC meeting on 14 May 1997. However, the furore over the closure of the Renault Vilvoorde plant somewhat overtook these deliberations and highlighted the gaps in existing consultative arrangements in current domestic and transnational companies.

The Commission had suggested measures in three areas:

- mechanisms that allow early identification of negative social consequences of changes in work organisation;
- the establishment of permanent, structured mechanisms for informing/ consulting workers;

• the introduction of effective sanctions to be applied in cases of violation of the workers' right to be informed and consulted.

The proposals were fed into the 'social dialogue process' that has in the past two years successfully introduced directives on Parental Leave and Atypical Work. The hope was that this emerging 'social dialogue process' could allow disparate views to be heard, provide agreed workable solutions and avoid a top-down imposition of legislation. However, this has been dealt a blow due to the dissension over the need for information and consultation rights at national level. Union des Industries de la Communauté Européene (UNICE) (the European employers' peak association) backed by the CBI and German, Portuguese and Greek employers bodies have indicated their outright opposition to such a directive and have refused to start negotiations with the unions on the issue (*The Guardian*, 17 March 1998). More surprisingly to many is the support given to this coalition by the British Labour government which is insisting that this is not a European matter and under the principles of subsidiarity is the province of national law. Peter Mandelson further underlined this opposition when taking over from Margaret Beckett at the Department for Trade and Industry. In an interview with *The Independent* newspaper he said:

> **We have signed up to the Social Chapter and we support it ...**
> **but it is not a back door means of winning rights through Europe**
> **that the Government here is unwilling to legislate upon.** (*The*
> *Independent*, **15 September 1998**)

Such a position of favouring the Social Chapter but not the specific reforms it contains has led many to consider that the Blair government's commitment to employment rights reform is hollow and minimalistic. Labour is seen as actively taking up the neo-liberal cause and trying to dissuade other member states from enacting anything that might increase labour costs:

> **Arguing that a stronger Social Chapter might threaten jobs, Blair**
> **appears content with the Tory legacy of a national economic**
> **strategy which has attempted to secure competitive advantage**
> **through low labour costs, low social security charges and legal**
> **repression of trade unions.** (Gray, 1998, p 3)

In this particular instance there is now great uncertainty about whether a Framework Agreement can be reached in this area and the larger consequences have been described as a "serious setback for the Social Dialogue" by Jacques Santer (*Guardian*, 17 March 1998). It is yet to be seen whether the Commission will adopt the consultation track and implement a directive against the views of the opposing coalition (EIRR, March 1998, p 2).

Conclusion

In the areas explored here it does appear that the Labour government has made an ambivalent start. In its 'Third Way' approach, it has taken up measures that have a distinctly free-market character, with large vestiges of voluntarism and deregulation. On the other hand it wishes to be seen as a social reformer, ending youth unemployment and enforced idleness while also bringing in a floor of basic rights into the employment and labour market area. Hence the government can describe its overall 'Fairness at work' package as "a balanced approach consistent with enabling employers to find ways of ensuring that their companies are competitive" (DTI, 1998). The reiteration of the needs of companies, of the new competitiveness and of globalised pressures bearing on the labour market does echo much of the managerialist language heard within enterprises. Such rhetoric has displaced an emphasis on fairness and exploitation and also more fundamentally it has ceded control of the economy to those forces. New Labour can no longer intervene and control in the interests of equity. Nor can it put forward solutions based on older varieties of collective ownership or industrial democracy. For Coates and Barratt Brown (1996) the New Labour agenda individualises people in the market. It individualises them in terms of taking responsibility for training and for job search. Class is replaced by community which has numerous stakeholders and interest groups all of whom have legitimate demands.

Gray sees this ideological shift coming out strongly in relation to the new policies on employment and the labour market. For her the continuance of Tory policies are disguised by a different rhetoric but essentially they represent an attack on the poor and working class from three directions.

The first is a hardening of the work discipline to be imposed upon the unemployed. The second is to postpone even what

little improvement in trade union rights had been promised. The third is to embrace the neo-liberal 'labour market flexibility' agenda, resisting most attempts to improve social protection of labour at European and at UK level. (Gray, 1998, p 1)

In the areas of the New Deal for employment, the development of adequate training structures, trade union rights and European social reform the evidence is of ideological support for advance while at the same time offering little practical enablement for that to happen. The resultant compromises are alienating the traditional supporters of the Party while not producing the necessary wherewithal to keep the new supporters happy. It is still too early to say what the out come of many of the policies will be, but the gathering pressures in many areas of New Labour's employment policy may erupt if the real divisions of poverty and social exclusion are not tackled.

NINE

The new politics of law and order: Labour, crime and justice

Sarah Charman and Stephen P. Savage

> I know I sometimes go into prisons feeling tough but I always come away feeling that 90% of the people there are not evil but somehow inadequate. The roots of crime are still social deprivation, broken homes and all the rest. (James Callaghan, Labour Home Secretary, 1970)

Paul: Number 28's been burgled. I bet it's that gang of yobbos again.

Helen: Even if they catch them they get off scot-free.

Voiceover: Already crime has doubled under the Tories.

Paul: If they get back next time there'd be more criminals getting off.

(Labour Party political broadcast, January 1997)

Introduction

To an extent 'law and order' policy has presented New Labour with one of its biggest challenges. Labour may have had to fight extremely hard to establish itself as a Party seen as capable of managing the economy, or as being held to be reasonably sound on defence, but particular difficulties applied when it came to policies on crime, policing and criminal justice. After all, it has had to compete with the Conservatives' apparently natural status as the 'Party of law and order'. Traditionally, the Conservative Party has been able to point to its 'tough not tender' approach to law and order as evidence that it, not Labour, is to be trusted with waging a war on crime. Conservative policies in the years running up to the 1997 General Election were notably more 'tough' in the accepted sense than at any time in the post-war period. At the very least, this presented New Labour with an uphill task.

Seen in this light it is difficult to deny that Labour has, by some standards, been remarkably successful. Labour managed to enter the General Election having at least neutralised the Conservatives' identity as the natural Party of law and order. As the key elements of its crime policy began to unfold in the early years of office, it could claim not only to have gained the backing of senior police officers and senior prison managers ('Editorial', *Prison Service Journal*, May 1998) but also to have won over some of its former critics on the Left (see below). This was no mean achievement. On the way, spearheaded in opposition first by Shadow Home Secretary Tony Blair and then by Jack Straw, the Party had decided to break from tradition and throw down new gauntlets. In any inventory of the 'newness' of New Labour, law and order policy would have to occupy a leading position.

This chapter will outline, explain and assess Labour's policies on law and order. The first section will provide a backcloth to this discussion by documenting key phases in Conservative policy on crime from 1979-97. It will be argued that Labour's shifting agenda for law and order can only be fully understood in the light of these developments. The chapter will then move on to examine the policy agenda within key stages of the criminal process. In so doing it will attempt to contrast New Labour policy with the dominant ethos of earlier Labour approaches to crime and criminal justice. While supporting the view that Labour has in some ways moved sharply away from its former 'liberal' stance on criminal justice, it will conclude that a fuller assessment points to the danger of overstating this shift. Not only is it important to be careful not to conflate Labour's *rhetoric* on crime with its *policies*, it is also necessary to acknowledge the 'liberal' philosophy underpinning much of Labour's strategy for 'community safety'. On balance, Labour's crime policy has been essentially radical, but it is not the sort of radicalism that can easily be associated with a drift to the Right.

Law and order under the Conservatives: tough–tender–tough again

The essence of Labour's strategy for criminal justice is set out in the 1998 Crime and Disorder Act (Home Office, 1998d). This piece of legislation, as will be argued below, constitutes a veritable paradigm shift in the discourse of crime control. In criminal justice terms, it might be seen as a form of 'New Deal'. However, elements of the Act were inherited from the previous Conservative administration and certain features were shaped by the political battles which took place when Labour stood in opposition. It is difficult to appreciate New Labour policy on crime without examining the destiny of crime policy under the Conservatives. What such an examination reveals is a policy agenda subject to quite remarkable sea changes and reversals (Savage, 1998a).

The Conservatives took office very much on a 'law and order' ticket. On the eve of the 1979 General Election Margaret Thatcher exclaimed: "What the country needs is less tax and more law and order" (see Savage, 1990). That sentiment set in motion the first stage of what can be seen as the 'three phases' of Conservative policy on law and order stretching from 1979 to 1997. The policy agendas in each case were shaped by the political and economic configurations of that period; in the politics of the 1980s and 1990s, crime policy has in many ways held centre stage.

The Tory agenda for crime which emerged during their first period in office bore very much the marks of a 'get tough' approach. Commitments were made to increase the resources available to the police and increase police numbers; pledges were also made to increase police powers in the 'war against crime'. New sentences were made available to the courts, mainly targeted at young offenders which, when applied to the newly revamped detention centres, complied with the rhetoric of the 'short sharp shock'. To complete the deterrent package, the government announced a huge prison-building programme to ensure that sentencers were not to be constrained by a shortage of prison places. A strengthened police force, stiffer sentences and a more expansive penal regime were to spearhead the Conservatives' early crime policy.

Despite the heavily authoritarian rhetoric of this era and the plethora of nakedly deterrent measures, it is important not to ignore the fact that the legislation largely responsible for the tougher approach, the 1982 Criminal Justice Act (Home Office, 1982), also heralded steps to divert some classes of offenders from custody and to stiffen the conditions under which custodial punishments could be metered out (Savage, 1990). Quietly, and certainly away from the gaze of the Conservative Party Annual Conference (at which 'red meat' has traditionally been thrown from the platform), the strategy of 'bifurcation' or 'twin-tracking' was emerging. Bifurcation, as Hudson (1987) has argued, is an approach to crime policy which strengthens sentences for some groups of offenders/offences while reducing them, or orienting them in a non-custodial direction, for others. This approach was to be sustained through much of the Conservatives' time in office, at least until the arrival of Michael Howard as Home Secretary (as shall be seen later).

As the 1980s wore on, a rather different emphasis in crime policy began to emerge. Above all, there was a definite shift in attitude within the Home Office to the role of custody in criminal justice. In official papers criticisms of the effectiveness of imprisonment (for all but the most serious offenders) appeared. Preference was expressed for the more extensive application of tougher *non-custodial* forms of punishment, *community penalties*. Community service and supervision orders were to take priority over prisons as weapons in the war against crime. Alongside this 'liberal' development, the government also began to place value on *crime prevention* as an effective strategy for crime reduction. Criminologists had long argued that crime policies focused on reducing opportunities for crime, such as 'target hardening' (better security of premises, alarm systems, and so on) would reap more rewards in cost-benefit terms than focusing on punishing offenders. The Home Office began to take seriously the principles of 'situational crime prevention'; the launch of 'Crime Concern' in 1987, set up to mobilise partnerships between public and private agencies for crime prevention purposes, was at least a symbolic expression of this. It is not without significance that the Home Secretary for much of this period was Douglas Hurd, very much on the liberal ('wet') wing of the Party. Again, the process of bifurcation during this phase should not be ignored. The 1988 Criminal Justice Act actually toughened sentences for sex and drugs-related offences. However, in this case the pendulum had swung in the opposite direction: it was the non-custodial measures which were in the limelight. While this shift may have been disguised to an extent by the right-wing dressing of notions such as 'just deserts' (see Savage and Nash, 1994), it was difficult to deny that what was taking place was a definite move towards a more liberal criminal justice strategy – more 'tender' than 'tough'.

The legislative expression of this phase – the 1991 Criminal Justice Act – was also to mark its zenith. The political upheavals of the early 1990s were to see to that. It was no accident that the cultural shift which took place from the mid-1980s, heralding a much more 'reasoned' policy approach – one less red in tooth and claw and more steeped in criminological research – took place during a period in which the Conservatives were politically secure. The opposition Parties offered little threat and internal dissent within the Conservative Party was muted and ineffectual. That was certainly not to be the case by the early 1990s. Criminal justice policy was to bear the brunt of that.

It is difficult to envisage a policy reversal in any area of public policy on a par with that which took place in criminal justice policy under Michael Howard. From a point somewhere in 1992, the whole edifice of the late-1980s agenda began to crumble. The factors underpinning this shift are discussed elsewhere (Savage, 1998a; Dunbar and Langdon, 1998; Wilson and Ashton, 1998), but they include the traumas and public anxieties associated with the killing of James Bulger, a two-year-old murdered by two young boys, internal dissent within the Conservative Party over Europe and the rapid decline in public support for the Conservatives relative to Labour post the 1992 General Election. Law and order policy was to become a key player as this crisis unfolded.

At the 1993 Conservative Party Annual Conference Howard announced his notorious '27 measures' to combat crime. These covered virtually every aspect of the criminal justice process, from amendments to the right of silence – against the recommendations of the 1993 Royal Commission on Criminal Justice, suspects were to lose their unfettered right to remain silent (judges could now comment negatively on a suspect's decision to remain silent) – to a clamp-down on squatting, anti-hunt demonstrations and even 'rave' parties! However, it was Howard's declaration that 'prison works', discussed later, which attracted most attention. At a stroke it created clear blue water between the Howard regime and the Conservative criminal justice policy which immediately preceded it. The prison had returned as the key weapon against crime. We were back to getting 'tough' again.

Howard had dramatically raised the stakes of the law and order debate. Some would say he had to. Whereas as late as April 1992 opinion polls were showing that 41% of those polled thought that the Conservative Party had 'the best policies on crime', by March 1993 that figure had dropped to 19% (*The Guardian*, 21 March 1994). The 'Party of law and order' was losing ground fast. The potential electoral fall-out from this threatened to be disastrous. 'Regaining the high ground' on law and order had become a number one priority. However, Howard's pledges set in motion a spiral of rhetoric into which the Labour Party in opposition was soon to hurl itself.

Rather than seek to counter Howard's new agenda with a critique of the effectiveness of custody as a penal strategy, Labour chose a very different tack: it decided to take him on at his own game.

New Labour and the new politics of law and order

It is difficult to summarise Labour's 'traditional' stance on law and order. As Downes and Morgan (1997) have argued, there was for much of the post-war period something of a policy vacuum of in this area. Put simply, law and order was not high on Labour's list of priorities or concerns. A review of Labour's posturings on law and order during much of the 1980s would reveal more concern with questions of civil liberties, prisoners' rights, or police accountability than with particular policies on crime reduction. Typically, Labour discourse on the issue crime took more the character of a *critique* than a strategy – a critique of inequities in criminal justice, of limitations to prisoners' rights, of shortcomings in the system of police accountability, or of lack of protections for suspects of crime (Goddard, 1997). Alongside this, what effort went into the law and order debate was concentrated on emphasising the *social basis of crime* in terms of the linkage between crime and unemployment, deprivation and so on. When it came to finding ways of actually confronting the problem of crime from *within* the criminal justice system, as distinct from problems relating to the agencies charged with controlling crime (such as the police and prisons), there was often silence.

That was to change dramatically in the political discourse that emerged between the 1992 and 1997 General Elections. The hallmark of this was Blair's much mocked dictum 'Tough on crime, tough on the causes of crime' (*The Independent*, 4 December 1993), a slogan expressed while Blair was Shadow Home Secretary. This seemingly simple maxim, later to be a key slogan within the Labour Party manifesto (Labour Party, 1997a) in fact was loaded with meaning. Not only was Labour concerned to tackle the (social) causes of crime, fairly familiar traditional territory (whereby crime policy is a sub-set of social policy), but it was to go a step further and enter into the less familiar discourse of 'blame', 'condemnation' and 'personal responsibility'. Indicative of this new politics was Blair's later statement as leader:

> We should [not] seek to disavow personal responsibility for crime. That is, ultimately, to deny individuality. Those who commit crime should be brought to justice. Not to do so is unjust to their victims. (Blair, 1996a)

A legitimate place was being carved out for 'action' against offenders. It was Labour's way of avoiding the old accusation from the Right that in focusing solely on the causes of crime it was in effect *excusing crime*. This was never a justified (or indeed logical) deduction. However, it was an accusation which, in the high stakes of the Howard agenda, Labour was anxious to deflect. The counter rhetoric was aimed at neutralising this potential Achilles' heel. 'Excusing crime' was to law and order policy what unilateral nuclear disarmament was to defence policy. Scotching this one would enable Labour to be able to claim, as it did in the Party manifesto, "Labour is the party of law and order in Britain today" (Labour Party, 1997a).

However, it would be erroneous to lay Labour's new politics of law and order simply at the feet of political outscoring. Indirectly, a heated debate within Left-wing criminology, over the issue of how to approach crime, had laid some of the foundations of Labour's new discourse. A group of criminologists known as 'Left Realists' set out a platform in the mid-1980s which attacked key features of the radical-Left paradigm for crime analysis (Lea and Young, 1984; Young, 1997). Most significant to this chapter was the accusation that radical analysis had tended to see the 'crime control industry' as more of a 'problem' than crime itself (Young, 1997, p 475). It had, the Realists argued, focused more on deficiencies and inequities within the machinery for law enforcement and criminal justice than it had on the problem of crime. Alternatively, it 'talked down' crime by seeing crime problems as media-led exaggerations of reality, as nothing more than a 'moral panic' (Young, 1997, p 478). The Left Realist retort was straightforward: *crime really is a problem*, and furthermore, *crime is a problem which disproportionately harms the weakest and most vulnerable in the community*. In other words, the Left should take crime seriously as a problem to be addressed, for it is the constituencies which the Left seeks to represent who suffer most from crime and disorder. 'Taking crime seriously' became a slogan differentiating one tradition of Left-wing criminology from another. It would seem that this sentiment did infiltrate the discourse of New Labour as it sought to formulate the agenda for crime policy. This was not the only example of an 'academic' criminological debate finding its way into the new politics of law and order, as shall be seen later.

As Jack Straw took over as Shadow Home Secretary, the head-to-head with Howard became, if anything, more pronounced. Often to the dismay of liberals and sectors of the Left (see later), Straw waded into the game of outgunning on rhetoric. For example, he attacked 'squeegee merchants' and 'winos' as part of his attack on 'antisocial behaviour':

> In conjunction with tackling the underlying causes of crime, the
> community has the right to expect more responsible and less
> anti-social behaviour from its citizens. That means less
> intimidation, bullying and loutish behaviour on the streets and
> in our towns and city centres. (Straw, 1995)

What was often associated with these sentiments was support for the idea
of 'zero-tolerance' policing (Bratton, 1998). This policing philosophy
emerged in the early 1990s in New York and was based on the principle
that if the police crack down on petty crimes and incivilities, that will
stop them escalating into more serious criminal problems – tolerate nothing
and 'stop the rot'. This in turn drew on what is known as 'broken windows'
theory (Wilson and Kelling, 1982) which, crudely put, postulates that
small-scale damages, if left untreated, will before long develop into major
damages – leave a broken window unrepaired and the whole building
will eventually be destroyed. However, it is important not to exaggerate
the extent to which Straw's attack on 'squeegee merchants' and the like
was engaging with a particular theory of crime and crime reduction. It
had much more to do with a nakedly political agenda. What was often
ignored by critics of Straw's stance was that, however inappropriate some
of these sentiments might have been, they seldom got above the rhetoric.
On matters of actual *policy*, an agenda very different in tone was emerging.
Rightly or wrongly, Straw seemed to be using certain, easy, targets to win
public support or at least neutralise the Tory's campaign. In that sense the
strategy seemed to have worked. In the months running up to the 1997
General Election public opinion polls had the two parties running neck-
and-neck in terms of public support for their approach to law and order
(*The Times*, 28 February 1997). On winning the election, it was now a
question of which policies were to follow.

Law and order policy I: law enforcement

The Labour Party manifesto had highlighted a number of priorities for
future action. These included: fast-track punishment for persistent young
offenders, a crackdown on petty crimes and 'neighbourhood disorder',
reform of the Crown Prosecution Service, crime prevention and more
police officers 'on the beat'. Whatever the populist flavour of some of the
measures proposed, what underpinned the new agenda was a serious and

far-reaching programme to tackle crime, employing strategies far more radical than many liberal critics had, at that stage at least, realised.

It is revealing that Labour should think to declare in its manifesto, "The police have our strong support". This was perhaps not just a message to the electorate. It could just as well have been directed at the Labour Left and the police themselves. The clashes between Labour-dominated metropolitan authorities and certain chief constables in the early- to mid-1980s, over the question of 'who controls the police?' (Reiner, 1992) had been such that Labour could easily be dubbed 'anti-police'. That would have been unfair, or even meaningless. However, it is appropriate to argue that much of the Labour-led discourse on British policing had focused more on means of *controlling* the police, in terms of increased accountability, than on the role of the police in controlling crime. Its concerns with policing were less about the extent to which the police were effective and more with whether the police were *accountable*. Whatever the merits of this approach, it created a situation in which the relationship between Labour and the police service was less than warm.

The thaw in this relationship began with the heated debate which surrounded the passage through Parliament of the 1994 Police and Magistrates' Courts Act. This Act introduced radical changes to the relationship between central government, local police authorities and the police (see Leishman et al, 1996). For many, it was a step towards government control of policing and a significant loss of local accountability. What the legislation did was help form some unusual campaign alliances (Cope et al, 1996), including one between senior police officers, in the shape of the Association of Chief Police Officers (ACPO), and Labour politicians, who together fought against central features of the Act, with some success (Cope et al, 1996). Tony Blair, as Shadow Home Secretary, made a keynote speech at the ACPO Conference in 1993, one apparently well received by the audience. A new understanding seemed to be in the air; Labour could begin to dismantle its image as 'anti-police'. From that point onwards Labour, first in opposition and subsequently in government, has worked closely with organisations representing the police in developing a policy for policing. Things had moved so far as to cause some on the Left to argue that Labour had become too close to the police and too prepared to accept the police view on policy from crime and policing. This was an issue which arose in the debate over the 1996 Police Bill, when until a late U-turn, it seemed Labour had accepted the police case that chief constables should have the capacity to authorise intrusive surveillance of premises (see Savage et al, 1997). Labour's 'support' for the police was another expression of the new 'realism' which was part and parcel of the new politics of law and order.

Labour's actual policy on policing as developed within this framework has been both consistent with and a departure from the policies of the Conservatives. Labour has accepted the constitutional reforms of the Police and Magistrates' Court Act but has seen within the Act the potential, perhaps underestimated by its critics (see Savage, 1998b), for *increasing* local influence over policing. For example, the Home Office has encouraged local police authorities to engage in extensive local consultation in drawing up the 'local policing plan' for the area. More generally, the Home Secretary has made clear his view that local police authorities should move from being the 'cinderella' of the tripartite system (in comparison to the Home Office and the chief constable) to becoming a central player in the development of policing policy. This is highly likely to be reinforced by the relatively greater assertiveness emerging from within by the new body representing all police authorities, the Association of Police Authorities (APA). This was apparent in the first Annual Report of APA, which stated that the establishment of the Association was "the first time police authorities have been able to speak with one authoritative voice, *alongside our tripartite partners*, ACPO and the Home Office" (APA, 1998, p 1; emphasis added) There would seem to be a process of 'power sharing' at work which could have profound implications for the concept and practice of 'constabulary independence', the sacred cow of British policing.

Another emergent feature of Labour policy, with its own implications for constabulary independence, is the process of *regionalisation*. Labour's commitment to regional assemblies will, it could be argued (APA, 1998), mean that in the not too distant future 'regional police forces', perhaps as few as 10, could replace the existing 43 separate forces in England and Wales. The Conservatives had caused consternation by including provisions for amalgamations of police forces in the Police and Magistrates' Court Act; regionalisation could dwarf that agenda. While the Conservatives' interest in amalgamation was largely driven by the concern for efficiency savings, the regionalisation of policing would be more concerned with the process of 'power sharing' through devolution and, arguably, involve the diminution of central controls over policing (APA, 1998).

There are signs that in terms of *expenditure* on policing, Labour is not prepared to 'bankroll' the service in the way the Conservatives did. Throughout the 1980s and early 1990s, the police were made very much a 'special case' vis-à-vis the rest of the public sector and levels of spending were kept above the going rate for other public services, and were not subjected to anything like the VFM (value-for-money) regimes of their colleagues in the other sectors. Although Labour has not fully reversed this trend, the fact that in the 1998 spending review the police were required to achieve efficiency savings of 2% over the year sent out the message that they are to be brought more in line with the rest of the public sector; this will in many ways be a painful process for the police, particularly so in the light of the relative laxity of financial regimes of the past.

However, the major departure from Conservative policy on policing comes in the form of the 1998 Crime and Disorder Act. This single piece of legislation, concerned in part with policing but with a lot more besides, threatens to transform the way we think about crime and the response to crime. Central measures contained in the Act include:

- an obligation placed on local authorities, the police, police authorities, health authorities and probation committees to work *in partnership* to develop and implement a strategy for tackling crime and disorder in their area; they will have a joint and formally stated responsibility for protecting the public and for maintaining *community safety*;
- as part of the process of forming a strategy for tackling crime and disorder, a requirement for the police and the local authorities to conduct a *crime audit* for their areas, which reviews patterns of crime and problems of disorder in those areas and will form the basis of action against crime;
- a requirement for local authorities to establish *Youth Offending Teams* and for the statutory bodies to formulate annual youth justice plans; a range of measures will be taken to speed up the process of youth justice;
- giving the courts new powers to pass *antisocial behaviour orders* in an attempt to counter those who harass or cause disturbance or disruption in their area; 'sex-offender orders', which will impose conditions on sex-offenders at large in the community; 'reparation orders', requiring young offenders to make reparation to victims of the community in general; 'parenting' orders requiring parents to abide by certain conditions set out by the court, including obligatory counselling;
- the Lord Chancellor setting up an advisory body which will help establish *sentencing guidelines* for the courts to strengthen the framework within which sentencing can take place and to introduce greater consistency in sentencing.

An analysis of the Crime and Disorder Act and its surrounding agenda leads to a number of conclusions. Firstly, that Labour sees the problems of law and order not just in terms of crime but against the wider backcloth of *community safety*. It recognises that 'social harm' and victimisation can come about as a result of non-criminal as well as criminal activities – the scenario, perhaps, of 'neighbours from hell'! The broader framework of 'public protection' or community safety is one which seeks to reduce fear and insecurity as well as criminal activity. Secondly, it is clear that Labour views the police as only *one* key agency in the fight against crime. This rests on the belief, well founded in criminological discourse, that without community support the police cannot succeed in controlling crime, hence the emphasis on 'partnerships'. Although many forces had worked towards developing partnerships with other agencies, they are now required to do so and in effect will have to learn to share power and decisions with those agencies. Thirdly, and most evidently, a central place is reserved for *local authorities* in controlling crime. This is highly influenced by the recommendations of the Morgan Report (Home Office, 1997) which advocated the partnership principle and the pivotal role for local authorities in fighting crime – a report which the Conservatives largely ignored.

Underpinning these factors is Labour's effective endorsement of the principle of *social crime prevention*. This places emphasis on early intervention and support for young persons at risk of future or further offending (hence the focus on youth offender teams and the plethora of measures on youth justice) and the importance of families and communities as networks of social control (see Pease, 1997). In turn this articulates with Labour's wider strategy to tackle 'social exclusion', an approach discussed elsewhere in this text (particularly Chapter Six and the Conclusion). Social crime prevention stands in contrast to the Conservative strategy for crime control, which was based on *deterrence* for individual offenders through stiffer sentencing and using the police as the front-line agency in the fight against crime. As further evidence of the philosophical gap between Conservative and Labour, the creation of 'reparation orders' is consistent with the notion of *retributive justice*, which focused on 'constructive punishments' which aim to reintegrate the offender into the community, rather than banish them from the community. Unfortunately, as shall be seen shortly, Labour's insistence on remaining faithful to imprisonment as a tool for crime control somewhat undermines this 'liberal' approach.

Taken together, the measures contained in the Crime and Disorder Act constitute a radical departure from the previous Conservative agenda (although perhaps less so than the agenda pre-Howard as outlined earlier).

Law enforcement is recast in the form of 'public protection'. The police, probation and the prisons might all become different branches of a coordinated 'public protection agency'.

Law and order policy II: sentencing and penal strategies

Labour and Tories do battle

It would seem that the piles of paperwork in Mr Straw's office marked 'police', 'courts', 'prisons' and so on show distinct differences in terms of their size. The 'prisons' file could be held with a small paper clip. While the new Labour administration has been talking of the importance of the police, community relationships, working in partnership, juvenile justice and more, the state of the prison service has been largely ignored. While to some, the state of British prisons has always been one of 'crisis', in recent years with prison numbers rising by 40% in the years 1993-97, an avoidable, manufactured crisis may now be emerging. Yet Labour has been strangely quiet about its penal policies and after a year in government the situation, with regard to prison numbers at least, has not improved.

The same could certainly not be said about Jack Straw's predecessor, Michael Howard. As mentioned earlier, the Conservative government during its 18-year reign, followed a circular policy of 'tough–tender–tough' with regard to criminal justice, the latter stage the 'toughest' seen for many years (Dunbar and Langdon, 1998). The arguments about the causes of the Conservatives' abrupt changes in punitiveness are documented elsewhere (Savage, 1998a; Newburn, 1995) but can be in part attributed to financial pressures, political pressures, public pressures and also the pressures from the new sounding Labour Party, which Blair at the 1993 Labour Party Annual Conference termed, "the Party of law and order". Michael Howard responded to these pressures by turning his back on the ground-breaking work of the fairly liberal measures contained in the 1991 Criminal Justice Act by announcing, famously, that 'prison works'. Delegates at the Conservative Party Conference were delighted, so too were the sections of the media which had so vociferously fought the campaign to convince the public that this country was 'soft' on criminals. This simple yet ambiguous statement designed to win over the Tory faithful and convince the public that they were winning the 'tough' stakes brought about a 25% increase in the prison population in just three years.

By using this statement, Howard was throwing the gauntlet to the newly 'toughened up' Labour Party. Nobody could deny that prison did indeed work by stopping criminals from committing crime while they were locked up. Nobody dared deny that the protection of the public was paramount in a democratic system of criminal justice. Howard played a clever political game and waited patiently for Labour to deny this was true so the champion of 'toughness' could be crowned. Labour not only resisted the temptation but irritated the Conservative Party further by going ahead of them in the polls. Labour was being taken more and more seriously in terms of its penal policies, achieved through a change in emphasis from a concentration on a reductionist policy in terms of imprisonment and on the improvement of prison conditions to a twin-track policy where there is a legitimate role for the prison for those who deserve it but that community penalties can be equally if not more effective (see earlier comments about bifurcation). The latter part of this strategy could prove more difficult for the Labour Party in terms of convincing the public as shall be seen later on.

The battle between the two Parties continued and strengthened in the years running up to the 1997 General Election. Both Parties aimed to portray the other as 'soft' on crime culminating in an extraordinary Labour Party political broadcast which cast the Tories as 'letting criminals off the hook' as seen in the opening quote of this chapter. Liberal commentators were worried but believed that the rhetoric would give way to sensible penal strategies once the election was won. Polly Toynbee in *The Guardian* said that "in liberal circles, there are few names more reviled than that of Jack Straw: ... they shudder and wave garlic at the sound of his name" (P. Toynbee, *The Guardian*, 20 January 1997). However, she finished the article by arguing, perhaps hoping, that "Jack Straw is nothing like as illiberal as he pretends to be now".

A strangely similar story occurred in the 1995 election campaign in New South Wales, Australia between the two major political parties there, both trying to be the 'toughest' on crime. When one Party argued that it would bring in 'three strikes and you're out', based on the American model of a life sentence for a person's third serious conviction, the opposing Party responded with 'one strike and you're out'! (White and Haines, 1996). While the situation was not reduced to that level of farce in this country, commentators were surprised at the lengths to which Jack Straw went to secure the support of voters.

The 1996 Crime (Sentences) Bill and subsequent 1997 Act was a good example of this. Michael Howard announced a series of penal measures which it was estimated would have increased the prison population by

11,000 (*The Guardian*, 20 July 1997). However, the White Paper conversely estimated that the measures would reduce the prison population by 20% through deterrence (Dunbar and Langdon, 1998). The measures included mandatory life sentences, the abolition of parole or early release, the increasing use of the private sector and the building of 12 'super' prisons. Mandatory sentences have always been greeted with dismay by the judiciary and the Lord Chief Justice is no exception:

> ... **one sentence and one sentence only can be passed, whatever the nature of the crime, however strong the mitigating circumstances, whatever the position of the offender, the victim and the victim's family, however minimal the need to prevent the offender from re-offending or to deter others from offending in the same way, however negligible, on the particular facts, the need to protect the public. (Lord Bingham, 1998)**

Howard was asserting his authority, ensuring that everyone knew who was in charge, by presenting the case as 'protection of the public'. It was 'the public' Howard insisted he listened to and not the judiciary.

A Bill that was so heavily criticised by so many sections of the criminal justice system had a surprisingly smooth passage through Parliament. There were fierce arguments, especially in the House of Lords, but the Labour Party made it clear that it would not oppose the passing of the Act. Faulkner argued that "optimism has again given way to anxiety" (1997).

Labour achieved its objectives, it 'won' the law and order battle, it convinced the public, or enough of them, that it was not 'soft' on crime and it won the General Election of 1997 with the biggest majority this century. Whether it sacrificed any of its ideals and principles in order to achieve its momentous success is subject to debate, but already it had appeared to have moved a long way from the sentiments expressed by James Callaghan in the opening quote.

Labour's approach to sentencing

The Labour Party began its term of office on a wave of euphoria and optimism. Most sectors of the criminal justice professions were confident that the rhetoric of the election campaign would be quickly displaced by a twin-track penal policy of the prison as a legitimate punishment, but by no means the only punishment, with an increasing emphasis on the community as a place of punishment for many offenders. Labour did not disappoint and got off to a blistering start. Jack Straw announced that he would take full responsibility for prisons thus ending one of the many confusions that characterised Michael Howard's relationship with the Director General of the prison service Derek Lewis (before he was sacked). Straw also indicated that he was looking for ways to reduce the prison population and would do this by promoting punishment in the community and by speeding up the criminal justice process (thus reducing the numbers in prison on remand and awaiting trial). Without delay he announced the extension of three pilot electronic tagging programmes. Interestingly, Straw initially announced that one of the more controversial aspects of the 1997 Crime (Sentences) Act, the mandatory sentence for a third conviction for burglary, would be shelved. This was the aspect of the Act that would have led to the biggest increase in the prison population. The Home Secretary was clearly under pressure to reduce the prison population, not least because of the escalating costs and concerned noises coming from the Treasury. However, once again penal policy was to be subjected to political expediency. In response to the political crisis of late 1998 relating to high profile ministerial resignations, Labour's attempt to 'relaunch' itself was to be expressed in law and order terms through a 'get tough' approach to burglary. Straw was to resurrect the prospect of the mandatory sentence for repeat burglary. Unsurprisingly, penal reformers were aghast, with the Prison Reform Trust arguing that the penalties were "wrong in principle and likely to be disastrous in practice" (*The Guardian*, 13 January 1999). Alan Travis, the Home Affairs Editor asks us to consider Mr Straw as a first-time offender (*The Guardian*, 13 January 1999).

With this exception, more generally a positive stance seems to have been taken now towards Labour. There are anxieties and concerns over some issues that will be discussed later but overall the talk is of open debate, respect and consultation:

> **There is much greater openness, there is much greater willingness to consult and involve on the part of officials and Ministers, there is a pluralistic approach. There is a willingness to discuss and debate which was not there. (Shaw, 1998)**

While a part of this must be attributed to relief at the departure of a Home Secretary who was deeply unpopular and mistrusted by the criminal justice professionals, there was and still is a general sense of optimism about the future. An editorial in the *Prison Service Journal*, not always a natural supporter of governments, talked positively about improved resources, improved effectiveness and signs that changes to help the service with reintegration for offenders would be forthcoming ('Editorial', *Prison Service Journal*, May 1998). Straw (1998) refers to this in the foreword to his path-breaking *Prisons–probation review* where he states the importance of changing behaviour and rehabilitation during imprisonment: "Community sentences and work with offenders during custody ... have a central part to play in changing offending behaviour, reducing crime and protecting the public" (Straw, 1998).

While the new Home Secretary could hardly disagree with his predecessor that the amount of crime that can be committed by a person in prison is severely limited, he could and does argue that in order to maximise the potential to 'protect the public', work must be done within the prison. The *Prisons–probation review* aims to achieve this through closer consultation between the two sectors and an increasing role for the probation service *within* the prison. However, apart from the possible reorganisation of the prison service areas to be in line with the Government Offices for the Regions and apart from an agreement in principle, that it is preferable to house prisoners close to their home towns, the review is in the main a document concerned with changes to the system of probation.

Labour's approach to prisons

This brings us back to the question of the 'prisons file' in Jack Straw's office held neatly with a paper clip. The prison system was the Samson to Michael Howard's Delilah, suitably cut down to size. The legacy of the prison population left by Howard and the damage that was done through political whim to the prison system more generally cried out for more positive steps to remedy the situation. Yet despite the optimism, that does still prevail, all is relatively quiet and the prison population continues to rise. In April 1998 the figure stood at 66,800 and continued to rise at a rate of more than 1,000 per month (*The Guardian*, 10 April 1998). Yet this is despite the fact that this was the fifth consecutive year that recorded crime has fallen (due more, arguably, to falling unemployment rather than 'prison works'). This concern is incomparable to the despair that was felt towards the previous government's penal policies but there is mild anxiety among many that not enough is being done or being said by this government to redress the balance and restore equity to a system that has seen so many changes in recent years.

Concern seems to centre around three issues. Firstly, the lack of direction from the Home Office in encouraging sentencers to use custodial sentences less and less. Secondly, and as a direct result of the first point, the burgeoning prison population, and thirdly the decision by Labour not only to extend the existing contracts between the private sector and the Home Office to provide prisons but to seek out new ones.

When Douglas Hurd took over as Home Secretary in 1987 one of his first jobs was to use emergency powers to reduce the prison population by giving 50% remission to those sentenced to 12 months or less. He then stated loud and often that the prison population was growing at too fast a rate and that there were other forms of punishment. This was in line with the White Paper which followed shortly afterwards and the 1991 Criminal Justice Act. The prison population fell from 51,000 in 1987 to a low of 40,600 in December 1992. This was achieved not just by legislation but by public pronouncements and pressure on magistrates and the judiciary that custodial sentences were not the only option. The White Paper, *Crime, justice and protecting the public*, preceding the 1991 Criminal Justice Act stated that:

> **For most offenders, imprisonment has to be justified in terms of public protection, denunciation and retribution. Otherwise it can be an expensive way of making bad people worse. The prospects of reforming offenders are usually much better if they stay in the community. (Home Office, 1990, para 2.7)**

This is why some commentators see their red rose of New Labour wilting at the sides a little and needing water. While it is feasible to suspect that the Home Secretary does believe in similar sentiments to those expressed in the White Paper, he has appeared reluctant to say so. Douglas Hurd has recently said that Jack Straw must do more to change penal policy. He argues that "you cannot win a battle on tiptoe" (Hurd, 1998).

Yet Jack Straw has insisted that despite the increases in the prison population he will not tell judges what sentences they should pass (*The Guardian*, 14 July 1998). He *hints* that community sentences are the preferable option. He *suggests* that if only public confidence in punishment in the community were higher it could be used more frequently. He even includes in the 1998 Crime and Disorder Act a caveat that sentencers must take notice of the cost of different sentences and their impact with regard to preventing reoffending (Home Office, 1998d, Section 80). Yet he will not *tell* the judges that he does not believe in this continued rate of high imprisonment. After the bullishness of Michael Howard, the judiciary must be pleased that they are no longer being told what to do. However, Jack Straw can provide a *lead* and he is not doing this to the exasperation of many:

> **Where Hurd led, the people followed. That's what politicians are supposed to do.... He has to say out loud what he says to the professionals within the system: that prison does not work for many ... but like so many ministers in this government, psychologically he is still in opposition ... still terrified of some imaginary backlash. (P.Toynbee, *The Guardian*, 18 February 1998)**

The public is not as punitive as some believe. With gentle steers from the government and a belief that community punishments are a viable yet still 'punishing' option, the public could be re-educated away from the 'prison works' policies. Lord Bingham has argued that both the public and the judiciary need to be convinced that community punishments are not a 'soft' option but stresses that this is a political task (Bingham, 1997). Judges argue that they are sending more people to prison because that is what 'the people' want (A. Marr, *Observer*, 28 June 1998). 'The people' believe that sentences are much more lenient than they actually are (Hough and Roberts, 1998). Jack Straw believes that he must quietly attempt to reduce the prison population so as not to upset 'the people' (P. Toynbee, *The Guardian*, 18 February 1998). Yet 'the people' according to Andrew Marr do not care "we have a situation of public apathy" and a "vicious circle of ignorance and mental sloth" (A. Marr, *Observer*, 28 June 1998). There appears to be a vicious circle.

For a start, a public pronouncement from Jack Straw would save the Treasury enormous sums of money. The cost of a community sentence is estimated to be one sixth of that of a prison place (*The Guardian*, 20 July 1997). The Home Secretary has already, and very quietly, had to give the prison service firstly £70 million in February 1998 and then £47 million a few months later merely to cope with the numbers in prisons. When there are such strict budgetary controls elsewhere in the public sector, it appears incongruous that the government is prepared to finance a policy of which it apparently does not approve of and one which will show no signs of improved effectiveness.

A further area of concern mentioned earlier is that of prison privatisation or 'contracting-out'. Since coming to power, the Home Secretary Jack Straw has given his approval to more prison privatisation, for adults, juveniles and asylum seekers than all of his Conservative predecessors combined (Wilson and Ashton, 1998). This includes the new 'child jail' opened this year for 12- to 14-year-old persistent offenders and run by the security firm Group 4 at a cost of £250,000 per child per year (*The Guardian*, 15 April 1998). Again, this was a policy that was begun by the Conservative Party and opposed by the Labour Party. It is estimated that by the year 2002, more than 6,200 prisoners will be held in private prisons in England and Wales. This means that England and Wales have one of the largest commercial penal industries in the world (*The Guardian*, 26 August 1998).

These facts are startling given that the first privately-run prison in this country was not opened until 1992. However, what is perhaps even more startling is that this expansion of the private sector within imprisonment comes from a government who in 1993 described private companies profiting from state punishment as "morally repugnant" (Labour Party, 1993). The history of the privatisation of prisons in England and Wales is documented elsewhere (Ryan and Ward, 1989; Shaw, 1992; Matthews, 1989) but needless to say the Labour Party has opposed it all the way. The tone of Labour began to change during the 1997 General Election campaign. Rather than the State taking back control of all privately-run prisons, which John Prescott had announced in 1994, Labour would instead not allow any *new* contracts to be signed. The message from Labour was still one of principled objection to the privatisation of imprisonment. The final stage to completely reverse 'Old' Labour's policy came after the General Election, where in this case the actual policy was further to the traditional 'Right' than the rhetoric. The Home Secretary announced that despite the moral objections to privatisation, the practical necessity to provide more prison places had to take precedence and the bidding was opened.

In the early stages of privately-run prisons in this country, a useful lesson could have been learned about the unacceptable state of British prisons. However, that lesson does not appear to have been learned. The privatisation of prisons and the acceptance of Jack Straw to allow new contracts to be granted to private companies should not be hailed as a cure to the problem. What would be much more difficult to achieve would be a move to a 'reductionist' policy with far less reliance on the prison system and more reliance on the community punishments that the Home Secretary *hints* that he would like to see developed. As

Rutherford (1998) argues, "the Government might attempt to build its way out of the prison numbers crisis but should it?"

Stephen Shaw, Director of the Prison Reform Trust, has argued that the prison system is the "black hole" in Labour's criminal justice reforms (Shaw, 1998). While the energy of New Labour has been channelled very effectively into other areas of policy, most notably youth justice, the prison system appears to have been left behind. The General Secretary of the Prison Governors' Association describes the feeling after Michael Howard left office as one of "sitting in a bombsite after the air-raid" (Roddan, 1998). After the bomb must come the often slow process of rebuilding, to at least give the impression that work is being done. The positive effects that have been felt through reforms by the new administration into other areas of criminal justice must be extended to a system that is in desperate need of attention.

Some signs indicate that things may be starting to change. A recent Home Office research study (1998e) argues that custody is the most expensive sentence yet is no more effective at reducing reoffending than any other sentence. A Home Affairs Select Committee report has warned of the burgeoning prison population and argued that prison is an expensive means merely of containing people (*The Guardian*, 11 September 1998). Maybe finally, although slowly, the ethos of 'prison works' will finally be laid to rest. Prison doesn't work, a fact of which many people are aware. It is now time for this government to say so.

Despite the continued anxiety about the prison population there are also penal strategies that have come from the Labour government which must be applauded. To those commentators who thought that Jack Straw was trying to "out-Howard Howard" (Roddan, 1998), it should be noted that Section 36 of the Crime and Disorder Act abolishes the death penalty for all remaining civilian offences – a clear example of the *policy* being quite different to the *rhetoric*!

Conclusion

The whole New Labour package on law and order together presents a rather uneven picture. On the one hand there is a strategy for 'community safety' which draws on criminologically sound principles such as social crime prevention, social control networks and early intervention. It is surrounded by notions of coherence, coordination, research-based planning and concerted action. On the other hand there is a penal strategy which is still all too inseparable from the policies Labour inherited. Custody continues to be used extensively for a wide range of offences and offenders. If Labour is so committed to the idea of 'what matters is what works', then it is difficult to understand why the prison remains such a central option within the penal system. We have yet to see a radical attack on the prison to equate with the radicalness of the community safety agenda. Until Labour feels politically comfortable enough to 'think the unthinkable' about the custodial end of law and order policy the picture will remain an uneven one.

However, the law and order agenda will not simply be left to the vagaries of political calculation. The government has also had to respond to, rather than set out, agendas. In the criminal justice context a major emergent issue in this respect is the whole debate surrounding the case of Stephen Lawrence, which involved the deficient response of the Metropolitan police after the murder of a black teenager. The inquiry by Lord Macpherson into the Lawrence case (Home Office, 1999) has opened up a can of worms regarding race and racism, not just in the policing and criminal justice context but also more widely across the public sector. Certainly the impact of Lawrence on the world of policing will be widespread. It has called into question not just the specific question of the way in which the police deal with racially motivated crimes, but also more generally selection, training and management within the police service. It has heralded something close to a paradigm shift in the development of British policing, the effects of which will be felt for many years to come. Alongside Labour's own agenda for policing and criminal justice reform, the Lawrence case has ensured that the face of law and order in this country will never be the same again.

TEN

Citizenship

Hartley Dean

Introduction

Central to any discussion of the changing role of the State in relation to welfare provision is the concept of citizenship, both as a status attributed to individual members of society and as a social practice involving participation and governance. Citizenship is a fundamentally contested concept that has lately re-emerged as a subject of political discourse and academic inquiry. Prior to the 1992 General Election, Britain's main political parties vied with each other to establish different visions of a 'citizen's charter' (Dean, 1994, pp 103-4). Although such rhetoric did not feature so explicitly in the 1997 election campaign, the language of citizenship continues to lie at the heart of New Labour's project, and in particular, in its proposals for welfare reform. The welfare reform Green Paper, for example, envisages a forthcoming age in which "the new welfare contract between government and the people will give all our citizens the means to achieve their full potential" (DSS, 1998a, p 21). Meanwhile, there has been a daunting proliferation of literature on citizenship theory (for example, Culpitt, 1992; Roche, 1992; Turner, 1993; Oliver and Heater, 1994; Twine, 1994; van Steenbergen, 1994; Bulmer and Rees, 1996; Lister, 1997b).

This chapter will:

* outline the competing traditions which underpin concepts of citizenship, the different ways in which notions of 'social citizenship' have informed modern welfare state regimes and the manner by which conceptions of citizenship were reconstructed within New Right thinking prior to New Labour's election;
* analyse the significance of New Labour's communitarian agenda and the extent to which this represents an emerging new orthodoxy with regard to the basis of our citizenship;
* draw on evidence from recent research in order to discuss the relationship between popular expectations of the welfare state and

New Labour's political discourse and the possible implications of New Labour's approach.

Competing traditions of citizenship

Conceptual legacy

In its original meaning 'citizenship' denoted residence in a city, or more precisely, the status of the free men of that city. Citizenship implied freedom: the freedom reserved to a self-governing patrician elite, or a freedom 'earned' from feudal servitude. However, neither in the cities of ancient Greece or Rome, nor the early modern cities of Europe were women, slaves or servants counted as citizens. What is more, although the idea of citizenship was territorially delimited, its essence was not defined in relation to the city, the nation, the culture or the people, but in relation to the political practices of free men and the State which they created (see Habermas, 1994).

Having been fashioned by the outcome of political struggles, wars, migration and all types of social movement, modern citizenship is not simply a consequence of the rise of capitalism (Turner, 1986). None the less, it was the transition from feudalism to capitalism and the associated ideological upheavals of the Enlightenment which set the context in which from the 17th century onwards the ancient notion of citizenship re-established itself. At stake was the renegotiation of sovereignty – or, as Dahrendorf would have it, the 'domestication of power' (1996, p 41). Two distinct traditions were to emerge. One of these envisaged a form of social contract in which sovereign power is negotiated between the individual citizen and the State: this is the solution posed by classical liberal theory. The other sought to subordinate sovereignty to solidarity and the need for citizens to achieve social integration and mutual cohesion: this is the solution of civic republicanism. The three Enlightenment principles embodied in the French Revolutionary slogan – liberté, egalité, fraternité – expressed what Hobsbawm has called "a contradiction rather than a combination" (1962, p 284). The contractarian conception of citizenship which sought to protect the liberty of the individual subject is inimical to the solidaristic conception of citizenship which seeks to promote fraternity or belonging. Neither conception, as shall be seen, is necessarily concerned to uphold equality.

In the Western world, as modern civil and political regimes developed from the 18th century onwards, they tended to draw on one or a combination of these two strategies (cf Mann, 1987). One strategy was constitutionalist, subscribing to a contractarian notion of citizenship by which individuals are subject to the rule of law and constitutional governance: it is the strategy which came to typify the Anglo-Saxon world. The other was corporatist, subscribing to a solidaristic conception of citizenship by which the interests of individuals are brokered through negotiated compromise between different sources of coercive power: it is the strategy which came to typify continental Europe. In both types of regime administrative State power developed in ways which made it possible for governments to make provision for the welfare of their subjects or 'citizens'.

T.H. Marshall (1964) famously contended that in the 20th century citizenship came of age. In addition to the civil and political rights which had been important to achieve emancipation from despotism, the welfare state had ushered in an array of social rights – rights to healthcare, education and income maintenance – which would ensure that every citizen could enjoy a broad equality of status and opportunity. Citizenship, he argued, required a social element to be meaningful or effective. The idea of a 'social dimension' that complements the economic and political dimensions of citizenship has since become common currency even within the discourse of supranational bodies such as the European Union (EU) (EC, 1994).

However, in seeking to develop a social dimension the EU has been beset by the essential tensions which exist between the two conceptions of citizenship. As Room (1995) has pointed out, concerns about poverty reflect a characteristically liberal preoccupation with distributional issues, while corporatist concerns are characteristically about processes of 'social exclusion' and relational issues. Seminal theorists of poverty such as Townsend (1979) have sought to define relative poverty in relation to exclusion from social participation. This allows for an uneasy compromise or conflation between the two conceptual traditions (see also Levitas, 1996). That conflation has tended to obscure significant differences between egalitarian and non-egalitarian approaches to citizenship's social dimension; between approaches to social welfare which would secure either formal or substantive equality between citizens on the one hand and those which would either preserve or constructively regulate social hierarchies on the other.

Citizenship and welfare 'regimes'

It is differing understandings of the relations between the individual and the collectivity, a distinction between liberal or contractarian ideas (which are, by implication, exclusively focused on freely participating individuals) and republican or solidaristic ideas (which are, by implication, inclusively focused on the membership of a collectivity) which distinguish different approaches to citizenship. There are also differing evaluations of the constitutional basis on which social distribution occurs and a distinction between egalitarian and hierarchical values. In Figure 10.1 these distinctions are represented as the axes of a taxonomy of different types of welfare regime: the relational dimension is represented along the horizontal axis and the distributional dimension along the vertical axis. Three of the regimes so identified correspond to those identified through empirical analysis by Esping-Andersen (1990). The regimes are ideal types and the strategies adopted by political parties and nation states may represent a synthesis drawn from different quadrants of the taxonomy.

Although the validity, scope and rigour of Esping-Andersen's seminal typology of welfare regimes have been widely challenged, it still provides a model on which to build. Esping-Andersen's neo-liberal or residual welfare regime is found in quadrant A of Figure 10.1: it is formally

Figure 10.1: Taxonomy of political discourses and welfare regimes

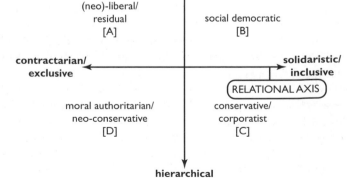

egalitarian

DISTRIBUTIONAL AXIS

(neo)-liberal/
residual
[A]

social democratic
[B]

contractarian/
exclusive

solidaristic/
inclusive

RELATIONAL AXIS

moral authoritarian/
neo-conservative
[D]

conservative/
corporatist
[C]

hierarchical

egalitarian, but substantively exclusive in the sense that it would aspire to be rigorously meritocratic; it would moblise welfare provision in order to secure the conditions for a free-market economy, but would be tolerant of social inequality. His social-democratic regime is found in quadrant B: it is both substantively egalitarian and substantively inclusive in the sense that it would seek to make universal provision for all its citizens; it would be concerned to redistribute resources so as to limit social inequality. His conservative or corporatist regime is found in quadrant C: it is substantively hierarchical, but only formally inclusive in the sense that it would make extensive provision for most citizens while sustaining established social relations of power; it would be concerned to supervise the distribution of resources in the interests of social cohesion, but it would not ensure equality nor necessarily protect the interests of the marginalised or powerless. The moral authoritarian or neo-conservative regime represented in quadrant D was not a part of Esping-Andersen's typology: it is both formally hierarchical and formally exclusive in the sense that it would aspire to sustain traditional authority; it would mobilise welfare provision in order to deter undesirable forms of individual behaviour and to enforce desirable ones and so promote a social order based on inequality.

The model represented in Figure 10.1 relates to the limited range of citizenship discourses which have been deployed within capitalist welfare states. The underlying organising principles of all such states, it may be argued, have been work, family and nation and the maintenance of the corresponding social divisions – based respectively on class, gender and 'race' – to which modern Western citizenry is subject (Williams, 1989). The model does not accommodate such alternative discourses that, for example, would argue for:

- the kind of emancipatory struggle against exploitative social relations by which Marx had evisaged we might ultimately realise, not citizenship but our true 'social humanity';
- the utopian social contract once envisaged by Rousseau or the radical communitarian agenda proposed by contemporary writers such as Walzer (1983);
- a differentiated but universalistic form of citizenship that could redress the systemic disadvantage to which women are subject (Lister, 1997b);
- a non-racialised or even global form of cititizenship that would redress the systemic disadvantages to which aboriginal and minority ethnic groups are subject or which might transcend the distortions of immigration and nationality law (Turner, 1990; Falk, 1994).

Shifting orthodoxies

The value of the model outlined above is that it makes it possible to characterise underlying shifts in prevailing ideological orthodoxy. To the extent that modern welfare states had been developing before the Second World War, these had been essentially Bismarckian in nature, drawing most strongly on the citizenship discourse of quadrant C in Figure 10.1. The Keynes/Beveridge orthodoxy which emerged after the Second World War and which is associated with the principles of the 'modern' welfare state drew strongly (but by no means exclusively) on quadrant B. Certainly, throughout most of the Western world, it was discourses from quadrants B and C which held sway until the so called 'crisis' of the welfare state in the 1970s (see, for example, Mishra, 1984).

After the 1970s, the Western world witnessed the emergence of what might be called the Thatcher/Reagan orthodoxy, which drew on discourses from quadrants A and D of Figure 10.1. On the one hand, there was a concerted attempt to 'privatise' citizenship (Lister, 1990). On the other hand, there was a significant movement towards 'workfare' and neo-conservative pro-familism (Roche, 1992). To the extent that 'Thatcherism' embodied an intelligible ideology it entailed a simultaneous belief in the virtues of a free economy and a strong State (Gamble, 1988): it was both liberal and authoritarian.

During the years of Conservative rule which preceded the election of New Labour there was a significant shift towards 'welfare pluralism' and a welfare model consistent with the regime characterised in quadrant A in Figure 10.1 above (see Chapter One and, for example, Johnson, 1987; Taylor-Gooby and Lawson, 1993). Increasingly, the burden of welfare provision was shifted from the State to the informal, voluntary and commercial sectors and the character of welfare transactions became, if not literally private, more akin to contractual relations in the marketplace. They came increasingly to equate with the civil rights, rather than the social rights of citizenship (Dean, 1996). At the same time, government ministers began in the 1980s to promote the concept of 'active citizenship', which they portrayed as "a necessary complement to that of the enterprise culture" (Hurd, 1989). This attempt to encourage voluntary service and charitable good works is redolent of the feudal principles of noblesse oblige and one-nation Toryism. None the less, the initiative is more properly understood in the light of the neo-liberal injunction that those who fail to prosper have no rights against those who succeed (Hayek, 1976). The appeal to active citizenship was an explicit signal that such responsibilities as comfortable citizens might feel they owe to those who are less fortunate are a matter of choice and individual conscience and ought not to be collectively discharged through the payment of taxes. However, in the 1990s the new orthodoxy crystallised under the premiership of John Major, whose Citizen's Charter (Prime Minister's Office, 1991) sought to subject all public services to the type of performance standards which might properly be demanded by paying customers in the marketplace. The citizen was no longer to be the helpless client of the welfare state, but a 'heroic consumer' (Warde, 1994) whose sovereignty is vested not in social entitlements, but in her/his power to choose or to complain.

The other element of the new orthodoxy, drawn from quadrant D, related to the increasingly coercive nature of State welfare provision for certain social groups and, in particular, for unemployed people and lone parents. It has been argued that during the 1980s, the social security system was made in many ways more punitive towards the poor (Andrews and Jacobs, 1990). Certainly, with a major shift towards means-testing, the system became more conditional. Once again, it was under John Major's premiership that change was to crystallise. The introduction of Job Seekers' Allowance (JSA) signalled an altogether more rigorous regime intended to promote the work ethic, to direct unemployed benefit claimants into employment and to impose sanctions on those who failed to comply. The introduction of the Child Support Agency represented the culmination of a 'back to basics' campaign by which ministers had sought to promote the values of the 'traditional family', to privilege the liabilities of biological parenthood above those of social parenthood and wherever possible restore lone-parent households to dependency on the 'absent parent' (see Dean, 1995). When New Labour came to power it inherited a State apparatus which, far from being residual, had been recently developed in ways which were explicitly intended to control the behaviour of certain citizens.

The New Labour agenda

The birth of New Labour has been associated with the revision in 1995 of Clause 4 of the Labour Party constitution (see Chapter One). The original Clause 4, drafted in 1918, had committed the Party to social equality on the basis of common ownership and popular administration. The revised clause committed the Party to the creation of "a community in which power, wealth and opportunity are in the hands of the many not the few, where the rights we enjoy reflect the duties we owe, and where we live together freely, in a spirit of solidarity, tolerance and respect". The concept of citizenship which is implied by these words is deeply ambiguous. The assertion that "the rights we enjoy reflect the duties we owe", is a refrain which the Labour Leader Tony Blair portrays as key to New Labour's project (see, for example, Blair, 1995).

The policy documents which began to emerge from New Labour (for example, Labour Party, 1996b) began to speak of 'Labour's contract for a new Britain', of building both a 'stakeholder economy' and a 'one-nation society'. The Labour manifesto (Labour Party, 1997a), to which the electorate subsequently gave its endorsement, perpetuated this mixture of discourses, drawing on contradictory notions of citizenship. In his introduction to the manifesto, Blair draws on solidaristic discourse when he speaks of wanting "a Britain that is one nation, with shared values and purpose". However, he also draws very explicitly on contractarian discourse, not least in his final flourish, which claims: "This is our contract with the people". The 'bond of trust' which Labour seeks to forge is with "the broad majority of people who work hard, play by the rules [and] pay their dues". By implication, it would seem, the contract is conditional on behaviour and there will be those who are not included. In this context it is significant that the New Labour government's Social Exclusion Unit (see Chapters One and Six) has to date been concerned not with the potentially exclusionary effects of social inequality for citizens in general, but with the plight of particular groups whose excluded status is characterised by their behaviour: school truants, rough sleepers and teenage lone-mothers.

The welfare reform agenda outlined in New Labour's manifesto is "based on rights and duties going together". This is not the unconditional language of social justice, nor of the 'Old' Labour Party which had presided over the creation of the modern welfare state. It is a discourse which flows from the Party's qualified acceptance of key recommendations of the Commission on Social Justice, originally established by the late John Smith, Blair's predecessor as Labour Leader (see Chapter One). This had called for an "investors' strategy" which would "combine the ethics of community with the dynamics of a market economy" (Commission on Social Justice, 1994, p 95). This is the makings of a regime which draws on discourses from both quadrants A and C of Figure 10.1: on both economic liberalism and social conservatism.

In a perceptive commentary on New Labour's first year in power,

Marquand (1998b) has observed that while New Labour "has turned its back on Keynes and Beveridge ... [and] ... is manifestly unshocked by the huge and growing disparities of income engendered by the late twentieth century capitalist rennaissance", it has managed, in a way that the Conservatives had not, to embody a national consensus:

> **In place of the Thatcherite cold shower, it offers a warm bath, administered by a hegemonic people's party appealing to every part of the nation. This may have nothing in common with social democracy, but is the nearest thing to Christian democracy that modern British politics have known. And Christian democracy is light years away from Thatcherism. (Marquand, 1998b)**

However, if New Labour has abandoned social democracy and is combining the economic liberalism of the Thatcher/Reagan orthodoxy with something approaching socially conservative Christian democracy, there remain other elements of its agenda which are more difficult to explain. Marquand (1998b) notes that "[u]nderpinning the individualistic, mobile, competitive society is a dirigiste workfare state that would have warmed the cockles of Beatrice Webb's heart". Before returning to this additional contradiction, this chapter will now explore the particular brand of communitarianism that informs the emerging political orthodoxy, in Britain, the USA and, potentially, around the globe (see also Chapter Twelve).

Blair/Clinton orthodoxy

There is a strand of communitarian thinking, emanating particularly from writers such as the American political scientist Etzioni (1995), that appears to have been influential both with New Democrats in the USA and with New Labour in Britain (Gray, 1995; Campbell, 1995). Bill Jordan (1998) has argued that the appeal of this form of communitarianism to the present politics of welfare stems from the connections it seeks to establish between individual choice and collective responsibility. It is an almost nostalgic appeal to the rural village or the close-knit working-class neighbourhood; it speaks to the moral intuitions of small-town America or traditional English values, and it seeks to translate the principles of reciprocity appropriate to membership of a small association to the realisation of the common good within a national community. This, Jordan suggests, lies at the heart of a newly emerging and increasingly hegemonic Blair/Clinton orthodoxy. In an age when it is apparently accepted that the 'golden age' of welfare state protectionism is past (Esping-Andersen, 1996), all prescriptions for welfare reform are informed by a perceived need to limit public spending and sustain labour market flexibility. There is a role for governmental intervention, especially in stimulating the supply side of the economy, but it is necessary that the rights of citizens should strictly reflect their observance of duties and obligations to the community.

Communitarianism, it has been suggested, "offers Labour modernizers a political vocabulary which eschews market individualism, but not capitalism; and which embraces collective action, but not class or the state" (Driver and Martell, 1997, p 33). Driver and Martell point out that there is not one form of communitarianism, but many. New Labour's policies in many respects do reflect the communitarianism that is implicit in old fashioned Christian democracy, but there are important exceptions. Driver and Martell suggest that New Labour is essentially conservative rather than progressive, in so far that it is profamilial and more authoritarian than permissive; it is prescriptive rather than voluntaristic in so far that it will countenance compulsion in the interests of social cohesion; it is moralistic in so far that it has eschewed increased socioeconomic redistribution in favour of policies to promote opportunity. In spite of a certain commitment to pluralism, constitutional reform and the devolution of power, New Labour has a tendency to be conformist in that it seeks to retain power centrally in certain key policy areas and, on occasions, appears rhetorically to conflate the powers and responsibilities of 'the community' with its own powers and responsibilities as a government. However, in two respects New Labour communitarianism is unlike that of conventional Christian democracy.

First, as already indicated, it is a strictly conditional communitarianism. The reciprocal and proportionate nature of rights and responsibilities are determined with reference to a narrow calculus. In spite of New Labour's insistence that vulnerable people will always be protected, the overwhelming implication is that social rights can be conceded only if they are earned or, exceptionally, deserved. There are no unconditional rights of citizenship. Although it has been claimed that Labour's new direction reflects a move away from socialist dogma and towards substantive social justice (Plant, 1995; Blair, 1996b), Blair himself insists that "the most meaningful stake anyone can have in society is the ability to earn a living and support a family" (Blair, 1996b). Such a 'stake' becomes in effect the sine qua non of social justice. Jordan (1998) has argued that the Blair/Clinton orthodoxy may be seen, in the name of social justice, to be extending the surveillance and control of 'deviant' minorities; to be expanding processes for counselling and compelling unemployed people, lone parents and disabled people towards the labour market. In this, Jordan suggests, New Labour is observing regulatory principles espoused in the 19th century by the utilitarian philosopher, Jeremy Bentham. Here Jordan may be correct, not because Bentham was a communitarian (on the contrary he famously denied that there is any such thing as community), but in the sense that the disciplinary techniques associated with the development of administrative power are continuously available to be refined and applied (Foucault, 1977; Dean, 1991) and because utilitarianism, as a corrupted interpretation of the classical liberal project, approved of coercion in the cause of the greater good. New Labour thinking here chimes with that of Mead who had argued that the goal of social policy should be to promote 'equal citizenship', a process which:

> ... does not require that the disadvantaged 'succeed', something not everyone can do. It requires only that everyone discharge the common obligations, including social ones like work. All competent adults are supposed to work or display English literacy, just as everyone is supposed to pay taxes or obey the law. (Mead, 1986, p 12)

Second, according to Driver and Martell (1997) New Labour's communitarianism is more individualistic than corporatist. By this they mean that New Labour's concept of 'stakeholding' is less about the corporate economic responsibilities of companies and organisations (as advocated, for example, by Hutton, 1996) as about the personal moral duties of individuals. However, it is at this point that the synthesis which has been identified as the Blair/Clinton orthodoxy meets and becomes conflated with a rather different political discourse exemplified in the pronouncements of Frank Field, who served as New Labour's Minister for Welfare Reform until his unceremonious departure from the government during Blair's first ministerial reshuffle in July 1998.

It is a reflection of the reality that Field functioned along a different axis to the New Labour mainstream that it was he who was appointed to 'think the unthinkable' and to formulate proposals for welfare reform (cf Alcock, 1997b). The proposals which Field had proposed before New Labour's election victory had been based on a wholesale onslaught against means-tested provision (see 1995, 1996b). To this end he advocated individualised stakeholder pensions on the one hand and an extended but 'mutualised' form of National Insurance provision on the other. However, he coupled this with a 'proactive' approach to Income Support in order to compel those who are able to work to do so and to eliminate fraud. It is in this latter respect that Field's influence on New Labour's Welfare to Work policy and on the Green Paper (DSS, 1998a) is evident. Of the rest of Field's agenda little has been translated into policy. Means-testing is to be retained in the longer term and the government's pension reform proposals (see Chapter Seven), which were delayed until after Field's departure from office, fell conspicuously short of his aspirations. The paradox would seem to be that Field himself drew on discourse from quadrants B and D from Figure 10.1. His was a mixture of social democratic concern for universal mechanisms coupled with a deeply moral authoritarian approach founded on an essentially Hobbesian view of human nature: it is self-interest, he has argued, not altruism that is "mankind's main driving force" (1996b, p 19), and social policy must therefore harness the motivations of the individual citizen. To this extent, Field had much in common with early Fabians, such as Beatrice Webb, and it is precisely this tendency to state dirigism which Marquand detects (see above). In the same sense that Benthamism was a corruption of the liberal project, so Fabianism was a corruption of the socialist project, yet, practically speaking, these two schools of thought had much in common (see, for example, Thompson, 1968). It is the coercive techniques envisaged by each, rather than their ideological principles, which are evident in what appears to be an ineluctible shift towards a workfare state.

Workfare state

The Blair/Clinton orthodoxy identified by Jordan (1998) is preoccupied with paid work (cf Chapters Seven, Eight, and Twelve). That orthodoxy, Jordan argues, is premised on three theses: that work contributions provide the only sustainable claims to social welfare; that the worst type of social injustice stems from the 'freeriding' of some on the efforts of others; that all social rights imply obligations to labour for the good of others (1998, Chapter 2). This is what gives rise to what might justifiably be called a workfare state.

Although New Labour may eschew the term 'workfare' because of its pejorative connotations, paid work is self-evidently central to the terms on which it envisages the relationship between citizen and state. Lister (1998) has identified the emergence of New Labour with three principal shifts in the concerns of the Party:

* from promoting equality to ensuring equality of opportunity;
* from combating poverty to addressing social exclusion;
* from creating rights to enforcing social obligations and responsibilities.

However, in each instance the reason for the shift relates to the perceived importance of paid work to the individual citizen. The emphasis is on education, training and employment rather than redistribution through the tax and benefits system; on paid work as the principal mechanism for ensuring social inclusion; on work as the primary social obligation.

Important elements of such a shift had been foretold by Jessop (1994) who identified a tendential process of transition, associated with the global tendency towards the 'hollowing out' of nation states, from a Keynesian welfare state to a Schumpeterian workfare state. The Keynesian welfare state was characterised by commitment to full employment through the management of aggregate demand and universalistic welfare provision on a centralised 'Fordist' model. The Schumpeterian workfare state would be characterised by commitment to market opportunity through supply-side economic management and selectivist welfare provision on a pluralist 'post-Fordist' model. Rather than using the power of the nation state to shape the international economy in accordance with the social and political objectives of the government, the role of government would be restricted to that of creating labour markets that will conform to the demands of global economic forces (cf Whiteside, 1995). The space between the individual and the State is itself 'hollowed out' as it is subordinated to economic forces and made increasingly conditional on the citizen's individual 'stake' in the economy as a paid worker.

There are other theorists who have suggested that the role of the State in welfare must inevitably change in so far that one of the consequences of the global process of 'reflexive modernisation' (see Beck et al, 1994) is that the calculation and management of risk is a central preoccupation of every citizen: we now live, not in a class society, but a 'risk society' (Beck, 1992). The downside of the increasing range of choices made available to the citizens of the late or post-modern age are the risks they must face. The downside of the reflexivity which people acquire as they come to place their trust in advanced technical and administrative systems and maintain social relations across indefinite spans of time and space is the anxiety that is entailed in the maintenance of self-identity and ontological security in a society full of social hazards, environmental risks and economic uncertainty (see Giddens, 1990, 1991). Giddens, a British academic with influence within the Blair government, has argued that the primary role for the welfare state can no longer be the provision of services; it should become the management of risk (1994).

In practice, the key risks to be managed relate to paid work and the labour market. T.H. Marshall's seminal account of citizenship (see above) had supposed that the welfare state would ensure that citizenship would supersede class as an organising principle. This has never come about. Neither has risk, however salient it may have become, replaced class as the primary determinant of life chances. The global ascendancy of capitalism means that – for the vast majority – labour markets and labour market location (class) remain the ultimate determinants of life chances, albeit in sometimes circuitous and indirect ways (see, for example, G. Marshall, 1997). In opposition to T.H. Marshall's account, Offe has argued that the role of state welfare has always been critical to the maintenance of labour markets: "[t]he owner of labour power first becomes a wage-labourer as a citizen of a state" (Offe, 1984, p 99). This, it would seem, applies as much under New Labour as it ever did.

Popular discourse and citizenship

These theoretical concerns with the nature of citizenship do have relevance for the way in which people have experienced or interpreted the nature of New Labour in government. This is not because popular discourse engages with the idea of citizenship, but because there is within popular discourse a variety of corresponding 'moral repertoires' which inform people's understanding of social inequality and their expectations of the welfare state.

Moral repertoires

Offe (1993) argues that there is a range of different moral repertoires on which to draw to validate any particular pattern of rights and obligations. He has constructed a taxonomy of repertoires somewhat arbitrarily from an analysis of dominant political and philosophical traditions. He identifies three such repertoires: 'the utilitarian', 'the Kantian' (subscribing to the ideal of moral universalism) and the 'conservative communitarian', loosely corresponding to Esping-Andersen's liberal, social democratic and corporatist welfare regimes (see above). It is possible to add a fourth moral repertoire, which might be called 'the Hobbesian', corresponding to what has been identified above as the moral authoritarian ideal-type welfare regime.

With a colleague, I have recently sought to derive an alternative taxonomy of popular moral repertoires from a qualitative study of popular discourse. The study was conducted in 1996, the year that led up to New Labour's general election victory (see Dean with Melrose, 1999). It involved interviews with working adults, with widely differing levels of income and from various parts of England. The interviews explored the participants' perceptions of social inequality and their understandings of the rights and responsibilities of citizenship. It was evident that the important differences between participants related not only to the substance of the explanations or justifications they used, but also to the strategies of understanding and expression – or 'voices' – on which they were able to call. Popular discourse is, in its nature, a complex mixture of competing explanations and voices and it is these which inform the various ways in which individuals bind themselves in to social structures. To construct our taxonomy of the popular discourses through which dominant moral repertoires are constituted we called on the work of two very different theorists: the sociologist Giddens (referred to above) and the anthropologist Mary Douglas.

It is possible to articulate Giddens' particular concepts of reflexivity and anxiety (or rather anxiety's converse, ontological security) with the concepts of 'grid' and 'group' in the work of Douglas (1978). 'Grid' and 'group' are the dimensions in Douglas' system of cultural typologies. 'Grid' relates to the extent to which systems of classification in society are either shared or private; to which codes of discourse are either restricted and tradition bound or elaborated and radical. 'Group' relates to the extent to which individuals in society are either controlled by other people's pressure or are free to exert pressure; to which they are either integrated through reciprocal group social relations or largely independent (or alienated) from them.

Where Douglas is describing the ways in which some individuals, groups or societies may come to depend less on ritual and more on elaborated communicative codes, Giddens would speak of reflexivity. Where Douglas is describing the ways in which some individuals, groups or societies become less bounded by collective power and more alienated,

Giddens would speak of anxiety or loss of ontological security. Figure 10.2 incorporates Douglas' and Giddens' respective theoretical distinctions as intersecting dimensions or continua. The taxonomy represented in Figure 10.2 supersedes the notions of grid and reflexivity with the above-mentioned concept of voice: this is represented along the vertical axis. The taxonomy supersedes the notions of group and ontological security by articulating them with the realm of ideology, as the medium through which individual perceptions of social existence are apprehended or shaped: this is represented along the horizontal axis.

Figure 10.2 relates not to the personalities of the people who participated in our study, but to the discourses on which they drew. At issue is the extent to which they drew on reflexive or mythologising modes of expression on the one hand, or on autonomistic (behaviourally situated and risk-embracing) or collectivist (structurally situated and risk-averse) modes of explanation on the other. So, for example, people who drew on autonomistic modes of explanation would characteristically blame poverty on the poor themselves. Of these, those who drew on reflexive modes of expression were characteristically entrepreneurial – for them, the way to resist poverty is through individual merit and the seizing of opportunity; but those who drew on mythologising modes of expression were characteristically survivalist – for them, resisting poverty is a matter

Figure 10.2: Taxonomy of popular moral repertories and discourses

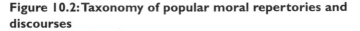

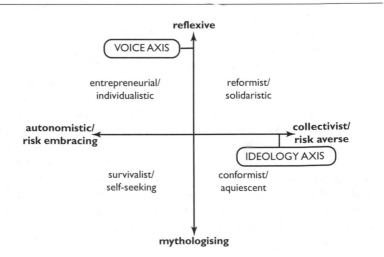

of good luck and of keeping ahead of the competition. In contrast, people who drew on collectivist modes of explanation would characteristically regard the poor as the victims of social circumstance. Of these, those who drew on reflexive modes of expression were characteristically reformist – for them, resisting poverty is a matter of social justice and is a policy question; but those who drew on mythologising modes of expression were characteristically conformist – for them, although the poor might be deserving of help, poverty was an inevitable occurrence.

Popular perceptions of citizenship

It is important to emphasise that the participants in our study were seldom able to engage coherently with the concept of 'citizenship'. Almost one third said they did not know what being a citizen meant or that it didn't mean anything much. Others could only define citizenship in its narrowest sense by equating it with nationality. The horror with which participants regarded poverty and the sceptical fascination with which they regarded wealth were far more tangible than their concepts of citizenship. Even among those on very low or very high incomes, it was their imagined distance from the extremes of poverty and riches, coupled with their aspiration to a 'comfortable' lifestyle, which defined their inclusion within the pale of social convention; as citizens, not by virtue of civic status, but because they believed themselves to be neither rich nor poor, but 'ordinary' (cf Scott, 1994). Nonetheless, participants could and did convey what they understood with regard to rights and responsibilities and the nature of their and other people's relationships as individuals to society.

In their attitudes to redistributive state welfare, participants tended to exhibit an ostensibly contradictory mixture of guarded altruism and pragmatic instrumentalism (cf Rentoul, 1989; Brook et al, 1996). Although participants generally valued key elements of the solidaristic or collectivist principles on which the welfare state was established, they were predisposed to ideological principles which would underpin more individualistic self-sufficiency. Judged in terms of their explicit opinions, this sample on balance was more individualist than collectivist in outlook. The way they answered questions conformed by and large to the expectations of public opinion on which New Labour policy is being constructed. However, close examination of the participants' underlying discourses revealed a subtler reality.

As in Runciman's study 30 years before (1966), participants were seldom able to locate themselves within the social distribution of incomes. Asked to place themselves on a scale between rich and poor, few were able to do so with any accuracy (although they were able, by and large, to locate themselves in terms of their social or occupational class). In particular, participants with middle to higher incomes tended grossly to underestimate their relative standing. To a degree, it would seem, in an unequal society people may in fact be subject to the same 'veil of ignorance' about their relative material standing as that which Rawls (1972) had sought artificially to impose on the imaginary participants in his famous thought experiment, where they did not know their position in the income distribution. Ontological insecurity might incline people just as much as calculative rationality to subscribe to certain principles of social justice. The people in our sample feared poverty more strongly than they aspired to wealth and, by implication, their preference was for a form of citizenship which protects against poverty before it secures the opportunity to pursue wealth.

In daily speech, all of us draw on a multiplicity of often variable and sometimes contradictory discursive repertoires, but by taking account of the relative extent of different discourses within the text generated during each interview and identifying the dominant discourse, it was possible to assign each of the participants to one of the four quadrants in Figure 10.2. In the event, the participants were distributed between the quadrants in broadly equal proportions. No single underlying moral repertoire is dominant; rather there is a fundamental tension within popular discourse between:

- belief in meritocratic principles and an entrepreneurial impulse which would seize the potential for personal self-advancement;
- concerns for social justice and a reformist impulse which stem largely from a pragmatic desire for the predictability and security that flow from greater equality;
- commitment to social cohesion and an essentially conformist impulse which are fueled by an implicit conservatism and desire for certainty and stability;
- a sense of fatalism and a survivalist impulse based on a presumption that inequality is to be contended with as an inevitable hazard.

Implications of New Labour's approach

Popular discourse relating to citizenship is no more coherent or consistent than political discourse. There is plainly a sense in which the discourse of the liberal welfare regime speaks to the entrepreneurial repertoires within popular discourse; social democratic regime speaks to reformist repertoires; conservative regime speaks to conformist repertoires; moral Right regime speaks to survivalist repertoires. However, the associations are not in every respect simple or unambiguous. What is more, in spite of its broad popular appeal, New Labour is by no means 'in step' with popular discourse. There is no evidence that popular discourse naturally embraces the particular combination of economic liberalism and social conservatism which characterises New Labour's approach (see also Dwyer, 1998).

Attempting to shift the underlying basis of a welfare regime cannot be undertaken without a clearer understanding of the complex ways in which the moral and practical significance of citizenship is socially constructed and popularly understood. New Labour claims that its approach will work with the grain of popular aspirations, but it is not clear that such aspirations are properly understood. While certain of the repertoires identified above sit more easily than others with New Labour's agenda, none provide a sufficient basis for moral consensus.

Popular entrepreneurial moral discourse resonates with New Labour's rhetoric concerning the need to realise individual potential. It endorses the centrality accorded to paid work within the Blair/Clinton orthodoxy. However, the equality of opportunity that is underwritten within the contract between citizen and State must be effective. There is ample evidence that people are by and large motivated to participate and to succeed in the world of paid work. However, the inherent value which people place on work as a source of identity and self-esteem can be undermined if they are coerced into poor quality placements which provide neither dignity nor opportunity (see, for example, Dean and Taylor-Gooby, 1992). Whatever the influence of the entrepreneurial repertoire, our evidence demonstrates (Dean with Melrose, 1999) that it seldom equates with unbridled ambition. Generally speaking, the participants in our study wanted to be 'comfortable' rather than rich and their fascination for the privilege and conspicuous consumption that can accompany material success was usually tempered by caution, if not distaste.

Popular reformist discourse is substantially at odds with New Labour's rejection of the Keynesian welfare state. It may be seen that surviving within popular discourse in Britain there is a paradigm which accepts a role for a redistributive welfare state and that the solidaristic values necessary to support that paradigm have by no means been eclipsed. Such discourse is not merely a residual vestige from some bygone age, but reflects fears and aspirations which are current and immediate.

Popular conformist discourse is clearly attracted to New Labour's rhetoric concerning the need for a 'one-nation society'. All of us want to belong. However, the evidence suggests that in this 'age of anxiety' (Pahl, 1995) the fear of poverty extends up the income scale to people on middle and even high incomes (Dean with Melrose, 1999). New Labour is not offering the type of security for which the corporatist welfare states of continental Europe are renowned. Even if it were, it must be borne in mind that in countries such as Germany, for example (see Clasen, 1997), questions are being raised about the sustainability of the trust on which solidaristic mechanisms must depend. The communitarianism of the Blair/Clinton orthodoxy apparently fails to recognise that the forces of globalisation are bound, as Gray (1995) has put it, "to undermine communities and to endanger the cohesion of society as a whole". New Labour may speak to people's fears, but it seems unlikely that it can quell them. How long will it be before the 'warm bath' of which Marquand speaks begins to go cold?

Popular survivalist moral discourse is able to engage with some of the moral certainties offered by New Labour; with the prospect that idlers will be made to work and that scroungers will be punished. However, the idler or scrounger is always somebody else and the fickle nature of survivalist discourse is such that it can always be summoned in defence of a very conservative form of resistance (see Dean and Melrose, 1997). One of the consequences of a more coercive welfare regime may be that more citizens will defect from their contract with the State, in the sense that they will 'disappear' into the shadowy world of the informal economy. If welfare reform does not work with the grain of everyday survival strategies the result may be more not less social exclusion.

Conclusion

The argument of this chapter has been that New Labour gives expression to an emerging orthodoxy that draws on a blend of long established discourses of citizenship. It is a blend that resonates with some aspects of the moral repertoires of popular discourse, but not with others. New Labour has correctly read the prevailing instrumentalism that inhabits popular discourse, but it has failed properly to read some of the accompanying insecurities or their deeper consequences. People are capable of both selfishness and altruism, but what most aspire to above all is ontological security. If there is a lowest common denominator, it is that people seek a degree of material security that is not necessarily selfish and a degree of social security based in belonging and reciprocity that is not strictly altruistic. This is what the 'social dimension' of contemporary citizenship might reasonably be expected to provide. It would not seem that New Labour's conception of citizenship fully accommodates that expectation.

ELEVEN

Accountability

John Rouse and George Smith

Introduction

This chapter explores the changing nature of public accountability in the welfare state since 1979. The particular emphasis is on the position of the Labour Party in opposition as the radical agenda of public sector reforms progressed through the four terms of Conservative governments to its current position following its election victory in May 1997. Although this is a complex journey, the key theme of this chapter will be to identify and explain the shift from the traditional forms of public accountability associated with the social democratic period of post-war consensus on the welfare state to the more diverse mechanisms associated primarily with the new accountability of neo-liberalism and its associated managerialism. It would be rash, however, to claim that these changes have been wholly accepted and incorporated into New Labour thinking. However, there is much to suggest that the changes being made and proposed so far by the government indicate an attempt to absorb managerialism within a model of public accountability that has been revived principally through the 'democratic renewal' agenda with its emphasis on institutional reform, greater decentralisation and a focus on citizenship and participation. Whether this is convergence or the multiple realities of a post-modern public administration (a third way?) is a major area for debate (Fox and Miller, 1995). The chapter begins by defining key terms relevant to the subsequent discussion.

Defining accountability

The idea of accountability is an inherently ambiguous one. It is a complex phenomenon with a number of dimensions. There are innumerable classifications of accountability in the literature and each author tends to give a slightly different twist to apparently the same term. However, the view of John Stewart that the prime accountability in the public sector is "public accountability" since "the exercise of [public] power can only be justified by public accountability" (Stewart, 1995a, p 289) is accepted here. The legitimacy of public choice rests on consent and consent is tested and confirmed through public accountability (Ranson and Stewart, 1994). Stewart also stresses that there are two differing elements in public accountability, both of which are required if it is to be fully developed:

* those who control public institutions should *give an account* to the public of their exercise of power so as to ensure discourse within the polity;
* there should be a means by which the public can *hold them to account* thereby ensuring relations of control and consent (Stewart, 1995a).

This public, or political, accountability depends on the existence of other forms of accountability such as managerial, professional, contractual and client (customer) accountability as well as financial, budgetary and legal accountability. The issue becomes complex because not only are there different definitions of each of these sub-accountabilities in different periods of time, but each is often weighted differently so as to constitute an 'accountability paradigm' relevant to a particular era. The range of definitions and meanings is indicative of the fundamental issues surrounding the multiple stakeholders and competing domains that characterise the public sector. Accountability is a 'wicked problem' in that it is one which is complex, ambiguous and intractable and, by its nature, given definition and substance by different groups who approach the problem from different perspectives at different times (Jackson, 1998). The fundamental controversy concerns which set of stakeholders should be given prominence and in what way their interests are best represented, since different models of accountability have different implications for the distribution of power and also for organisational design (Ferlie et al, 1996). The key questions are around values, discourse and politics (Ranson and Stewart, 1994).

Social democratic consensus and its critics

The traditional model of public accountability which dominated thinking throughout the years of post-war welfare state consensus until the mid-1970s was, according to Rhodes (1997), based on the essential organising perspective which he refers to as the Westminster model.

It focuses on: parliamentary sovereignty; strong cabinet government; accountability through elections; majority party control of the executive (that is, Prime Minister, cabinet and the civil service); elaborate conventions for the conduct of parliamentary business; institutional opposition, and the rules of debate. (Rhodes, 1997, p 5)

In terms of the services of the welfare state, the line of accountability runs from service deliverers to elected representatives at both national and local levels who are responsible to elected assemblies. The relevant minister must both give an account to the Chamber and can be held to account by the House of Commons, appearing before the House of Commons Public Accounts Committee and the various departmental select committees and ultimately the electorate. In local government responsibility is to the relevant committee and then to the appropriate minister in Whitehall. Through the electoral chain of command the public is given the opportunity to question the workings of the delivery agencies of the welfare state. The post-war consensus on public service delivery was supplemented by an administrative model where:

... emphasis was upon the bureaucratic ideal of efficient and impartial administration characterised by hierarchical structure, clearly defined duties and rule-based procedures, in which tasks which could not easily be controlled by rules were carried out by professionally qualified staff who were given 'bounded discretion'. (Butcher, 1995, p 2) (see also Hadley and Young, 1990; Clarke and Newman, 1997)

Hence, political accountability was bolstered by bureaucratic administration and professional accountability, with the latter being of increasing importance in the post-war era. Additionally, administrative processes would also secure legal accountability (judicial review), financial and managerial accountability (accounting for internal organisational processes), particularly via the process of national and local audit. This is referred to here as *the public administration paradigm*. It centred on the political and professional domains, with administration acting in an essentially mediatory role (Painter, 1995). It was the stuff of consensus, at least until the mid-1970s, although the minor skirmishes around interpretation and emphasis within the different areas of the welfare state should not be underestimated.

The reasons for the collapse of the post-war consensus and rise of dissatisfaction with the public administration paradigm are well documented (Hadley and Hatch, 1981; Mishra, 1984). It became apparent that theory and practice increasingly deviated since the assumptions of continuity and growth on which the public administration paradigm was based began to be challenged. The huge growth in the scale and size of government put accountability upwards, via ministerial responsibility, under immense strain. This was brought to a head by the public expenditure crisis of 1976 (Elcock, 1983). Public apathy at the polls, particularly the local ones, compromised the electoral chain of command. Inefficiency and waste, as found by the Public Accounts Committee and others, seemed to suggest a failure of financial, managerial and even legal accountability. There was also a perception that accountability outwards, to colleagues within the profession and relevant local authority departments, had become too controlling, leading to services being dominated by professionals and bureaucrats with consequential compromise to accountability both upwards to politicians and downwards to users and consumers of public services. There were critics on both the Left and the Right attacking the traditional approach to welfare service delivery and its increasing lack of accountability to key stakeholders in the community.

Although there was a chorus of criticism from across the political spectrum at the time, it was critics on the Right that gained the political and intellectual ascendancy in the late 1970s debate. The image portrayed by the neo-liberal theories of public choice and neo-Austrian political economy of the New Right was of a passive public dominated by a professional culture within organisations managed according to the bureaucratic principles of hierarchical control, delivering uniform and ever-expanding services. Their particular emphasis was on the inefficiencies and bureaucratic waste in public services and their insensitivity, even hostility, to user/customer interests. The election of Margaret Thatcher provided the opportunity for the next four Conservative administrations, inspired by the New Right, to introduce major changes during the 1980s and 1990s under the banner of new public management (Hood, 1991). These changes to the organisation of the welfare state challenged and confronted traditional forms of public accountability, replacing the public administration paradigm with one more focused on efficiency and consumerism, emphasising managerial and consumer accountability based on market processes, contracts and explicit performance standards. A whole series of challenges to the traditional routes of accountability were made at both central and local level, as more market-based approaches to welfare delivery were introduced.

New managerial accountability

The hallmark of new managerialism during the Thatcher-Major era was increasing emphasis on the individual as consumer and the development of market-type transactions in the public services. The result was a more confined and bounded notion of accountability than that represented by the public administration paradigm, with legitimacy seen as a matter of efficiency rather than consent and mutual commitment (Walsh, 1995). Emphasis moved from process politics to managerial performance with the State seen as one that steers not rows, enabling service delivery by private or autonomous organisations, increasingly differentiated, relating to each other through contracts rather than hierarchies, with performance monitored by various agencies of evaluation (Osborne and Gaebler, 1992; Henkel, 1991). In this vision, the delivery of welfare services is essentially a private issue for the individual user. It is the role of the politician to set the broad framework within which services operate and to observe a clear separation of powers between this policy role and the managerial/ operational one of implementation within autonomous agencies, "Politics is replaced by management, which, in turn, is replaced by audit" (Walsh, 1995, p 250).

The first phase, from 1979 until 1987, of the Conservatives' reforms of the welfare state in the 1980s, excluding the utilities, was largely concerned with improving their efficiency within the existing organisational framework using essentially neo-Taylorist managerial techniques of inspection and control (Pollitt, 1993). Focus was on transforming the administrative role into a managerial one to achieve value for money, mainly defined in economy and efficiency terms, while retaining largely traditional bureaucratic structures. The later more market-based phase, from 1987 onwards, centred more overtly on the consumer, challenging both the political and professional domains and traditional organisational principles and structures. It centred on more formal contracting, internally and externally, by the establishment of quasi-markets, commercialisation and consumerism. This resulted in a blurring of boundaries between public and private sectors as the number of appointed agencies grew and service delivery fragmented.

Throughout the Conservative years there occurred an increasing centralisation of responsibilities for political decisions as significant changes were made in local government, the National Health Service and other areas of the welfare state. In local government, for example, 'reforms' ranged from rate capping, the poll tax, compulsory competitive tendering

(CCT), removal of responsibilities in education, health and housing to outright abolition as in the case of the Greater London Council and metropolitan counties. The result was the erosion of the influence of intermediary tiers of government, notably the local authority, a strengthening of the centre and a proliferation of agencies, local and central, governed by appointed members and forming what Stewart (1993a) calls a 'new magistracy'. These took the place of elected councillors/politicians. This unelected or 'quango' state made increasing inroads in health, housing, education and training, social services, criminal justice and economic development. For example, at the national level, semi-autonomous 'Next Steps' executive agencies were set up, such as the Benefits Agency in 1991, so as to create a clearer division between policy and administration. The agencies would undertake responsibilities within the framework laid down for them by the responsible departments. These departments would set the agencies' objectives, their relations with the department and with Parliament, with other departments and other agencies and their performance criteria (Greer, 1994). Internal market reforms, in health, education and housing for example, also led to loosening connections in the public sector at the local level. As a result, semi-independent, non-profit making bodies appeared such as health authorities and hospital trusts, grant maintained schools (GMS), Training and Enterprise Councils, housing associations, further and higher education corporations. In particular, local authorities were separated from responsibilities previously theirs, either directly by losing functions or indirectly through losing representation on the new bodies. The structure of local government fragmented into what Rhodes (1997) calls the 'differentiated polity' of local governance, with services increasingly delivered by a network of semi-autonomous organisations.

The key rationale for much of this reform was in terms of managerial accountability, defined as "making those with delegated authority answerable for carrying out agreed tasks according to agreed criteria of performance" (Day and Klein, 1987, p 27). The outcome would be more results orientation, better performance and quality service delivery. By introducing new sets of incentives such as performance indicators, league tables, devolved budgets, competition, external monitoring and inspection, and ultimately the Citizen's Charter, public officials and politicians would be forced to respond to service users in a more economic, efficient and effective way. The Conservative government saw responsiveness to the individual citizen as consumer as a more direct, more democratic, form of accountability which would restore the democratic deficit of the discredited public administrative paradigm with its attenuated electoral chain of command. Not only would increasing reliance on managerial and quasi-market reform guide resources into the uses desired by the customer, it would also deliberately marginalise overtly political forms of accountability, seen as particularly dangerous if, as in so many 'looney left' local authorities, it fell into the wrong hands. William Waldegrave, the minister in charge of the Citizen's Charter initiative, provided the most coherent rationale for the new accountability:

> ... **services are not necessarily made responsive to the public simply by giving citizens a democratic vote, and a distant and diffuse one at that.... They** *can* **be made responsive by giving the public choices or by instituting mechanisms which build in public approved standards and redress when they are not attained.... We have strengthened th[e] formal lines of accountability by making our public services directly accountable to their customers. (Waldegrave, 1993)**

Hence, the welfare state reform programme was seen to create a democratic gain not a loss, with efficiency offered as a substitute for more traditional forms of accountability.

This managerial/market-based accountability approach came under increasing attack as it spread to previously inviolable tracts of the public services. Centralisation and the spectacular rise of non-elected agencies nationally and particularly locally, had increased the burden of responsibility for accountability on ministers to undeliverable levels, since it was only by ministers that these agencies could be held to account. Greer (1994), with regard to executive agencies for example, emphasised their confused accountability given the high degree of ambiguity as to whom or what the agencies owed responsibility. The sacking in October 1995 by Michael Howard (the then Home Secretary) of Derek Lewis, the Director General of Prisons, illustrated the confusion and the impossibility of separating powers for policy from those of implementation. By transferring accountability for outputs from politicians to officials the danger was that accountability became reduced to meeting pre-stated performance targets, rather than pursuing desired outcomes. It also meant that activity could be manipulated to show these targets had been achieved (Walsh, 1995). Quasi-market fragmentation and the resulting rise of quangos at the local level raised even more problems for the ministerial route to accountability. This was seen to represent a threat to local accountability and representative democracy (Davis, 1993; Davis and Stewart, 1993; Stewart, 1993a). Although such agencies could choose to give an account to local people and although the traditional legal requirements on them to do this were much less rigorous than on elected local councillors, "there [was] no means by which local people can hold them to account" through the electoral process (Stewart, 1995a, p 292). The absence of what Painter (1995, p 246) refers to as "the formidable array of constraints on the abuse of public power" which applied to local government meant that accountability could be severely compromised. These constraints ranged from the ultimate sanction of the election through the range of statutory regulations such as the need to keep a register of council members' interests, scrutiny by the local ombudsmen and surcharge possibilities for councillors. Although such agencies had a formal organisational autonomy, the appointment system for the quango boards offered all sorts of informal networks of influence that could operate through the patronage system of ministerial appointment to ensure the implementation of central policy. With the 'new magistracy' outnumbering local government councillors by more than 2:1 in the early 1990s (Weir and Hall, 1994) this was by no means an insignificant possibility.

The result can be, and certainly has been, cases of financial mismanagement and other misdemeanours and scandals summed up in the word 'sleaze'. The later years of Conservative rule were strewn with examples of impropriety and the abuse of public power. Eventually there was recognition that action was needed. The Nolan Committee's report on *Standards in public life*, published in May 1995, suggested a more consistent legal framework for propriety and accountability in public bodies. However, in the case of non-elected agencies (NEAs), it represented merely a changing and tightening of procedures rather than a return to more traditional accountability via some form of directly elected control (Stewart, 1995b).

There were other issues too as the supposed consumer accountability advantages of quasi-markets were increasingly questioned. The new markets were, for example, not only administratively expensive as a bureaucracy of hierarchy was replaced by a bureaucracy of contract, as was so well illustrated in the new NHS. Most were also at best quasi-markets which remained virtual monopolies dominated by producer values and agency relationships with the consumer given little real choice. There was little evidence that public services, certainly local ones, were meeting the new accountability and succeeding in becoming more customer and performance driven. Indeed, their study of local quangos, Painter et al (1995) found some insensitivity to local views, with prominence being given to performance outputs prescribed by central government and more commercial values prevailing to the detriment of public service ones such as equity, participation and openness. Their study also found a variety of practices on openness and participation, some impressive others not, suggesting a rather voluntaristic or piecemeal notion of accountability, often motivated by legitimacy-seeking in the absence of the consent provided by the ballot box. Within the fragmenting structure of local governance the study also observed the emergence of new networks of cooperation cutting across elected and non-elected agencies, representing a haphazard and informal form of reintegration. Although such alliances had the potential to mitigate against some of the coordination problems associated with fragmentation, they presented their own problems of unaccountable structures with the possible emergence of a new élite with personal ties and shared cultural outlook exerting undue power and influence, unconstrained by traditional lines of accountability (Rouse, 1997).

The new fragmented structure of governance, the "differentiated polity" as Rhodes (1997) calls it, had become increasingly incoherent and unaccountable as a range of government, quasi-government, voluntary and private sector bodies took responsibility for service delivery. The result has been the emergence of an 'organisation mess', manifest in both central and local government and the NHS, where it has become almost impossible to assign responsibilities and where there are doubts about delivery, even on its own managerial performance terms. The legitimacy of the new accountability has been seen as wanting since, as Stewart (1995a, p 290) claims, "consumer responsiveness is no substitute for public accountability". Citizens' wants do not necessarily coincide with citizens' needs and the requirements of the collective good defined in terms of the multiplicity of stakeholders (Walsh, 1995). In this view, citizenship is more than consumption in the private realm. Democratic accountability goes well beyond the attenuated notion of contract accountability with its barriers to communication and learning, incentives to distort and conceal, possible impropriety and its insensitivity to the distinctive purposes, values and conditions of the public domain (Stewart, 1993b; Rhodes, 1997).

Before discussing the extent to which New Labour is introducing a new accountability paradigm, focused perhaps on a third way, it is necessary first to trace the changing approach to accountability of the Labour Party during its 18 years in opposition.

Labour's journey

The approach of the Labour Party to accountability in the welfare state was in the year of its electoral defeat, 1979, essentially unchanged from that held at the inception of the welfare state in the 1940s. The Labour Party subscribed to the Westminster model and the public administration paradigm.

Prior to 1979, critical discussion within the Labour Party had occurred regarding its traditional approach to accountability in the welfare state. The outcome of this was a shift in support both for more participative democratic methods (Richardson, 1983) and a decentralisation of representative democracy (Marquand, 1992). Nonetheless, at the 1979 and 1983 Elections the Labour Party showed only minor changes in its traditional approach to accountability. The Westminster model and public administration paradigm remained largely intact with only tokenistic support for participative democracy and consumer accountability. The manifesto of 1983 renewed promises made in 1979 for a Scottish Assembly and a Freedom of Information Bill, to give local communities much more say about how their services were run. It also referred to making public services more responsive to users and improving procedures for complaints (Craig, 1990).

It was only by the end of the 1980s that significant change had occurred in Labour's approach to accountability as a result of several factors. These were principally:

- its involvement in local government;
- the social and economic changes that impinged on its involvement;
- its successive election defeats;
- the policy review which the election defeats prompted;
- the radical changes made by the Conservative government to the welfare state with their implications for accountability.

Through the local authorities that it controlled, the Party continued to exercise power in the welfare state. Here, initiatives were taken to extend the accountability of services through various arrangements which afforded more direct links between the users of services and the service deliverers. Pioneering councils included Walsall, Islington and Glasgow and the new arrangements included greater consultation, decentralisation of services and greater local democratic control (Gyford, 1991; Hill, 1994; Lansley et al, 1989). Increasingly also, consumerism became a concern of the Party during the 1980s. This followed the pioneering work of several local authorities, such as York and Lewisham, that introduced charters or contracts of service. As a result, the specification of standards and availability of information for the user of services became a Labour Party proposal in 1986 and was confirmed in subsequent policy documents (Hill, 1994).

A revised concept of accountability became accepted throughout the Labour Party during the 1980s as a result of its experience in local government. Two sources of pressure that impinged on all local authorities, irrespective of the Party in control, were the cause of this change. These were from de-industrialisation and the increasing diversity and assertiveness of the public (Gyford, 1991).

Massive employment and population change that accompanied de-industrialisation resulted in greater social differentiation and diversity than had prevailed hitherto. The customary methods used by local government to keep in touch with the needs and wishes of the public were no longer adequate. New means to regain contact with consumers were sought (Richardson, 1983). A more positive interest in new methods of managerial accountability also developed in the ranks of Labour councillors when they realised that many of their ambitious and idealistic schemes were frustrated because of the obsolete nature of the administrative procedures at hand (Lansley et al, 1989).

By the 1980s major economic and social changes had occurred in Britain, as in many other post-industrial societies. As a result of these changes the population enjoyed a higher standard of living on average than ever before, was much better educated and had greater expectations of services delivered by the welfare state (Taylor-Gooby and Lawson, 1993; Glennerster and Le Grand, 1994). The political culture in Britain that had been a deferential civic culture (Almond and Verba, 1963) had by the 1980s become much less deferential and accepting of decisions made by élites and hierarchies (Kavanagh, 1980). The response of the Labour Party to demands for consumer accountability in the welfare state was inhibited in the early 1980s by the traditional concern of the Party to protect the interests of public service employees. That concern was accentuated as a result of the threats presented to the public sector at large from the Conservative government of the day. However, there was realisation in the Labour Party eventually that the largely uncritical defence of public service employees was jeapordising the support of voters. Consequently, concern with the quality of services came to the fore in the Party's appeal to the public.

By the time of the 1987 Election, the Labour Party's evolution in thinking about accountability showed in its manifesto. The decentralisation of democracy promised in the manifestos of 1979 and 1983 was renewed and tentatively extended. Firm support was given to both consumer and managerial accountability. The manifesto of 1987 promised a new strategic authority for London and suggested regional authorities for England and Wales. The pledge to make public bodies respond better to their users was renewed and the promise was made for a quality commission for local government to ensure that good practices, high standards and efficiency were widely observed (Craig, 1990).

The election defeat of 1987 prompted the appointment of a policy review to look hard at Party policy in its entirety. The review responded to negative electoral feedback about policies such as the lack of priority for users' needs in public service provision. Various initiatives were endorsed such as public quality commissions, social audits and customer contracts for welfare services (Alcock, 1992). The general ideological shift in the Party that the review legitimated, permitted support for improvement in public services from the consumer's point of view rather than the producer's point of view (Seyd, 1992). The review also led to proposals being supported for changes in the system of government of the welfare state that implied considerable decentralisation (Marquand, 1992). These proposals for a more decentralised form of representative democracy were inspired by the continuing domination of the welfare state by the Conservative government. Although the Conservative Party had only little more than 40% of the popular vote after the 1987 Election it was able to drive through radical and controversial policies (Seyd, 1992). Constitutional changes were supported to ensure greater protection from the further onslaught of Thatcherite policy (Marquand, 1992).

The reappraisal of the system of government of the welfare state continued after the review was officially completed in 1989. Pressure groups such as Charter 88, the Constitutional Convention in Scotland and new academic thinking about accountability that was prompted by bodies such as the Left-wing think tank, the Institute for Public Policy Research (IPPR), all exercised an influence on the Labour Party. The ferment of thinking and debate in and around the Labour Party at the end of the 1980s culminated in a new perspective on accountability. That new perspective was a broader and more complex understanding of accountability than had existed hitherto and was fashioned to empower the public in different guises. It included approaches to management that were adapted from private industry as well as diverse ideas to ensure that citizens and users had greater rights to the welfare state. The development of this perspective was further stimulated by the introduction, by the Conservative government after 1987, of internal or quasi-markets in health, housing, personal social services and education. These new markets all accentuated the importance of managers and consumers contributing to decision making about services.

When the 1992 Election arrived, the Labour Party had an extensive programme for the enhancement of accountability. This included a programme of decentralisation of representative democracy and a strengthening of participative democracy. Earlier promises were renewed and proposals made for a Welsh Assembly, a Bill of Rights and a review of the electoral system (Labour Party, 1992). Significant innovations were proposed in the manifesto to enhance considerably managerial and consumer accountability. A Health Quality Commission, an Educational Standards Commission and a Quality Commission for local government were proposed to monitor quality and improve standards throughout the welfare state. Opted-out schools and hospitals would be returned to their respective local authorities. Local management of schools was accepted but CCT would end.

The election defeat of 1992 prompted a further policy review. Benefits and taxes were a source of some electoral unpopularity and a Commission on Social Justice was appointed to review the whole breadth of social policy (Taylor, 1997). The Commission considered accountability within the welfare state and largely confirmed established policy. It affirmed that power was overcentralised and a broad programme of measures was endorsed to strengthen public accountability (Commission on Social Justice, 1994). The analysis made by the Commission that the system of government was centralised, inefficient and bureaucratic was also upheld by the 1997 election manifesto. The manifesto also shared the Commission's prescription for a comprehensive programme of democratic renewal of the welfare state in which both representative and participative processes would be furthered. Managerial and consumer accountability were upheld but through different means from those promised in the 1992 manifesto. No mention was made of the Education, Health and Quality Commissions promised in the previous manifesto. The promise of raised standards was now to be fulfilled through existing authorities. Opted-out schools would be linked to local authorities but the internal market would be abolished in health (Labour Party, 1997a).

Democratic renewal

By the time New Labour was elected to office in May 1997, it had revised its thinking considerably about the means by which accountability was best secured within the welfare state. The approach since then has been a fusion of new ideas, the legacy of unimplemented proposals for reform from the past and a response to changes that were made by the Conservative government. However, the new approach has been more evident as an emergent strategy for accountability in the welfare state than as a fully designed strategy of change.

Pivotal to New Labour's new approach to accountability is its belief that there is a crisis of confidence in the political system (Labour Party, 1997a). That belief is the basis of a programme of revision of the political system, the purpose of which is to restore to people the power that has ebbed away from them. The programme seeks to revive the sense of ownership by the public and its willingness to participate in public affairs. It is a programme for democratic renewal. The management and control of the welfare state is to be made more fully and firmly accountable to the public through innovations that restore the democratic process. This is to be achieved through a decentralisation of power away from Westminster and changes to the procedure of the political system. These changes are intended to provide easier and more accessible opportunities for all to participate politically. None are to be excluded or marginalised. A token of the spirit of inclusivity has been given in the co-option of Liberal Democrats onto a Cabinet committee deciding constitutional reform.

Much of the programme of constitutional change was announced in the Queen's Speech of May 1997, confirmed in the Queen's Speech of November 1998 and foreshadowed by the 1997 manifesto. A start has been made to the process of its implementation. Power is being devolved to Scotland, Wales and Northern Ireland through the creation of elected assemblies. The creation of these three new assemblies bring to closer account the relevant central government departments, Scottish Office, Welsh Office and Northern Ireland Office and the quangos for which they have responsibility. The Welsh Assembly will oversee the welfare state in Wales. It will set the priorities and determine the direction, involving £7 billion of expenditure. In Scotland, the transfer of power is greater, with the creation of a Parliament that has tax-raising and law-making powers. A strategic authority for London will be established. This authority will comprise an elected mayor overseen by a separately elected assembly. The Greater London Authority will assume responsibility for various services that have been run by unelected committees since the abolition of the Greater London Council. The introduction of a chief executive for the capital is an innovation in regional government. In addition, nine Regional Development Agencies (RDAs) in England outside London are being created. The agencies are being accompanied by the voluntary formation of regional chambers, comprising councillors, business people and trade unionists. In the short term, these chambers will serve as advisory bodies to the RDAs. In the longer term, a system of elected regional assemblies may evolve that resembles the precedent of the Greater London Authority.

Constitutional reform has also been pursued in the use of referenda and a shift away from the traditional first-past-the-post electoral system. Referenda were arranged to ensure that there was public support for the introduction of assemblies for Scotland, Wales, Northern Ireland and Greater London. Proportional representation is invoked by the electoral arrangements for these assemblies and is proposed for election of UK members to the European Parliament. Proportional representation to replace the first-past-the-post system is also recommended by the Jenkins Commission, appointed to review the system for election to the House of Commons. A more democratic and representative upper House has been promised through the abolition of the voting rights of hereditary peers and the appointment of a royal commission to investigate alternatives to the present House of Lords.

The government has expressed its support for participatory democracy through reforms to the local government system, for which legislation is expected in due course. Consultative proposals have been made for greater participation of the public in decision making through the use of information technology to obtain the views of voters, directly-elected mayors, citizens' juries, focus groups and referenda. Ironically, some of these practices have been pioneered by quangos and were created by the Conservative reforms of the welfare state (Rouse, 1997). The government also favours local authorities taking a more proactive role with regards to community planning, through, for example, public forums, whereby matters that concern local communities are addressed, even if other public bodies are largely responsible for them.

In its attempt to revive the confidence of the public in the political processes of the welfare state, the government has continued with the belated efforts made by the previous Conservative government to combat dishonesty by those in public office. It referred the funding of political parties to the Committee on Standards in Public Life and is now considering its response to the report from the Committee, which recommends substantial changes. The campaign against corruption has been extended by the government to the sphere of local government. Consultative proposals have been made that include the adoption of codes of conduct for councillors and employees and the creation of an independent standards board to investigate corruption claims.

Labour government proposals to enhance democratic control of the welfare state have been complemented by measures to maintain and enhance managerial and consumer accountability. The management revolution brought about by the Conservative government is not to be reversed by New Labour. There will be no return to the public administration paradigm as the template for the organisation of the welfare state. Instead, the Labour government has accepted many of the changes made by the Conservatives that have improved managerial accountability and has introduced some of its own. The performance management ethos has become even more pronounced under New Labour.

The Conservative legacy that has been accepted has included the separation of policy making from management. The Next Steps executive agencies (Greer, 1994) have been retained because they are considered to offer greater accountability to ministers than the previous unified system (Theakson, 1998). The purchaser/provider split has been endorsed although not the internal market, as shown in plans for reform of the health service. Partnership between the public and private sectors is approved, as shown in the introduction of action zones, Best Value approach to services and in the continuation of the private finance initiative. Performance indicators will be retained as a valuable managerial tool for the improvement of services. In plans for health and education particularly, the government's zealous concern to raise standards is dependent on a range of managerial devices and in making information readily available to the public, for example in the form of school performance tables. The Citizen's Charter has being relaunched and renamed Service First (Cabinet Office, 1998). There is every prospect that the guarantors of standards, in the form of auditors, most notably the Audit Commission, Ofsted, and Social Services Inspectorate will have a busy time in promoting efficiency and high standards in many services. They will be strengthened by a new Commission for Health Improvement and a local government inspectorate attached to the Audit Commission.

Changes that are more distinctive to New Labour are its pragmatic and experimental approach to the delivery of services, enthusiasm for collaboration and cooperation throughout the welfare state and commitment to greater openness. Pragmatism is shown in the maintenance of market testing and contracting out which has resulted in several privately-financed jails and the sale of the Social Security property estate and the Benefits Agency medical service to the private sector (Theakston, 1998). The application of this pragmatic approach to local government has led to the rescinding of CCT and its replacement with a regime to obtain Best Value (DETR, 1998b). Local authorities are required to show that they have conducted an overall assessment of their performance strengths and weaknesses judged in terms of objective indicators and the more subjective views of the local community. As such, Best Value represents a form of continuous improvement management. Councils will need to convince central government that they are providing Best Value in terms of targets set. Failure to do so will result in the imposition of controls from outside. Guidance about Best Value has been promised from the piloting of schemes in several local authorities (Gray and Jenkins, 1998). Best Value is meant to move service provision from a cost-effectiveness approach to effectiveness based on a broader stakeholder definition of quality. Effectively, Best Value provides the green light for the mixed economy of local government service provision with no presumption that the service should be private or public.

The action zones for education, employment and health that are being created are also characterised by experimentation. Collaboration between organisations will be required in these zones to break down the usual institutional barriers. It is possible that valuable lessons will be learned about the delivery and ultimately the accountability of services. Consultative proposals for local government reform suggest new powers may be given to local authorities to work in partnership with other agencies to deliver a wider range of services. The formation of the Social Exclusion Unit, with close links with the Prime Minister, is also expected to promote the integration of organisations within the welfare state. Collaboration has been a conspicuous practice of the government from the start. It has been exhibited in the admission of outsiders to government in the multiplicity of review groups that have scrutinised many aspects of policy. Greater openness has been promised through legislation for freedom of information, albeit delayed. Individual members of the public will be entitled to see information that is kept about them by government departments. Where information is refused, individuals may appeal to an independent and powerful Information Commissioner. The rights of individuals have also been strengthened through the incorporation of the

European Convention on Human Rights into British Law and the passage of the Public Interest Disclosure Act.

Conclusion: New Labour, the differentiated polity and the Third Way

During the short time it has been in office, New Labour has already demonstrated a search for more effective accountability in the welfare state. Changes that are being made seek to bring about a new relationship between citizens and the welfare state. More accessible opportunities are being created for the public, through representative and participative means, to contribute to the shaping and control of the welfare state. The providers of welfare are being encouraged to innovate and be cooperative, to maintain high standards of performance that are publicly demonstrable, to be efficient in their work and to maintain opportunities for users to be informed and feel satisfied with the services delivered to them. The changes are in part an attempt to overcome those elements of the New Right legacy of accountability that are widely seen as deficient and damaging. This legacy is characterised by fragmentation, secrecy, lack of trust, dishonesty, the decline of democratic control and a dogmatic approval of the supply of welfare by market principles. While some of New Labour's approach to accountability has been based on the principles and values of the New Right, much of it has not.

The constitutional reform programme represents a strategy for political change where New Labour diverges markedly from the New Right which opposed constitutional reform as part of its antipathy to political processes. Those aspects of new public management that New Labour upholds, distinguish them also from the New Right perspective on accountability. Nor can the approach be likened to the approach to accountability that characterised the social democratic consensus, prior to 1979, when the Westminster model and public administration paradigm were wholeheartedly accepted, with minor reforms only. The approach of New Labour to accountability in the welfare state is sufficiently different from both the social democratic consensus and the New Right to consider at least provisionally, that it belongs to a Third Way (see Table 11.1).

The institutional changes that have been initiated have promoted the democratisation of democracy and the renewal of civil society. Both of these principles have been identified as intrinsic to the pursuit of a third way (Giddens, 1998). New Labour has accepted the widely-shared view

Table 11.1: Approaches to accountability in the welfare state

Dimension	Social democratic consensus	Third Way	New Right
Principles	Traditional political control upheld. Chain of command from elected assemblies through elected representatives office, down to officials and professionals. Bureaucratic, unitary, wholly public organisations delivering services. Supplementary procedures for legal and financial affairs.	Revival of political control through decentralised elected assemblies, electoral reforms and participative democracy. Subordination of managerialism to politics. Public–private partnerships. Collaboration in public sector. Revived probity in political conduct. Pragmatism in service delivery. Openness.	Contraction of political control through substitution by managerial processes and market principles. Separation of political and managerial spheres. Contracts and performance standards. Separation of finance from provision of services. Plurality of providers, both public and private.
Chief stakeholders	Electorate, politicians, administrative officials, professionals, trade unions.	Electorate, politicians, managers, auditors, professionals, users of services, citizens.	Consumers, managers, appointed representatives, entrepreneurs, auditors.
Values	Equity, impartiality, consistency, reliability, expertise (public service values).	Inclusivity, quality and performance, trust, self-governance, civil empowerment, cooperation, opportunity.	Individualism, choice, performance, variety, economic freedom (customer values).
Key problems	Non-compliance of the officials and professionals with instructions. Unresponsiveness of services to social diversity and change. Disaffection of the public. Wastefulness.	Incoherence of the overall approach. Relationships between plurality of elected bodies. Effectiveness of the diffusion of power. Passive citizenry. Efficiency versus democracy.	Fragmentation, élitism, secrecy, dishonesty. Exclusion of the wishes of the electorate. Confusion of political and managerial spheres.

that a revival of civil society is required. However, it has not endorsed several specific alternative prescriptions that have been offered to achieve that. A strategy canvassed by Hirst (1998) for associative democracy through the conversion of state welfare bureaucracies to a plurality of self-governing associations which are given public funds to provide services to the public, has been eschewed. Also rejected, has been the proposal made by Green (1996) for a contraction of direct provision of welfare by government in order that space be created for action by an independent voluntary sector. Similarly, there has been little demonstrable enthusiasm for the project advocated by Field (1996b) to transform the welfare state through the rebuilding, extension and creation of new mutual aid organisations that recognise fully the importance of self-interest. The existence of an approach to accountability from a third way becomes more distinct when consideration is given to the chief stakeholders implicitly recognised by the three approaches (see Table 11.1). The Third Way approach to accountability has emerged from the recognition made by New Labour that its conception of democratic control of the welfare state has to be in keeping with a much more complex and diverse society than in the past, with a much less deferential culture. The Third Way approach to accountability has also been inspired, in part, by a belated recognition of the value of some aspects of the new public management. This has been adapted to uphold accountability to users in the context of community and not as separate atomised consumers. The approach taken by the Third Way to accountability is founded on the premise that a differentiated polity of local governance (Rhodes, 1997) is the prevalent pattern of the welfare state. It seeks to construct a new relationship of accountability, based more on intentional collaboration and networking between the separate but linked authorities that deliver welfare and the citizens that they all serve – effectively acting as a joined-up government.

New Labour's approach to accountability owes a debt to communitarianism. For communitarianism seeks to move beyond the traditional Left-Right divide and to attach greater importance to the building of inclusive communities. The communitarian testament is predicated on three principles: cooperative inquiry, mutual responsibility and citizen participation (Tam, 1998). These three principles are evident in much of the programme of New Labour from its early days in office. However, the centralised search to improve performance throughout the welfare state, so ardently pursued by New Labour, cannot be attributed to communitarianism and appears to be at variance with it.

The emergent approach to accountability that New Labour has

- embraced is only beginning to be implemented. Its separate identity is not yet clear, nor can the full implications of the approach be appreciated. However, from the initiatives that have been launched so far it is possible to recognise several potential problems in the emergent approach to accountability made by the Third Way.

There is the overall destination of the changes made and the extent to which there is coherence in the various initiatives. Are the various political and managerial developments fully compatible with one another so that accountability to citizens is made more effective? A new democratic system for control of the welfare state is evolving but the exact nature of the relationships between all the elected bodies (including many local authorities) has yet to be established. Will all these bodies respect each others' domain or will damaging conflict prevail with all that follows for services? The extent to which these changes actually decentralise power and empower citizens and users remains to be seen. The effective devolution of power might not be realised unless new democratic institutions are created, at regional or neighbourhood level, or both. More immediately, the decentralisation espoused by the government appears to be at odds with the same government's firm centralised control to contain public spending and promote efficiency through strict performance management. Effective decentralisation of power challenges the centralist tradition that has long characterised the governance of the welfare state (Bochel and Bochel, 1998). The willingness and ability of citizens to avail themselves of the new opportunities to participate politically has also yet to be realised. A revival of the political process, of a civic culture, may be very difficult to achieve after such a long period of political decline.

TWELVE

Bridging the Atlantic: the Democratic (Party) origins of Welfare to Work

Desmond King and Mark Wickham-Jones

Introduction

In January 1988, the National Executive Committee of the Labour Party endorsed *The Charter against workfare* (NEC, 1988). The Charter had been agreed by a number of trade unions and local authorities, laying out four principles for participation in government schemes to reduce unemployment. The most important was a commitment to make all initiatives voluntary:

> ... people should join the scheme because they want to, not because they fear they will lose all or part of their benefits if they don't. Compulsion is a recipe for lower standards, resentment and discrimination. (*Charter against workfare*, PD 1201/December 1987, p 1, NEC, 1988)

Labour's rejection of workfare, an arrangement under which claimants must take work in exchange for social security benefits, was unequivocal.

Labour's approval of the voluntary principle was uncontroversial. The idea that benefit entitlement should be unconditional was at the core of Marshallian social rights of citizenship. This commitment to universal social rights was a benchmark of the Party's welfare programme between 1945 and 1992 (Marshall, 1964; Lister, 1997b; see Deacon, 1996, for a critical view). Labour ministers criticised the various schemes floated by the Conservatives during the late 1980s and early 1990s which attached conditions to receipt of benefit (King, 1995). For example, Robin Cook was blunt in defending the benefit rights of those who voluntarily left work: "Those people's families are entitled to the same diet, clothes and heating allowances as the families of other unemployed people" (*The*

Sunday Times, 6 March 1988). He later criticised the "humiliating hoops" through which the Conservatives wanted claimants to jump by making benefit conditional (*The Times*, 23 November 1988). When the Tories edged towards workfare in 1992 and 1993, Tony Lloyd, a member of Labour's frontbench described such arrangements as "socially unacceptable" (*The Times*, 5 February 1993). These schemes were irrelevant to the needs of the unemployed and they were unfair: they would create a two-tier labour force. It was "demeaning", claimed Frank Dobson, to demand that people "work for next to nothing" (*Financial Times*, 5 February 1993).

On 9 November 1995, Gordon Brown, Shadow Chancellor of the Exchequer, announced an ambitious plan, called Welfare to Work, to tackle the problem of youth unemployment (Brown, 1995). Four options would be designed for those aged between 18 and 25 who had been out of work for six months. Private employers would be offered subsidies to take them on for six months. There would be opportunities for training and further education. There would be the chance of voluntary work and the new administration would establish an environmental taskforce which the unemployed could join. In a break with Labour's existing trajectory, Brown introduced an element of compulsion to the scheme. As has already been mentioned in Chapter Eight, penalties were planned for those who refused to participate: "simply remaining unemployed and permanently on benefit", Brown stated, "will no longer be an option" (*Financial Times*, 10 November 1995). Those who rejected the four options would lose 40% of their benefit entitlement indefinitely. The Shadow Chancellor told *The Daily Telegraph*, "young people have a responsibility to work and to train" (9 November 1995).

The Labour Party was quick to deny that the new proposal amounted to workfare. However, the introduction of compulsion into the Party's policies did mark a departure. Rather than benefit entitlement being unconditional, the core of social democratic citizenship, Labour claimed, was that rights must be balanced by responsibilities (Deacon, 1997a). Those expecting receipt of benefits must discharge their obligations towards society and make use of any opportunities to work that they were offered. If they rejected those opportunities, they would lose some benefit entitlement. Predictions about the impact of compulsion varied. Once Labour was in office, one internal paper anticipated that up to 40,000 individuals would reject the options and so lose their benefit (*The Independent*, 8 July 1998). By the spring of 1999, after nearly two years in government, Labour's enthusiasm for such arrangements, including greater compulsion, had escalated. The penalties on those who refused to participate in the Welfare to Work programme were increased. In January, *The Times* reported further moves by the administration towards workfare, indicating that all benefit claimants would have to attend interviews. With few exceptions (including disabled people), they would have to seek paid employment and take up any offers of work (13 January 1999, see also *Financial Times*, 19 January 1999). In February, the government's much-anticipated Welfare Reform and Pensions Bill was published outlining stricter conditions for the receipt of benefits, especially for disabled people and lone parents (DSS, 1999a; press anticipations include *The Times*, 27 and 29 October 1998; *The Independent*, 29 October 1998). Alistair Darling, Secretary of State for Social Security wrote bluntly and defiantly about the new measures:

> **The new regime will be far tougher than people thought.... We will end the something-for-nothing approach that has characterised the past.... Our new contract will require people to attend an interview as a condition of receiving benefit and to consider the options available to them. (Darling, 1999)**

This remarkable turnaround is surprising even in terms of Tony Blair's New Labour (for an introduction see Driver and Martell, 1998). Many of the reforms of Blair's project are less abrupt and sweeping than is claimed by their proponents. However, in this case the Party had broken a long-held conviction that benefit entitlement should be unconditional, replacing it with a much tougher and more-market orientated approach. In February 1999, Blair promised the readers of the *Daily Mail* that the welfare reforms marked "a fundamental break with the past" (Blair, 1999). How this point was reached is the subject of this chapter.

Electoral politics and policy development after 1992

Labour's defeat in the April 1992 General Election raised question marks about the Party's capacity to return to office. In the run-up to the poll, Neil Kinnock had carried out a series of detailed reforms to the party's policy commitments and to its structure. Although the Conservative majority in the House of Commons fell from 101 to 21, such moderations failed to ensure that Labour won. The unexpected size of the defeat (the worst outcome many had considered was a hung Parliament with no Party able to command a majority) added to its members' feelings of despair.

Some commentators and leading figures within Labour, the so-called 'modernisers', were quick to conclude that new policies were essential if it was to triumph electorally. Others, often called 'traditionalists', were cautious about further reforms. From the modernisers' perspective, Labour's Shadow Budget, launched at the start of the 1992 election campaign, was one of the Party's most significant mistakes. The Budget had promised limited increases in income tax and National Insurance in order to fund higher pensions and Child Benefit payments. In themselves the increases were modest and most voters would have been better off. However, the starting point for the tax increases was relatively low and well within the salary bracket aspirations of many voters, a point exposed by the Conservative Party. If Labour was to abandon even the most limited of tax increases, what policies could it offer in terms of welfare to the worst-off in society? The Party's existing approach used benefits to ameliorate poverty. Some Labour politicians concluded that other ways, rather than general tax rises and increases in benefit, had to be found to help the living standards of the worst-off. Tax increases threatened middle-class voters and prevented the Party from winning much-needed votes (see, for example, Radice, 1992).

The stark conclusion reached by modernisers was that a party so imbued with welfarism of the type with which Labour was associated simply could not win a general election. Labour had been committed to universalist entitlements, benefits for all regardless of income or status. However, welfare budgets had skyrocketed despite the determined efforts of Conservative administrations since 1979. Such spending was costly in terms of tax revenues. Even more problematic it acted as an electoral disincentive by alienating middle-class voters. Paul Thompson, editor of the journal *Renewal*, produced by the Labour Coordinating Committee (an important internal group within the party), concluded of the election defeat: "What Labour was left with as the centrepiece of election strategy was old-fashioned welfarism" (Thompson, 1993, p 3). There was an electoral imperative for the Party to adopt a new line on welfare, one which broke with its commitment to universal benefits: by so doing Labour could demonstrate it was no longer a threat towards the ambitions of ordinary middle-class voters. One estimate claimed that Welfare to Work could reduce the social security budget by 18% (cited by Oppenheim, 1998a, p 31). Such a move would free up resources for allocation towards other areas of the welfare state without necessitating tax increases.

The imperative to alter the Party's pledges on welfare was given added impetus by Tony Blair's accession to the Labour leadership in July 1994. John Smith, his predecessor, had sought to steer the Party clear of potentially divisive policy issues. Smith's focus was on the equally contentious subject of organisational reform. He established the Commission on Social Justice, under Sir Gordon Borrie, to delay problematic decisions on welfare and so limit internal policy disputes within the Party. Tony Blair's position as a leading moderniser was well established by 1994, largely through his command of the home affairs brief within the Shadow Cabinet. As leader, Blair was less concerned about consensus within Labour and he quickly emphasised a new set of underpinnings for the Party's outlook on welfare. He spoke not of entitlements, but of 'rights' matched with 'responsibilities'. Blair's Spectator lecture of 1995 was titled, 'The rights we enjoy reflect the duties we owe' (Blair, 1995). When Blair outlined the opportunities available to individuals, he noted the obligations accompanying them. Given such language (and the changes that Blair promoted to the Party's structure), it was apparent from the early days of his leadership that there would be important changes to policy.

Labour's abandonment of universalistic-type entitlements can be explained in terms of domestic developments following the 1992 General Election. In standard Downsian terms (Downs, 1957), the Party had to move further to the centreground to attract middle-class voters. It had to break with its welfarist image. Support for the most deserving groups in society could no longer be funded by general taxation increases but only by savings in public spending elsewhere. (The Welfare to Work programme provided Labour with an ingenious solution to this dilemma.) Under Tony Blair, Labour's shift was dramatic: his language broke directly with the Party's existing image. Labour opposed, reviewed and then accepted the adoption of the Job Seekers' Allowance (JSA) which tightened the conditions for the receipt of benefit. By 1995, both Labour and the Conservative Parties were moving in the same direction in terms of policy on work and welfare, partly as a direct result of electoral impulses and the perceived preferences of voters.

The success of the New Democrats in the United States

In the late 1980s the Democratic Party in the United States was perceived by many observers to be in a similar impasse to that in which the British Labour Party found itself. The Democrats had lost three elections in a row (and could, in many ways, count themselves lucky to have won in 1976 in the aftermath of Watergate). In 1990, the question some commentators asked was, what could the Democrats learn from the Labour Party and the modernisation programme launched by Neil Kinnock? Within two years the direction of that question was reversed.

Bill Clinton's 1992 presidential campaign marked a departure for the Democrats which proved successful in capturing the White House in the November election (Pomper, 1993). He made a series of changes to the Party's policy outlook, ideas and campaigning strategy. The cumulative effect of these changes was conveyed in the epithet 'new' to describe the Democratic Party.

Clinton supported the market mechanism and prioritised growth before distribution (Peele, 1996). He talked of entrepreneurial government – but it was clear that such a stance marked a break with the type of big government approach so often associated with the Democrats. He took a tough line on crime (returning to Little Rock, Arkansas, to sign a death penalty during the campaign) and on welfare. He noted that welfare rights must entail responsibilities and promoted some form of workfare as a solution to welfare dependency. This line on welfare reflected the position taken by the Democratic Leadership Council, an internal group within the party of which Clinton was an active member and which advanced the type of reforms he espoused as part of his presidential bid. Clinton chaired the National Governors' Association during the 1988 reform of welfare (which resulted in President Reagan's Family Support Act) when workfare was mandated federally (MacGregor, 1998). One commentator noted, "The group [Democratic Leadership Council] believes, for example, that welfare payments are justified only if recipients accept training or jobs" (*Financial Times*, 12 October 1992). Clinton's language was not only of responsibility but also of opportunity and community. Some members of the Democratic Leadership Council went so far as to see the group as successfully charting a 'third way' between the Republicans and the old Democrats.

Clinton's policy reforms were accompanied by changes to the Democrats' electoral strategy. He targeted middle-class voters. The Democrats could no longer afford to be associated with either special interests or the decaying constituencies of industrial areas. His tough line on welfare was crucial in establishing this middle-class electoral base, in reassuring voters that personal tax levels would not be threatened by social budgets. One observer, Joe Rogaly concluded, "The Clinton programme, which centres around 'workfare', is politically saleable as a hand-up, not a hand-out" (*Financial Times*, 27 November 1992). Clinton had long held such views. Speaking in Congress in 1987 to welfare reform hearings, then Governor Clinton stated: "We believe that every welfare recipient should sign a contract with the State, making a personal commitment in return for benefits to pursue an individually developed path to independence" (US Senate, 1987, p 17). Other features of Clinton's 1992 electoral strategy included the use of focus groups to refine the campaign message and the deployment of an organised 'war room' to direct the campaign from Little Rock. The effect of Clinton's programme was to transform policy areas in which the Democrats had been historically weak into ones which were electoral strengths for the Party.

The Democrats' tough line on welfare was underpinned theoretically by the work of such academics as Lawrence Mead (1992, 1997a). Mead's argument was straightforward. The main cause of unemployment was not economic and the problem could not therefore be tackled by economic programmes. Unemployment and welfare dependency originated from a culture of poverty which meant that the poor lacked the competence to work. Mead concluded: "A great number [of unemployed] are simply defeatist about work or unable to organise their personal lives to hold jobs consistently" (1997b, p 12). Mead's argument suggested not only that there were electoral benefits to workfare-type arrangements but that such schemes were an important means of cutting unemployment. The State should prepare people for work through advice and assistance in preparation for the labour market but it should also ensure strict conditions for eligibility so that individuals were forced to make use of such help.

In the first years of office, Clinton's performance disappointed many supporters of the New Democratic approach. Hampered by the institutional weaknesses inherent in the United States system, the Clinton presidency lacked a vision as to what New Democratic meant in practice. The administration pursued too many initiatives, some of which appeared far removed from the parsimony of the election campaign: its health reform plan disintegrated. The result was a huge reversal at the mid-term elections in 1994. Subsequently, Clinton followed a more coherent programme which was reflected in his approach to welfare. Compulsion was emphasised, particularly to induce single mothers back into the labour market. Under welfare reforms in 1996 (the Personal Responsibility and Work Opportunities Reconciliation Act), single mothers must accept job offers or lose benefits. Robert Reich, Clinton's Secretary of Labor during the first term, concluded that the harsh approach was motivated by the President's electoral fears. Reich commented critically: "Instead of smoothing the transition from welfare to work, then the new law simply demanded that people get off welfare" (Reich, 1999, p 3). Signing the law, President Clinton declared that "today we are ending welfare as we know it" (*The New York Times*, 23 August 1996). A lifetime limit of five years on benefit was established and states were given the discretion to attach tougher conditions. Some states went further in the drive towards workfare by organising job schemes.

Lessons of Clinton's New Democrats for Labour

Party members and media commentators immediately noted the potential for Labour to draw important lessons from Bill Clinton's success in the 1992 presidential election (Rentoul, 1995, pp 271-82). The Democratic victory boosted confidence that Parties of the Left could win. It was much less certain what the exact message was, given the differences both between the Democratic and Labour Parties and between the political systems within which they operated. Accordingly, the 1992 Democratic victory sparked a fierce debate within Labour. Many of the leading modernisers – such as Tony Blair – felt that there was much the Party could acquire from Democrats' approach. More traditional figures, who felt that the reforms had gone far enough, were unconvinced. They feared that Clinton's victory could be used to jettison long-held values and policies as part of a myth that only through such modifications could victory be secured. Clare Short, one Left-wing frontbencher, criticised

> ... the secret, infiltrating so-called modernisers of the Labour party [who] have been creating myths about why Clinton won, in order to try and reshape the Labour party ... they have very little understanding of Labour's traditions. (Rentoul, 1995, p 274)

John Prescott, later to become the Party's deputy leader, was reported as maintaining that Clinton's success masked a hidden agenda to end the Party's links with the unions and end its socialist ideology (*The Times*, 1 January 1993). He claimed of the Democrats' approach:

> It's not about strengthening a party: all the ideas from Clinton are an élite few running a party on the basis of the information they get from the polls. That is not the way the Labour Party has

been run, and while we've tried it in the last couple of elections, it does seem to be that we've lost, doesn't it [sic]. (C. Brown, 1997, p 273)

Prescott went on, revealing a tenuous grasp of American politics: "I do not think it's been proven that Clinton won the election because he broke his contacts with the trade unions" (C. Brown, 1997, p 276). The American approach was seen to rely too much on polling and adopting policies to the whims of the electorate. Short stated:"I am not a conspiracy theorist, but it is now clear to me that there are well-placed people in our midst who want to model the British Labour Party on the American Democratic Party" (Anderson and Mann, 1997, p 320). It was not a development that Left-wingers welcomed and the phrase 'Clintonisation' of the Party was employed pejoratively.

Modernisers established close links with the new Democratic administration in Washington. Blair (seen as the arch-Clintonite within the Party) together with Gordon Brown spent time in Washington during the transition in January 1993. Soon after, leading members of the Clinton campaign came to London and addressed the Party Leader's committee (as well as a Transport and General Workers' Union conference). Further meetings ensued. Brown was an especially frequent visitor to Washington, often for discussions with senior economists in the Democratic administration, facilitated by links established by his US-educated adviser, Ed Balls. In April 1996, Blair's first official visit as Leader of the Opposition to the United States was immensely successful in terms of press coverage of his meetings with Clinton and with senior business figures. A close personal relationship between the two leaders was established. It was a marked contrast to the hostile reception given to Neil Kinnock on his visit to the Reagan White House in 1987. When Clinton and Blair had met earlier in the UK, one commentator claimed they talked 'like twins separated at birth' (*The Guardian*, 13 April 1996). In the US, Blair emphasised the links between the Parties, arguing that they faced a common challenge and that "the values that brought us into politics are the same" (*Daily Telegraph*, 13 April 1996). Once in office, Gordon Brown also stressed these 'shared values' (Brown, 1998a). Prime Minister Blair noted the "ideology that links Labour and the Democrats", and claimed "we really are talking about the same things" (*The Guardian*, 7 February 1998).

In January 1993, Patricia Hewitt (previously a senior member of Neil Kinnock's staff) and Philip Gould (who advised Labour on polling) published an assessment of Clinton's campaign. It was a significant report, not just because of their status within the ranks of Labour's modernisers: Gould had spent some time working with Clinton campaigners in Little Rock, assisting them in avoiding the type of mistakes which had dogged Labour's campaign in 1992 (Gould, 1998, pp 162-9). He was not alone: several senior Party officials, including Margaret McDonagh who was to become Labour's General Secretary in 1998, spent time in the United States helping and studying the Democrats' campaign. On his return Gould was enthusiastic about what could be learned from the American experience. Hewitt and Gould argued that Labour should focus on the *process* of the Democrats' success and not on its *content* (1993, p 45). They made a myriad of points about Clinton's success which reflected on *both* content and presentation. The lessons Labour needed to learn included the:

- repackaging of the Democratic Party's identity by Clinton;
- use of think-tanks;
- deployment of particular themes via voter friendly language;
- employment of focus groups to identify key themes;
- development of symbolic policies on such matters as welfare and crime;
- need for reforms to the Party's structure;
- emphasis on women in the campaign;
- open and accessible style of campaigning – portraying Clinton as an ordinary individual;
- careful management of the campaign;
- establishment of a coordinated war room;
- ability to hit back quickly at opposition attacks through the use of a databank of quotes and information.

Hewitt and Gould attributed Clinton's success to such features. The implication of their article was straightforward: to win, Labour needed to mimic the Democratic campaign. Labour would only succeed, Gould was convinced, "when we have changed as the Democrats have changed" (Gould, 1998, p 170). The Party needed a fresh identity around which new issues would attract middle-class support. Commenting on the Democrats' coordination of campaigning and use of a databank, Hewitt and Gould argued, "the comparison with Labour is depressing" (1993, p 51). Gould wrote a private version of the paper co-authored with Hewitt directly for Labour: it was not well received by the Smith leadership (Gould, 1998, p 175). Another internal report was compiled by John Braggins, a Party official, which listed the aspects of the Democrats' approach which could be copied. Just before Christmas 1992, a debrief was held for those who had been in the United States. The subsequent paper (Braggins, 1993) emphasised the use of telephone banks in canvassing voters. Some of Hewitt and Gould's features had already been adopted by Labour. The Party had made extensive use of think-tanks, especially since the foundation of the Institute for Public Policy Research (IPPR) in 1988. From the late 1980s, it had endorsed measures to promote the status of women within the Party – these were part of a whole package of sweeping reforms initiated under Kinnock's leadership. Some proposals included in Hewitt and Gould's article had been made much earlier by Gould alone. In 1985, he had compiled the detailed report about Labour's campaigning strategy which led to the foundation of the Shadow Communications Agency (the body which had guided Labour's polling and electoral strategy between 1986 and 1992). In the report, Gould called for the development of simple symbolic themes to dominate campaigning and for the establishment of a 'rapid reactions unit' to allow an instant response to Conservative attacks (Gould, 1985, p 12; see also Gould, 1998, pp 54-6). The Shadow Communications Agency went on to make extensive use of focus groups and to work on the type of language that Labour politicians should marshal in vote-seeking. Some of Hewitt and Gould's points were novel: for example, the call for a new identity and the extent of changes to policy. The Party had never before attempted the type of 'counter-scheduling' Hewitt and Gould proposed in which new policies were laid out without compromises to old allies. Elsewhere Gould called for Labour to tackle economic issues (perceived to have done so much damage to the party in April 1992). The approach should be as direct as Clinton's with the Party radically moderating its stance and orientating policy explicitly towards middle class voters (Gould, 1992). Altogether Hewitt and Gould had designed a far-reaching reformulation of the Party's electoral approach.

The main policy implication of Clinton's victory was that the Party must appropriate tough stances on particular issues in order to reassure the middle-class voters. The key issues were fiscal conservatism, crime and welfare. On economy and law and order, Labour had historically been weak. The Party's task was to win over voters through articulating a new stance. Likewise on welfare, the Party had to reassure voters about the limits to Labour's egalitarian aspirations. Such policies would provide the Party with the middle-class support that electoral victory demanded (Collins, 1996).

Tony Blair quickly took up the type of policy stance which Clinton had exploited. Three days after his return from the United States in January 1993, he gave his most famous soundbite on the Today BBC Radio 4 programme when discussing crime. Labour would be, he said, "tough on crime and tough on the causes of crime" (Anderson and Mann, 1997, p 243). A week later Blair spelled out his support for further organisational reform in the Party, including the extension of "one member one vote". His desire to reduce the role of the unions – the type of special interest from which Clinton had distanced the Democrats – was manifest (Rentoul, 1995, p 308). In July 1994, when campaigning for the Party leadership, Blair addressed welfare dependency: "I quite understand the resentment of every taxpayer who has to pay £20 a week in taxes to keep three million unemployed". He went on: "work and welfare go together ... welfare must enhance duties and responsibilities and not be a substitute for them" (*Financial Times*, 15 July 1994). As leader, Blair's policies reflected the "new mix of interventionism and social conservatism" that Hewitt and Gould had suggested Labour adopt (Hewitt and Gould, 1993, p 46). Observers noted the parallels between Blair and Clinton. Within two months of Blair becoming leader, Peter Riddell commented: "Labour leaders have had close contacts with the Clinton team. Much of the rhetoric of the 'modernisers' has echoes of Bill Clinton's campaign two years ago" (*The Times*, 22 August 1994). Clare Short took Blair and Brown's tough approach on pensions and Child Benefit to be a direct emulation of Clinton's success (Rentoul, 1995, p 274).

Blair's determination to reforge Labour's identity in much the same way that Clinton had relocated the Democrats was clear at the Party's 1994 conference. Not only was the Labour leader talking the same language as the US president with his focus on responsibilities and rights, he also adopted the epithet 'new' to indicate the extent of the breach wrought with the Party's historic trajectory. The BBC programme Newsnight noted the shared phrases and themes of the two leaders (Sopel, 1995, p 145). In his first speech as Labour leader, Blair told his Party that "with opportunity must come responsibility" (Labour Party, 1994a, p 102). The Labour leader announced his intention to jettison Clause 4 of the Party's constitution which marked its long-standing commitment to public ownership. Six months later at the special conference which ditched Clause 4, Blair was blunt: "today a new Labour Party is being born" (Labour Party, 1994a, p 292). Subsequent conferences in 1995 and 1996 saw both Blair and Brown engage in the type of 'counter-scheduling' that Hewitt and Gould had proposed: the Labour leaders were blunt in telling

Party members about the need to cap their aspirations and the limited resources that would be available in office. The linkage of rights and obligations became a central theme of the Labour leadership (for a discussion see Dwyer, 1998).

In terms of campaigning, the lessons of Clinton's victory concerned the use of focus groups, carefully directed advertising and the coordinated management of the media via spin doctors. All three measures had been assembled by Labour before 1992. All three were intensified and prioritised as pivotal to the Party's efforts in the run-up to the 1997 General Election. In December 1995, the Party set up a new campaigning centre at Millbank near Westminster. The new office became the basis for Labour's election campaign, the kind of war room for which Hewitt and Gould had called. The war room housed 'Excalibur', Labour's computerised database, which allowed the Party to refute instantly claims made by the Conservatives. At Labour's existing headquarters, John Smith house in Walworth Road, much space was given over to telephone banks from which volunteers canvassed voters in marginal constituencies throughout the country.

In office, Labour's policies and their presentation have reflected those of the Clinton administration. Gordon Brown's emphasis on economic stability as the core aim of policy was influenced by the performance of the Democratic administration. His decision to grant operational independence over monetary policy to the Bank of England was determined by a visit to the US and meetings with officials including Allan Greenspan, Chairman of the Federal Reserve, in March 1997. Brown announced, "We have learnt a great deal from America and the Federal Reserve Bank" (Brown, 1998b, p 3). The Chancellor told one interviewer: "I think it's interesting that the success of America over the past few years has been built on that [stability] and I think it's interesting too that this is pursued in every other major industrialised country" (*Sunday Business*, 15 February 1998). The Chancellor's second Budget was heavily influenced by the US with its emphasis on tax credits. Blair has adopted an increasingly presidential-style of managing both Party and government. He also sought to ensure that the government has remained focused in a way that the Democratic administration did not in its first years, thus learning from its failures as well as its successes (Mandelson, 1994; Collins, 1996; Gould, 1996). Blair was also critical of Clinton's failure to live up to the expectations generated during the 1992 presidential election: "you don't run on one basis and govern on another" (Rentoul, 1995, p 81).

Blair's close personal relationship with Clinton continued to flourish after Labour's election victory in May 1997. The US President was quick to visit the UK where Blair invited him to address the Labour Cabinet. Their mutual admiration was undeniable. This meeting was followed by talks in Washington in February 1998, which included a 'brainstorming' session about the future of the centre-Left. Blair was accompanied by intellectuals purported to have influenced his 'Third Way' framework. The so-called 'wonkathon' followed an earlier meeting at Chequers in December 1997. The Washington session, dubbed 'Chequers 2', proposed the establishment of a standing conference of centre-Left Parties, one which would include European social democrats but would be based initially around an 'Anglo-Saxon' axis of Labour and the Democrats (*The Guardian*, 7 February 1998). A further meeting was held in September 1998. As president, Clinton has held annual meetings with groups of eminent intellectuals; Blair too has indicated considerable interest in academic work, largely through his encouragement of Nexus, a group of Left-inclined scholars. In his articulation of the 'Third Way', Blair has regularly emphasised that European economies must learn from the achievements of the US, especially the flexibility of its labour markets. Likewise Gordon Brown concluded, "We are also working with our European partners to create a New Europe – more dynamic, competitive, and open, and thus learning from the entrepreneurial and flexible labour markets of the American economy" (Brown, 1998a).

Labour's Welfare to Work

Welfare to Work was the most ambitious proposal articulated by Labour during the years in opposition from 1992 to 1997. It was by far the most expensive initiative advanced by the Party. In reflection of the problems public spending and taxation had caused Labour in 1992, all other new spending commitments were to be met from savings within existing budgets. Welfare to Work, also called the New Deal, was to be funded by a one-off windfall tax on the excess profits of the privatised utilities (see Deakin and Parry, 1998; Driver and Martell, 1998, pp 108-13). Gordon Brown announced the new project in November 1995 as a determined attempt to tackle youth unemployment: the objective was to provide work or training for 250,000 during the first Parliament of a Labour government. The scheme had the added advantage that it demonstrated the Party's new stance on welfare, thereby establishing its credentials as a moderate party on matters of spending and taxation. The proposal built on two Conservative schemes, 'Workstart' and 'Project Work' (Finn, 1998).

The policy recast in a fundamental fashion Labour's strategy to tackle poverty: previously, Labour administrations and social democratic thinkers had placed much weight on the amelioration of general destitution through State-directed public spending programmes. New Labour, by contrast, emphasised paid work, seemingly to the exclusion of other approaches. By 1999, Alistair Darling was categoric: "Benefits cannot remove the causes of poverty" (Darling, 1999).

At the launch of Welfare to Work, the Shadow Chancellor denied that the element of compulsion in the plans represented a departure from the Party's existing commitments. He contended: "This is not a lurch to the right. It is the Labour Party stating the values of decent hard-working people in this country – that in a modern society rights are matched by responsibilities" (*Financial Times*, 10 November 1995). Brown dismissed the claim that it was coercive: "This is not workfare in the sense that it is understood, as in the penalising of the unemployed for being unemployed and asking people to work in return for their benefit" (*The Times*, 10 November 1995). Making a rather fine distinction, he told the *Daily Telegraph*, that "it is not workfare because they will not be working for their benefit. People will be paid a wage of benefit plus a fixed sum for six months" (9 November 1995). Commentators were much less certain about the direction of the Party's policy. Noting the Party's shift towards workfare, Joe Rogaly concluded, "'Fine', says New Labour, 'but we may ease the pain by calling it welfare to work'" (*Financial Times*, 26 April 1997).

Welfare to Work was devised by Brown and his advisers. The proposal was not discussed by the Shadow Cabinet before its launch. There was immediate concern within the Party over the adoption of such measures. *The Guardian* quoted a leading member of the Shadow Cabinet as saying, "Senior people have been taken totally by surprise by these proposals. We have been taken aback because it runs counter to what we have been saying about the government's coercive approach" (*The Guardian*, 10 November 1995). The source denied that the plans were Party policy. Brown's scheme caused 'consternation' in John Prescott's office (C. Brown, 1997, p 277) and was opposed by Michael Meacher, the Party's employment spokesperson (*The Guardian*, 19 November 1995). Up to half of the Shadow Cabinet were reported to be angered by the plans – as much, it should be noted, because of the unilateral manner of their formation by Brown as for their content. Those registering concern included Robin Cook, Frank Dobson, Mo Mowlam, and Chris Smith (Kampfner, 1998, p 107; *The Spectator*, 25 November 1995).

In November 1994, a year before the launch of Welfare to Work, Labour's Budget submission had adopted a less coercive approach to the availability of benefits: "We recognise not only the responsibility of the long-term unemployed to seek work, but that these objectives must be matched by the government's responsibility" (Labour Party, 1994b, p 10). The focus of policy was on improving incentives to persuade individuals back into the labour market. Criticising the Conservatives' approach, the Party had attacked "this blunt Tory strategy of compulsion" which "undermined claimant confidence" and "forced people on to inappropriate schemes" (Labour Party, 1994c, p 28). By the time of the draft manifesto, on which Party members voted in 1996, Labour was forthright: "There will be no fifth option of remaining permanently on full benefit", the document stated frankly. "We believe that is fair: rights and responsibilities must go together" (Labour Party, 1996b, p 17). The emphasis was now on a combination of incentives and pressures to get individuals into work. A document issued during the run-up to the 1997 General Election echoed Brown's words from 1995 in stating, "Young people have a responsibility to seek work and to train" (Labour Party, 1997d, p 2).

In January 1998 the details of the New Deal were finalised. Employers would be offered a subsidy of £60 a week for six months and given a grant of £750 to cover training costs. Considerable attention was given by senior figures within the government to persuading businesses to participate (and much of the publicity surrounding the New Deal focused on this issue). Entrants to the scheme would be prepared via a 'gateway' in which they would be given advice on job applications. The DfEE intended that all four options would be available to each participant but this could not be guaranteed. In some cases a restricted choice of two options would apply and in a very small minority there might be no choice of option (DfEE, 1997c, p 11). The training and education option was applicable only to those without certain relatively basic qualifications. Some locations would be unable to provide either the voluntary work or the environmental taskforce options. In some situations an individual would be offered a choice within a particular option. Individuals who failed to accept a place would "towards the end of the four-month gateway period ... be mandatorily referred to an option" (DfEE, 1997c, p 12). Under these contractual arrangements, "the notified place will not necessarily be the one the young person would have preferred" (DfEE, 1997c, p 12). Sanctions fell on those who failed to start or complete the programme. Some groups of young people could opt into the New Deal before being required to join: those choosing to participate would be subject to the same commitment to take up a place in one of the options and, if necessary, accept direction. The new government toughed its position on sanctions: young unemployed people without dependants who failed to participate would now lose all their benefit (and not just 40% of it as originally proposed). Sanctions would also be applied to young people with children, carers, those with disabilities and pregnant mothers in the 18-24 age group. These individuals could claim limited support on grounds of hardship.

After the government's election the New Deal was expanded beyond the young unemployed (partly because falling unemployment levels limited the numbers available to join the scheme). Childless spouses of unemployed individuals would be included: at the time of writing the question of whether participation will be compulsory is undecided. The New Deal would also cover those older than 25, lone parents, disabled and pregnant women (*Financial Times*, 4 July 1997). Those aged above 50 were added in the spring of 1998. At first participation was voluntary for lone parents and disabled people, though press reports indicated that these groups might also be subject to the same tough conditions as the New Deal for 18- to 24-year-olds. The New Deal for those aged 25 and above was not as coercive as that for those younger than 25. Attending interviews would be compulsory as under the existing job-seeking regulations. However, the government retained the capacity to enforce sanctions for those who "persistently refuse all offers of help" (DfEE, 1997d, p 9). Such individuals could be required to take up a specified activity and would face benefit sanctions if they refused.

A leaked memorandum in the summer of 1997 demonstrated the government's inflexibility. Harriet Harman (Blair's first Secretary of State for Social Security) and Stephen Byers (the Department for Education and Employment) argued: "We need by our approach to force change in the attitude of young people to benefits and work". They continued: "Penalties must be of clear and sufficient weight either to deter them from rejecting opportunities or to ensure that they reconsider their position and take up the options available" (*Independent on Sunday*, 6 July 1997). From December 1997 the government put considerable pressure on lone parents to find work by cutting their benefit entitlement. Labour had opposed the reduction when in opposition and the implementation of it proved politically problematic, generating considerable disquiet within the Party and among backbench MPs (*The Observer*, 4 January 1998). Early reports indicated limited success for the New Deal in persuading lone parents off benefit (*The Guardian*, 20 July 1998). A further reflection of the difficulties involved in welfare reform came with Tony Blair's first ministerial reshuffle in July 1998: in a surprise move, both Harriet Harman and Frank Field, the Minister of State at Social Security, key architects of the government's efforts to restructure the benefits system, were sacked. Harman was replaced by Alistair Darling who proved to be far tougher and more politically astute than his predecessor.

In January 1999, the government widened the scope of the New Deal. Welfare claimants would be given a personal adviser as the gateway process was extended to all those on benefit (*The Times*, 13 January 1999: see also DfEE/DSS, 1998). These plans were formalised in the 109-page Welfare Reform and Pensions Bill, published in February 1999 (DSS, 1999a). Attendance at interviews "to discuss the steps they [claimants] might take to move closer back to the labour market" and job seeking would be conditions of benefit (DSS, 1999b, p 74). Both disabled claimants and lone parents would be required to attend while exemptions from work would be based on more rigorous criteria than in the past. The proposals gave the Secretary of State for Social Security sweeping powers to require claimants to attend such interviews regularly, to determine any acceptable delays and to decide the appropriate occasions on which to call individuals back for further discussions. For the young the interval between these interviews was likely to be no more than months. Such compulsory work-focused interviews were designed to encourage individuals back into employment. Pilot schemes had demonstrated, for example, that under voluntary arrangements 94% of single parents would not attend. Of those that did, 80% went on to leave benefits. The new regulations would apply, the government indicated, to all claimants and not just new ones. There was some discussion within the government as to whether Welfare to Work should be institutionalised as a permanent programme to reduce unemployment (*The Times*, 2 October 1998). The new proposals, contained in the Queen's Speech in November 1998, would be piloted during 1999 and extended nationally in 2001. It remains uncertain what the impact on the numbers claiming benefits of these measures will be in practice. Alongside their uncompromising stance, and at odds with it, ministers repeated safeguards that those unable to work, such as single parents and genuinely disabled people, would not be forced to work (*The Guardian*, 11 February 1999). Despite such protestations, the BBC commented, "many will see this [welfare bill] as the first step into forcing people into work" (BBC News, 10 February 1999). Other claimants would be expected, according to *The Times*, to take a job within a certain time or forfeit benefit (11 February 1999). According to Alistair Darling:

"no one has an unqualified right to benefit" (Darling, 1999). He told *The Independent*: "We want a sea change in the culture of the system" (10 February 1999). The Secretary of State argued that such arrangements did not amount to workfare because "we are not forcing people to work" (*The Times*, 29 October 1998). He went on: "People will no longer ask of the system, 'what can you do for me?' but 'what can I do to help myself'". With the publication of the Welfare Reform and Pensions Bill, the government anticipated further dissent within the Party.

A variety of influences can be detected in the development of Welfare to Work. Labour claimed that the new proposals were closer to Swedish arrangements than those prevalent in the United States. Clinton had earlier argued that Swedish experience had influenced his own approach. In any case, the Swedish policy involved much greater activism in terms of labour market interventions and much higher levels of benefit relative to wages. The Borrie Commission on Social Justice, which reported in the autumn of 1994, supported a tougher line on benefits, but had rejected workfare schemes: "Of course, someone who unreasonably turns down a job or training cannot expect to continue claiming full benefit" (Commission on Social Justice, 1994, p 239). The Commission proposed the establishment of an environmental taskforce to give work-type experience to the unemployed. A year before the Conservatives' (1997) electoral defeat, the House of Commons Select Committee on Employment issued a substantial report on workfare, endorsing such schemes in principle (Employment Committee, 1996). Mead's influence can be noted in the New Deal's combination of compulsion and direction: the emphasis placed by the government on the gateway is an indication of the need to prepare individuals for the labour market and the demands of regular jobs. Frank Field accepted much of Mead's argument (albeit with some qualification) and defended the need for compulsion in benefit availability: "The threat of penalisation begins to affect the culture in which people consider how they should respond and, indeed, what their responsibilities are" (Field, 1997c, p 62). The influence of radical American ideas on British social policy was also a feature of the Thatcher years, epitomised in the importation of Charles Murray's concept of an underclass (Murray, 1990; Murray 1994; Dolowitz, 1997; see also Parsons, 1989 on economic policy). The rhetoric, contractualism and coercion of the New Deal echoes American practice – as does New Labour's emphasis on the work ethic (see Social Security Committee, 1998, p vi). By the summer of 1998 one commentator concluded: "It would be hard to think of a more American feature of the highly Americanised Blair government than its much trusted new deal on welfare to work" (*Sunday Times*, 31 May 1998). James McCormick, a researcher for the IPPR, argued:"Britain's New Deal programmes borrow heavily from accumulated international experience of welfare reform, especially from Australia and the USA" (McCormick, 1998, p 88).

Conclusion

Welfare to Work is one of the flagship policies of the Blair administration. Its success or failure will affect Labour's future electoral prospects. It is more ambitious than the schemes of previous Conservative administrations. At present, the outcome is uncertain so it is not possible to assess its chances of meeting its goals. Academic opinion about schemes utilising subsidies and compulsion is divided (see, for example, Richard Layard and Patrick Minford's separate evidence before the Education and Employment Committee, 1998, pp 19-28). Criticisms of job subsidies highlight their potential deadweight effects (unemployed individuals are paid to take work who would have got jobs anyway) and displacement impact (those who get subsidised jobs push others out of work). Other problems concern 'churning' as recipients on the programme fail to find permanent jobs and return to benefit and market distortion as those firms receiving subsidies out-perform those that do not. Criticisms of compulsion highlight the demoralising impact on claimants, the generation of insecurity among those on benefits, the uncertain quality of the labour force that results and the potential for injustice, especially on dependent relatives (see Deacon, 1997b). Long-term reductions in unemployment may depend more on the demand for labour than on its supply: on the basis of an examination of US arrangements, Simon Crine concluded in a Fabian pamphlet, "the transition from welfare to work depends more on the supply of jobs than it does on the motivation of the non-working poor" (Crine, 1994, p 25). The record of similar arrangements elsewhere is mixed. Some, including ones more generous and much costlier than the UK's Welfare to Work, appear to have little impact on rates of unemployment (for a general discussion see Solow, 1998). Since these schemes are expensive, social security spending need not fall (Social Security Committee, 1998, p vii). The impact of subsidies on poverty may be disappointing because such schemes may depress wage levels by increasing the supply of labour. (The newly-introduced minimum wage may offset such depression in the UK.)

Some early results from the New Deal are encouraging: Trades Union Congress (TUC) statistics indicated a big fall of 28% in the number of unemployed aged between 18 and 24 during 1998 (*The Guardian*, 22 December 1998). The DfEE reported that 52,000 jobs had been found for youngsters on Welfare to Work by November 1998 (DfEE, 1999). Three quarters of these went into unsubsidised employment. Only 10,000 had been placed on the option of subsidised work offered by private employers. Of those leaving the New Deal, nearly 50% found work. Critics claimed that there remained a high proportion of drop-outs – up to 40% – among participants (*The Sunday Telegraph*, 25 October 1998). The bureaucracy and overall costs of the programme were further points raised by those hostile to the programme. Businesses complained about the slow rate of referral to them of potential participants from the gateway (*Independent on Sunday*, 1 November 1998). (The lack of coverage given to Welfare to Work and the criticisms raised of it, led the Labour administration to adopt a new strategy in February 1999 of dealing with the press, one which focused largely on local papers.)

The Blair administration's New Deal presents a recasting of the Labour Party's notion of social citizenship. Previously the Party had adopted a version of Marshall's citizenship, based on universal and unconditional entitlement. Under the logic of Welfare to Work and Labour's current social policy, this universalistic approach has been superseded with a market-based one (see Jordan, 1998 for a discussion of what he terms the Blair–Clinton orthodoxy). Individuals must accept responsibility for their own well-being in terms of entering labour markets and contributing to society through paid work. Alistair Darling stated: "We will do something to help people but, in turn, they have got to do something to help themselves" (*The Independent*, 9 February 1999). Repeating phrases spun by his ministers, Blair was equally forthright in trumpeting "the end of a something-for-nothing welfare state. The days of an automatic right to benefit will go" (Blair, 1999).

The illiberal potential of these programmes is far from trivial and may come to haunt their architects. They break with the liberal premise of equality of treatment acquired as a correlate of citizenship (King, 1999). A *Financial Times* leader described Labour's welfare reform bill as containing "draconian powers" (11 February 1999). As critics have pointed out, New Labour's position assumes an individual can contribute to society through working as a paid childcarer but not as an unpaid mother, though both individuals carry out the same tasks and make identical contributions. Time and again, the Blair administration emphasises the importance of work and employment. The government's annual report defined "work as the best route out of poverty for those who can" (*Government's Annual Report*, 1998, p 50; see also DSS, 1998c). Labour's 1998 conference document noted: "We want to rebuild the [welfare] system around work and security. Work for those who can; security for those who cannot" (Labour Party, 1998, p 67). David Blunkett argued, "Nobody without a disability or a good case should give up the option of earning their own living" (*Financial Times*, 4 July 1997). He claimed that paid work was one of Labour's traditional values (*Observer*, 1 November 1998). Gordon Brown has called for a "welfare state built around the work ethic" (*Observer*, 11 May 1997). On another occasion, he outlined his desire to "re-establish the work ethic at the centre of our welfare system" (G. Brown, 1997a, p 10). The Prime Minister articulated the need for a "fundamental change in the culture, attitude, and practice of the welfare state" (Blair, 1997b, p 4). One commentator, Victor Keegan, concluded: "Fifteen years ago the very idea of 'workfare' was anathema to the Labour party. Now the principle has been accepted. The argument is about the detail" (*The Guardian*, 1 January 1998; King, 1999, pp 226-57). The recasting of New Labour's conception of citizenship and the emphasis placed on employment may be as important as other shifts in the Party's welfare policy such as the relegation of equality as a social democratic objective and the prioritisation of social inclusion as an objective (Levitas, 1998).

A word of caution needs to be noted about just how far reaching this recasting of the social democratic basis of citizenship is likely to be in the short run. The government's tough stance is evident in theory. It remains to be seen what impact such policies will have in practice and whether many of those concerned will simply evade the conditions imposed on them. Tony Blair reported that the rate of increase in social security had been halved under his administration compared with its predecessors. However, estimates of the numbers who will be denied benefit as a result of Welfare to Work vary considerably. One report in May 1998 stated that 35 out of 16,400 processed so far had been forced off benefit and that 135 cases were pending adjudication (*The Independent*, 28 May 1998). Another report in July put the number of those denied benefit at 151 (*The Independent*, 8 July 1998). These figures do not include those coerced into work or participation against their will. It is probable that those entering the New Deal during its first months of operation will be the most likely to benefit from it: tougher cases and tougher decisions will follow later in this Parliament. By November 1998, Andrew Smith, Minister of

Employment, stated that 1,352 individuals had lost benefits because of their failure to participate (*Financial Times*, 5 November 1998).

As to the US influence on Labour, many journalists have noted the parallels between the New Democrats and New Labour. In 1996 the *San Francisco Chronicle* commented that Labour was:

> ... not just watching but emulating. The Labor Party has adopted many techniques employed by the Democrats ... first and foremost claiming to be new. (*San Francisco Chronicle*, 28 August 1996)

Joe Rogaly went so far as to conclude of Blair that: "he designed and built New Labour, using blueprints faxed from Little Rock" (*Financial Times*, 26 April 1997). Philip Stephens argued, "In spite of ritual disavows, the party has borrowed heavily from the successes of President Bill Clinton's New Democrats" (*Financial Times*, 11 April 1997). Labour's efforts to learn from the Democrats represent a notable realignment of the Party's outlook: in the late 1980s and early 1990s under Neil Kinnock Labour sought to orientate itself towards European social democratic parties (King and Wickham-Jones, 1998). Blair's articulation of a third way has indicated his antipathy towards the conventional European model of social democracy and his belief that important lessons can be acquired from the US.

This chapter has laid out some significant similarities between the Democrats and the Labour Party. Perceiving close personal links between the two Parties, it has indicated areas where Labour has imitated the electoral strategy and policy platform of Bill Clinton. The Party's Welfare to Work programme reproduces the Democrats' tough stance on welfare issues. It is an approach which has paid electoral dividends for Labour, helping the Party to win over middle-class voters. However, just how important the American experience has been for Labour is difficult to assess. As noted above, there was a powerful electoral impulse behind the adoption of Welfare to Work, following the Party's defeat in the 1992 General Election. The Party's decision to focus on work and job subsidies reflects the results of academic research indicating that previous initiatives to tackle poverty through benefit programmes have failed. Labour leaders were especially struck by the number of households, nearly one in five, without any wage earners (Brown, 1996, p 4; Blair, 1997a, p 6; Gregg, 1998; Labour Party, 1998, p 67). Under the last Conservative government eight million individuals lived in households with no incomes. The focus on job subsidies in the Welfare to Work programme is also reminiscent of the employment measures of the 1974-79 Labour government (Bowen, 1991). Some of the economists who have endorsed Labour's approach have long articulated the case for job subsidies (Layard, 1997). Such proposals have been the subject of much attention from UK-based think-tanks such as the IPPR (McCormick and Oppenheim, 1998; Oppenheim, 1998b). (American measures may have been an important influence on such think-tanks in turn – see Crine, 1994 on the Fabians, and Nye, 1996, on the Social Market Foundation.)

However, one striking feature of much of this support for Welfare to Work is the opposition contained within it to any coercive element. Many media commentators, the Borrie Commission on Social Justice, the IPPR, the Fabians, and the Scottish Affairs Committee of the House of Commons have opposed the use of compulsion (see Oppenheim, 1998a, pp 60-1; Crine, 1994, p 25). The latter described coercive measures as 'counter-productive' (Scottish Affairs Committee, 1998, p 30). James McCormick concluded: "There is little enthusiasm for compulsion [among participants and prospective employers]" (McCormick, 1998, p 108). The Labour Party itself is divided on the issue. Outlining Welfare to Work in 1998, Frank Dobson took a much softer line that some of his colleagues: "We should also make sure that the benefit rules encourage people to work if they can.... Some benefit rules place obstructions in the way of people who are trying to improve their chances of getting a job" (Dobson, 1998, p 2). As well as reflecting the electoral imperatives of post-1992 political alignment, Labour's enthusiastic espousal of such a tough position emulates the Democrats' experience in the US. Just how far Tony Blair's government is prepared to go down the American route remains to be seen.

Note

Some of the research for this paper was funded by the Harold Wincott Foundation and the Nuffield Foundation. Their support is gratefully acknowledged by Mark Wickham-Jones.

THIRTEEN

Conclusion

Martin Powell

Introduction

Labour's first 600 days of office has seen significant moves in many parts of the welfare state. For example, in the area of 'welfare' Tony Blair (1998c, col 365) stated that in its 15 months of office Labour had:

- reformed student finance;
- brought in proposals to reform legal aid;
- changed lone parent benefits;
- introduced £3.5 billion for young people getting off benefit and into work;
- proposed a fundamental reform of the Child Support Agency;
- proposed the Working Families Tax Credit scheme, and action to get disabled people off benefit and into work;
- put together the first ever comprehensive strategy on benefit fraud.

He claimed that Labour accomplished more welfare reform in 15 months than the Conservatives did in 15 years. Areas to be reformed in the forthcoming year included:

- Disability Living Allowance;
- Incapacity Benefit;
- a minimum income guarantee for pensioners;
- a single work-focused gateway into the benefit system;
- asylum and legal aid (Blair, 1998c, col 368).

In its first Annual Report the Labour government claimed that it had been "a year of welfare reform" (*Government's Annual Report*, 1998). The government had set a 'cracking pace' in delivering its 177 manifesto commitments: 50 had been carried out, 119 were under way and on course and only 8 had yet to be timetabled. Despite contrary claims from the Conservatives, the five key 'card' pledges were being delivered (Jones, 1998).

In the debate on the Queen's Speech in November 1998, Blair (1998d, col 27) stated that in the previous Parliamentary session the government had proposed 22 Bills and delivered 52 Acts. In the shorter forthcoming Session, nearly 20 Bills were promised. He continued that the centrepiece of the Queen's Speech was the set of measures to improve the health service, schools, law and order and to reform welfare. Taken together, the measures – both the investment and the reform – amount to the largest programme of change in our public services for many years. He also pledged that the government would tackle subjects which were ducked when the Conservatives were in office (Blair, 1998d, cols 30-2).

As the contributors to this book show, Labour's period of office has seen substantial reform in many areas as shown by a number of White Papers, Green Papers, Parliamentary Bills, policy announcements and keynote speeches. However, with Labour arguably still in its self-proclaimed 'post-euphoria, pre-delivery' mode, what does all of this mean for the welfare state? This chapter summarises the main themes of the book and attempts to address the questions posed in the introduction. Is there evidence of policy continuity with Old Labour or policy convergence with the Conservatives? Can a third way be detected? Will New Labour lead to a new welfare state? Is it possible to advance some tentative explanations for any changes?

Old Left

Few commentators have pointed out much policy continuity with Old Labour. This view appeared to be restricted largely to a handful of articles in newspapers such as the *Daily Telegraph* (for example, Lawson, 1997) but has become more prominent since the comprehensive spending review (CSR). In an editorial, 'Return to spender', the *Sunday Telegraph* (19 July 1998, p 40) argued that underlying Brown's strategy was "a very old assumption: that public spending is an intrinsic good". Shadow Chancellor Francis Maude (1998, col 195-6) claimed that Labour cannot control public spending, had raised tax 17 times and made families £1,000-a-year worse off: the central pillars of the myth of the iron Chancellor have rusted away. Former Conservative Chancellor Kenneth Clarke (1998, col 201) remarked on Brown's 'U-turn' from the iron Chancellor to the big-handed Chancellor: "Will he tell the cheering ranks of old Labour behind him that they may ring the bells today, but they will wring their hands hereafter?" Mentions made of policy continuity with old Labour by the

writes that in the personal social services, New Labour has adopted many of the major principles of Conservative policy. Paton (Chapter Three) argues that as it was not possible to return health policy to 1979 – to unscramble the eggs in the Conservative omelette – it does not so much mean a convergence between Labour and Conservative policy as either adoption or adaption by Labour.

However, it is important to bear in mind the difference between policy rhetoric and reality; between stated intentions and outcomes (a point particularly emphasised by Paton [Chapter Three], and by Charman and Savage [Chapter Nine]). In a number of areas, Labour was slow to make the transition from opposition to government, setting up a large number of policy reviews (cf Kemp, Chapter Six). Critics of Frank Field, the minister told to "think the unthinkable" argued that he "thought the unworkable". It is claimed that he "generated lots of thinking on reform, but the government has to produce a policy" and that "his proposals were largely at an analytical level, they were not policy" (Grice, 1998; Wintour, 1998; Watt and Webster, 1998). It is possible that there will be significant 'policy slippages' or 'implementation gaps' between broad outlines and implemented schemes. For example, Paton (Chapter Three) argues that to a certain extent, 'old radicalism' (the socialism that dare not speak its name under New Labour) was to have more of a place in the pantheon of the National Health Service than elsewhere in society – but was to be linked to an alleged new pragmatism. There is a difference between New Labour's approach to the NHS and other areas of social and economic policy. New Labour is more like Old Labour in terms of the goals it believes in for the NHS, yet in practice, its approach to the NHS is more in tune with the philosophy of the Conservatives than in other areas of social policy. That is: more Old Labour in theory; more Tory in practice. This difference between theory and practice is increased by the redefinition of familiar welfare terms. For example 'New Labour's 'full employment' appears to mean something very different to its traditional usage (Powell and Hewitt, 1998). Other terms such as citizenship and equality may also be undergoing 'modernisation' or translation into 'NewLabourspeak' (see also McElvoy, 1997; Daniel, 1998).

The Third Way

Blair (1998a, p 7) claims that "In New Labour's first year of government we have started to put the Third Way into practice". However, as Halpern and Mikosz (1998, p 43) point out, the term does not yet have a universally accepted definition. The *Economist* (1998, p 47) argues that the Third Way has an "obfuscatory fog of generalities". It is easiest to define the Third Way negatively: by what it is not. Johnson quotes Driver and Martell (1997): "if communitarianism is New Labour's answer to Thatcherism, so too is it Tony Blair's rebuff to Old Labour". He suggests unequivocal responses to the two major questions of continuity and convergence posed by this book. In this respect, at least, New Labour departs from both Old Labour and the Conservative Party. According to Driver and Martell (1998, pp 169, 178, 184), New Labour is defined by, but departs from Thatcherism. It has moved to the Right, but with anti-Thatcherite emphases. In this sense, it is post-Thatcherite. Rather than being beyond Left and Right, it attempts, with some success, to combine them in a balance. Cressey (Chapter Eight) notes many continuities with the Conservatives, but some discontinuities. Johnson (Chapter Four) sees many New Labour policies as being between the Old Left and the New Right, but argues that New Labour leans towards the Right rather than centre-Left of this spectrum. According to Muschamp et al (Chapter Five) there has been no reversal of Tory reforms with the return of a Labour government and yet it is not possible to argue that the differences between the two Labour manifestos are the result of Labour adopting Tory policies. Labour's concept of a 'third way' would appear to be evident in the new gloss given to old policies. Charman and Savage (Chapter Nine) hint at a third way: "Labour's crime policy has been essentially radical, but it is not the sort of radicalism that can easily be associated with a drift to the Right". The authors of two chapters attempt to define the Third Way for their subject matter (Rouse and Smith on accountability in Chapter Eleven; Hewitt for social security in Chapter Seven). Rouse and Smith claim that while some of New Labour's approach to accountability has been based on the principles and values of the New Right, much of it has not. They continue that "the approach of New Labour to accountability in the welfare state is sufficiently different from both the social democratic consensus and the New Right to consider at least provisionally, that it belongs to a third way".

In spite of attempts to clarify the Third Way (Chapter One; see also Blair, 1998a; Halpern and Mikosz, 1998; Le Grand, 1998; White, 1998; Giddens, 1998; *Economist*, 1998), the coherence of the term must be questioned. It does not seem to be based on a clear ideology or a ' big idea' like the Old Left or the New Right. "The big idea is that there is no big idea" (*Economist*, 1998; cf Wright, 1996). Instead, it appears to be used in an eclectic, negative and pragmatic manner. It has been claimed that it is defined, like Herbert Morrison's famous definition of socialism, as what a (New) Labour government does. In this sense it is 'post-ideological' and may be best summed up by the New Labour phrase 'what counts is what works'. As Blair argued in the introduction to the 1997 manifesto (Labour Party, 1997a): "Some things the Conservatives got right. We will not change them. It is where they got things wrong that we will make change". While some commentators compared the election victory of 1997 to that of 1945, Crouch (1997, pp 352-3) argues that it was more like 1951 when the Conservatives showed that they could adjust to and succeed in a political world which was not of their making. For example, as Burchardt and Hills show, some public/private partnerships inherited from the Conservatives such as PFI were continued, but others such as nursery vouchers and the Assisted Places Scheme were abandoned. It is difficult to account for this on any clear arguments of principle. The difference seems to be that Labour considered the former to work while the latter did not. Neither does the Third Way appear to be internally coherent. Paton (Chapter Three) points out the different agendas in Labour's health policy. As Powell (1999) notes, different parts of the White Paper on the NHS stress greater power to doctors, ministers, representatives, patients, which suggest tensions, if not inconsistencies. However, none of this may be entirely surprising, for as Dean (Chapter Ten) points out in relation to citizenship, "popular discourse ... is no more coherent or consistent than political discourse". He also states that "in daily speech all of us draw on a multiplicity of often variable and sometimes contradictory discursive repertoires".

In addition to pragmatism, the Third Way seems to be characterised by an attempted populism. According to Dean, a combination of economic liberalism and social conservatism characterises New Labour's approach. Labour claims that its approach will work with the grain of popular aspirations, but as Dean shows New Labour is not always in step with popular discourse. Some writers are critical of the gauging of public opinion. For example, Heffernan and Marqusee (1992) are contemptuous of the 'focus group' approach of New Labour. McKibbin (1997, p 5) argues that "labour ministers cannot spend every day scanning the tabloids to see whether their government is acceptable to the press". However, this 'government by headline' approach is important to Labour: headlines such as 'DSS cheats to be "named and shamed"', 'Ministers to clamp down on "lying" lone parents', 'Field targets workshy' and 'Blair in welfare war on the idle' show their determination to take 'tough choices'. New

Labour's views that idlers will be made to work and that scroungers will be punished has parallels with the 'tough approach' in the US (King and Wickham-Jones, Chapter Twelve). Gordon Brown, commenting on Welfare to Work plans, contended that: "This is not a lurch to the right. It is the Labour party stating the values of decent hard-working people in this country" (quoted in King and Wickham-Jones). This appeal to the politics of decency of 'ordinary' people has been used elsewhere (Mandelson and Liddle, 1996).

In the last analysis, the importance of the Third Way for Labour is that it will work. Compared to the Conservative period of office, and previous Labour administrations (see for example, Ponting, 1989) Labour claims that there will be no 'breach of promise': the government will deliver its pledges and restore some faith in politics. Labour will be judged on results rather than philosophy. In a democratic society, the ultimate test of success is election and re-election: if the Third Way delivers a second term, then it will have served its purpose.

New welfare state?

In 1997 *The Guardian* (1997a) noted that the final form of the restructured welfare state is unclear. Most contributors in this book stress that it is too early to tell whether New Labour is leading to a new welfare state. The warning about not confusing policy rhetoric with outcomes bears repeating here (Chapters Three and Nine). For example, Burchardt and Hills remind us that the pledge made by the Conservative government of 1979 to limit public expenditure was not turned into reality. Bearing in mind this important caveat, it is possible to argue that the outline of a new design for welfare can be detected. Some themes emerge from a number of chapters. First, there is the the centrality accorded to paid work within the Blair/Clinton orthodoxy (Dean, Chapter Ten). Hewitt (Chapter Seven) has pointed out that New Labour's first objective of "work for those who can" has witnessed more attention than their second of "security for those who cannot". He warns that Labour is in danger of creating two welfare states for the different clienteles of workers and non-workers (cf Jessop, 1994). This "rebuilding of the welfare state around work" is linked to the "more coercive welfare regime" (Dean, Chapter Ten) and moves towards a more conditional citizenship, with its changing balance between rights and responsibilities (Chapters Four, Seven, Ten, Eleven and Twelve) following the line of the Democrats in the US. In

1987 then Governor Clinton stated "We believe that every welfare recipient should sign a contract with the State, making a personal commitment in return for benefits to pursue an individually developed path to independence" (quoted in Chapter Twelve). As President, Clinton emphasised compulsion for groups such as single mothers to return to the labour market, bringing in a new Act in 1996 under which single mothers must accept jobs or lose benefits, Clinton declared that "today we are ending welfare as we know it" (quoted by King and Wickham-Jones in Chapter Twelve). They point out that:

> **The idea that benefit entitlement should be unconditional was at the core of Marshallian social rights of citizenship. This commitment to universal social rights was a benchmark of the Party's welfare programme between 1945 and 1992. (but see Deacon, 1996)**

The new welfare state seems to redraw the boundaries between the individual and the State, leading to a different mix within the mixed economy of welfare (Chapter Four). There may be a reduced role for the State and an increased role for private and mutual organisations (Chapters Two, Five and Seven), involving a more localised and community-based revived civic society (Chapter Eleven; cf Field, 1996a, 1996b, 1997a, 1997d) or associational welfare (Hirst, 1994, 1998). The exact role of the State in finance, production and regulation remains unclear, but there may be greater scope for "DIY welfare" (Klein and Millar, 1995; Grice, 1997a). People are urged to become more responsible and make provision for the risks that they and their families face. This generally fits with the New Labour version of communitarianism (see Driver and Martell, 1998; Tam, 1998; Chapters Four, Ten and Eleven). However, the private pensions misselling scandal and the Maxwell pension fund scandal, let alone the Conservatives changing the rules of SERPS and New Labour taxing pension credits make DIY welfare a risky business. As Hewitt and Powell (1998, p 100) warn, like all DIY jobs, it can go disastrously wrong.

Labour clearly wants to develop a more rational welfare state. Blair in the introduction to the Welfare Green Paper (DSS, 1998a, p v) states: "We must return to first principles and ask what we want the welfare state to achieve". According to Miliband (1994, p 88), "we need to redefine welfare, and turn our understanding of the role of the welfare state ... on its head".

The Commission on Social Justice (1994) declared that welfare should be supportive of both social justice and economic efficiency, which are "two sides of the same coin". While it is argued that the Old Left emphasised the former and the New Right emphasised the latter, the Third Way views social justice as good for business (see Driver and Martell, 1998; Pierson, 1998). Perhaps the most significant implication of this may be found in education. As Blair argued: "Education is the best economic policy there is.... Unless we get our education system right, our children will not be prosperous and our country will not be just" (in Driver and Martell, 1998, pp 57, 107). He later added: "The main source of value and competitive advantage in the modern economy is human and intellectual capital. Hence the overriding priority New Labour is giving to education and training..." (Blair, 1998a, p 10). A further linking of social and economic policy may be seen in Welfare to Work (Chapters Seven, Eight and Twelve; see also Driver and Martell, 1998). However, this fusing of social and economic policy places a heavy burden on economic performance (cf Chapter Two). Traditionally the welfare state has been seen as protection against the vagrancies of the labour market. The economic problems suffered by previous Labour governments in 1947, 1967 and in the late 1970s led to pressures on welfare spending. These problems may be intensified as work is now seen as partially replacing welfare. In placing the welfare eggs in the economic basket, if the economy catches a cold, then the welfare state gets a dose of influenza.

Labour wishes to promote an active rather than a passive welfare state, and to fund investments in services such as education and health by reducing the bills of economic failure. This active welfare state is to be achieved by 'active government'. Government must be reinvented, with a greater clarity about goals and problems and a greater readiness to make changes to address them (Blair, 1998a, pp 15-16). The first dimension may be shown by the CSR (see especially Chapters Two and Six) which suggests a greater rational, rather than incremental, basis for expenditure. Instead of merely spending extra increments to achieve 'more of the same', Brown (1998c, col 188) states that each spending department will have a 'contract' with the Treasury which sets out the objectives and targets that have to be met, the stages by which they will be met, how departments intend to allocate resources to achieve those targets and the process that will monitor results. The contract "requires reform in return for investment". Money will be released only if departments keep to their plans. This implies a return to first principles; to rethinking objectives.

Perhaps the most important advantage of conducting a comprehensive spending review is the opportunity that it allows

for individual services to put in place a substantial reallocation of resources within Departments – from bureaucracy to front-line services, from dealing with the symptoms of problems to dealing with their causes – and to consider a coordinated approach that breaks free from the old departmental fragmentations and duplication. (Brown, 1998c, col 189)

This last objective is linked with the New Labour phrase of 'joined-up government' at both central and local levels (Chapters Six and Eleven). At central levels, the Social Exclusion Unit is a 'new cross-departmental group set up to tackle urgent problems which were neglected because no Whitehall department 'owned' them. At local levels there is a commitment to devolution and local governance which makes use of public–private partnerships and promotes strong communities within a strong civil society (Blair, 1998a). It is perhaps here that there may be something genuinely new. For example, it has been claimed that the action zone approach captures the Third Way in practice (see Gerwirtz, 1998; Power and Whitty, 1999; Chapter Three). Similarly, Kemp suggests that "where Labour has a new story to tell it is in respect of social exclusion" (Chapter Six). Many previous interventions were highly fragmented, with too little investment in people. Initiatives were parachuted in rather than harnessing community commitment (Social Exclusion Unit, 1998b). Rather than emphasising paternalist policies and producer interests such as the Old Left or responding to atomised consumers, the Third Way seeks to empower communities (see Driver and Martell, 1998). New Labour seeks to "intervene in inverse proportion to success" (Blair, 1998a, p 16). Ministers have been given tough powers to intervene in the case of failing education and health institutions, but they are increasing the autonomy of the majority – those who are doing a good job. Rouse and Smith (Chapter Eleven) suggest that there will be no return to the old public administration template. With devolution to Scotland and Wales, a different pattern of local authorities and different processes of accountability will emerge. However, they point out that a clear tension remains between devolution and greater centralisation. In their emphasis on new central institutions to enforce change, 'name and shame' and 'hit squads', Labour – contrary to its Third Way – is aiming for more effective 'command and control' (Paton, Chapter Three; see also Klein, 1998; Boyne, 1998).

Blair's views about intervention may also apply to individuals. Responsibility has been rescued from the clutches of the Right:

Rights and opportunity without responsibility are engines of selfishness and greed. Where duties are neglected, we should not hesitate to encourage and even enforce them, as we are seeking to do with initiatives such as our 'home-school contracts' between schools and parents.... The Third Way approach is to give support where it is needed most, matching rights and responsibilities. (Blair, 1998a, pp 4, 12-13)

However, 'support' alone may not match rights and responsibilities. Driver and Martell (1998, p 119) point out that Labour espouses firm, even punishable, ideas about duties, with a resort to legislative solutions to social problems. A necessary corollary of greater responsibility in welfare must entail more severe consequences for failure: there must be some stick with which to beat the 'irresponsible' – and their families. It is difficult to see how the circle linking responsibility and inclusion can be squared.

It can be argued that many of the ingredients of the 'new welfare state' are not particularly 'new'. For example, building the welfare state around work – "work for those who can; security for those who cannot" (DSS, 1998a) – is little more than a more humane version of the 'less eligibility' concept of the New Poor Law. Work incentives were seen as vital by Beveridge. The Beveridge welfare state nominally incorporated notions of the obligations of actively seeking work, which were not rigidly enforced during periods of relatively low levels of unemployment. Similarly, the importance of a voluntary and private 'extension ladder' of voluntary and private benefits and services above a state minimum would be familiar to Beveridge (see *The Guardian*, 1997b; Hewitt and Powell, 1998; Powell and Hewitt, 1998). In some ways, the new welfare state has merely taken some old policies from the shelf, dusted them down and given them a new gloss. Viewed in this light, the Third Way is simply a new mix of carrots and sticks (see Hewitt, Chapter Seven). McKibbin (1997) argues that in some respects New Labour has parallels with 'Very Old Labour' (the Party of Ramsay MacDonald of the 1920s). Similarly, in some ways, the new welfare state is the very old welfare state of Chadwick and Beveridge.

There have clearly been some moves towards a 'new welfare state', but progress has been far from uniform both between and within service sectors. Progress has been faster in areas such as employment than in others such as housing and personal social services. Within services, Cressey (Chapter Eight) argues that New Labour has made an ambivalent start in the area of employment, while Charman and Savage (Chapter Nine) claim that New Labour's law and order package represents a rather uneven package. Rouse and Smith (Chapter Eleven) state that Labour has made a complex journey towards "democratic renewal". Similarly, Hewitt (Chapter Seven) points to a complex journey in social security of:

> ... **two steps forward and one step back: each step back representing something of a rearguard action by Old Labour; each step forward furthering parts of the Tory agenda, and each second step forward an advance for New Labour.**

The appropriate analogy might appear to be not a journey in one direction, but rather ballroom dancing in two dimensions.

Driver and Martell (1998, p 86) suggest three questions associated with Labour's rethinking of social policy:

* Who pays and who benefits from social policy?
* How should welfare be delivered?
* What should social policy aim to achieve?

While it is too early to give any definitive answers, this section concludes by summarising the provisional verdicts to these questions.

First, who pays and who benefits from social policy. Despite closing the front-door traditional route of income tax, there has been some changes in the funding of services through the backdoor (Chapters One and Two), with some degree of redistribution by stealth. Against warnings of writers such as Field (1995, 1996a, 1996b) and Lister (1997a), Labour appears to be increasing the emphasis of means-testing (Chapter Seven). It is also following an area-based strategy by focusing on the most deprived areas in terms of health, education, employment and 'social exclusion'. However, access to these rights is becoming more conditional.

Second, how should welfare be delivered? There has certainly been a change in the mix of the mixed economy of welfare. This is most apparent in terms of production. New Labour is happy to see greater pluralism, with greater use of private and voluntary agencies. There has been a smaller move with respect to finance. New Labour is more tolerant of the purchased service, with the result that those with deeper pockets may have access to better private schools, healthcare and pensions. Delivery will largely be left to local 'quasi-market' agencies – so long as they conform to central directions.

Finally, what should social policy aim to achieve? As Driver and Martell (1998, p 104) recognise, this goes to the heart of the new Labour welfare agenda. There has been an attempt to marry social justice and economic efficiency within the parameters of an active welfare state. While not fully subscribing to Jessop's (1994) notion of a transition from a Keynesian welfare state to a Schumpeterian workfare state in which social needs are subordinated to productive capacities (see Chapters Seven and Ten), there has at the margins been a move away from need towards 'desert', with the reward of carrots and the punishment of sticks. In other words, there are some tendencies to move from a distribution based on pattern (need) to one taking into account some aspects of process (behaviour). All will be included, but some will be more included than others.

Explanations

There is continuing debate about the significance of changes in the Labour Party. As Kenny and Smith (1997, p 220) write, Blair has been presented as a one-nation conservative, a Thatcherite conservative, a moderniser completing the mission of previous leaders such as Gaitskell and a Labour politician still committed to the traditions of labourism. Similarly, there are long-running debates about the extent to which Labour ever was a socialist party (for example, Thorpe, 1997; Shaw, 1996) The next section addresses a more limited set of issues: providing an explanatory framework relevant to understanding changes in social policy. A useful starting point is the differences between electoral, ideological and external factors. Have policies been adopted because they are perceived as vote-winners, because they reflect fundamental changes in political ideology (a policy choice) or because external factors such as changed economic and social structures have limited the room to manoevure (policy constraints)?

Electoral

Kenny and Smith (1997) argue that a powerful interpretation of Blair which has been offered by commentators from a political science background stems from the Downsian view of Party competition. Like ice-cream sellers on a beach, it is argued that political parties will move to the position of the 'median voter'. More specifically, it was necessary for Labour to appeal to the voters in the marginal constituencies. In particular,

Labour had to capture seats in southern, affluent areas: to claim back 'Essex Man' into the Labour fold. At first sight, this appears an apt description of Labour's move to the political middle ground, jettisoning unpopular 'Left' policies. However, as noted in Chapter One, Labour's welfare policies were generally popular. This meant that the electoral explanation may have an indirect impact on welfare. It means that New labour cannot reverse Conservative policies which were electorally popular such as the right to buy legislation (Chapters Two and Six). It may account for a general change of tone. As Blair put it: "The new right had struck a chord. There was a perception that there was too much collective power, too much bureaucracy, too much state intervention and too many vested interests around it" (Sopel, 1995, p 209). It may explain an emphasis on key pledges limiting taxation and a trend away from overt redistribution (Chapters One and Two). According to leading moderniser Giles Radice an egalitarian tag was a vote-loser, "a fatal electoral handicap in a 'two-thirds, one-third' society" (Shaw, 1996, pp 196-8). Both perspectives are hinted at by King and Wickham-Jones. They quote Thompson who writes of the 1992 election defeat: "what Labour was left with as the centrepiece of its election strategy was old-fashioned welfarism". They point out the need to attract the middle class, like the New Democrats in the US. In standard Downsian terms, the Party was perceived by many as needing to move to the centreground to win over middle-class voters. Finally, it may account for the stress on delivering promises. In his introduction to the 1997 manifesto (Labour Party, 1997a), Tony Blair argued that in contrast to the Conservatives' broken promises, Labour would introduce a 'new politics': "our guiding rule is not to promise what we cannot deliver, and to deliver what we promise". By making a limited set of important promises and achieving them, New Labour aims to renew faith in the ability of government to deliver. In return, it seeks more than one term of office in government and hopes to emulate the long periods of Conservative office (1951-64 and 1979-97).

Ideological

Some commentators see New Labour as changing its ideology. However, there is little consensus as to the beginning and end points. There remains considerable disagreement as to what extent Labour was a 'socialist' party. There were a number of versions of 'Old Labour' (Crouch, 1997) and the category arguably includes individuals as diverse as Attlee, Bevan, Crosland

and Benn. Similarly, it is unclear whether Labour has moved towards social democracy, socialism or liberalism. In the space of not many pages, Shaw (1996, pp 201, 203, 228) mentions trends towards European-style social democracy, pre-Keynesianism and "the American vision of an economically and socially mobile society". Although Giddens (1998), Blair (1998a, 1998e) and Wright (1996, p 136) appear to align Labour with European social democracy, King and Wickham-Jones (Chapter Twelve) illustrate the influences on the Party from the US New Democrats and the way in which it learned from US policy. They quote Rogaly who claimed that Blair "designed and built New Labour, using blueprints faxed from Little Rock" (quoted in King and Wickham-Jones, Chapter Twelve; cf Jordan, 1998; Driver and Martell, 1998). However, as Cressey (Chapter Eight) clearly illustrates, New Labour's policy learning resembles a jackdaw's search for shiny objects, with pieces from Europe, the United States, as well as Old Labour. Shaw (1996, p 218) claims that the old objectives of full employment, equality and social justice have either been abandoned or diluted. However, it would be more accurate to say that objectives have been re-defined. The emphasis on retreat rather than redefinition misses a number of important developments in welfare such as the 'new moralism', greater conditionality and some revival in variants of Christian socialism/ethical socialism.

External

Labour has argued that the welfare state has to change because of changing social and economic pressures. In his introduction to the Welfare Green Paper (DSS, 1998a, p iv) Blair states that "the system must change because the world has changed, beyond the recognition of Beveridge's generation. We need a system designed not for yesterday, but for today". Later, it is claimed (DSS, 1998a, Chapter 1) that the welfare system has failed to keep pace with profound economic, social and political changes. The machinery of welfare has the air of yesteryear and has failed to take account of changing work, working women, changing families, an ageing society and rising expectations.

Just as the social sphere has changed since Beveridge, it can be argued that the economic sphere has changed since Keynes. The key concept here is 'globalisation' which "has been called upon to do an extraordinary amount of explanatory work in accounts of recent social and political change and, as such, it has generated a vast literature and a great deal of disagreement" (Pierson, 1998, pp 62-3). The global economic environment means that 'Keynesianism in one country' no longer appears to be a feasible policy option. However, Keynesianism was abandoned by the Labour government of the 1970s. In his speech to the 1976 Labour Party Conference, Prime Minister James Callaghan stated that, "We used to think that you could spend your way out of recession.... I will tell you in all candour that that option no longer exists" (Shaw, 1996, p 134). Shaw (1996, p 158) claims that the government gave an impression of "struggling to do its best in extremely bleak conditions, where the familiar landmarks were vanishing and where few of the levers used in the past to control events any longer worked".

Blair's view that "macro-economic policy can do little to change the underlying growth rate of the economy" (Sopel, 1995, p 210) may be compared with that of Denis Healey that "in the end markets decide" (Shaw, 1996). Brown's speech to the Labour Party Conference of 1997 echoed Callaghan: "Just as you cannot spend your way out of a recession, you cannot, in a global economy, simply spend your way through a recovery either" (Riddell, 1997). This is essentially the same economic framework as the Right (Shaw, 1996, p 201). As Blair (1998e) summed up, "we are all globalists now". This new consensus is due in part to a new end of ideology thesis: external factors such as demographic pressures and the globalisation of work patterns have persuaded politicians of all Parties of the merits of the affordable welfare state (Dean, 1994, p 106; George and Miller, 1994, pp 218-19). The social policy agenda has been written with an economic pen in both a direct and indirect sense. First, governments have less room to manoeuvre because of globalisation. Keynesianism in one country has been rejected and one of the central goals of the post-war welfare state, full employment, is no longer a realistic policy option. Second, politicians believe that the electorate does not want to pay higher taxes to finance growing demands of the welfare state, with the result that in order to square the welfare circle they have to restructure the welfare state. In other words, the 'affordable welfare state' is due to a perceived fiscal crisis.

The final external factor is that politicians have to respond to a new political landscape. Labour could not wish away its inheritance from the Conservatives. It has therefore adapted many Conservative policies, or has 'reformed the reforms.' It had to start from 'here' rather than with a blank piece of paper. Just as the Conservatives in 1951 could not turn back the clock to the 1930s, Labour in 1997 could not undo the Conservative changes such as the Right to Buy legislation.

There are no clear dividing lines between the explanations. For example, it is not clear whether the rejection of full employment is due to ideological or external factors; a policy choice or an external constraint. It does appear that many of Labour's policies are flowing with the international tide. For example, giving control over interest rates to an independent national bank fits in with long-standing arrangements in countries such as Germany and the US. However, does it make a difference if the same result came about for different reasons: choice versus constraint; ideology versus pragmatism; internal versus external factors?

Conclusion

There are few simple answers to the questions posed at the start of this book. This is partly due to the provisional nature of the early verdicts given by the contributors and partly because some of the contributors are clearly more sympathetic to New Labour's policies than others. Nevertheless, in general, New Labour has a distinctive approach from Old Labour. Some clear trends of policy convergence with the Conservatives have been noted, particularly in the areas of public expenditure, the mixed economy of welfare and Welfare to Work. However, it may be more accurate to use the term policy adoption or adaption, as Labour realised that in many cases it would be difficult to turn back the clock to 1979. Labour inherited a welfare landscape not of its making. Its pragmatic response was to accept or modify the reforms that appeared to work and reject those that did not. While it is possible to argue that New Labour has moved further in areas such as Welfare to Work than others such as housing, there appear to be differences in pace within policy sectors. For example, while 'opting out' of local education authorities (LEAs) into grant-maintained status was disallowed, 'opting-out' into an Education Action Zone has been introduced.

Labour has claimed that the Third Way is a new and distinctive concept that can be mapped out for different policy areas. However, while some contributors have tentatively suggested some evidence of a 'third way', it is not a coherent concept that can be applied more or less uniformly to different policy sectors. Instead, it appears to be all things to all people: a poorly specified, pick and mix strategy, largely defined by what it is not. Neither does it appear to be new: arguably some of its key components such as the centrality of work and civil society have their historical roots in the New Poor Law and in the writings of New Liberals such as Beveridge.

Finally, most of the contributors stress that it is too early to tell whether Labour's welfare reforms are leading to a new welfare state, although a new relationship between citizens and the welfare state seems to be emerging. This caution is due to a number of reasons. Many terms used by New Labour such as 'full employment' are ambiguous and may be redefined from their traditional welfare usage. In the 'pre-delivery' phase, there may be significant differences between policy intentions and the eventual policy results. Nevertheless, a number of themes appear in different chapters. These include the centrality of work, the redefinition of citizenship and the redefinition of redistribution and equality. It is no secret that Tony Blair wishes his government to be remembered as one of the great 'left of centre' reforming governments of the 20th century along with the Liberals in 1906 and Labour in 1945. It seems likely that the volume of change will place Blair's government in the company of the governments of 1906, 1945 and the Thatcher government of 1979. The jury is still out on the direction of change. Nevertheless, it is likely that the welfare state of the next millennium may be very different from that of 1979, or even that of 1997.

Bibliography

Acheson, D. (1998) *Independent Inquiry into Inequalities in Health*, London: The Stationery Office.

Adnett, N. and Davies, P. (1999) 'Schooling quasi-markets: reconciling economic and sociological analyses', Paper presented at *Eighth Quasi-market Research Seminar*, University of Bath, 6-7 January.

Alcock, P. (1992) 'The Labour Party and the welfare state', in M.J. Smith and J. Spear (eds) *The changing Labour Party*, London: Routledge.

Alcock, P. (1997a) 'Consolidation or stagnation? Social policy under the Major Governments' in M. May, E. Brunsdon and G. Craig (eds) *Social Policy Review 9*, London: Social Policy Association.

Alcock, P. (1997b) 'Making welfare work: Frank Field and New Labour's social policy agenda', *Benefits*, no 20.

Alexander, R. (1997) *Policy and practice in primary education*, London: Routledge.

Almond, G.A. and Verba, S. (1963) *The civic culture*, Princeton, NJ: Princeton University Press.

Anderson, P. and Mann, N. (1997) *Safety first*, London: Granta Books.

Andrews, K. and Jacobs, J. (1990) *Punishing the poor: Poverty under Thatcher*, Basingstoke: Macmillan.

Armstrong, H. (1998) 'Speech by Hilary Armstrong', presented to the Annual Conference of the Chartered Institute of Housing, Harrogate, 16 June.

APA (Association of Police Authorities) (1998) *Annual Report 1998*, London: APA.

Audit Commission (1986) *Making a reality of community care*, London: HMSO.

Audit Commission (1993) *Taking care: Progress with care in the community*, London: HMSO.

Audit Commission (1994) *Taking stock: Progress with community care*, London: HMSO.

Auer, P. (1996) 'The monitoring of labour market policies in EU member states', *InfoMISEP*, no 53, Spring, Berlin.

Back, G. and Hamnett, C. (1985) 'State housing policy formation and the changing role of housing associations in Britain', *Policy & Politics*, vol 13, no 4, pp 393-411.

Baldock, J. (1998) 'The personal social services and community care', in P. Alcock, A. Erskine and M. May (eds) *The student's companion to social policy*, Oxford: Blackwell.

Baldock, J. and Ungerson, C. (1994) *Becoming consumers of community care: Households within the mixed economy of welfare*, York: Joseph Rowntree Foundation.

Bartlett, W., Propper, C., Wilson, D. and Le Grand, J. (eds) (1994) *Quasi-markets in the welfare state*, Bristol: SAUS Publications.

Beck, U. (1992) *Risk society: Towards a new modernity*, London: Sage Publications.

Beck, U., Giddens, A. and Lash, S. (1994) *Reflexive modernization*, Cambridge: Polity Press.

Bell, D. (1993) *Communitarianism and its critics*, Oxford: Clarendon Press.

Best, R. (1991) 'Housing associations 1890-1990', in S.G. Lowe and D.J. Hughes (eds) *A new century of social housing*, Leicester: Leicester University Press.

Best, R. (1997) 'Housing associations: the sustainable solution?', in P. Williams (ed) *Directions in housing policy*, London: Paul Chapman Publishing.

Beveridge, W.H. (1942) *Social insurance and allied Services*, Cmd 6404, London: HMSO.

Bingham, Lord (1997) 'The sentence of the Court', Speech given to the *Police Foundation*, 10 July.

Bingham, Lord (1998) 'The mandatory life sentence for murder', *Newsam Memorial Lecture*, given at the Police Staff College, 13 March.

Black, D., Morris, J., Smith, C. and Townsend, P. (1980) *Inequalities in health*, London: HMSO.

Blair, T. (1995) 'The rights we enjoy reflect the duties we owe', *The Spectator Lecture*, London: Labour Party, 22 March.

Blair, T. (1996a) *New Britain: My vision of a young country*, London: Fourth Estate.

Blair, T. (1996b) 'Battle for Britain', *The Guardian*, 29 January.

Blair, T. (1997a) 'The 21st century welfare state', Speech, Amsterdam, 24 January, London: Labour Party.

Blair, T. (1997b) 'Welfare reform', Speech, Sedgefield, 20 December, London: Labour Party.

Blair, T. (1998a) *The Third Way*, London: Fabian Society.

Blair, T. (1998b) *Hansard*, House of Commons, Prime Minister's Questions, 15 July.

Blair, T. (1998c) *Hansard*, House of Commons, Prime Minister's Questions, 29 July.

Blair, T. (1998d) *Hansard*, Debate on Queen's Speech, 24 November.

Blair, T. (1998e) 'Europe's left-of-centre parties have discovered the "third way"', *The Independent*, 7 April.

Blair, T. (1999) 'It really is the end of the something for nothing days', *Daily Mail*, 10 February.

Blake, J. (1998) 'Question time', *Roof*, September/October, pp 19-21.

Bochel, C. and Bochel, H. (1998) 'The governance of social policy', in E. Brunsdon, H. Dean and R. Woods (eds) *Social Policy Review 10*, London: Social Policy Association.

Bowen, A (1991) 'Labour market policies', in M. Artis and D. Cobham (eds) *Labour's economic policies 1974-79*, Manchester: Manchester University Press.

Boyne, G. (1998) 'Public services under New Labour: back to bureaucracy?', *Public Money and Management*, vol 18, pp 43-50.

Braggins, J. (1993) 'Presidential election de-brief', DO 31.1.93, 24 February, NEC.

Bramley, G. (1997) 'Housing policy: a case of terminal decline?', *Policy & Politics*, vol 25, no 4, pp 387-407.

Bratton, W. (1998) 'Crime is down in New York City: blame the police', in N. Dennis (ed) *Zero tolerance: Policing a free society*, London: Institute of Economic Affairs.

Brindle, D. (1998) 'Professionals should verify self-assessed beenfits claims', *The Guardian*, 14 March, p 18.

Brindle, D. and MacAskill, E. (1997) 'All change please: no room on board', *The Guardian*, 16 December, p 15.

Brine, J. (1998) 'The European Union's discourse of "equality" and its education and training policy within the post-compulsory sector', *Journal of Education Policy*, vol 13, pp 137-52.

Brook, L., Hall, J. and Preston, I. (1996) 'Public spending and taxation', in R. Jowell, J. Curtice, A. Park, L. Brook and K. Thompson (eds) *British social attitudes, the 13th report*, Aldershot: Dartmouth.

Brown, C. (1997) *Fighting talk*, London: Simon and Schuster.

Brown, G. (1995) 'Labour's New Deal for Britain's under 25s', Speech, London: Labour Party.

Brown, G. (1996) 'Equality of opportunity and the welfare state', Speech, 22 October, London: Labour Party.

Brown, G. (1997a) 'The Anthony Crosland Memorial Lecture', 13 February, London: Labour Party.

Brown, G. (1997b) *Hansard*, Budget Statement, 2 July, London: House of Commons.

Brown, G. (1998a) Speech, Federal Reserve Bank, New York, 17 April, London: HM Treasury.

Brown, G. (1998b) Speech to the British American Business Council, 28 April, London: Labour Party.

Brown, G. (1998c) *Hansard*, The Chancellor's Speech to the Commons on the Comprehensive Spending Review, 14 July.

Brown, P. (1997) 'The "Third Wave": education and the ideology of parentocracy', in A.H. Halsey, H. Lauder, P. Brown and A.S. Wells (eds) *Education, culture economy and society*, Oxford: Oxford University Press.

Brown, P. and Lauder, H. (1997) 'Education, globilization, and economic development', in A.H. Halsey, H. Lauder, P. Brown and A.S. Wells (eds) *Education, culture economy and society*, Oxford: Oxford University Press.

Bulmer, M. and Rees, A. (eds) (1996) *Citizenship today: The contemporary relevance of T.H. Marshall*, London: UCL Press.

Burchardt, T. and Hills, J. (1997) *Private welfare insurance and social security: Pushing the boundaries*, York: York Publishing Services.

Burchardt, T. and Hills, J. (1998) 'From public to private: the case of mortgage payment insurance in Great Britain', *Housing Studies*, vol 13, pp 311-23.

Burchardt, T., Hills, J. and Propper, C. (1999) *Private welfare and public policy*, York: York Publishing Services.

Burrows, R. (1997) *Contemporary patterns of residential mobility in relation to social rented housing in England*, York: Centre for Housing Policy.

Butcher, T. (1995) *Delivering welfare*, Buckingham: Open University Press.

Butler, J. (1992) *Patients, policies and politics*, Birmingham: Open University Press.

Cabinet Office (1998) *Service first: The new charter programme*, London: The Stationery Office.

CACE (Central Advisory Committee for Education) (1967) *Children and thier primary school* (Plowden report), London: HMSO.

Campbell, B. (1995) 'Old fogeys and angry young men', *Soundings*, no 1.

Carers National Association (1997) *Still battling? The Carers Act one year on*, London: Carers National Association.

Castle, B. and Townsend, P. (1998) 'Letter', *The Guardian*, 23 July, p 17.

Challis, L., Fuller, S., Henwood, M., Klein, R., Plowden, W., Webb, A., Whittingham, P. and Wistow, G. (1988) *Joint approaches to social policy*, Cambridge: Cambridge University Press.

Chatrik, B. and Convery, P. (1998) 'Nine out of ten jobless under 18s without an income', *Working Brief*, May, p 8.

Clarke, J., Cochrane, A. and McLaughlin, E. (1994) 'Introduction', in J. Clarke, A. Cochrane and E. McLaughlin (eds) *Managing social policy*, London: Sage Publications.

Clarke, J. and Newman, J. (1997) *The managerial state*, London: Sage Publications.

Clarke, K. (1998) *Hansard*, House of Commons, 14 July, col 201.

Clasen, J. (1997) 'Social insurance in Germany: dismantling or reconstruction?', in J. Clasen (ed) *Social insurance in Europe*, Bristol: The Policy Press.

Coates, K. and Barratt Brown, M. (1996) *The Blair revelation: Deliverance for whom?*, Nottingham: Spokesman Press.

Collins, D.J. (1996) 'Lessons from America', *Progress*, no 2, Summer, pp 26-7.

Commission on Social Justice (1994) *Social justice: Strategies for national renewal*, London: Vintage.

Committee on Standards in Public Life (1995) *Standards in public life* (Chair: Lord Nolan), London: HMSO.

Common, R. and Flynn, N. (1992) *Contracting for care*, York: Joseph Rowntree Foundation.

Conservative Party (1987) *The next moves forward: The Conservative Party Manifesto 1987*, Westminster: Conservative Central Office.

Cope, S., Leishman, F. and Starie, P. (1996) 'Reinventing and restructuring', in F. Leishman, B. Loveday and S. Savage (eds) *Core issues in policing*, London: Longman.

Copley, J. (1998) '£75 minimum for pensioners', *The Daily Telegraph*, 11 July, p 1.

Craig, F.W.S. (ed) (1990) *British General Election manifestos 1959-1987*, 3rd edn, Aldershot: Dartmouth.

Crine, S. (1994) *Reforming welfare: American lessons*, Pamphlet No 567, London: Fabian Society.

Crook, T. and Kemp, P.A. (1996) 'The revival of private rented housing in Britain', *Housing Studies*, vol 11, pp 51-68.

Crosland, C.A.R. (1964) (first published 1956) *The future of socialism*, London: Jonathan Cape.

Crouch, C. (1997) 'The terms of the neo-liberal consensus', *Political Quarterly*, vol 68, pp 352-60.

Crozier, G. (1998) 'Parents and school', *Journal of Education Policy*, vol 13, no 1, pp 125-36.

Cullingworth, J.B. (1979) *Essays on housing policy*, London: George Allen and Unwin.

Culpitt, I. (1992) *Welfare and citizenship: Beyond the crisis of the welfare state?*, London: Sage Publications.

Dahrendorf, R. (1996) 'Citizenship and social class', in M. Bulmer and A. Rees (eds) *Citizenship today: The contemporary relevance of T.H. Marshall*, London: UCL Press.

Daily Telegraph (1997) 'The party of the left', 5 April, p 15.

Dale, R. (1997) 'The State and the governance of education: an analysis of the restructuring of the state-education relationship', in A.H. Halsey, H. Lauder, P. Brown and A.S. Wells (eds) *Education, culture economy and society*, Oxford: Oxford University Press.

Daniel, C. (1998) 'The concise NewLabourspeak', *New Statesman*, 1 May, pp 28-34.

Darling, A. (1999) 'We make no apologies for our tough benefit regime', *The Independent*, 10 February.

Daugherty, R. (1995) *National Curriculum assessment*, London: Falmer Press.

Davey, K. (1998) 'The impermanence of New Labour', in M. Perrymen (ed) *The Blair agenda*, London: Lawrence & Wishart.

Davis, H. (1993) *A first guide to appointed local agencies in the West Midlands*, Birmingham: Institute of Local Government Studies.

Davis, H. and Stewart, J. (1993) *The growth of government by appointment*, Luton: LGMB.

Day, P. and Klein, R. (1987) *Accountabilities*, London: Tavistock.

Deacon, A. (1996) 'The dilemmas of welfare: Titmuss, Murray and Mead', in S.J.D. Green and R.C. Whiting (eds) *The boundaries of the State in modern Britain*, Cambridge: Cambridge University Press.

Deacon, A. (ed) (1997a) *From Welfare to Work: Lessons from America*, London: Institute for Economic Affairs.

Deacon, A. (1997b) 'Welfare to Work: options and issues', *Social Policy Review*, vol 9, pp 34-49.

Deakin, N. and Parry, R. (1998) 'The Treasury and New Labour's social policy', in E.Brunsdon, H. Dean and R.Woods (eds) *Social Policy Review 10*, London: Social Policy Association.

Dean, H. (1991) *Social security and social control*, London: Routledge.

Dean, H. (1994) 'Social security: the cost of persistent poverty', in V. George and S. Miller (eds) *Social policy towards 2000*, London: Routledge.

Dean, H. (1995) 'Paying for children: procreation and financial liability', in H. Dean (ed) *Parents' duties, children's debts: The limits of policy intervention*, Aldershot: Ashgate.

Dean, H. (1996) *Welfare, law and citizenship*, Hemel Hempstead: Prentice Hall/Harvester Wheatsheaf.

Dean, H. and Melrose, M. (1997) 'Manageable discord: fraud and resistance in the social security system', *Social Policy and Administration*, vol 31, no 2, pp 103-18.

Dean, H. with Melrose, M. (1999) *Poverty, riches and social citizenship*, Basingstoke: Macmillan.

Dean, H. and Taylor-Gooby, P. (1992) *Dependency culture: The explosion of a myth*, Hemel Hempstead: Harvester Wheatsheaf.

Denny, C. (1998) 'Is the New Deal tackling old problems?', *The Guardian Jobs*, 1 August, p 16.

DfEE (Department for Education and Employment) (1997a) *Excellence in schools*, London: HMSO.

DfEE (1997b) *Connecting the learning society. National Grid for Learning. The Government's Consultation Paper*, London: DfEE.

DfEE (1997c) *Design of the New Deal for 18-24 year olds*, London: DfEE.

DfEE (1997d) *New Deal for long-term unemployed people aged 25 plus*, London: DfEE.

DfEE (1997e) *The European Social Fund; A plan for Objective 4 in Great Britain, 1998-1999*, London: DfEE.

DfEE (1998a) *Teachers meeting the challenge of change*, London: DfEE.

DfEE (1998b) *Professional conduct, competence, appraisal, raising standards in school*, London: DfEE.

DfEE (1999) *Statistical First Release*, 2 February, London: DfEE.

DfEE/DSS (1998) *A new contract for welfare: The gateway to work*, Cm 4102, London: The Stationery Office.

DES (Department of Education and Science) (1977) *Education in schools: A consultative document*, London: HMSO.

DES (1991) *The Parent's Charter*, London: DES.

DoE (Department of the Environment) (1977) *Housing policy: A consultative document*, London: HMSO.

DoE (1987a) *Housing: The government's proposals*, London: HMSO.

DoE (1987b) *Housing and constructive statistics 1976-86*, London: HMSO.

DETR (Department of the Environment, Transport and the Regions) (1998a) *Modernising local government: Improving local services through Best Value*, London: DETR.

DETR (1998b) *Modern local government: In touch with the people*, London: HMSO.

DETR/Welsh Office (1997) *Replacing CCT with a duty of Best Value: Next steps*, unnumbered circular, London: HMSO.

DHSS (Department of Health and Social Security) (1981) *Growing older*, London: HMSO.

Disney, R., Bellman, L., Carruth, A., Franz, W., Jackman, R., Layard, R., Lehmann, H. and Phillpot, J. (1992) *Helping the unemployed: Active labour market policies in Britain and Germany*, London: Anglo-German Foundation.

Dobson, F. (1998) Speech, Liverpool, 12 February 1998, London: Labour Party.

DoH (Department of Health) (1989a) *Working for patients*, Cmnd 555, London: HMSO.

DoH (1989b) *Caring for people: Community care in the next decade and beyond*, Cm 849, London: HMSO.

DoH (1991) *Working together under the Children Act 1989*, London: HMSO.

DoH (1992) *The health of the nation*, London: HMSO.

DoH (1995) *Community care monitoring: Report of 1994 National Exercises*, London: HMSO.

DoH (1996) *Functions and manpower review*, London: DoH.

DoH (1997) *The new National Health Service: Modern, dependable*, London: HMSO.

DoH (1998a) *Statistical bulletin: Community care statistics 1997*, London: HMSO.

DoH (1998b) *Modernising social services: Promoting independence, improving protection, raising standards*, Cm 4169, London: HMSO.

DoH (1998c) *Our healthier nation*, London: HMSO.

Dolowitz, D. (1997) *Learning from America*, Falmer: Sussex Academic Press.

Douglas, M. (1978) *Natural symbols*, Harmondsworth: Penguin.

Downes, D. and Morgan, R. (1997) 'Dumping the "Hostages to Fortune"? The politics of law and order in post-war Britain', in R. Reiner, R. Morgan and M. Maguire (eds) *Oxford handbook of criminology*, Oxford: Oxford University Press.

Downs, A. (1957) *An economic theory of democracy*, New York, NY: Harper Row.

Doyal, L. and Gough, I. (1991) *A theory of social need*, Basingstoke: Macmillan.

Driver, S. and Martell, L. (1997) 'New Labour's communitarianisms', *Critical Social Policy*, vol 17, no 3, pp 27-44.

Driver, S. and Martell, L. (1998) *New Labour: Politics after Thatcherism*, Cambridge: Polity Press.

DSS (Department of Social Security) (1998a) *A new contract for welfare: New ambitions for our country*, Cm 3805, London: The Stationery Office.

DSS (1998b) *Welfare reform focus files 1-7*, London: DSS.

DSS (1998c) *A new contract for welfare: Principles into practice*, Cm 4101, London: The Stationery Office.

DSS (1998d) *A new contract for welfare: Support for disabled people*, Cm 4103, London: The Stationery Office.

DSS (1998e) *A new contract for welfare: Partnership in pensions*, Cm 4179, London: The Stationery Office.

DSS (1998f) *Income support statistical quarterly enquiry, November 1997*, Press Release, 28 May, DSS Analytical Services Division.

DSS (1998g) *Family credit statistical quarterly enquiry, August 1997*, Press Release, 13 January, DSS Analytical Services Division.

DSS (1998h) *Children first: A new approach to child support*, Cm 3992, London: The Stationery Office.

DSS (1999a) *Welfare reform and pensions bill*, House of Commons, Bill 44 52/2, London: The Stationery Office.

DSS (1999b) *Welfare reform and pensions bill explanatory notes*, House of Commons, London: The Stationery Office.

DTI (Department of Trade and Industry) (1998) *Fairness at work*, London: HMSO.

Dunbar, I. and Langdon, A. (1998) *Tough justice: Sentencing and penal policies in the 1990s*, London: Blackstone Press Ltd.

Dunleavy, P. (1981) *The politics of mass housing in Britain 1945-1975*, Oxford: Clarendon Press.

Dwyer, P. (1998) 'Conditional citizens? Welfare rights and responsibilities in the late 1990s', *Critical Social Policy*, vol 18, pp 493-517.

Economist (1998) 'Goldilocks politics', 19 December, pp 47-9.

Education and Employment Committee (1998) *The New Deal/The New Deal Pathfinders*, House of Commons session 1997-98, London: The Stationery Office.

Edwards, P.K. (1998) 'Minimum pay', Internet feature article, European Industrial Relations Observatory, Dublin: European Foundation. (eiro@eurofound.ie)

Elcock, H. (1983) 'Disabling professions: the real threat to local democracy', *Public Money*, vol 3, pp 23-7.

Elliott, G. (1993) *Labourism and the English genius*, London: Verso.

Ellison, N. (1997) 'From welfare state to post-welfare society? Labour's social policy in historical and contemporary perspective' in B. Brivati and T. Bale (eds) *New Labour in Power*, London: Routledge.

Ellison, N. and Pierson, C. (eds) (1998) *Developments in British social policy*, Basingstoke: Macmillan.

Employment Committee (1996) *The right to work/workfare*, House of Commons Sessions 1995-96, Employment Committee Second Report, London: HMSO.

Esping-Andersen, G. (1990) *The three worlds of welfare capitalism*, Cambridge: Polity Press.

Esping-Andersen, G. (ed) (1996) *Welfare states in transition*, London: Sage Publications.

Etzioni, A. (1995) *The spirit of community*, London: Fontana Press.

EC (1994) *European social policy: A way forward for the Union*, Luxembourg: EC.

EC (1995) *White Paper: Education and training: Teaching and learning: Towards the learning society*, Luxembourg: OOPEC.

European Industrial Relations Review (1998) March, London.

Evans, M. (1998) 'Social security: dismantling the pyramids?', in H. Glennerster and J. Hills (eds) *The state of welfare*, Oxford: Oxford University Press.

Falk, R. (1994) 'The making of global citizenship', in B. van Steenbergen (ed) *The condition of citizenship*, London: Sage Publications.

Farnham, D. and Lupton, C. (1994) 'Employment relations and training policy', in S. Savage, R. Atkinson and L. Robins (eds) *Public policy in Britain*, New York, NY: St Martins Press.

Faulkner, D. (1997) 'A prison service for the 21st century', *Prison Service Journal*, no 109.

Ferlie, E., Pettigrew, A., Ashburner, L. and Fitzgerald, L. (1996) *The new public management in action*, Oxford: Oxford University Press.

Field, F. (1995) *Making welfare work: Reconstructing welfare for the millennium*, London: Institute of Community Studies.

Field, F. (1996a) *How to pay for the future: Building a stakeholders' welfare*, London: Institute of Community Studies.

Field, F. (1996b) *Stakeholder welfare*, London: Institute of Economic Affairs.

Field, F. (1997a) 'Welfare: the third way', Speech at Victoria and Albert Museum, 24 September.

Field, F. (1997b) The Warwick Debate, University of Warwick, 21 October.

Field, F. (1997c) 'Re-inventing welfare: a response to Lawrence Mead', in A. Deacon (ed) *From welfare to work: Lessons from America*, London: Institute of Economic Affairs.

Field, F. (1997d) 'How Labour will shake up the welfare state', *Sunday Times*, 4 May, p 37.

Field, F. (1998) 'An almost criminal waste of welfare', *Sunday Times*, 2 August.

Finegold, D. and Soskice, D. (1988) 'The failure of training in Britain: analysis and prescription', *Oxford Review of Economic Policy*, vol 4, no 3, pp 21-53.

Finn, D (1998) 'Labour's "New Deal" for the unemployed and the stricter benefit regime', in E. Brunsdon, H. Dean and R. Woods (eds) *Social Policy Review 10*, London: Social Policy Association.

Ford, J. and Kempson, E. (1997) *Bridging the gap: State and private safety-nets for mortgages*, York: York Publishing Services.

Forder, J., Knapp, M. and Wistow, G. (1996) 'Competition in the mixed economy of care', *Journal of Social Policy*, vol 25, pp 201-21.

Forrest, R. and Murie, A. (1988) *Selling the welfare state*, London: Routledge.

Forrest, R., Murie, A. and Williams, P. (1990) *Home ownership: Differentiation and fragmentation*, London: Unwin Hyman.

Foucault, M. (1977) *Discipline and punish: The birth of the prison*, Harmondsworth: Penguin.

Fox, C.J. and Miller, H.T. (1995) *Postmodern public administration*, London: Sage Publications.

Freedman, E.S., Muschamp, Y.M., Jones, S., Thompson, J.J. and Daugherty, R. (1997) *Evaluation of Key Stage 2 assessment in England and Wales 1996 Outcomes Report*, London: School Curriculum and Assessment Authority.

Galbraith, J.K. (1992) *The culture of contentment*, London: Sinclair-Stevenson.

Gamble, A. (1988) *The free economy and the strong state*, Basingstoke: Macmillan.

Gennard. J. (1998) 'Labour government: change in employment law', *Employee Relations*, vol 20, no 1.

George, V. and Miller, S. (1994) '2000 and beyond: a residual or a citizens' welfare state', in V. George and S. Miller (eds) *Social policy towards 2000*, London: Routledge.

George, V. and Wilding, P. (1976) *Ideology and social welfare*, London: Routledge and Kegan Paul.

Gewirtz, S. (1996) 'Post-Welfarism and the reconstruction of teachers' work', Paper given at British Educational Research Association Annual Conference, Lancaster.

Gewirtz, S. (1998) 'Education policy in urban places: making sense of Action Zones', Paper presented at Social Policy Association Annual Conference: 'Social Policy in Time and Place', University of Lincolnshire and Humberside, 14–16 July.

Gewirtz, S., Ball, S.J. and Bowe, R. (1995) *Markets, choice and equity in education*, Buckingham: Open University Press.

Giddens, A. (1990) *The consequences of modernity*, Cambridge: Polity Press.

Giddens, A. (1991) *Modernity and self-identity: Self and society in the late modern age*, Cambridge: Polity Press.

Giddens, A. (1994) *Beyond Left and Right: The future of radical politics*, Cambridge: Polity Press.

Giddens, A. (1998) *The Third Way*, Cambridge: Polity Press.

Gillborn, D. (1998) 'Racism, selection, poverty and parents: New Labour, old problems?', *Journal of Education Policy*, vol 13, no 6, pp 717–35.

Ginsburg, N. (1992) *Divisions of welfare*, London: Sage Publications.

Gipps, C. (1994) *Beyond testing*, London: Falmer Press.

Glatter, R., Woods, P.A. and Bagley, C. (eds) (1997) *Choice and diversity in schooling: Perspectives and prospects*, London: Routledge.

Glendinning, C. (1998) 'From general practice to primary care: developments in primary health care 1990-1998', in E. Brunsdon, H. Dean and R. Woods (eds) *Social Policy Review 10*, London: Social Policy Association.

Glennerster, H. (1998a) 'New beginnings and old continuities', in H. Glennerster and J. Hills (eds) *The state of welfare*, Oxford: Oxford University Press.

Glennerster, H. (1998b) 'Education: reaping the harvest?', in H. Glennerster and J. Hills (eds) *The state of welfare*, Oxford: Oxford University Press.

Glennerster, H., Matsaganis, M., Owens, P. with Hancock, S. (1994) *Implementing GP fundholding – wild card or winning hand?*, Buckingham: Open University Press.

Glennerster, H. and Hills, J. (eds) (1998) *The state of welfare*, 2nd edn, Oxford: Oxford University Press.

Glennerster, H. and Le Grand, J. (1994) *The development of quasi-markets in welfare provision*, London: STICERD.

Goddard, J. (1997) 'New Labour: the party of law and order?', Unpublished paper presented to Political Studies Association Conference, April.

Goodchild, B. and Karn, V. (1997) 'Standards, quality control and house building in the UK', in P. Williams (ed) *Directions in housing policy*, London: Paul Chapman Publishing.

Goode, J., Callender, C. and Lister, R. (1998) *Purse or wallet? Gender inequalities and income distribution within families on benefit*, London: Policy Studies Institute.

Goodlad, R. (1997) *Housing and the Scottish Parliament*, ESRC Centre for Housing Research and Urban Studies Occasional Paper, Glasgow: University of Glasgow.

Goss, S. and Miller, C. (1995) *From margin to mainstream: Developing user- and carer-centred community care*, York: Joseph Rowntree Fondation.

Gould, P. (1985) *Communications Review*, Kinnock Papers, 22 December, Cambridge: Churchill College, University of Cambridge, Box 304.

Gould, P. (1992) 'The politics of victory', *The Guardian*, 6 November.

Gould, P. (1996) 'Tunes of glory', *The Guardian*, 9 November.

Gould, P. (1998) *The unfinished revolution*, London: Little Brown.

Government's Annual Report (1998) Cm 3969, London: The Stationery Office.

Gray, A. (1995) 'Hollowing out the core', *The Guardian*, 8 March.

Gray, A. (1998) 'New Labour – new labour discipline', *Capital and Class*, no 65, pp 1-8.

Gray, A. and Jenkins, B. (1998) 'New Labour, new government? Change and continuity in public administration and government 1997', *Parliamentary Affairs*, vol 51, no 2, pp 111-30.

Green, D. (1996) *Community without politics*, London: IEA Health and Welfare Unit.

Greer, P. (1994) *Transforming central government*, Buckingham: Open University Press.

Gregg, P. (1990) 'The evolution of special employment measures', *National Institute Economic Review*, 132, May, pp 49-58.

Gregg, P. (1998) 'Comment', in C. Oppenheim (ed) *An inclusive society*, London: IPPR, pp 129-36.

Gregg, P. and Wadsworth, J. (1996) 'More work in fewer households', in J. Hills (ed) *New inequalities: The changing distribution of income and wealth in the United Kingdom*, Cambridge: Cambridge University Press.

Grice, A. (1997a) 'Blair aims for DIY welfare state', *Sunday Times*, 9 November.

Grice, A. (1997b) 'Council tax will soar as Labour hits the rich', *Sunday Times*, 30 November.

Grice, A. (1998) 'Ministers call Frank Field "a failed joke"', *Sunday Times*, 2 August.

Grice, A. and Smith, D. (1997) 'Blair launches crusade for welfare reform', *Sunday Times*, 4 May.

Griffiths, E.R. (1983) Letter to the Secretary of State, 6 October, London: DoH.

Griffiths, Sir Roy (1988) *Community care: Agenda for action*, London: HMSO.

Guest, D. (1997) 'Towards jobs and justice in Europe: a research agenda', *Industrial Relations Journal*, vol 28, no 4.

Gyford, J. (1991) *Citizens, consumers and councils*, Basingstoke: Macmillan.

Habermas, J. (1994) 'Citizenship and national identity', in B. van Steenbergen (ed) *The condition of citizenship*, London: Sage Publications.

Hadley, R. and Hatch, S. (1981) *Social welfare and the failure of the state*, London: George Allen & Unwin.

Hadley, R. and Young, K. (1990) *Creating a responsive public service*, Hemel Hempstead: Harvester Wheatsheaf.

Hall, M. (1997) 'Fairness at work', European Industrial Relations Observatory, Internet feature article, European Foundation, Dublin (eiro@eurofound.ie).

Halpern, D. and Mikosz, D. (eds) (1998) *The Third Way: Summary of the Nexus on-line discussion*, London: Nexus.

Hamnett, C. (1987) 'Conservative government housing policy in Britain, 1979-85', in W. van Vliet (ed) *Housing markets and policies under fiscal austerity*, Westport, CT: Greenwood Press.

Hargreaves, I. (1998) 'A step beyond Morris dancing: the third sector revival', in I. Hargreaves and I. Christie (eds) *Tomorrow's politics: The Third Way and beyond*, London: Demos.

Hargreaves, I. and Christie, I. (eds) (1998) *Tomorrow's politics: The Third Way and beyond*, London: Demos.

Harloe, M. (1995) *The people's home: Social rented housing in Europe and America*, Oxford: Basil Blackwell.

Harman, H. (1998) 'Welfare reform: theory into practice', *Fabian Review*, vol 110, pp 2-3.

Hawksworth, J. and Wilcox, S. (1995) *Challenging the conventions: Public borrowing rules and housing investment*, Coventry: Chartered Institute of Housing.

Hayek, F. (1976) *Law, legislation and liberty, Volume 2: The mirage of social justice*, London: Routledge and Kegan Paul.

Heath, A. and Curtice, J. (1998) 'New Labour, new voters?', Paper presented to PSA Annual Conference, April.

Heath, A., Jowell, R. and Curtice, J. (1994) 'Can Labour win?', in A. Heath, R. Jowell, and J. Curtice with B. Taylor, *Labour's last chance? The 1992 election and beyond*, Aldershot: Dartmouth.

Heffernan, R. (1998) 'Labour's transformation: a staged process with no single point of origin', *Politics*, vol 18, pp 101-6.

Heffernan, R. and Marqusee, M. (1992) *Defeat from the jaws of victory: Inside Kinnock's Labour party*, London: Verso.

Hencke, D. (1998) 'Harman surrenders savings', *The Guardian*, 15 July, p 6.

Henkel, M. (1991) *Government, evaluation and change*, London: Jessica Kingsley.

Henwood, M. (1995) *Making a difference? Implementation of the community care reforms two years on*, Leeds/London: Nuffield Institute/King's Fund Centre.

Hewitt, M. (1993) 'Social movements and social needs', *Critical Social Policy*, issue 37, pp 52-74.

Hewitt, M. (1998) 'Social policy and human need', in N. Ellison and C. Pierson (eds) *Developments in British social policy*, Basingstoke: Macmillan.

Hewitt, M. and Powell, M. (1998) 'A different back to Beveridge: welfare pluralism and the Beveridge welfare state', in E. Brunsdon, H. Dean and R. Woods (eds) *Social Policy Review 10*, London: Social Policy Association.

Hewitt, P. and Gould, P. (1993) 'Learning from success – Labour and Clinton's New Democrats', *Renewal*, January, vol 1, pp 45-51.

Higgins, J. (1998) 'HAZs warning', *Health Service Journal*, 16 April, pp 24-5.

Hill, D. (1994) *Citizens and cities*, Hemel Hempstead: Harvester Wheatsheaf.

Hillman, J. (1996) *University for Industry: Creating a national learning network*, London: IPPR.

Hills, J. (1996) 'Tax policy: are there still choices?' in D. Halpern, S. Woods, S. White and G. Cameron (eds) *Options for Britain: A strategic policy review*, Aldershot: Dartmouth.

Hills, J. (1998) 'Housing: a decent home within the reach of every family?', in H. Glennerster and J. Hills (eds) *The state of welfare*, Oxford: Oxford University Press.

Hirst, P. (1994) *Associative democracy*, Oxford: Polity Press.

Hirst, P. (1998) 'Social welfare and associative democracy', in N. Ellison and C. Pierson (eds) *Developments in British social policy*, Basingstoke: Macmillan.

HM Treasury (1979) *The government's expenditure plans 1980-81*, Cm 7746, London: HMSO.

HM Treasury (1997) *Equipping Britain for our long-term future: Financial statement and budget report*, HC 85, London: The Stationery Office.

HM Treasury (1998a) *New ambitions for Britain: Financial statement and budget report*, HC 620, London: The Stationery Office.

HM Treasury (1998b) *Stability and investment for the long term: Economic and fiscal strategy report 1998*, Cm 3978, London: The Stationery Office.

HM Treasury (1998c) *Modern public services for Britain: Investing in reform (Comprehensive Spending Review)*, Cm 4011, London: The Stationery Office.

HM Treasury (1998d) *Public Expenditure Statistical Analyses 1998-99*, Cm 3901, London: The Stationery Office.

HM Treasury (1998e) *The code for financial stability*, London: HM Treasury.

Holmans, A.E. (1995) *Housing demand and need in England, 1991-2011*, York: Joseph Rowntree Foundation.

Hobsbawm, E. (1962) *The age of revolution 1789-1848*, New York, NY: Mentor.

Home Office (1982) *Criminal Justice Act 1982*, London: HMSO.

Home Office (1990) *Crime, justice and protecting the public*, Cm 965, London: HMSO.

Home Office (1997) *Safer communities: The local delivery of crime prevention through the partnership approach*, Morgan Report, London: Home Office.

Home Office (1998a) *Supporting families*, London: HMSO.

Home Office (1998b) *Reducing offending*, Home Office Research Study 187, London: HMSO.

Home Office (1998c) *Compact: Getting it right together*, London: Home Office.

Home Office (1998d) *Crime and Disorder Act, 1998*, London: HMSO.

Home Office (1998e) *Research Study 187*, London: HMSO.

Home Office (1999) *The Report of the Stephen Lawrence Inquiry*, London: The Staionery Office.

Hood, C. (1991) 'A public management for all seasons?', *Public Administration*, vol 69, pp 3-19.

Hough, M. and Roberts, J. (1998) *Attitudes to punishment: Findings from the British Crime Survey*, Home Office Research Study 179, London: Home Office.

Hudson, B. (1987) *Justice through punishment*, London: Macmillan.

Hudson, B. (1998) 'Prospects for Partnership', *Health Service Journal*, 16 April, pp 26-7.

Hughes, C. and Wintour, P. (1990) *Labour rebuilt*, London: Fourth Estate.

Hughes, G. and Lewis, G. (eds) (1998) *Unsettling welfare*, London: Routledge.

Hughes, M., Wikeley, F. and Nash, T. (1994) *Parents and their children's schools*, Oxford: Blackwell.

Hunter, D. (1997) *Desperately seeking solutions: Rationing health care*, London: Longman.

Hurd, D. (1989) 'Freedom will flourish where citizens accept responsibilities', *The Independent*, 13 September.

Hurd, Lord (1998) 'Jack Straw's battle on tiptoe', *Prison Service Journal*, no 117, May, pp 2-3.

Hutton, W. (1996) *The state we're in*, revised edn, London: Vintage.

Jackson, P. (1998) 'Public sector value added: can bureaucracy deliver?', Unpublished conference paper, Public Services Research Unit 1998 Conference, Cardiff Business School.

Jenkins, S. (1995) *Accountable to none: The Tory nationalisation of Britain*, London: Hamish Hamilton.

Jessop, B. (1994) 'The transition to post-Fordism and the Schumpeterian workfare state', in R.Burrows and B.Loader (eds) *Towards a post-Fordist welfare state?*, London: Routledge.

Johnson, N. (1987) *The welfare state in transition: The theory and practice of welfare pluralism*, Brighton: Harvester Wheatsheaf.

Johnson, N. (1990) *Reconstructing the welfare state*, Hemel Hempstead: Harvester Wheatsheaf.

Johnson, N. (1998) *Mixed economies of welfare*, Prentice Hall.

Jones, G. (1997) 'Blair warns of welfare curbs', *Daily Telegraph*, 15 May.

Jones, G. (1998) 'We've set a cracking pace, says Blair', *Daily Telegraph*, 31 July, p 11.

Jones, G. and Shrimsley, R. (1997) 'Basic pension plus: the pressing questions', *Daily Telegraph*, 6 March, p 4.

Jones, H. and MacGregor, S. (eds) (1998) *Social issues and party politics*, London: Routledge.

Jones, T. (1996) *Remaking the Labour Party*, London: Routledge.

Jordan, W. (1998) *The new politics of welfare: Social justice in a global context*, London: Sage Publications.

Judge, K., Mulligan, J.-A. and New, B. (1997) 'The NHS: new prescriptions needed?', in R. Jowell, J. Curtice, A. Park, L. Brook, K. Thompson and C. Bryson (eds) *British Social Attitudes, the 13th report: The end of Conservative values?*, Aldershot: Ashgate.

Kampfner, J. (1998) *Robin Cook*, London: Victor Gollancz.

Karn, V. and Sheridan, L. (1994) *New homes in the 1990s*, Manchester/York: University of Manchester/Joseph Rowntree Foundation.

Kavanagh, D. (1980) 'Political culture in Great Britain: the decline of the civic culture', in G.A. Almond and S. Verba (eds) *The civic culture revisited*, Boston, MA: Little Brown and Company.

Kemp, P.A. (1989) 'The demunicipilisation of rented housing', in M. Brenton and C. Ungerson (eds) *Social policy review 1988-9*, London: Longman.

Kemp, P.A. (1991) 'From solution to problem? Council housing and the development of national housing policy', in S.G. Lowe and D.J. Hughes (eds) *A new century of social housing*, Leicester: Leicester University Press.

Kemp, P.A. (1997) *A comparative study of housing allowances*, London: The Stationery Office.

Kemp, P.A. (1998) *Housing benefit: Time for reform*, York: Joseph Rowntree Foundation.

Kenny, M. and Smith, M.J. (1997) '(Mis)understanding Blair', *Political Quarterly*, vol 68, pp 220-30.

King, D. (1987) *The New Right: Politics, markets and citizenship*, Basingstoke: Macmillan.

King, D. (1995) *Actively seeking work:The politics of unemployment and welfare policy in the United States and Great Britain*, Chicago, IL: University of Chicago Press.

King, D. (1999) *In the name of liberalism: Illiberal social policy in Britain and the United States*, Oxford: Oxford University Press.

King, D. and Wickham-Jones, M. (1998) 'Training without the state? New Labour and labour markets', *Policy & Politics*, vol 26, no 4, pp 439-55.

Klein, R. (1995) *The new politics of the NHS*, 3rd edn, Harlow: Longman.

Klein, R. (1998) 'Clinincal depression', *The Guardian*, 29 April, p 6.

Klein, R. and Millar, J. (1995) 'Do-it-yourself social policy: searching for a new paradigm?', *Social Policy and Administration*, vol 29, pp 303-16.

Knapp, M., Wistow, G., Forder, J. and Hardy, B. (1994) 'Markets for social care: opportunities, barriers and implications', in W. Bartlett, C. Propper, D. Wilson and J. Le Grand (eds) *Quasi-markets in the welfare state*, Bristol: SAUS Publications.

Labour Market Trends (1998) *Labour market trends*, December, London: HMSO.

Labour Party (1979) *The Labour way is the better way*, London: Labour Party.

Labour Party (1983) *The new hope for Britain*, London: Labour Party.

Labour Party (1987) *Britain will win*, London: Labour Party.

Labour Party (1989) *Meeting the challenge, make the change:A new agenda for Britain*, Final Report of Labour's Policy Review for the 1990s, London: Labour Party.

Labour Party (1992) *It's time to get Britain working again*, London: Labour Party.

Labour Party (1993) *Selling our security*, London: Labour Party.

Labour Party (1994a) *Annual Conference Report*, London: Labour Party.

Labour Party (1994b) *Budget action for investment, jobs and fairness: Labour's Budget Submission*, London: Labour Party.

Labour Party (1994c) *Jobs and social justice*, London: Labour Party.

Labour Party (1996a) *Building prosperity: Flexibility, efficiency and fairness at work,* London: Labour Party.

Labour Party (1996b) *New Labour new life for Britain,* London: Labour Party.

Labour Party (1997a) *New Labour because Britain deserves better (1997 General Election Manifesto),* London: Labour Party.

Labour Party (1997b) *Teacher 2000,* Labour Party Policy Statement London: Labour Party.

Labour Party (1997c) *New Labour, new Britain, policy guide,* General Election Edition, London: Labour Party.

Labour Party (1997d) *New Deal for a new Britain,* 18 March, London: Labour Party.

Labour Party (1998) *National Policy Forum report to Conference,* London: Labour Party.

Lansley, S. Goss, S. and Wolmar, C. (1989) *Councils in conflict,* Basingstoke: Macmillan.

Lauder, H., Green, A. and Brown, P. (1999) 'Competitiveness and the problem of low skill wquilibria: a comparative analysis', High Skills Economy Research Group, Occasional Paper, London: Post-16 Centre, Institute of Education, London University.

Lauder, II. and Hughes, D., Watson, S., Waslander, S., Thrupp, M., Strathdee, R., Simiyu, I., Dupuis, A., McGlinn, J. and Hamlin, J. (1999) *Trading in futures: Why markets in education don't work,* Buckingham: Open University Press.

Lawson, D. (1997) 'New or old, Labour's labour', *Daily Telegraph,* 7 December, p 34.

Layard, R. (1997) *What Labour can do,* London: Warner Books.

Layard, R. and Phillpot, J. (1991) *Stopping unemployment,* London: Employment Policy Institute.

Le Grand, J. (1982) *The strategy of equality,* London: George Allen and Unwin.

Le Grand, J. (1990) 'The state of welfare', in J. Hills (ed) *The state of welfare,* 1st edn, Oxford: Clarendon Press.

Le Grand, J. (1997) 'Knights, knaves or pawns? Human behaviour and social policy', *Journal of Social Policy*, vol 26, pp 149-69.

Le Grand, J. (1998) 'The third way begins with CORA', *New Statesman*, 6 March, pp 26-7.

Le Grand, J. and Bartlett, W. (eds) (1993) *Quasi-markets and social policy*, Basingstoke: Macmillan.

Lea, J. and Young, J. (1984) *What is to be done about law and order?*, London: Penguin.

Leibfried, S. (1993) 'Towards a European welfare state?', in C. Jones (ed) *New perspectives on the welfare state in Europe*, London: Routledge.

Leishman, F., Loveday, B. and Savage, S. (eds) (1996) *Core issues in policing*, London: Longman.

Levitas, R. (1996) 'The concept of social exclusion and the new Durkheimian hegemony', *Critical Social Policy*, vol 16, pp 5-20.

Levitas, R. (1998) *The inclusive society? Social exclusion and New Labour*, Basingstoke: Macmillan.

Lilley, P. (1995) *Winning the welfare debate*, London: Social Market Foundation.

Lister, R. (1990) *The exclusive society: Citizenship and the poor*, London: Child Poverty Action Group.

Lister, R. (1997a) 'From fractured Britain to one nation?: the policy options for welfare reform', *Renewal*, vol 5, pp 11-23.

Lister, R. (1997b) *Citizenship: Feminist perspectives*, Basingstoke: Macmillan.

Lister, R. (1998) 'From equality to social inclusion: New Labour and the welfare state', *Critical Social Policy*, vol 18, no 2, pp 215-25.

LGA (Local Government Association)/ADSS (Association of Directors of Social Services) (1998) *Social services ADSS/LGA budget survey*, London: ADSS/LGA.

LLoyd, J. and Bilefsky, D. (1998) 'Transatlantic wonks at work', *New Statesman*, 27 March, pp 33-4.

Low Pay Commission (1998) *The national minimum wage: First report of the Low Pay Commission*, Cm 3976, London: The Stationery Office.

McCartney, J. and Jamieson, B. (1997) 'So how do you feel now?', *Sunday Telegraph*, 27 July, p 18.

McCormick, J. (1998) 'Brokering a New Deal: the design and delivery of Welfare to Work', in J. McCormick and C. Oppenheim (eds) *Welfare in working order*, London: IPPR, pp 86-122.

McCormick, J. and Oppenheim, C. (eds) (1998) *Welfare in working order*, London: IPPR.

McElvoy, A. (1997) 'An A-Z of New Labour', *Daily Telegraph*, 29 December, p 20.

McKibbin, R. (1997) 'Very old Labour', *London Review of Books*, 3 April, pp 3-6.

McSmith, A. (1993) *John Smith*, London: Verso.

MacAskill, E. (1998) 'Brown shrugs off welfare protests', *The Guardian*, 3 February, p 2.

MacDermott, T., Garnham, A. and Holtermann, S. (1998) *Real choices for lone parents and their children*, London: Child Poverty Action Group.

Macgregor, A. et al (1996) *The intermediate labour market and area regeneration: An evaluation of the Wise Group*, York: Joseph Rowntree Trust.

MacGregor, S. (1998) 'A new deal for Britain?', in H. Jones and S. MacGregor (eds) *Social issues and party politics*, London: Routledge.

Maclennan, D. (1997) 'The UK housing market: up, down and where next?', in P. Williams (ed) *New directions in housing policy*, London: Paul Chapman Publishing.

Malpass, P. (1990) *Reshaping housing policy*, London: Routledge.

Malpass, P. (1998) 'Housing policy', in N. Ellison and C. Pierson (eds) *Developments in British social policy*, Basingstoke: Macmillan.

Malpass P. and Murie, A. (1994) *Housing policy and practice*, 4th edn, Basingstoke: Macmillan.

Mandelson, P. (1994) 'Clinton's lessons for Labour', *The Guardian*, 11 November.

Mandelson, P. and Liddle, R. (1996) *The Blair revolution: Can New Labour deliver?*, London: Faber & Faber.

Mann, M. (1987) 'Ruling class strategies and citizenship', *Sociology*, vol 21, no 3.

Marginson, P. (1998) 'Industrial relations under New Labour: an update', EIRO Feature, December, Dublin: European Foundation. (eiro@eurofound.ie)

Marquand, D. (1992) 'Half-way to citizenship?', in M.J. Smith and J. Spear (eds) *The changing Labour Party*, London: Routledge.

Marquand, D. (1998a) 'The Blair paradox', *Prospect*, May, pp 19-24.

Marquand, D. (1998b) 'What lies at the heart of the people's project?', *The Guardian*, 20 May.

Marr, A. (1998) 'You think judges are too soft', *Observer*, 28 June.

Marsh, P. and Fisher, M. (1992) *Good intentions: Developing partnership in social services*, York: Joseph Rowntree Foundation.

Marshall, G. (1997) *Repositioning class: Social inequality in industrial societies*, London: Sage Publications.

Marshall, T.H. (1964) *Class, citizenship and social development*, New York, NY: Doubleday.

Matthews, R. (1989) *Privatising criminal justice*, London: Sage Publications.

Maude, F. (1998) *Hansard*, House of Commons, 14 July, cols 195-8.

Mays, N., Goodwin, N., Melbon, G., Lease, B., Mahon, A. and Wyke, S. (1998) *What were the achievements of first-wave total purchasing pilots...?*, London: King's Fund.

Mead, L. (1986) *Beyond entitlement: The social obligations of citizenship*, New York, NY: Free Press.

Mead, L. (1992) *The new politics of poverty*, New York, NY: Basic Books.

Mead, L. (ed) (1997a) *The new paternalism*, Washington, DC: Brookings Institute.

Mead, L. (1997b) 'From welfare to work: Lessons from America', in A. Deacon (ed) *From welfare to work: Lessons from America*, London: Institute for Economic Affairs.

Meager, N. (1998) 'Evaluating active labour market meaures for the long-term unemployed', *Misep Employment Observatory*, 62, Spring, EU.

Mendelson, M. (1998) *The WIS that was: Replacing the Canadian Working Income Supplement*, York: Joseph Rowntree Foundation.

Menter, I., Muschamp, Y.M., Nicholls, P. and Ozga, J. with Pollard, A. (1997) *Work and identity in the primary school: A post-Fordist analysis*, Buckingham: Open University Press.

Merrell, C. and Durman, P. (1997) 'Millions hit by tax raid on pensions schemes', *The Times*, 3 July.

Merrett, S. (1979) *State housing in Britain*, London: Routledge and Kegan Paul.

Mikosz, D. (1998) 'The third way', *Fabian Review*, vol 110, p 13.

Miliband, D. (1994) 'From welfare to wealthfare', *Renewal*, vol 2, pp 87-90.

Mishra, R. (1984) *The welfare state in crisis*, Brighton: Harvester Wheatsheaf.

Morris, E. (1998) 'Future of teacher and head teacher appraisal', Speech to British Appraisal Conference by Parliamentary Under Secretary of State, 26 January.

Mortimore, P. and Mortimore, J. (1998) 'The political and the professional in education: an unnecessary conflict?', *Journal of Education for Teaching*, vol 24, no 3, pp 205-19.

Mortimore, P. and Whitty G. (1997) *Can school effectiveness overcome the effects of disadvantage*, London: Institute of Education.

Mullard, M. and Spicker, P. (1998) *Social policy in a changing society*, London: Routledge.

Mullins, D., Niner, P. and Riseborough, M. (1995) *Evaluating large scale voluntary transfers of local authority housing*, London: HMSO.

Murie, A (1997) 'The social rented sector, housing and the welfare state in the UK', *Housing Studies*, vol 12, pp 437-61.

Murray, C. (1984) *Losing ground: American social policy 1950-1980*, New York, NY: Basic Books.

Murray, C. (1990) *The emerging British underclass*, London: Institute of Economic Affairs.

Murray, C. (1994) *Underclass: The crisis deepens*, London: Institute of Economic Affairs.

NEC (National Executive Committee) (1998) 'Minutes of 27 January meeting', London: Labour Party.

Newburn, T. (1995) *Crime and criminal justice policy*, Essex: Longman.

Newton, C. and Marsh, P. (1993) *Training in partnership: Translating intentions into practice in social services*, York: Joseph Rowntree Foundation.

NHS Executive (1995) *Community care monitoring report: Findings from local authority self-monitoring and NHS surveys*, London: HMSO.

Nye, R. (1996) *Welfare to work: The America works experience*, London: Social Market Foundation.

OECD (1996) *The OECD jobs strategy: Evaluating the effectiveness of active labour market policies*, Paris: OECD.

Offe, C. (1984) *Contradictions of the welfare state*, Cambridge, MA: MIT Press.

Offe, C. (1993) 'Interdependence, difference and limited state capacity', in G. Drover and P. Kerans (eds) *New approaches to welfare theory*, Aldershot: Edward Elgar.

Ofsted (Office for Standards in Education) (1999) 'Setting in primary schools', *Times Educational Supplement*, 15 January, p 7.

O'Leary, J. (1999) 'The end is nigh for "state" education', *The Times*, 20 March, pp 16–17.

Oliver, D. and Heater, D. (1994) *The foundations of citizenship*, Hemel Hempstead: Harvester Wheatsheaf.

ONS (1998) *Social Trends 28*, London: The Stationery Office.

Oppenheim, C. (1997a) 'The post-Conservative welfare state', Paper presented at the Social Policy Association Annual Conference, University of Lincolnshire and Humberside, 16–17 July.

Oppenheim, C. (1997b) 'Welfare and work', *Renewal*, vol 5, pp 50–62.

Oppenheim, C. (1998a) 'Welfare to work: taxes and benefits', in J. McCormick and C. Oppenheim (eds), *Welfare in working order*, London: Institute for Public Policy.

Oppenheim, C. (ed) (1998b) *An inclusive society*, London: IPPR.

Osborne, D. and Gaebler, T. (1992) *Reinventing government*, Reading, MA: Addison Wesley.

Pahl, R. (1995) *After success:* Fin-de-siécle *anxiety and identity*, Cambridge: Polity Press.

Painter, C. (1995) 'Management by the unelected state: the rise of quangocracy', in K. Isaac-Henry, C. Painter, and C. Barnes (eds) *Management in the public sector: Challenge and change*, London: Chapman and Hall.

Painter, C., Rouse, J., Isaac-Henry, K. and Munk, L. (1995) *Changing local governance: Local authorities and non-elected agencies*, Luton: LGMB.

Panitch, L. (1980) 'Recent theorisations of corporatism: reflections on a growth industry', *British Journal of Sociology*, vol 31, no 2, pp 159-87.

Parsons, W. (1989) *The power of the financial press*, Aldershot: Edward Elgar.

Paton, C. (1992) *Competition and planning in the NHS*, 1st edn, London: Chapman and Hall.

Paton, C. (1995) 'Present dangers and future threats: some perverse incentives in the NHS reforms', *British Medical Journal*, vol 310, 13 May, pp 1245-8.

Paton, C. with Hunt, K., Birch, K. and Jordan, K. (1998) *Competition and planning in the NHS. The consequences of the NHS Reforms*, 2nd edn, Cheltenham: Stanley Thornes.

Pawson, H. (1998) 'The growth of residential notability and tenancy turnover', Paper presented to a Conference on 'Housing Abandonment in the English Inner City', University of York, 13 July.

Pease, K. (1997) 'Crime prevention', in R. Reiner, M. Maguire and K. Morgan (eds) *Oxford handbook of criminology*, Oxford: Oxford University Press.

Peele, G. (1996) 'Social policy and the Clinton presidency', in E. Brundson, H. Dean and R. Woods (eds) *Social Policy Review 10*, London: Social Policy Association.

Personnel Publications (1997) 'How the main political parties line up on employment issues', *People Management*, vol 3, no 8.

Pierson, C. (1996a) 'Social policy', in D. Marquand and A. Seldon (eds), *The ideas that shaped post-war Britain*, London: Fontana.

Pierson, C. (1996b) 'Social policy under Thatcher and Major' in S. Ludlam and M.J. Smith (eds) *Contemporary British conservatism*, Basingstoke: Macmillan.

Pierson, C. (1998) *Beyond the welfare state*, 2nd edn, Cambridge: Polity Press.

Plant, R. (1995) 'Market place for everyone', *The Guardian*, 20 March.

Plant, R. (1997a) 'Citizenship, employability and the labour market', *Basic Income Bulletin*, no 24, pp 2-3.

Plant, R. (1997b) 'Rights, obligations and the reform of the welfare state', in A. Morton (ed) *The future of welfare*, Edinburgh: Centre for Theology and Public Issues, University of Edinburgh.

Plant, R. (1998) 'So you want to be a citizen?', *New Statesman*, 6 February, pp 30-2.

Pollard, A. (1997) *Reflective teaching in the primary school*, London: Cassell.

Pollitt, C. (1993) *Managerialism and the public services*, Oxford: Blackwell.

Pomper, G.M. (ed) (1993) *The election of 1992*, Chatham NJ: Chatham House Publishers.

Ponting, C. (1989) *Breach of promise*, London: Hamilton.

Powell, M.A. (1995) 'The strategy of equality revisited', *Journal of Social Policy*, vol 24, pp 163-85.

Powell, M.A. (1997a) *Evaluating the NHS*, Buckingham: Open University Press.

Powell, M.A. (1997b) 'Socialism and the British NHS', *Health Care Analysis*, vol 5, pp 187-94.

Powell, M.A. (1999) 'New Labour and the "Third Way" in the British NHS', *International Journal of Health Services*, vol 29, pp 353-70.

Powell, M.A. and Hewitt, M. (1997) 'The new welfare state', Paper presented to the Social Policy Association Annual Conference, University of Lincolnshire and Humberside, 14-16 July.

Powell, M.A. and Hewitt, M. (1998) 'The end of the welfare state?', *Social Policy and Administration*, vol 32, pp 1-13.

Power, S. and Whitty, G. (1999) 'New Labour's education policy: first, second or third way?', Paper presented at Eighth Quasi-market Research Seminar, University of Bath, 6-7 January.

Prescott, J. (1998) 'Housing and regeneration policy', A Statement by the Deputy Prime Minister, London: DETR.

Prime Minister's Office (1991) *The Citizen's Charter: Raising the standard*, Cm 1599, London: HMSO.

Radice, G. (1992) *Southern discomfort*, London: Fabian Society.

Rafferty, F. (1999) 'Downing Street to rule on councils', *Times Educational Supplement*, 15 January, p 1.

Ranson, S. and Stewart, J. (1994) *Management in the public domain*, Basingstoke: Macmillan.

Rawls, J. (1972) *A theory of justice*, Oxford: Oxford University Press.

Reich, R. (1999) 'Clinton's leap in the dark', *Times Literary Supplement*, 22 January, pp 3-4.

Reiner, R. (1992) *Politics of the police*, Brighton: Harvester Wheatsheaf.

Rentoul, J. (1989) *Me and mine: The triumph of the new individualism?*, London: Unwin Hyman.

Rentoul, J. (1995) *Tony Blair*, London: Little Brown.

Rhodes, R. (1997) *Understanding governance*, Buckingham: Open University Press.

Richardson, A. (1983) *Participation*, London: Routledge and Kegan Paul.

Riddell, P. (1997) 'New Labour messages sound reassuringly old', *The Times*, 30 September.

Robertson, D. (1998) 'The University for Industry – a flagship for demand led training, or another doomed supply-side intervention?', *Journal of Education and Work*, vol 11, pp 5-22.

Roche, M. (1992) *Rethinking citizenship: Welfare, ideology and change in modern society*, Cambridge: Polity Press.

Roddan, D. (1998) 'Prison policy under Labour a year after the election', *The Howard League Magazine*, no 1.

Room, G. (ed) (1995) *Beyond the threshold: The measurement and analysis of social exclusion*, Bristol: The Policy Press.

Rouse, J. (1997) 'Performance inside the QUANGOs: tensions and contradictions', *Local Government Studies*, vol 23, pp 59-75.

Runciman, W.B. (1966) *Relative deprivation and social justice*, London: Routledge and Kegan Paul.

Rutherford, A. (1998) 'One year on', *The Howard League Magazine*, no 1.

Ryan, M. and Ward, T. (1989) *Privatisation and the penal system*, Milton Keynes: Open University Press.

Saraga, E. (ed) (1998) *Embodying the social: Constructions of difference*, London: Routledge.

Savage, S.P. (1990) 'A war on crime? Law and order policies in the 1980s', in S.P. Savage and L. Robins (eds) *Public policy under Thatcher*, London: Macmillan.

Savage, S.P. (1998a) 'The politics of criminal justice policy', in I. McKenzie (ed) *Law, power and justice in England and Wales*, New York, NY: Praeger.

Savage, S.P. (1998b) 'The changing geography of police governance', *Criminal Justice Matters*, June.

Savage, S.P. and Nash, M. (1994) 'Yet another agenda for law and order', *International Criminal Justice Review*, vol 4.

Savage, S.P., Charman, S. and Cope, S. (1997) 'ACPO: a force to be reckoned with?', *Criminal Lawyer*, April.

Scott, J. (1994) *Poverty and wealth: Citizenship, deprivation and privilege*, Harlow: Longman.

Scott, S. and Parkey, H. (1998) 'Myths and reality: anti-social behaviour in Scotland', *Housing Studies*, vol 13, pp 325-45.

Scottish Affairs Committee (1998) *Welfare to work in Scotland: The New Deal*, House of Commons session 1997-98, First Report, London: HMSO.

Scottish Office (1998) *New housing partnerships*, Edinburgh: Scottish Office.

Selbourne, D. (1997) *The principle of duty*, 2nd edn, London: Abacus.

Seyd, P. (1992) 'Labour: the great transformation', in A. King (ed), *Britain at the polls*, Chatham, NJ: Chatham House.

Shaw, E. (1984) *The Labour Party since 1979*, London: Routledge.

Shaw, E. (1996) *The Labour Party since 1945*, Oxford: Blackwell.

Shaw, S. (1992) 'A short history of prison privatisation', *Prison Service Journal*, no 87.

Shaw, S. (1998) 'Interview with Stephen Shaw', *Prison Service Journal*, no 117.

Shrimsley, R. (1997) 'Right-wing think-tank applauds Labour', *Daily Telegraph*, 10 December, p 7.

Silva, E. and Smart, C. (eds) (1999) *The new family*, London: Sage Publications.

Smith, C. (1996) 'Social justice in a modern world', Lecture to IPPR.

Smith, M.J. (1992a) 'The Labour Party in opposition', in M.J. Smith and J. Spear (eds), *The changing Labour Party*, London: Routledge.

Smith, M.J. (1992b) 'A return to revisionism? The Labour Party's policy review', in M.J. Smith and J. Spear (eds), *The changing Labour Party*, London: Routledge.

Smith, M.J. (1992c) 'Continuity and change in Labour Party policy', in M.J. Smith and J. Spear (eds), *The changing Labour Party*, London: Routledge.

Smith, M.J. and Spear, J. (eds) (1992) *The changing Labour Party*, London: Routledge.

Social Exclusion Unit (1998a) *Rough sleeping – Report by the Social Exclusion Unit*, London: The Stationery Office.

Social Exclusion Unit (1998b) *Bringing Britain together: A national strategy for neighbourhood renewal – Report by the Social Exclusion Unit*, London: The Stationery Office.

Social Security Committee (1998) *Social Security Reforms: Lessons from the United States of America*, House of Commons Session 1997-98, Second Report, London: The Stationery Office.

Solow, R, (1998) *Work and welfare*, Princeton, NJ: Princeton University Press.

Sopel, J (1995) *Tony Blair: The moderniser*, London: Michael Joseph.

Squires, P. (1990) *Anti-social policy*, Hemel Hempstead: Harvester Wheatsheaf.

SSAC (Social Security Advisory Committee) (1997) *Social security provision for disability: A case for change?*, London: The Stationery Office.

Standing, K. (1997) 'Scrimping, saving and schooling', *Critical Social Policy*, vol 17, pp 79-99.

Stevenson, O. and Parsloe, P. (1993) *Community care and empowerment*, York: Joseph Rowntree Foundation.

Stewart, J. (1993a) 'Advance of the new magistracy', *Local Government Management*, vol 1, no 6, pp 18-19.

Stewart, J. (1993b) 'The limitations of government by contract', *Public Money and Management*, vol 13, pp 7-12.

Stewart, J. (1995a) 'Accountability and empowerment in welfare services', in D. Gladstone (ed) *British social welfare: Past, present and future*, London: UCL Press.

Stewart, J. (1995b) *Local government today - An observer's view*, Luton: Local Government Management Board.

Straw, J. (1995) 'Straw and order', *New Statesman and Society*, 15 September.

Straw, J. (1998) 'Foreword', *Joining forces to protect the public – Prisons–probation review*, London: HMSO.

Sutherland, H. (1998) *Poverty*, no 99, Spring, pp 13-17.

Sylva, K. (1997) 'The early years curriculum: evidence based proposals', in *Developing the primary school curriculum: The next steps*, London: School Curriculum and Assessment Authority.

Tam, H. (1998) *Communitarianism*, Basingstoke: Macmillan.

Tawney, R.H. (1964) (first published 1931) *Equality*, London: George Allen and Unwin.

Taylor, G.R. (1997) *Labour's renewal?*, Basingstoke: Macmillan.

Taylor-Gooby, P. and Lawson, R. (eds) (1993) *Markets and managers*, Buckingham: Open University Press.

The Guardian (1997a) 'The new welfare state', 2 October.

The Guardian (1997b) 'Back to Beveridge', 13 October.

Theakston, K. (1998) 'New Labour, new Whitehall?', *Public Policy and Administration*, vol 13, pp 13-34.

Thompson, E.P. (1968) *The making of the English working class*, Harmondsworth: Penguin.

Thompson, P. (1993) 'Labour – the natural party of opposition?', *Renewal*, vol 1, pp 1-10.

Thorpe, A. (1997) *A history of the British Labour Party*, Basingstoke: Macmillan.

Timmins, N. (1996) *The five giants: A biography of the welfare state*, London: Fontana Press.

Towers, B. (1994) 'Unemployment and labour market policies and programmes in Britain: experience and evaluation', *Industrial Relations Journal*, vol 25, no 4.

Townsend, P. (1979) *Poverty in the United Kingdom*, Harmondsworth: Penguin.

Toynbee, P. (1997) 'Why I trust Jack Straw to do the right thing', *The Independent*, 20 January.

Toynbee, P. (1998) 'Speak to us Jack', *The Guardian*, 18 February.

Turner, A. (1998) *Social Partners respond to fairness at work White Papers*, EIRO feature. (www.eiro.eurofound.ie)

Turner, B. (1986) *Citizenship and capitalism: The debate over reformism*, London: Allen and Unwin.

Turner, B. (1990) 'Outline of a theory of citizenship', *Sociology*, vol 24, no 2, pp 189-217.

Turner, B. (ed) (1993) *Citizenship and social theory*, London: Sage Publications.

Twine, F. (1994) *Citizenship and social rights: The interdependence of self and society*, London: Sage Publications.

US Senate (1987) *Welfare reform*, Hearings before the committee on finance, Part One, 9 April.

van Steenbergen, B. (ed) (1994) *The condition of citizenship*, London: Sage Publications.

Waldegrave, W. (1993) *The reality of reform and accountability in today's public services*, London: Public Finance Foundation.

Walker, M. (1998) 'The third way international', *New Statesman*, 27 March, pp 30-2.

Walsh, K. (1995) *Public services and market mechanisms: Competition, contracting and the new public management*, Basingstoke: Macmillan.

Walzer, M. (1983) *Spheres of justice*, Oxford: Basil Blackwell.

Warde, A. (1994) 'Consumers, consumption and post-Fordism', in R. Burrows and B. Loader (eds) *Towards a post-Fordist welfare state*, London: Routledge.

Watt, N. and Webster, P. (1998) 'Ministers attack Field for "thinking the unworkable"', *The Times*, 3 August.

Webster, P. (1997) 'Blair pledges shake-up for welfare state', *The Times*, 15 May.

Weir, S. and Hall, W. (eds) (1994) *Ego trip: Extra-governmental organisations in the United Kingdom and their accountability*, London: Charter 88 Trust.

Wells, A.S. (1993) 'The sociology of school choice: why some win and others lose in the educational marketplace', in E. Rasell and R. Rothstein (eds) *School choice: Examining the evidence*, Washington, DC: Economic Policy Institute.

White, M. (1996a) 'Blair lays ghost of old Labour', *The Guardian*, 5 July, p 1.

White, M. (1996b) 'Hard sell on the road to Downing St', *The Guardian*, 5 July, p 13.

White, R. and Haines, F. (1996) *Crime and criminology*, Oxford: Oxford University Press.

White, S. (1998) 'Interpreting the "third way"', *Renewal*, vol 6, pp 17-30.

Whitehead, C. (1983) 'Housing under the Conservatives', *Public Money*, June, pp 15-16.

Whitehead, C. (1997) 'Changing needs, changing incentives: trends in the UK housing system', in P. Williams (ed) *Directions in housing policy*, London: Paul Chapman Publishing.

Whitehead, M. (1987) *The health divide*, London: Health Education Council.

Whiteside, N. (1995) 'Employment policy: a chronicle of decline?', in D. Gladstone (ed) *British social welfare: Past, present and future*, London: UCL Press.

Whitty, G. (1997) 'Marketisation, the state, and the re-formation of the teaching profession', in A.H. Halsey, H. Lauder, P. Brown and A.S. Wells (eds) *Education, culture, economy and society*, Oxford: Oxford University Press.

Wilcox, S. (1997) *Housing finance review 1997/98*, York: Joseph Rowntree Foundation.

Wilding, P. (1992) 'The British welfare state: Thatcherism's enduring legacy', *Policy & Politics*, vol 20, no 3, pp 201-12.

Wilding, P. (1997) 'The welfare state and the Conservatives', *Political Studies*, vol 45, pp 716-26.

Wilkinson, H. (1998) 'The family way: navigating a third way in family policy', in I. Hargreaves and I. Christie (eds) *Tomorrow's politics: The Third Way and beyond*, London: Demos.

Williams, F. (1989) *Social policy: A critical introduction*, Cambridge: Polity Press.

Wilson, D. and Ashton, J. (1998) *What everyone should know about crime and punishment*, London: Blackstone Press Ltd.

Wilson, J.Q. and Kelling, G. (1982) 'Broken windows', *The Atlantic Monthly*, March.

Wintour, P. (1998) 'Blair's team launches ferocious attack on "incapable" Field', *Observer*, 2 August.

Wistow, G., Knapp, M., Hardy, B. and Allen, C. (1994) *Social care in a mixed economy*, Buckingham: Open University Press.

Wright, A. (1996) *Socialisms*, London: Routledge.

Young, J. (1997) 'Left realist criminology: radical in its analysis, realist in its policy', in R. Reiner et al (eds) *Oxford handbook of criminology*, Oxford: Oxford University Press.

Index

A

accountability 235–55
and Labour 244–7
on education 116–19
in government 248–55
and New Right 238–43, 252, 253
of NHS 55
and social democratic consensus 236–8, 240–1, 244, 252, 253
Acheson Report 12, 68
action zones 251, 291
for education 20, 108–9
for health 65–6, 110
'active citizenship' 218–19
Adam Smith Institute 284
Alcock, P. 8
Alexander, R. 105–6
ALMPs 174–6
America see US
antisocial behaviour 138–9, 202
orders 201
Armstrong, Hilary 134–6, 137, 138
Assisted Places Scheme 4, 33, 110
abolition 20, 47, 107, 283
Association of Chief Police Officers (ACPO) 199, 200
Association of Directors of Social Services 85, 86–7
Association of Police Authorities 200
Attlee, Clement 23, 295
Atypical Work: directive 188
Audit Commission 95, 97, 250
on community care 81, 83
and Housing Inspectorate 139
Australia 172, 204

B

Baldock, J. 77, 86
Balls, Ed 265
Barratt Brown, M. 178, 189
Bartlett, W. 83
Beacon Schools Initiative 107–8

Beckett, Margaret 56, 183
Bell, D. 92
benefits *see* social security
Benefits Agency 240
Bentham, Jeremy 223
Benthamism 224
Best Value 21, 94–5, 139–40, 147, 251, 284
Bevan, Aneurin 18, 295
Beveridge, W.H. 16, 154, 292, 299
Report (1942) 2, 3, 167, 169
changes since 3, 169
and national minimum/subsistence 2, 22, 162, 164
bifurcation: in crime policy 193–4, 204
Bingham, Lord 6, 205, 209
Black Report 67, 68
Blair, Tony 6, 7, 294
and Clinton/New Democrats 264, 265, 268–70
communitarianism 91, 92, 98
and crime/police 26, 196, 199, 268
on education 116, 118
on employment regulation 171–2
on family 93
on globalisation 297
leadership style 7, 261
as moderniser/reformer 41, 56, 264, 265, 268–9, 299
and New Labour as reforming government 282, 296, 299
on NHS 58
on poverty/exclusion 49, 141
pragmatism 23, 287
on rights/duties 19, 21, 139, 168, 220, 261, 268, 277, 291–2
on social security 22, 152, 278
on stakeholding/inclusion 18, 220, 222–3
on taxation/public spending 21, 24, 39, 42
on Third Way 13, 14, 19, 23, 48, 285
on welfare state 94, 289

reform(s) 11, 154, 259, 278, 281, 282, 296
Blair/Clinton orthodoxy 221–4, 231, 232, 277
Blunkett, David 56, 118, 278
Boateng, Paul 88
Borrie Commission *see* Commission on Social Justice
Bottomley, Virginia 68
Braggins, John 266–7
Bramley, G. 147
Brine, J. 114–15
British Social Attitudes Survey 37, 39
'broken windows' theory 198
Brown, Gordon 10
    on Industry University 115, 116
    on public spending 21, 22, 37, 282, 290–1, 297
    US influence 265, 268, 269, 270
    and welfare reforms 11, 17–18, 166, 278
    New Deal 258, 270, 271, 288
Brown, P. 103, 107, 110, 111, 113
Budgets (1997/98) 17, 42–3, 45
Bulger, James: killing 195
Burchardt, Tania 24, 29–49, 283, 284, 287, 288
Business Connect 181
Business Link 181
Butcher, T. 237
Byers, Stephen 273

C

Callaghan, James 101, 104, 191, 297
Calman-Hine Report 63
carers: support 88–9
Carers National Association 88
Carers (Recognition and Services) Act (1995) 88
Carvel, J. 109
Castle, Barbara 163
Central Arbitration Committee 184
Central Council for Education and Training in Social Work 90
centralisation: and Labour 97, 291
Charman, Sarah 26, 191–212, 283, 285, 286, 293

Charter 88 246
Chartered Institute of Housing 130
Chief Police Officers, Association of (ACPO) 199, 200
Child Benefit: 1998 changes 166
Child Support Act (1991) 4
Child Support Agency 219
Child Tax Credit 157
childcare: and New Labour 12, 16, 89–91, 157
Childcare Tax Credit 16, 91, 157
Children Act (1989) 82, 83, 85
children's rights officers 89–90
Christian democracy 221, 222
'churning' 178, 179, 276
Citizen's Charter 213, 219, 240, 241, 250
citizenship 213–33
    contractarian view 214, 215, 220
    and New Labour 19, 168–9, 213, 219–24, 231–2, 277–8
    and popular discourse 226–32
    solidaristic view 214, 215, 220, 232
    traditions 214–19
    and welfare regimes 216–19, 220
    vs consumerism 243
    and workfare state 224–6
civil society 21, 252, 254, 298–9
Clarke, Kenneth 282
class, social 92, 226, 230
class sizes (in school) 106–7
'classic welfare state' 2–3, 5 *see also* Beveridge
Clause 4: amendment 7, 74, 219–20, 268
Clinical Excellence, National Institute for 63, 66
Clinton, Bill
    and Blair 265, 268, 269–70
    policies 262–4, 275
    and Labour 13, 150, 264–70, 279
    see also Blair/Clinton orthodoxy
Coates, K. 178, 189
collaboration *see* partnerships
'command and control' 291
    in NHS 60, 61, 65, 73, 74
Commission for Health Improvement 63–4, 250

Commission on Social Justice (Borrie Commission) 7, 22, 114, 261
policy approaches 14–15, 39, 41, 220
and welfare reform 150, 247, 275, 280, 289–90
Committee on Standards in Public Life (Nolan) 242, 249–50
communitarianism 91–3, 98, 217, 254, 286
vs individualism 92, 96–7
see also Blair/Clinton orthodoxy
community care 80–4, 86, 88
and mental health 78–9, 87
White Paper *(Caring for people)* 81, 82, 89, 90
community safety 139, 201, 202
competition: in services 21, 94–6 *see also* Best Value; compulsory competitive tendering; quasi-markets
comprehensive schools 102, 103–4, 112, 120
Comprehensive Spending Review (CSR) 12, 22, 43–4, 45, 48–9, 149–50, 290–1
and communities new deal 87
for housing 123, 134, 135, 142–3
compulsion: in welfare 280, 289 *see also* workfare
compulsory competitive tendering (CCT) 21, 33, 81–2, 251
Confederation of British Industry (CBI) 184, 185, 188
Conservative Governments (1979-97) 10, 97, 246, 297, 298
and accountability 238–43
and consumerism 55, 81, 219, 240–1
and New Deal 178, 261, 270–1
and New Labour 284–5, 286, 295, 297, 298
and pensions/benefits 34, 156, 160, 164
policies 3–5
on education 101, 105–6, 111–12
on employment 173–4, 175–6, 181
on housing 4, 32, 123, 126–34
on law/order 138–9, 191–2, 193–5
on NHS 52–6

and privatisation 32–5, 36, 37, 111–12, 153, 218
public spending 29–32, 77, 127
on welfare 29, 30, 31–2, 35–7, 151–2, 158
Constitutional Convention (Scotland) 246
consumerism 243
and Conservatives 55, 81, 219, 240–1
and Labour 244–5, 284
Policy Review 93, 95–6, 98, 246
contracting-out *see* Best Value; compulsory competitive tendering
Cook, Robin 257–8, 271
council housing 124–5, 126–8, 133–4
see also Right to Buy
Cressey, Peter 25–6, 171–90, 286, 292–3, 296
Crime and Disorder Act (1998) 139, 192–3, 201–3, 208–9, 211
crime audits 201
'Crime Concern' 194
Crime (Sentences) Act (1997) 204–5, 206
criminal justice
and Conservatives 138–9, 191–2, 193–5
and Labour 191, 192–3, 196–212
Blair on 26, 196, 268
Criminal Justice, Royal Commission on (1993) 195
Criminal Justice Acts
(1982) 193
(1988) 194
(1991) 194, 203, 208
Crine, Simon 276
Crosland, Anthony 18, 72, 295
Crouch, C. 287
Crozier, G. 112, 117
CTCs 107, 110

D
Daily Telegraph 282
Dale, R. 116, 118
Darling, Alistair 12, 259, 271, 274–5, 277
Daugherty, R. 104
Davey, K. 172

Davignon Group 187
day centres 79, 85
deadweight: in job creation 179, 276
Dean, Hartley 26, 213–33, 287, 288
decentralisation: and Labour 97, 246, 248–9
de-industrialisation 245
Democratic Leadership Council 262
democratic renewal: and New Labour 247, 248–52
Democratics, New (US) 261–4
and Labour 264–70, 279
demunicipalisation: of housing 128–9, 136–7
devolution 244, 248, 291
Directors of Social Services, Association of 85, 86–7
Disability Living Allowance (DLA) 158, 159
Disability Rights Commission 90, 159, 167
disabled people 45–6, 152, 157–9
and New Deal 157–8, 159, 273, 274
Disabled Person's Tax Credit 157
displacement, job 179, 276
'DIY welfare' 20, 289
Dobson, Frank 67, 87, 258
and Welfare to Work 271, 280
Douglas, Mary 227–8
Downes, D. 196
Driver, S. 93, 292, 293, 294
on communitarianism 91, 92, 96–7, 222, 223, 286
on Third Way 13, 14, 16
Dunleavy, P. 136
duties *see* rights: and duties
Dwyer, P. 139

E

Early Years Development and Childcare Plans 106, 111
Economist: on Third Way 286
education 32, 101–3, 120–1
and accountability 116–19
action zones 20, 108–9
and choice 110–13
comprehensive 102, 103–4, 112, 120

lifelong learning 113–16, 181–3
standards 103–10, 120
see also Assisted Places Scheme
Education Act (1980) 4
Education Action Zones 20, 108–9, 110
Education Development Plans 113
Education Priority Areas (EPAs) 108
Education Reform Act (1988) 106, 110, 113
Educational Standards Commission 247
Edwards, P.K. 186
elderly people: care 167
in community 80–1
residential 79, 84–5, 87, 88, 89
Elliott, G. 8
Emergency Programme of Action 37–8
employment 171–90
and employee relations 183–4
White Paper *see Fairness at work*
and EU policies 187–9
and job creation 173–80 *see also* New Deal
and training 173–4, 180–3
Employment, Select Committee on 275
Employment Relations Bill 171
environmental work 275
in New Deal 46, 177, 258, 272, 275
equality: of opportunity 17–19
in schools 108, 120–1
Esping-Andersen, G. 1, 216–17, 227
ethnicity: and citizenship 217
Etzioni, Amitai 91–2, 221
Euro-Bonds 179
Europe/European Union
and citizenship 215
and New Labour 279, 296
and employment 172, 178–9, 182, 183, 187–9
European Commission 187–8
European Company 187
European Convention on Human Rights 252
European Parliament: and PR 249
'Excalibur' 269

Excellence in schools (White Paper) 11, 106, 115, 117
exclusion *see* social exclusion

F
Fabianism 224
failing schools 118
Fairness at work 12, 171–2, 183, 184, 189
families 19, 90–1, 93, 98–9, 284 *see also* lone parents
Family and Parenting Institute 93
Family Credit 154, 157, 166
Family Support Act (US: 1988) 262
Farnham, D. 173, 181
Faulkner, D. 205
Field, Frank 17, 18, 45, 178, 223–4, 275, 285
    and communitarianism/mutual aid 20, 91, 93, 254
    on means-testing 153, 223–4, 293
    on pensions 45, 160, 161, 224
    resignation/sacking 12, 223, 274
    on spending cuts 11, 22
Financial Services Authority 167
Finegold, D. 120
'Fiscal Stability Code' 43
Fisher, M. 83
focus groups 269, 287
Foot, Michael 6, 37, 40
Forder, J. 127
Forrest, R. 127
fraternity strategy (Tawney) 19, 91
Freedom of Information Bill 244
Friendly Societies 11
'FT 54' 17

G
General Social Care Council 90, 98
Gennard, J. 183
Gewirtz, S. 109, 110–11, 112–13, 117
Giddens, Anthony 18, 19, 167, 296
    on risk/security 226, 227–8
    on Third Way 13, 14, 15, 20, 21
Ginsburg, N. 2
Gipps, C. 101
Glasgow: and accountability 244

Glennerster, H. 30
globalisation 68–9, 296–7
Gloucestershire Council 87–8
Gould, Bryan 10
Gould, Philip 265–6, 267, 268, 269
GPs
    Fund Holding (GPFH) 21, 53–4, 55
    and PCGs 59, 64–5, 67
Gray, A. 178, 188, 189–90, 232
Greater London Authority 248–9
Green, D. 254
Green Papers: on welfare (reform) 151, 169 *see also New contract for welfare; Welfare reform focus files*
Greenspan, Allan 269
Greer, P. 241
Gregg, P. 176
Griffiths Report 52–3, 81
Group 4 210
Guest, D. 172–3

H
Hall, M. 185
Halpern, D. 14, 16, 19, 285–6
Hargreaves, I. 20–1
Harman, Harriet 90, 166, 273
    sacking 12, 274
Healey, Denis 10, 297
Health Action Zones 65–6, 110
Health Improvement, Commission for 63–4, 250
Health Improvement Programme 60
health insurance: tax relief 47, 283
Health of the nation 69
health policies 67–71
    see also NHS
Health Quality Commission 247
Heffernan, R. 287
Hewitt, Martin 8, 25, 149–70, 284, 286, 288, 289, 293
Hewitt, Patricia 265–6, 267, 268, 269
Hillgate Group 105
Hillman, J. 115
Hills, John 24, 29–49, 132, 147, 283, 284, 287, 288
Hirst, P. 254
Home Office

on criminal justice 194, 211
on partnerships 88, 200
home ownership 124, 125, 127, 128,
137 *see also* Right to Buy
homecare services 79, 85
homelessness *see* rough sleeping
House of Lords: reform 249
housing 123–47
pre-1979 124–6
under Conservatives 4, 32, 126–34
under New Labour 19, 134–43
CSR 123, 134, 135, 142–3
and Old Labour: compared 144–7
and Right to Buy 41, 42, 137, 146
Housing, Chartered Institute of 130
Housing Acts
(1974) 125
(1980) 4
(1996) 139
housing associations 125, 129, 133, 136
Housing Benefit 32, 130, 143
Housing Corporation 125, 138
Housing Inspectorate 139–40
Howard, Michael 26, 195, 203–4, 207,
211
and Derek Lewis 206, 241
Hudson, B. 193
Human Rights, European Convention
on 252
Hurd, Douglas 194, 208
Hutton, W. 223

I

Incapacity Benefit 46, 158, 159
inclusion *see* social inclusion
Income Support 224
and lone parents 149, 154, 155
mortgage benefit (ISMI) 130, 164
and pensioners 161, 165
income tax: and New Labour 10
independent schools 104, 107
Individual Learning Accounts 115, 116,
182
individualism 92, 96–7, 168
Industry, University for 115–16, 182–3
Inequalities in Health: Acheson inquiry
68

Inequalities in health (Black Report) 67,
68
Information Commissioner 251
inspection: of schools 117
Institute for Public Policy Research
(IPPR) 246, 267, 280
Integrity Benefits Project 158
Invalidity Benefit 4
'Investor's Britain' strategy 14, 39, 220
Investors in People 182
Islington: and accountability 244

J

Jamieson, Ian 25, 101–21, 283
Jenkin, Patrick 67
Jenkins Commission 249
Jessop, B. 153, 225, 294
job creation: schemes 173–83
job displacement 179, 276
Job Seekers' Allowance (JSA) 4, 164,
176, 219
New Labour retention 150, 168, 261
Johnson, Norman 25, 77–100, 283,
284–5, 286
Jordan, W. (Bill) 13, 16, 221–2, 223, 224,
277
Jospin, Lionel 178–9

K

Keegan, Victor 278
Kemp, Peter A. 25, 123–47, 283–4, 285,
291
Kenny, M. 294
Keynesianism 225, 294, 297
and Beveridge 2, 3, 218
King, Desmond 26, 257–80, 283, 288,
289, 296
King's Fund Centre 83
Kinnock, Neil
reforms 6, 37, 38, 93, 259, 267
on health/welfare 41, 56
and US/Europe 262, 265, 279
Klein, R. 23
Knapp, M. 83

L

'Labour listens' campaign 6
Labour Party (pre-1997) 295–6
and accountability 244–7
Clinton influence 13, 150, 264–9, 279
and health/welfare 56, 95–6, 257–8,
259–61
and law/order 196–7, 199
and New Deal 270–2
and New Labour: continuity 282–4
and 1997 election 10–11
policy changes 5–8
on public spending 37–40
on public/private mix 40–2
see also Commission on Social
Justice; Policy Review
see also manifestos; *and for 1997- see*
New Labour
large-scale voluntary transfers 129
Lauder, Hugh 25, 101–21, 107, 283
law/order *see* criminal justice
Lawrence, Stephen: murder 212
Layard, Richard 276
Le Grand, J. 14, 83
Left Realists 197
'less eligibility' 16, 22, 292
Levitas, R. 18
Lewis, Derek 206, 241
Lewisham: service contract 245
Liberal Democrats 10
lifelong learning 113–16, 181–3
Lifelong Learning Initiative 182–3
Lister, Ruth 18, 22, 166–7, 225, 293
literacy hours 120
Lloyd, Tony 258
Local Authority Social Services Act
(1970) 82
Local Enterprise Companies 181
local government
accountability 242, 243, 244–5
and Best Value 21, 94–5, 139–40, 147,
251, 284
and decentralisation 22–3, 248–9
Quality Commission 247
structural fragmentation 240, 243
Local Government Association 85, 86–
7

London: local government 248–9
London Underground 20
lone parents 149, 154–5
and New Deal 155, 273, 274
in US 263, 289
Lords, House of: reform 249
Low Pay Commission 183, 186
Lupton, C. 173, 181

M

McCormick, James 276, 280
McDonagh, Margaret 266
MacDonald, Calum 136
MacDonald, Ramsay 10, 292
McKibbin, R. 10–11, 287, 292
Macpherson, Lord: inquiry 212
Major, John 97, 219
'Making Work Pay' 16, 155–6
Mandelson, Peter 188
manifestos, election (Labour)
(1979) 244, 246
on education 101, 102, 104, 106–7,
109, 111, 117
(1983) 37, 40, 244, 246
(1987) 38, 246
(1992) 247
(1997) 7, 8–10, 48, 86, 220, 287
on crime 196, 197, 198–9
on decentralisation/democratic
renewal 97, 247, 248
on education 101, 102, 103, 107, 114
on employee relations 183
on public spending 21
Manpower Services Commission 181
Marginson, P. 181, 185
markets *see* quasi-markets
Marquand, D. 123, 221, 224
Marqusee, M. 287
Marr, Andrew 209
Marsh, P. 83
Marshall, T.H. 215, 226, 277
Martell, L. 93, 292, 293, 294
on communitarianism 91, 92, 96–7,
222, 223, 286
on Third Way 13, 14, 16
Marx, Karl 217
Maude, Francis 282

Meacher, Michael 271
Mead, Lawrence 223, 263, 275
Meager, N. 178, 179–80
meals: provision 79, 85
means-testing 32, 154, 166–7
    and Frank Field 153, 223–4, 293
medical insurance: tax relief 47, 283
Mental Health Act (1959) 78
mental health services 78–9, 87
Menter, I. 110–11
Mikosz, D. 14, 16, 19, 92, 286
Milburn, Alan 64, 66, 74
Miliband, D. 16, 289
Minford, Patrick 276
minimum pay *see* national minimum
    wage
MIRAS 130
modernisers: in Labour 72, 260, 261
    and US influence 13, 264–70, 279
Modernising social services 12, 87, 88, 100
monetarism 31
Morgan, R. 196
Morgan Report 202
Morris, Estelle 117
Morrison, Herbert 287
Mortimore, J. 108, 118, 119
Mortimore, P. 108, 118, 119
Moser Committee 120
Mowlam, Mo 271
Murie, A. 127
Murray, Charles 150, 275
Muschamp, Yolande 25, 101–21, 283,
    286

N
National Association of Pension Funds
    17
National Childcare Strategy 155–6
National Curriculum 105, 106, 117
National Economic Development
    Office (NEDO) 181
National Family and Parenting
    Institute 93
National Governors' Association 262
National Grid for Learning 109
National Health Service *see* NHS

National Institute for Clinical
    Excellence 63, 66
National Insurance 159, 224
National Literacy Task Force 118
'national minimum': in Beveridge 2, 22,
    164
national minimum wage (NMW) 156,
    166, 183, 185–7, 283
National Numeracy Project 118
National Recovery Programme 37, 38
National Training Organisations
    (NTOs) 90
Natural Law Party 10
negative equity 130–1
neighbourhood renewal 140–2
neighbours, problem 138–9, 202
neo-liberalism *see* individualism
New contract for welfare (Green Papers)
    12, 13, 15, 19, 152, 165, 167, 213,
    224, 289, 296
    on pensions 12, 46, 160–1, 162
New Deal(s) 168, 177–80, 258–9, 260,
    270–80
    for Communities 87, 140, 142
    and disabled 157–8, 159, 273, 274
    influences 224, 280
    Conservatives 178, 261, 270–1
    US 150, 275–6, 279
    and lone parents 155, 273, 274
    and minimum pay 186
    and partnerships 46–7
    and unemployment 155, 156, 273
    and windfall tax 17, 44, 177, 178
    and work ethic 90, 152, 153–4
    workfare 178, 258–9, 271, 275
New Democrats (US) 261–4
    and Labour 264–70, 279
New Housing Partnerships 136–7
New Labour
    and accountability 248–55
    and childcare 12, 16, 89–91, 157
    and citizenship 19, 168–9, 213, 219–
        24, 231–2, 277–8
    and Conservatives 284–5, 286, 295,
        297, 298
    and criminal justice 191, 192–3, 196–
        204, 205–12
    development 5–11, 294–5

and education: compared with Old Labour 101–21
and employment 171–3, 177–90
health policy 21, 22, 23, 41, 56–67, 68–75
housing *see under* housing
and ideology 23, 295–6
and Old Labour: continuity 282–4
and personal social services 86–95, 96–100
public spending *see under* public spending
public/private mix 20, 45–8, 209–10 *see also* quasi-markets
and social security 149–70, 261 *see also* New Deal; workfare
and taxation 10, 24, 39–40, 42–4, 260
US influence 268–9, 279
welfare reforms: summarised 11–12, 281–2, 299 *see also* Third Way
'new management' 238–43, 254
New NHS 12, 23, 57, 58–63, 287
and policy implementation 63–6, 74
New Poor Law 16, 292, 299
New Right 14, 16, 168
and accountability 238–43, 252, 253
and New Labour 284–5
see also Conservative Governments
New South Wales: crime policy 204
New Statesman 23
Newsnight 268
Next Steps agencies 240, 250
Nexus 23, 270
NHS
under Conservatives 52–6
'internal market' 53–5, 61–2, 65, 73–4
and Labour 21, 22, 23, 41, 56–67, 68–75
Management Board/Executive 52, 70, 83
Royal Commission (1979) 51
'Socialist' character 2, 285
White Paper *see New NHS*
NHS and Community Care Act (1990) 53, 81–2, 84, 85
NHS Bill (1998) 65
NHS Primary Care Act (1997) 55, 65

Nolan Committee report 242, 249–50
non-elected agencies (NEAs) 241–3
Northern Ireland: and devolution 248
Nuffield Institute 83
numeracy hours 120
nursery vouchers scheme 20, 47, 111

O

Offe, C. 226–7
Ofsted 110, 111, 117, 118, 119, 250
Old Labour *see* Labour
older people *see* elderly people
O'Leary, J. 118
One Parent Benefit 149, 155
one parent families *see* lone parents
ontological (in)security 227, 230, 233
Open University 114, 115–16
Oppenheim, C. 18
opportunity
equality 17–19, 108, 120–1
and responsibility 262, 268, 292
Our healthier nation 12, 15, 60, 69
owner-occupation *see* home ownership; Right to Buy

P

paid work: centrality 15–16, 152–3, 222–3, 231, 277–8, 288, 298–9 *see also* workfare
Painter, C. 242–3
Panitch, L. 180–1
Parental Leave: directive 188
parentocracy 110, 111, 113
parents: and education 110, 111–13
Parent's Charter 110, 113
partnerships 20, 45, 250, 251
and community care 82–3, 88
in education 108–9, 110, 112
in health policy 65, 69–70 *see also* quasi-markets
in housing 136–7, 140
in New Deal 46–7
and pensions 19–20, 45, 160, 167
and police 200, 201, 202
Patient's Charter 55
Paton, Calum 24–5, 51–75, 285, 287

Patten, John 128
'Paying for Recovery' Programme 38
Pension Funds, National Association of 17
pensions 39, 150, 160–2, 224, 289
  under Conservatives 34, 160, 164
  Green Paper 12, 46, 160–1, 162
  and partnerships 19–20, 45, 160, 167
  and prices/earnings 20, 22, 38, 150
  types
    SSP 161–2, 165
    stakeholder schemes 161–2, 224
    see also SERPS
performance indicators 250
Personal Responsibility and Work Opportunities Reconciliation Act (US: 1996) 263–4, 289
personal social services 77–80
  1979-97 80–5, 95–8
  and New Labour 86–95, 96–100
Plant, R. 169
Plowden Report 108
police: and Labour 199–201, 202
Police and Magistrates' Courts Act (1994) 199, 200
Police Authorities, Association of (APA) 200
Policy Review (1989) 6, 8, 41, 246
  and consumerism 93, 95–6, 98, 246
Poor Laws 13, 16, 292, 299
poverty 22, 152, 153–62, 215
  fear of 229, 230, 232
  see also social exclusion
Powell, Martin 1–27, 65–6, 281–99
Power, S. 106, 107, 109, 118
Prescott, John 135, 210, 264–5, 271
primary care 55–6
  groups (PCGs) 58–60, 61, 64–5, 67, 71–2
  trusts (Scotland) 62–3
  see also GPs
Primary Care Act (NHS) 55, 65
Prison Governors' Association 211
Prison Reform Trust 206
Prison Service Journal 207
prisons 195, 203–4, 206–11, 212
private finance initiative (PFI) 20, 55, 250, 284

private renting 124, 137, 146–7
privatisation 34–5
  and Conservatives 32–5, 36, 37, 84–5, 111–12, 153, 218
  and Labour 20, 40–2, 45–8, 209–10
  see also quasi-markets
'Project Work' 178, 270
proportional representation 249
Public Accounts Committee 237, 238
public administration paradigm: of accountability 237–8, 241, 244, 252
Public Interest Disclosure Act 252
Public Policy Research Institute 246, 267, 280
public spending
  and Conservatives 29–32, 77, 127
  on welfare 29, 30, 31–2, 35–7, 151–2, 158
  and Labour 37–40
  in government 11, 21–2, 42–5, 160
    Gordon Brown on 21, 22, 37, 282, 290–1, 297
  and public/private mix 29–49
purchaser/provider split
  in community care 81
  in NHS 53, 54, 56
  vs market 57, 58, 250

Q
Qualification and Curriculum Authority 118, 119
Quality Commission (local government) 247
quangos 240, 241–3
quasi-markets 4, 240, 242
  in education 110–13, 117
  in housing 129, 135–8, 147
  and Labour 95–6, 247
  in government 94, 96, 135–8, 147
    and purchaser/provider split 57, 58, 250
  in NHS 53–5, 57, 58, 61–2, 65, 73–4
  and residential care 84–5

R
radicalism: *vs* modernisation 72

rationing: and NHS 66–7, 71, 72–3
Rawls, J. 230
Reagan, Ronald 262, 265
redistribution: and Third Way 17
referenda: and New Labour 249
Regional Development Agencies 249
regionalisation 200, 248–9
Reich, Robert 263–4
Renault Vilvoorde: closure 187
Renewal 23, 260
renting, private 124, 137, 146–7
residential care: of elderly people 79, 84–5, 87, 88, 89
responsibilities *see* opportunity; rights
Restart programme 176
Rhodes, R. 236–7, 240
Riddell, Peter 268
Right to Buy 33, 126–7, 128
and New Labour 41, 42, 137, 146
rights: and duties 19, 99–100, 168, 269, 272, 277
Blair on 19, 21, 139, 168, 220, 261, 268, 277, 291–2
Clinton on 262, 268
and communitarianism 91–2, 222
Gordon Brown on 271
'risk society' 225–6
'Road to the Manifesto' 7, 9
Rogaly, Joe 262–3, 271, 279, 296
Room, G. 215
Rough Sleepers Initiative 132, 134
rough sleeping/homelessness 132, 133, 134, 137–8
Rouse, John 26, 235–55, 286, 291, 293
Rousseau, Jean-Jacques 217
Rowntree (Joseph) Foundation 83
Royal Commissions
on Criminal Justice (1993) 195
on NHS (1979) 51
Runciman, W.B. 230
Rutherford, A. 211

S

San Francisco Chronicle 279
Santer, Jacques 189
Savage, Stephen P. 26, 191–212, 283, 285, 286, 293

School Curriculum and Assessment Authority 118
School Performance Award Scheme 119
schools *see* education
Scotland
and devolution 244, 248, 291
housing 133–4, 136–7, 146, 147
primary health care 62–3
Scottish Affairs Committee 280
security: and insecurity 225–6, 227, 230, 233
Selbourne, D. 91
Select Committee on Employment 275
self-help: and community 92–3
SERPS 34, 160, 161, 164
Service First 250
setting: in schools 107
Shadow Communications Agency 267
Shaw, E. 17, 18, 296, 297
Shaw, Stephen 206, 211
Short, Clare 264, 265, 268
Silva, E. 19
single parents *see* lone parents
Skills Task Force 120
sleaze: and Conservatives 242
Smart, C. 19
Smith, Andrew 46, 278–9
Smith, Chris 19, 22, 271
Smith, George 26, 235–55, 286, 291, 293
Smith, John 6–7, 266
and Borrie Commission 39, 41, 220, 261
Smith, M.J. 7–8, 294
Snowden, Philip 10
Social Charter 183, 187
Social Dialogue: of EU 188, 189
social exclusion 15, 147, 215, 232
Social Exclusion Unit 12, 15, 140–1, 220, 251, 291
on rough sleeping 137–8
Social Fund: under Conservatives 4
social housing: ownership 125 *see also* council housing; housing associations
social inclusion 18–19, 169, 278

Social Inclusion Partnerships 142
Social Justice Commission *see*
    Commission on Social Justice
social security 149–70, 261
    benefit levels 22, 162, 163, 278
    and disabled 45–6, 157–9, 273, 274
    and lone parents 154–5, 273, 274
    and 'Third Way' 151, 162–70
    and unemployment 155–7, 164
    see also New Deal; pensions
Social Security Advisory Committee
    157–8
Social Services Inspectorate 82, 83, 89,
    94–5, 97, 250
social work profession 97–8
Soskice, D. 120
Special Employment Measures 179
SSP 161–2, 165
'stakeholding' 222–3
    and accountability 253, 254
    and pensions 161–2, 224
Standards and Effectiveness Unit 117,
    119
Standing, K. 112
Stephens, Philip 279
Stewart, John 235–6, 240, 243
Straw, Jack 26, 91, 197–8, 204, 210
    on sentencing 206, 207, 208–9, 210–11
substitution *see* job displacement
Sure Start Programme 111, 141, 155–6
Sutherland, H. 156
Sweden: welfare regime 275

and taxation/public spending 29, 45
The Guardian: on Jack Straw 204
think-tanks 267, 280
Third Way 13–24, 99–100, 154, 285–8,
    298–9
    and accountabilty 252–5
    on employment 189–90
    and health policy 68–9, 73–5
    and pensions 45, 160–2
    in social security 151, 162–70
    and US 13, 262, 270
Thompson, Paul 260
Thorpe, A. 6
Timmins, N. 7
Today programme 268
Total Purchasing Pilot (TPP) 55–6
Townsend, Peter 22, 215
Toynbee, Polly 204, 209
trade unions
    under Conservatives 173, 181
    and Labour 171, 180, 183, 184–5
Trades Union Congress 184–5, 277
training 180–3
    'British problem' 173–4, 181
Training and Enterprise Councils 181
Training Organisation for the Personal
    Social Services 90
Travis, Alan 206
trust: and Labour 6, 10, 120
trusts: in healthcare 53, 62–3
Turner, Adair 184
twin-tracking *see* bifurcation

T

'Tadpole Society' 18
'target hardening' 194
Tawney, R.H. 18, 19, 91, 163
tax credits 152, 157, 166, 269 *see also*
    Childcare; Working Families
taxation: and New Labour 10, 24, 39–
    40, 42–4, 260
Teacher Training Agency 110, 119
Tenant Participation Compacts 138
Thatcher, Margaret (Thatcherism) 97,
    193, 218, 275
    and housing 123, 126
    and Labour 8, 286

U

underclass: concept 275
unemployment: and New Labour 155–
    7
Ungerson, C. 86
Union des Industries de la
    Communauté Européene
    (UNICE) 188
UNISON: on New Deal 180
University for Industry 115–16, 182–3
US: as influence 18, 172, 275–6, 280
    see also Clinton; New Democrats
utilitarianism 223

V

Viagra 67
voluntary sector 85, 92, 93

W

Waldegrave, William 128, 241
Wales: devolution 248
Walsall: and accountability 244
Walzer, M. 217
wealth: popular views 229, 230, 231
Webb, Beatrice 224
welfare (reform): Green Papers 151, 169
see also New contract for welfare; Welfare reform focus files
Welfare Reform and Pensions Bill (1999) 259, 274, 275
Welfare reform focus files 45–6, 47, 151
'welfare roadshow' 167–8
Welfare to Work *see* New Deal(s)
'welfarism': and Labour 260–1
Westminster model: of accountability 236–7, 244, 252
White, M. 7
White, S. 14
Whitehead, Margaret 68
Whitty, G. 106, 107, 109, 110, 118, 119
Wickham-Jones, Mark 26, 257–80, 283, 288, 289, 296

Wilding, P. 8
Wilkinson, H. 19
windfall tax 39, 48
and New Deal 17, 44, 177, 178
Wise Group (Glasgow) 180
Wistow, G. 83
women: and citizenship 217
Woodhead, Chris 106, 118
work: centrality *see* paid work
workfare 168, 218, 262–4
and Labour 16, 150, 153, 224–6, 257–8, 278
and New Deal 178, 258–9, 271, 275
Working Families Tax Credit 16, 44–5, 157, 165–6
Working for patients 53, 56, 62
Working Time Directive 183, 187
Workstart 270
Wright, A. (Tony) 7, 18

Y

York: service contract 245
Youth Offending Teams 88, 201
Youth Opportunity Programmes 104

Z

'zero-tolerance' policing 198